WITHDRAWN FROM
EMORY UNIVERSITY LIBRARY

LABOUR DISRUPTED

ŠKOLA PRIMERSKA PRIMORSKA
MILJENKOVIH LUCEN

LABOUR DISRUPTED

REFLECTIONS ON THE FUTURE OF WORK IN SOUTH AFRICA

EDITED BY
MALEHOKO TSHOAEDI, CHRISTINE BISCHOFF
AND ANDRIES BEZUIDENHOUT

WITS UNIVERSITY PRESS

EMORY UNIVERSITY LIBRARY

Published in South Africa by:
Wits University Press
1 Jan Smuts Avenue
Johannesburg 2001

www.witspress.co.za

Compilation © Malehoko Tshoaedi, Christine Bischoff and Andries Bezuidenhout 2023
Chapters © Individual contributors 2023
Published edition © Wits University Press 2023
Images © Copyright holders

First published 2023

http://dx.doi.org.10.18772/22023108226

978-1-77614-822-6 (Paperback)
978-1-77614-823-3 (Hardback)
978-1-77614-824-0 (Web PDF)
978-1-77614-825-7 (EPUB)

All rights reserved. No part of this publication may be reproduced, stored in a retrieval system, or transmitted in any form or by any means, electronic, mechanical, photocopying, recording or otherwise, without the written permission of the publisher, except in accordance with the provisions of the Copyright Act, Act 98 of 1978.

All images remain the property of the copyright holders. The publishers gratefully acknowledge the publishers, institutions and individuals referenced in captions for the use of images. Every effort has been made to locate the original copyright holders of the images reproduced here; please contact Wits University Press in case of any omissions or errors.

This publication is peer reviewed following international best practice standards for academic and scholarly books.

This work is based on research supported by the National Institute for the Humanities and Social Sciences. Opinions expressed are those of the authors and are not necessarily to be attributed to the NIHSS.

NATIONAL INSTITUTE
FOR THE HUMANITIES
AND SOCIAL SCIENCES

Project manager: Elaine Williams
Copyeditor: Karin Pampallis
Proofreader: Alison Paulin
Indexer: Margaret Ramsay
Cover design: Hybrid Creative
Typeset in 10 point Minion Pro

CONTENTS

FIGURES AND TABLES

ACKNOWLEDGEMENT

The editors would like to acknowledge and thank the National Institute for the Humanities and Social Sciences (NIHSS) for a generous grant that made the publication of this volume possible. The opinions expressed by authors in this volume do not necessarily reflect those of the NIHSS.

Amcu	Association of Mineworkers and Construction Union
AMSA	ArcelorMittal South Africa
ANC	African National Congress
B-BBEE	Broad-Based Black Economic Empowerment
CCMA	Commission for Conciliation, Mediation and Arbitration
Ceppwawu	Chemical, Energy, Paper, Printing, Wood and Allied Workers' Union
CHW	community health worker
CM	Continuous Miner
Cosatu	Congress of South African Trade Unions
Consawu	Confederation of South African Workers Union
CWAO	Casual Workers' Advice Office
CWIU	Chemical Workers Industrial Union
CWP	Community Work Programme
Denosa	Democratic Nursing Organisation of South Africa
ENGAGE	Empowerment and Capacity Building Network for Global Trade Unionists and Labour Activists [programme]
EPWP	Expanded Public Works Programme
ETI	Employment Tax Incentive
ETUC	European Trade Union Confederation
4.0 or 4IR	Fourth Industrial Revolution
FAK	Federasie van Afrikaanse Kultuurvereniginge
Fawu	Food and Allied Workers Union
Fedsal	Federation of South African Labour Unions
Fedusa	Federation of Unions of South Africa
Fosatu	Federation of South African Trade Unions
GLU	Global Labour University
Nehawu	National Education, Health and Allied Workers' Union
HPCSA	Health Professionals Council of South Africa

ICU	Industrial and Commercial Workers' Union
ILO	International Labour Organization
Imatu	Independent Municipal and Allied Trade Union
Iscor	Iron and Steel Corporation
ISI	import substitution industrialisation
Lacom	Labour and Community Resources Project
LRA	Labour Relations Act (No. 66 of 1995)
Mawu	Metal and Allied Workers Union
MCSA	Minerals Council South Africa
MHSC	Mine Health and Safety Council
MTS	Mamelodi Train Sector
MWU	Mineworkers Union
Nactu	National Council of Trade Unions
NEET	not in employment, education or training
Nehawu	National Education, Health and Allied Workers' Union
NGO	non-governmental organisation
NP	National Party
NRPI	Numsa Research and Policy Institute
NUM	National Union of Mineworkers
Numsa	National Union of Metalworkers of South Africa
Nupsaw	National Union of Public Service and Allied Workers
NYDA	National Youth Development Agency
Popcru	Police and Prisons Civil Rights Union
PPE	personal protective equipment
PSA	Public Servants Association
PSCBC	Public Service Co-ordinating Bargaining Council
SAA	South African Airways
Saawu	South African Allied Workers Union
Saccawu	South African Commercial, Catering and Allied Workers Union
Sacol	South African Confederation of Labour
SACP	South African Communist Party
Sactu	South African Congress of Trade Unions
Sactwu	South African Clothing and Textile Workers' Union
Sadtu	South African Democratic Teachers Union
Saftu	South African Federation of Trade Unions
Samwu	South African Municipal Workers Union
SAOU	South African Teachers' Union

Sarhwu	South African Railways and Harbour Workers Union
Satawu	South African Transport and Allied Workers' Union
SCU	social capital unionism
Seta	Sector Education and Training Authority
SIGTUR	Southern Initiative on Globalisation and Trade Union Rights
SMT	school management team
SMU	social movement unionism
SRWP	Socialist Revolutionary Workers Party
Stats SA	Statistics South Africa
TERS	Temporary Employer/Employee Relief Scheme
Tuacc	Trade Union Advisory Coordinating Council
Tucsa	Trade Union Council of South Africa
Uasa	United Association of South Africa
UIF	Unemployment Insurance Fund
Vesco	Vanderbijlpark Estate Company
VW	Volkswagen
WEF	World Economic Forum
YES	Youth Employment Service

Disruptions and New Directions in South African Labour Studies

Andries Bezuidenhout, Malehoko Tshoaedi
and Christine Bischoff

THE STATE OF LABOUR, THE STATE OF LABOUR STUDIES

This year marks the fiftieth anniversary of the 1973 Durban strikes, a strike wave that set in motion unprecedented dynamism in the South African labour movement after more than a decade of trade union decline. Because of apartheid legislation that curtailed union activities for black workers, as well as the persecution of union activists, trade unions were either incorporated into the government system of racialised collective bargaining (mostly through unions representing white workers), or had collapsed as formal organisations in the country and were forced to operate from exile. The strike wave of 1973 was a turning point in terms of workplace relations and the labour movement; the dynamism that followed eventually presented a significant challenge to the apartheid system as a whole when unions from the mining and manufacturing sectors merged to form the Congress of South African Trade Unions (Cosatu) in 1985. Ironically, labour law reforms that were intended to incorporate and tame the emerging militant unions opened up new spaces for organising; by the time the apartheid state wanted to roll back some of these laws, organised labour had become so strong that the state was forced to retreat (Friedman 1987; Baskin 1991).

Now, fifty years after this turning point, the dynamism of yore tends to be found in nostalgic reflections of the past rather than innovations in the present. To be sure, in so far as organised labour in South Africa is concerned, the past decade has been characterised by major disruptions in the order of things. As the country's dominant labour federation, Cosatu lost a large proportion of its manufacturing base when its metal union, the National Union of Metalworkers of South Africa (Numsa), left to form a rival federation, namely the South African Federation of Trade Unions (Saftu). In addition to this setback for worker unity and Cosatu's principle of 'one country, one federation', individual trade unions across the spectrum faced threats of deregistration. The Registrar of Labour started to take more seriously the Department of Labour's oversight of trade union financial governance and reporting after years during which labour factionalism had negatively impacted bureaucratic independence. This renewed enforcement of trade unions' reporting duties to the authorities, as required by labour law, revealed a number of dubious practices among an echelon of entrenched labour leaders who seemed more interested in political and entrepreneurial activity than in representing their members. All of this happened while workplaces and the economy more broadly were being restructured as a result of rapidly changing technology. In addition, state-owned companies reeled from large-scale and unchecked looting, also affecting the future of workers employed by these massive corporations.

As if this wasn't enough, a global pandemic broke out at the beginning of 2020. The government responded, as in the rest of the world, with restrictive lockdowns that had major economic and social fallouts. But this was not the only disruptor. In July 2021, still during the lockdown period, former president Jacob Zuma was sent to jail and large-scale protests broke out, primarily in the KwaZulu-Natal province, but also in other parts of the country.[1] Retail outlets, warehouses and businesses were looted, leading to an economic shock in the country as a whole. Still recovering from this, KwaZulu-Natal was hit by floods and landslides in April 2022, resulting in the deaths of nearly 500 people, with many more displaced. These floods, the drought that led to severe water shortages in cities such as Cape Town and Gqeberha (formerly Port Elizabeth), rolling electricity blackouts, and natural disasters in other parts of the world forced the climate crisis onto the mainstream agenda.

The Covid-19 pandemic and the subsequent lockdowns posed a number of direct challenges to the labour movement. First, unions had to step in to represent their members, especially those on the front line of the service and caring economy: nurses, teachers, retail and hospitality workers. Unions had to ensure that measures were taken to protect the health of their members in the country's response to the pandemic. But representing members who are not allowed to hold meetings in the way that unions typically do poses a serious challenge. Hence, like the rest of society, unions had to find new ways of communicating with members who were dispersed across various spaces and, often, isolated at home. Second, unions had to engage the state on measures put in place to support those members who had lost their jobs due to the lockdown. Again, it is very difficult to keep track of everything that is happening during a lockdown. As labour scholars, we were struck by how muted the labour response to the crisis was. Finally, at the level of human tragedy, unions sadly lost members and leaders due to the disease.

The Covid-19 pandemic affected an already weakened labour movement, relative to its influence and power in the past. But in spite of having to face up to the reality of a fragmented labour movement and weakened trade unions, South African labour studies has remained resilient and, one could argue, is entering a new phase of innovation. In our previous edited collection in this series of books on South African labour studies, *Labour Beyond Cosatu: Mapping the Rupture in the South African Labour Landscape*, we attempted to explain the break that had taken place when Cosatu split in two (Bezuidenhout and Tshoaedi 2017). Since the publication of that volume, there have been interesting and unexpected developments. During a strike at the Sibanye-Stillwater gold mining company at the beginning of 2022, the National Union of Mineworkers (NUM) and the Association of Mineworkers and Construction Union (Amcu) joined forces to embark jointly on strike action. They released joint press statements and even printed t-shirts with both unions' logos. The year before, the two unions had clashed violently over a strike at the same mining company. Also, during a 'national shutdown' in August 2022 (a rather muted one, we should add), Cosatu and Saftu cooperated and ran joint campaigns. During a strike in the civil service in November 2022, the Federation of Unions of South Africa (Fedusa) joined forces with Cosatu and Saftu, releasing joint press statements. In this volume we are interested in exploring the implications of a radically altered labour landscape by looking forward. As we hope to show, the Covid-19 pandemic has highlighted the crisis in the labour movement, which has sparked a range of new topics and research foci, sustaining the multi-disciplinary interest in labour and leading to new directions for labour studies by unlocking new questions.

Of course, some of these new topics have their roots in older concerns, research and debates. Roughly a decade ago Sakhela Buhlungu, one of the key figures in South African labour studies, had a dire reading of systematic attempts to understand labour (Buhlungu 2006, 2009; Buhlungu and Tshoaedi 2013). 'For many', he argued, 'labour has lost its glamour and intellectual attraction, and the focus has shifted to the state and business' – and, one might add, to an interest in social movements. Furthermore, he argued that 'the field of labour studies has not been particularly successful in attracting and producing black scholars', and that the bona fides of labour scholars have been questioned by labour leaders who 'had become accustomed to unquestioning support' from labour scholars, while most union leaders 'take offense and often respond defensively, in the process vilifying researchers and intellectuals' (Buhlungu 2009, 157–158).

Since then much has changed. A new generation of black scholars has taken the lead in the field, but there is no room for complacency. Buhlungu's critique on the representation of scholars in labour studies should not be limited to black scholars, but also the representation of women (especially black women), the disabled, the LGBTQI+ community, youth and migrant workers. The exclusion of these marginalised groups in South African labour studies reflects the hegemonic power dynamics in our academic and research institutions, where ideas and knowledge are a preserve of the elite few. This dominance of 'traditional scholars and voices' in labour studies runs the risk of producing stagnation and the recycling of old topics. At times, the focus continues to be traditional industrial issues, excluding the intersectional experiences and voices of these marginalised groups. In this volume, we attempt to infuse labour studies with a fresh set of perspectives. We do not present this volume as a definitive answer, but as a start in working towards a decolonial approach to labour studies (Nyoka 2013; Sitas 2004, 2014).

In *Labour Beyond Cosatu*, we emphasised the politics of difference in trade union mobilisation. If the labour movement wanted to regain some of its former dynamism, we argued, it had to re-evaluate its focus (or lack of it) on the politics of difference and new strategies in the representation of diverse interests (Bezuidenhout and Tshoaedi 2017). We are not calling for North American style identity politics, but rather a recognition that old solidarities structured around race and class do not always capture the complex and changing reality of our society (Tshoaedi and Hlela 2006). The student movement during the 2016 #FeesMustFall protests highlighted some of this, and ironically it was an alliance between students and workers that was able to strike a serious blow against the practice of outsourced services at universities that trade unions had been struggling with unsuccessfully for more than two decades (Hlatshwayo 2020). The student movement and their demand for decolonisation poses a challenge to us as labour scholars. Yet, the student movement also fractured along political and identity lines, so we are aware of the limitations of horizontal forms of mobilisation without clear mandates and elected leaders. In this current book, we make an argument for labour scholars to re-evaluate their perhaps comfortable positions on traditional labour issues. We challenge labour scholarship to transform and broaden its focus to include 'other voices' that are on the margins.

Sadly, where once the South African labour movement was routinely used as an example of social movement unionism, a model to emulate for unions in other parts of the world that were stagnating and fragmenting, this is no longer the case (Seidman 1994; Moody 1997). It is now often described as divided and fragmented, as a movement in crisis (Kenny 2020). In a perverse reversal of roles, the literature on trade unions in the Global North that drew inspiration for 'union revitalisation' from the South African example (Clawson 2003; Fantasia and Voss 2004; Phelan 2009), is now used to call for union revitalisation in South Africa (Pillay 2017). The idea of exporting South African social movement unionism (Bezuidenhout 2000), from a time when workers formed part of a much broader alliance against apartheid as a system, now seems somewhat quaint. South African social movement unionism was produced under unique conditions, and those conditions no longer exist (Von Holdt 2002). So the time when the South African labour movement had an important international reputation and stature is over. Not that the nostalgia for this long-lost time does not still play a role, but the stark realities of the present perhaps call for a different kind of understanding, one that still takes history seriously but is able to face up to present realities.

This sense that the labour movement is fragmented and weak is also reflected in popular opinion and public conversations. 'Far from being the forward-looking and clear-thinking force that it was in years gone by, the trade union movement has evolved into an intransigent bunch of perennial naysayers', wrote Mondli Makhanya (2019) in a *City Press* editorial at the end of 2019. He referred specifically to unions' roles in negotiating efforts to save South African Airways (SAA) and Eskom, the electricity parastatal, from liquidation, as well as threats to shut down parts of the civil service, saying that unions were being populist, while 'strangling the [economic] hen'. On the restructuring of state-owned enterprises he mentioned in particular a shutdown of SAA by trade unions, in which they rejected plans to retrench 900 employees, and demanded a salary increase of 8.5 per cent instead. This, he argued, in a context where the parastatal was in real crisis, with R20 billion of debt. Makhanya mentioned a similar situation in Eskom, where trade unions opposed cost-saving measures. 'The unions used their political muscle and the implicit threat of sabotaging the country's electricity supply to strong-arm management into giving them bankrupting increases', he wrote. Of course, one should point out that employees cannot be blamed for the need to salvage state-owned enterprises from the legacy of corruption and the impact of the coronavirus lockdown. Yet, as Makhanya argues, unions themselves were responsible for 'placing in power the chief enabler of state capture' and for driving 'the Polokwane revolution that got us to where we are'. He concluded: 'Granted, most of them saw the error of their ways, but the horse was far gone by then'.

The purpose of newspaper editorials is to inform but also to provoke, which Makhanya certainly did with this acerbic take on trade unions in contemporary South Africa. The aim of this book is to take stock of where the labour movement stands in a South Africa that has gone through a number of massive shocks, including the legacies of apartheid, state capture, the coronavirus pandemic, and the impact of the war between Russia and the Ukraine on the global economy. In most of these events, trade unions are both players and victims. In this book we draw on some of the best South African labour scholarship available to try to move beyond loaded rhetoric and to understand sympathetically but critically where the labour movement stands in relation to a number of issues. We also consider the future of the labour movement. A number of the chapters in this volume open up new fields of enquiry and highlight areas that have not always received attention.

Since Buhlungu (2009) wrote his assessment of labour studies as a field in decline, there have been a number of developments that we should note. The first is that it is exactly the fragmentation of labour and the crisis caused by this that has reinvigorated labour scholarship; this includes scholars in other parts of the world who want to understand how the changing nature of work and labour markets affects society, primarily through the rise of what some call the precariat (Standing 2011; Scully 2016a, 2016b; Milkman 2020). A second development is the transformation of a labour scholarship once dominated by white academics to a field of enquiry that has become more diverse in terms of race and gender. As pointed out, this represents significant progress, but diversity in its full range remains limited. Can we talk about a decolonised labour scholarship? Most probably not. A third change is a renegotiation of the relationship between labour scholars and the labour movement. Edward Webster (2002) referred to this as a relationship based on critical engagement, and the waning of Cosatu's dominance has opened up a whole range of research topics and new actors, rather than closing them down (Bezuidenhout, Mnwana and Von Holdt 2022). As Lucien van der Walt points out in his overview of South African labour scholarship (Chapter 1), unions that do not come from the Cosatu tradition are remarkably stable in terms of membership figures (the Public Service Association being one interesting example), and some even innovate with new approaches to trade unionism (see also Jantjie Xaba's chapter in this book). We think the chapters collected in this volume point to where labour studies is going in a labour landscape that has significantly opened up new ways of mapping the future of labour in South Africa.

As Gwede Mantashe was so fond of saying at public seminars when he was still a trade unionist, the unions have affected the transition, but the transition has also affected the unions. To be sure, there have been a number of massive shifts in South Africa's labour landscape over the past decades. Underlying these changes are three transitions, what Karl von Holdt (2003, 2–5) calls a triple transition. This refers to: (i) a political transition from apartheid to a nascent constitutional democracy, (ii) an economic transition from protectionism to trade liberalisation, and (iii) a social transition from a racialised order to one where diversity and economic redress is part of the country's constitutional aims. The three transitions are not necessarily mutually reinforcing, with rapid economic liberalisation putting severe strain on both the need for political democratisation and social decolonisation. The labour movement is an actor in each of these transitions, but how the triple transition plays out also affects the labour movement itself.

UNIONS, MEMBERSHIP AND POST-APARTHEID SOUTH AFRICA

Post-1994 labour legislation supports the rights of all to fair labour practices. Workers can establish, join and participate in the activities of trade unions, including going on strike and participating in collective bargaining. The Labour Relations Act (No. 66 of 1995) (LRA) sets out the guidelines for collective bargaining, offers a framework for dealing with conflict between employers and employees at the workplace, and entrenches and extends the system of wage determination by means of centralised bargaining. While the institutional improvements that emanate from the new labour regime have created favourable conditions for labour, a large proportion of workers are not covered by collective bargaining, and only just over a quarter of the workforce is unionised. Another factor to consider is the rise of the gig economy, where workers are turned into entrepreneurs linked to their clients through various web-based platforms (see Eddie Webster, Chapter 13). We are talking about a rapidly changing world of work that fundamentally challenges the idea that a contract of employment can form the basis of labour market regulation and collective bargaining (Elsley, Godfrey and Jacobs 2019; Webster 2020; Milkman et al. 2021).

In *Labour Beyond Cosatu* we outlined some of the shifts that have taken place in the labour movement, as well as the political, economic and social components of the landscape this movement occupies (Bezuidenhout and Tshoaedi 2017). We noted that there was a rapid shift in the composition of trade union members, including a general shift from the semi-skilled segments of the labour market to a large proportion of union members now possessing post-school qualifications (one in five Cosatu members has a post-school qualification). As illustrated by Figure 0.1, the skill levels of younger Cosatu members (18 to 34 years of age) shifted between 1994 and 2014. The proportion of unskilled and semi-skilled workers dropped from 60 per cent in 1994 to 29 per cent in 2014. The proportion of skilled Cosatu young members increased from 21 per cent in 1994 to 38 per cent in 2014. This is due to the restructuring of the labour market, which saw the traditional base of union membership being casualised, externalised and informalised, along with an inability of the labour movement to organise these precarious segments of the labour market. Where unions lost members in their traditional base, this was made up for by the rapid increase of union membership in the civil service (especially teachers and nurses) and in white-collar occupations. In part, this is due to the upward social mobility of black workers after the end of apartheid discrimination, the general increase in their formal qualifications, and employment opportunities in the civil service.

Yet, the youth unemployment rate remains high and is described as a crisis. According to the data from the Quarterly Labour Force Survey produced by Statistics South Africa, in quarter two of 2020, over half of those who were unemployed were considered to be part of the youth cohort (aged 15 to 34 years). In addition, the technological changes in workplaces pose further challenges for many workers in South Africa.

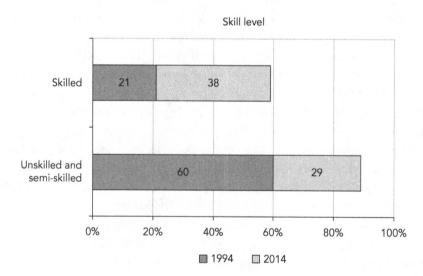

Figure 0.1: Skill level of Cosatu youth cohort (18–34 years of age), 1998 and 2014 (%)

Source: Bezuidenhout, Bischoff and Nthejane (2017)

The national lockdown in South Africa in March 2020 and the ones that followed had massive repercussions for workers and their organisations. From February to June 2020, workers who were poor, rural, female, unskilled and less educated were subjected to job losses (NIDS-CRAM September 2020). Those most affected were located predominantly in relatively low-skill occupations, such as manufacturing, cleaning and informal trading. This was in stark contrast to professionals and those with high levels of skills, who could work from home. In the context of what some call the 'Fourth Industrial Revolution' and the Covid-19 pandemic, the workplace is being remarkably transformed, and this is raising new issues for trade unions. The conversation on the challenges faced during this pandemic should move beyond just employment, and examine how to revolutionise the South African labour force in terms of skills and education.

UNIONS AND SOLIDARITY VS EXCLUSIVITY

Race and class identities have featured strongly in labour politics and have been the basis for solidarity in South African working-class struggles and trade union mobilisation (Tshoaedi and Hlela 2006; Tshoaedi 2008). The intersection of racial oppression and class exploitation in apartheid South Africa shaped the labour movement. The intersectional approach in labour politics during the apartheid era ensured solidarity on a wider basis. Common identity and shared experiences were the basis for solidarity. In a volatile context such as during apartheid, one could argue that this was a necessity. But strategic choices about the mobilisation of certain identities at the expense of others also led to the silencing of those who did not neatly fit into those categories. In observing the post-apartheid political context, it is critical to comment on the continuation of this type of strategy, which exclusively protects traditional members of the unions. There is a need for South African labour studies to reflect on the significance of new identities in the labour market – the youth, the LGBTQI+ community, persons with disabilities, women, migrant workers and the precariat. This area of study needs further focus by labour scholars, and we encourage young and upcoming scholars in this field to fill the gap (Maake 2019). We return to this matter in the concluding chapter. The neo-liberal post-apartheid labour market and globalisation have produced a more volatile context that puts the future of the unions and the working class into crisis. In such a crisis, where workers are displaced from their countries and where technological innovation is changing the nature of work and employment contracts, inclusion is key to the survival of workers (Webster 2020).

We conclude this chapter with a map of the chapters that are to follow and how these contribute to a comprehensive overview of the state of the South African labour movement and labour studies in the twenty-first century.

AN OVERVIEW OF THE BOOK

We start off with this chapter, which returns to the original impulse for 'Trade Unions and Democracy' research on organised labour in South Africa, namely the impact that trade union democracy has on democracy in society more broadly. In order to situate our intervention within the history of South African labour scholarship, we asked Lucien van der Walt to provide a critical overview of South African labour scholarship (see Chapter 1). As both historian and sociologist, he did not disappoint. His survey of the literature also provides those who are unfamiliar with South African labour scholarship with a map to guide them through some of the other contributions to the volume. He also makes a number of critical interventions on silences and knowledge gaps in the existing body of labour scholarship. Following on from this introduction and Van der Walt's overview of the field, the volume is organised in four sections. The first deals with the basis on which the labour movement structures its solidarities. The second returns to the labour process (Kenny and Webster 2021) in order to explore how trade unions deal with technology and skill. The third section looks at innovative ways in which unions are organising in response to the changing world of work. Finally, in the fourth part, we look at lockdown and the future of labour and labour studies.

Part 1: Changing Solidarities

In this section the contributors raise the issue of patriarchy and gender in the workplace, the extent to which a new generation of workers are joining the labour movement, and the challenge raised by the fact that a whole new category of people are joining the labour market but under the guise of welfare programmes. In Chapter 2, Asanda-Jonas Benya's detailed and engaged ethnographic work in the mining industry provides a devastating critique of the limits of patriarchal solidarities as a basis for working-class unity. It opens up issues of masculinities in unions and the need to engage movements from within the labour movement, as well as providing critique from other movements. After this focus on race and gender, we introduce the matter of generation. In Chapter 3, Christine Bischoff uses labour market survey evidence to show how South African trade unions have not been able to organise young members; she also critiques unions for being reactive when it comes to issues of youth unemployment, one of the major issues of our time. In Chapter 4, Nomkhosi Xulu-Gama and Aisha Lorgat open up the issue of volunteerism and work offered as a part of welfare programmes – the Expanded Public Works Programme (EPWP). With the rise of mass unemployment, these kinds of programmes will probably become more central to welfare systems across the world. This chapter is an important contribution to a volume about trade unions.

Part 2: Technology and Work

The four chapters in this section explore the impact that new technology has on work, and how unions in South African could engage with the impact of new technology on production and the working lives of their members. In Chapter 5, Siphelo Ngcwangu looks at the waning of union engagement with skill and technology in Numsa at a time when massive changes to the labour process are happening. It further examines how unions have lost much of their commitment and capacity, and what labour scholars and trade unions can learn from this. In Chapter 6, John Mashayamombe uses his ethnographic study of two mines to return to the labour process, but with insights from labour geography. Practical examples of how technology is transforming open cast mines are provided in this chapter. In Chapter 7, Mondli Hlatshwayo looks at the impact of new technology, arguing that companies in the Global North that build the robots, computers and other Fourth Industrial Revolution products are gaining as a result of technological change, while workers in the Global South are losing their jobs. Furthermore, in South Africa, unions have not engaged proactively with the issue of the impact of new technology on their members, as their focus is on bargaining over wages. We then shift our attention to new forms of work organisation in the public sector. In Chapter 8, Babalwa Magoqwana focuses on the public sector, the role of unions in organising workers in this sector, problems with service delivery and fighting for efficient services for communities. She draws on the notion of emotional labour to look at how citizens are used as 'customers' to monitor the work of civil servants. She also reflects on the idea of the consolidation of democracy and the role of workers in this process.

Part 3: New Forms of Organising

The five chapters that make up this section of our volume all deal with forms of organising and challenges posed to unions in the domain of solidarity and their relationship to society more broadly. In Chapter 9, Mpho Mmadi's historical ethnographic work on trade unions organising on trains shows how spaces of organising can be explored in order to overcome labour fragmentation. This innovative study explores an often-ignored issue related to the spaces of organising that are neither 'work' nor 'community', but the logistical spaces in between. Mmadi makes a case for returning to the idea of social movement unionism. In Chapter 10, Jantjie Xaba finds potential for progressive new approaches to trade unionism in an example that progressive labour scholars often ignore. Focusing on the trade union Solidarity, Xaba begins to fill this gap by using the notion of social capital unions to describe how unions use their resources in order to create their own institutions. In Chapter 11, Janet Cherry explores models and dynamics of organising specifically for the left labour movement, and provides a fresh perspective on the interaction between trade unions and issue-based movements in contemporary South Africa. Then, in Chapter 12, Sandla Nomvete critically examines the implications for trade unions and for unionism more broadly when trade union investment companies are set up, as subscription fees are insufficient for the unions' financial sustainability. The section is concluded in Chapter 13, where Edward Webster considers opportunities for global organising, a focus that has been on the back burner with the dominance of nationalist and factionalist politics in the major unions. He documents innovative new approaches to organising that involve the training of union activists in new forms of value chain and community mapping.

Part 4: Labour and Lockdown

The final section of the book systematically considers the further crisis for labour caused by lockdown, but it identifies a number of innovative responses to this. In Chapter 14, Christine Bischoff shows how Covid-19 exposed the labour movement to new challenges, forcing it to re-examine its role and intervention in the economy and health system, preservation of jobs, livelihoods and lives. Some of the responses to these issues are considered, along with what prospects there are for strengthening the labour movement. This section of the volume, as well as the volume as a whole, is concluded by the three editors: Andries Bezuidenhout, Malehoko Tshoaedi and Christine Bischoff. This chapter should be read in tandem with Lucien van der Walt's contribution. We examine the entire labour landscape, both in terms of recent events central to the fragmentation of labour and as a map for the future direction of research.

NOTE

1   Zuma was sentenced to a 15-month jail sentence by the Constitutional Court after he defied a summons to appear before the State Capture Commission in 2021. The commission, which was headed by Deputy Chief Justice Raymond Zondo, had been asked to investigate broad allegations of corruption and state capture involving several senior state officials, together with business leaders in the private sector.

REFERENCES

Baskin, Jeremy. 1991. *Striking Back: A History of Cosatu.* London and New York: Verso.

Bezuidenhout, Andries. 2000. *Towards Global Social Movement Unionism? Trade Union Responses to Globalization in South Africa.* Labour and Society Programme Discussion Paper 15 of 2000. Geneva: International Institute for Labour Studies.

Bezuidenhout, Andries, Christine Bischoff and Ntsehiseng Nthejane. 2017. 'Is Cosatu Still a Working-Class Movement?' In *Labour Beyond Cosatu: Mapping the Rupture in South Africa's Labour Landscape,* edited by Andries Bezuidenhout and Malehoko Tshoaedi, 48–61. Johannesburg: Wits University Press.

Bezuidenhout, Andries and Malehoko Tshoaedi, eds. 2017. *Labour Beyond Cosatu: Mapping the Rupture in South Africa's Labour Landscape.* Johannesburg: Wits University Press.

Bezuidenhout, Andries, Sonwabile Mnwana and Karl von Holdt, eds. 2022. *Critical Engagement with Public Sociology: A Perspective from the Global South.* Bristol: Bristol University Press.

Buhlungu, Sakhela. 2006. *Trade Unions and Democracy: Cosatu Workers' Political Attitudes in South Africa.* Pretoria: HSRC Press.

Buhlungu, Sakhela. 2009. 'South Africa: The Decline of Labor Studies and the Democratic Transition'. *Work and Occupations* 36 (2): 145–161.

Buhlungu, Sakhela and Malehoko Tshoaedi, eds. 2013. *Cosatu's Contested Legacy: South African Trade Unions in the Second Decade of Democracy.* Johannesburg: Wits University Press.

Clawson, Dan. 2003. *The Next Upsurge: Labor and the New Social Movements.* Ithaca, NY: Cornell University Press.

Elsley, Trenton, Shane Godfrey and Mario Jacobs. 2019. *Breaking the Chain: Value Chain Analysis as a Tool for Renewing Trade Union Bargaining and Organising Strategies.* Cape Town: Labour Research Services.

Fantasia, Rick and Kim Voss. 2004. *Hard Work: Remaking the American Labor Movement.* Oakland, CA: University of California Press.

Friedman, Steven. 1987. *Building Tomorrow Today: African Workers in Trade Unions, 1970–1984.* Johannesburg: Ravan Press.

Hlatshwayo, Mondli. 2020. 'Solidarity during the "Outsourcing Must Fall" Campaign: The Role of Different Players in Ending Outsourcing at South African Universities'. *Politikon* 47 (3): 305–320.

Kenny, Bridget. 2020. 'The South African Labour Movement: A Fragmented and Shifting Terrain'. *Tempo Social* 32 (1): 119–136.

Kenny, Bridget and Edward Webster. 2021. 'The Return of the Labour Process: Race, Skill and Technology in South African Labour Studies'. *Work in the Global Economy* 1 (1–2): 13–32.

Maake, Tshepo Bethuel. 2019. 'Spaces of Discrimination and Multiple Identities: Experiences of Black Homosexual Mineworkers'. Master's diss., University of Johannesburg.

Makhanya, Mondli. 2019. 'Shut Down the Shutdowns'. *City Press*, 18 November 2019. https://city-press.news24.com/Voices/mondli-makhanya-shut-down-the-shutdowns-20191118.

Milkman, Ruth. 2020. *Immigrant Labor and the New Precariat*. London: John Wiley & Sons.

Milkman Ruth, Luke Elliott-Negri, Kathleen Griesbach and Adam Reich. 2021. 'Gender, Class, and the Gig Economy: The Case of Platform-based Food Delivery'. *Critical Sociology* 47 (3): 357–372.

Moody, Kim. 1997. *Workers in a Lean World: Unions in the International Economy*. New York: Verso.

National Income Dynamics Study and Coronavirus Rapid Mobile Survey (NIDS-CRAM). 2020. *Synthesis Report NIDS-CRAM Wave 2*, September 2020. https://cramsurvey.org/wp-content/uploads/2020/10/1.-Spaull-et-al.-NIDS-CRAM-Wave-2-Synthesis-Report.pdf. Accessed 22 March 2021.

Nyoka, Bongani. 2013. 'Negation and Affirmation: A Critique of Sociology in South Africa'. *African Sociological Review / Revue Africaine De Sociologie* 17 (1): 2–24.

Phelan, Craig. 2009. *Trade Union Revitalisation: Trends and Prospects in 34 Countries*. Bern: Peter Lang.

Pillay, Devan. 2017. *Trade Union Revitalisation in South Africa: Green Shoots or False Dawns?* Global Labour University Working Paper No. 51, Berlin.

Scully, Ben. 2016a. 'Precarity North and South: A Southern Critique of Guy Standing'. *Global Labour Journal* 7 (2): 160–173.

Scully, Ben. 2016b. 'From the Shop Floor to the Kitchen Table: The Shifting Centre of Precarious Workers' Politics in South Africa'. *Review of African Political Economy* 43 (148): 295–311.

Seidman, Gay. 1994. *Manufacturing Militance: Workers' Movements in Brazil and South Africa, 1970–1985*. Oakland, CA: University of California Press.

Sitas, Ari. 2004. *Voices that Reason: Theoretical Parables*. London: Brill.

Sitas, Ari. 2014. 'Rethinking Africa's Sociological Project'. *Current Sociology* 62 (4): 457–471.

Standing, Guy. 2011. *The Precariat: The New Dangerous Class*. London: Bloomsbury.

Statistics South Africa. 2020. *Quarterly Labour Force Survey*. Quarter Two. September 2020. Pretoria: Stats SA.

Tshoaedi, Malehoko. 2008. Roots of Women's Union Activism: South Africa, 1973–2003. PhD diss., University of Leiden.

Tshoaedi, Malehoko and Hlengiwe Hlela. 2006. 'The Marginalisation of Women Unionists during South Africa's Transition'. In *Trade Unions and Democracy: Cosatu Workers' Political Attitudes in South Africa*, edited by Sakhela Buhlungu. Cape Town: HSRC Press.

Von Holdt, Karl. 2002. 'Social Movement Unionism: The Case of South Africa'. *Work, Employment and Society* 16 (2): 283–304.

Von Holdt, Karl. 2003. *Transition from Below: Forging Trade Unionism and Workplace Change in South Africa*. Pietermaritzburg: University of Natal Press.

Webster, Edward. 2020. 'The Uberisation of Work: The Challenge of Regulating Platform Capitalism. A Commentary'. *International Review of Applied Economics* 34: 1–10.

Webster, Edward. 2022. 'Choosing Sides: The Promise and Pitfalls of a Critically Engaged Sociology in Apartheid South Africa'. In *Critical Engagement with Public Sociology*, edited by Andries Bezuidenhout, Sonwabile Mnwana and Karl von Holdt, 44–60. Bristol: Bristol University Press.

1

Fragmented Labour Movement, Fragmented Labour Studies: New Directions for Research and Theory

Lucien van der Walt

Before the rise of studies of the modern labour movement in South Africa from the 1970s, studies of working-class struggles and of workers' movements were relatively rare. The major works on unions were written by unionists and other activists outside the academy (Gitsham and Trembath 1926; Andrews [1941] 1977; Meyer 1944; Forman [1959] 1992; Walker and Weinbren 1961). Within the academy, the working class was certainly studied, but rarely as an active agent of social change: it appeared in studies of stratification (Seekings 2009); in work on social problems, especially the poor whites (Jubber 1983; Webster 1985b); and in ergonomics, marketing, management and race relations, often with an emphasis on productivity issues (Silberbauer 1968; Tiley 1974).

There was a major shift from the early 1970s, marked by the rise of a more critical 'radical' school of social science, especially in history and sociology. Generally speaking, Marxist approaches took centre stage, including Braverman's labour process theory, Thompsonian-style 'new' labour history and various forms of structuralism; class analysis was the key (Saunders 1988, 2007; Bonner 1994; Webster 2004). Feminist thinking played a role, but it too was often deeply influenced by Marxism and concerned with political economy (Cock 1980; Bozzoli 1983). Labour history was an integral part of this project, and traditional boundaries between history and industrial sociology largely broke down.

This new body of work was closely associated with a new generation of scholars, mainly at the more liberal English-speaking universities, mostly white South Africans. It emerged against the backdrop of the global rebellions of the 1960s and, within South Africa, the 1973 Durban strikes and the 1976 uprising (Saunders 1988; Bonner 1994; Webster 2004).

It drew much of its energy from engagement with the struggles of the time, and there were notable efforts to reach beyond the academy by, for example, working with the new wave of unions, writing popular histories and holding Open Days at History Workshop conferences at the University of the Witwatersrand, which in 1987 hosted over 3 000 trade unionists and township activists. A complex network of labour service organisations, popular publishers and non-governmental organisations provided a key vector for the circulation of, and a key space for the further development of, the new work and growing emphasis on the importance of labour movements. The single most comprehensive national labour history to date appeared in 1987 (expanded in 1989: Lacom 1989b), not from a university but from, for example, the Labour and Community Resources Project (Lacom) of the South African Committee for Higher Education.[1]

These were key developments, although the innovations were sometimes exaggerated by contemporary commentators. Marxist and other left analyses of South African society such as revolutionary syndicalist accounts actually dated back to the 1910s, and they were largely developed outside of the academy before the 1970s (Saunders 1988; Nasson 1990; Van der Walt 2007a).

There were some overlaps: notably, work by communist exile Harold Wolpe (Alexander 2007, 111), and Trotskyist activist Martin Legassick (Saunders 1988, 172–176) was influential in academia. But generally speaking, these existing traditions and the new scholarship rarely intersected. For example, it is significant that the core South African Communist Party (SACP) theory – that South Africa was based on 'colonialism of a special type' – was almost completely absent in the new work. For its part, the party was inclined to dismiss the new radicals as living in an 'imaginary' South Africa, blinded by the dogmas of the 'armchairs of Europe' (Toussaint 1983, 43). Some of the Trotskyists felt their work had been marginalised, and viewed the new body of professionalised work with misgivings (Nasson 1990, 202–203).

Within the history discipline, it became commonplace to set up an unduly hard distinction between an older 'liberal' tradition and an emerging 'revisionist' school. In fact, key 'liberal' works anticipated 'revisionist' concerns with economic factors and the centrality of cheap, unfree black labour; many leading 'revisionists' came from liberal and Africanist schools stressing black history rather than from Marxism (Saunders 1988; Bozzoli and Delius 1990). Polemical debates elided the complexities and changes on both sides, as well as overlaps (Nattrass 1991).

It is true that by the late 1960s sociology was much influenced by Parsonian structural-functionalism, with its emphasis on stability (Webster 1985b, 2004; Jubber 2006, 332). It is also true that the new school sought to break with pluralist analyses that reduced South African history and society to an endless, supposedly self-explanatory conflict between neatly bounded and fixed nations and races, by examining the role of classes and the political economy (Slater 1976, Chapter 1). However, academic class analysis preceded the new school, emerging from a large tradition of Weberian-inflected work from the 1940s, which has been almost completely elided by accounts of the 1970s break (Seekings 2009).

Moreover, the older approaches often persisted in 'radical' work, but under new labels. Many History Workshop pieces in the popular *New Nation* newspaper showed little trace of class analysis: they were, basically, still pluralist accounts of relations between 'the Boers', 'the British', 'the whites', 'the Indians', 'the Xhosa', 'the Zulu', 'the blacks' and so on, also emphasising great men like kings, generals and governors (New Nation/History Workshop 1989). This tendency to a lack of systematic theory and conceptual clarity has long dogged modern South African labour studies.

Lastly, by no means all staff in fields like history and sociology hewed to the new approaches; for example, traditional approaches to industrial relations remained common (see the materials in Bendix 1988), while structural-functionalism was still widespread in Afrikaner and black institutions in the 1990s. Weberian approaches enjoyed a modest revival from the 1980s as well, as many sociologists found the new school's typically reductionist explanations of state activity unsatisfactory (Posel 1983, 1991; Hyslop 1992).

THE YEARS OF HOPE

That said, the new work *was* new. It was shaped, as noted, by the class struggles of the time, and it was interested in new issues. Earlier social policy work was concerned with solving social problems such as white poverty; the more critical industrial relations work of the past, such as that influenced by Elton Mayo, was interested in productivity issues (Webster 1985b, 44); the older Weberian class analyses were interested in stratification (and the black middle class) not class struggles.

By contrast, the new work focused on a radical critique of the existing order, and on recovering the history of earlier struggles, and this very often was with an eye on their lessons for contemporary movements (Bonner 1978). South Africa's racial and national questions were systemically explained as arising from a coercive labour and racist system, and late industrialisation taking place in a context where (to quote a key 'revisionist') 'capitalist relations of exploitation were constructed upon colonial relations of domination' (Bundy 1991, 32). Such work helped break down the distinction between history and sociology, enriching both.

The modern working class and its struggles took centre stage, with an emphasis on the unions in the Trade Union Advisory Coordinating Council (Tuacc 1974–1979), its successors the Federation of South African Trade Unions (Fosatu 1979–1985) and the Congress of South African Trade Unions (Cosatu 1985–). Within these federations, unions based on manufacturing and mining, such as the Metal and Allied Workers Union (Mawu) and its successor the National Union of Metalworkers of South Africa (Numsa), the National Union of Mineworkers (NUM), and the South African Clothing and Textile Workers' Union (Sactwu), received the most scholarly attention.

It was increasingly argued that unions should be understood not only in relation to older union traditions – South Africa's union movement is one of the oldest in Africa, dating to the 1880s (Andrews [1941] 1977) – but in terms of the ongoing transformation of the workforce through the changing labour process. From this perspective, the new wave of unionism from the 1970s was partly the result of the rise of big Fordist factories from the 1950s, run by local conglomerates and foreign multinationals: semi-skilled industrial workers, centralised in larger factories and townships, were seen as the core of the new unionism (Southall 1985). This was part of a larger body of work that linked changes in trade unionism to changes in the labour process, with emphasis on the 1920s to the 1950s (Lewis 1984) and the 1960s to the 1970s (Webster 1985a).

The increasingly overt political role of the new unionism in the 1980s was then explained as, in large part, arising from the unwillingness of an authoritarian state, presiding over relatively successful late industrialisation via import substitution industrialisation (ISI), to extend citizenship to a rapidly growing urban industrial working class. The coincidence of the economic exploitation faced by workers in despotic workplaces, and the political oppression faced by those same workers in grim working-class slums, helped build a bridge between 'economic' and 'political' demands, and a search for alliances (Seidman 2011, 95).

This supposedly fostered what was increasingly described as 'social movement unionism', referring to politicised unions forming alliances with other sectors of civil society to win democratic reforms (Seidman 2011). In South Africa, where racial and national oppression was integral to both exploitation and oppression, the effect was that unions became closely intertwined with national liberation struggles (Buhlungu 2010; Von Holdt 2003). Framing union politics around the contradictions of an authoritarian state, ISI and a growing Fordist working class invited comparisons with late-industrialising countries, first in Latin America (Cooper 1991; Seidman 1994) and then East Asia (Webster, Lambert and Bezuidenhout 2008). There was also a burgeoning literature making comparisons with the United States of America, mostly prompted by interest in black workers (for example, Cole 2018).

Cosatu unions played a key role in the democratic transition, winning major labour reforms at a time when union rights were under attack worldwide, and pushed for a 'left-Keynesian' progressive-competitive approach to capitalist globalisation (Webster and Adler 2000, 17). Given what was achieved by 1994 and how confident the unions were, and the policy and political capacities they had developed by this time, such hopes did not seem fanciful. The new wave of unions grew explosively in the state sector from the end of the 1980s, including in the civil service and the big state-owned corporations. Bodies like Cosatu's National Education, Health and Allied Workers' Union (Nehawu) eventually reached the size of NUM and Numsa, hitherto the biggest affiliates. Others, like the South African Municipal Workers Union (Samwu), became the dominant unions in their sectors. Union density reached 59 per cent in 1993 (up from 15.4 per cent in 1979), with 2 890 174 union members in total (Macun 2000, Table 3.1, 60).

It did not seem at all unreasonable to suppose that Cosatu's project of 'radical reform' would work. For a left battered by the fall of the Berlin Wall, the failure of the Keynesian welfare state, and the crisis in ISI everywhere – including South Africa's racial variant (Gelb 1991) – it was an immensely attractive, purportedly feasible approach (Godongwana 1992). It hinged, however, on union participation in pacts with employers, engagement in corporatist bodies like the National Economic Development and Labour Council, formed in 1994 at union urging, and winning influence in the Tripartite Alliance set up between Cosatu and the now-legal African National Congress (ANC) and SACP.

THE YEARS OF DISAPPOINTMENT

Enthusiasm for Cosatu, and work on the labour movement more generally, declined from the 2000s. The most notable change took place in historical work, where labour history (including work on the history of unions) almost completely disappeared. Internationally, the 'glory days' of labour history were the 1960s to the early 1980s; they were closely linked to the massive waves of workers' struggles in that period, including in South Africa. The defeats that followed, the crisis of the left, and neo-liberal globalisation, shook the optimism about the cause of labour that was very much a part of the field (Bonner, Hyslop and Van der Walt 2007, 138).

In South Africa, these coincided with the retreat of the great wave of struggle that had started in Durban in 1973. Unions remained active, but the biggest and most militant – that is, those affiliated to Cosatu – were now allied to the governing party. Many students' and residents' movements imploded, or were incorporated into the ANC apparatus, with the mass-based civil society coalition, the United Democratic Front, disbanded in 1991. The energy that had driven labour history in the 1970s and 1980s was dissipating, as student numbers in the discipline fell, posts closed and the concerns of the 1980s began to seem increasingly quaint (Bonner 1994; Saunders 2007).

Unlike the National Party (NP), the ANC was keen to work with the English-medium liberal universities and, especially, the radical scholars who had aligned with the anti-apartheid struggle and who were optimistic about the incoming ANC government. Erstwhile labour and social historians shifted to work on ANC biographies, local histories of townships, developing materials for the new school textbooks, and providing usable histories for government agencies.

A further blow came as ANC figures sought to establish a new patriotic history wherein modern South African history centred on a unified, essentially national-ist and ANC-led struggle. Viewed from this perspective, unions were bit players in a party story, either heroic (when led by the ANC or SACP), or foolish and/or reactionary (if not). There was little space for realities such as that the union move-ment was decades older than the ANC, consistently larger in terms of formal membership, had its own dynamics and impacts, and often sceptical of nationalism in favour of more class-based politics.

Patriotic history required distortions and fabrications to 'repress uncomfortable truths' in service of 'nationalist orthodoxy' – not least with regard to the 1970s wave of unionism (Legassick 2008, 241). Likewise, Fosatu's radical anti-capitalist 'workerism' – aiming at extensive workers' control of economy and society – was caricatured as yellow unionism or narrow economism because it criticised the pol-itics of the ANC, SACP and the South African Congress of Trade Unions (Sactu) (Byrne, Ulrich and Van der Walt 2017).

Labour history also largely disappeared within sociology. Many sociologists turned to policy development and commissioned studies, both for the unions and the new government. Studies of labour, including by postgraduates, focused primarily on contemporary challenges, such as the changing workplace (Von Holdt and Webster 2005; Bezuidenhout and Buhlungu 2011; Mosoetsa 2011), and the evolution of Cosatu post-apartheid (Webster and Adler 2000; Buhlungu 2010). The post-apartheid scholarship also saw to a focus on the history of women in Cosatu unions, including their involvement in the founding of unions and in workplace struggles for recognition of trade unions (Tshoaedi 2017). This work further highlighted women's struggles for gender equality during the 1970s and 1980s, and contestations for leadership positions in the post-apartheid Cosatu unions (Tshoaedi 2013, 2017).

Labour studies expressed some early concerns that the transition would itself change, indeed weaken, the unions in a fundamental way. Cosatu was losing leaders to the new ANC government, to an emerging black bourgeoisie and to endless collective bargaining meetings and to the National Economic Development and Labour Council; there was growing conflict between union leaders and members; the cohesion and vigour once provided by an escalating battle against a common enemy, apartheid, was fading; economic liberalisation, which was adopted from around 1979 by the old NP, was increasingly embraced by the ANC, with devastating effects on unionised sectors like textiles; there were indications of racial tensions in unions between coloureds, Indians and black Africans (on these issues see *inter alia* Surtee 1999; Webster and Adler 2000, 5, 10–11, 13–15; Von Holdt 2005, 66–69). Cosatu (1997) itself worried about these developments, and factored them into the scenario planning process of its 1997 September Commission on the future of the unions. Further noted by the September Commission was the federation's failure to address concerns of gender inequality within its ranks. The Commission criticised Cosatu for its double standards on women leadership and failure to adopt affirmative action policies to address inequities in leadership appointment (Cosatu 1997; Tshoaedi 2013, 2017).

Subsequent developments would bear out some of the most pessimistic projections, and lead directly to widespread disillusion among scholars. Research on efforts to transform the workplace – ending the cheap black labour system, and enabling global competitiveness and efficient state services through union-management pacts – revealed a dismal picture of authoritarianism, conflict, corruption and failure (Von Holdt 2005, 2010).

While Cosatu unions were able to win ongoing labour law reforms, they proved unable to affect major economic or social policy, yet stayed wedded to an ANC that was actively fostering free trade, flexible labour and corruption (Buhlungu 2010). Grumbling within the Tripartite Alliance went nowhere; instead, factional battles between rival ANC elites increasingly spilled over into the federation.

Having naively blamed the ANC's shifts almost entirely on then-President Thabo Mbeki, the leadership of the federation and of its affiliates, including Nehawu, NUM and Numsa, convinced itself that his main rival, Jacob Zuma, represented some sort of progressive alternative that would save the party (Van der Walt 2006). Like the SACP, Cosatu was largely swept up in the Zuma mobilisations; it suppressed dissent and backed Zuma's fateful victory at the ANC's Polokwane conference in 2007 (Pillay 2008). This was a disastrous miscalculation, as the Zumaites used privatisation schemes as channels for massive corruption, pushed austerity, unleashed the police against protestors and strikers, most notoriously at Marikana in 2012, and presided over rapid economic decline and the near-collapse of major state corporations.

Research also revealed that Cosatu and its affiliates were increasingly marred by the growing power of leaders, corruption scandals (especially in union investment companies), political intolerance and dogmatism, declining workers' democratic control of unions, and splits due to leadership infighting and members' frustrations (Buhlungu 2010; Mabasa and Chinguno 2018, 319–325; Mopeli 2021). The NUM, for example, suffered numerous breakaways from the 1990s onwards (Sefalafala 2010; Moodie 2016; Botiveau 2017). The most serious would prove to be the Association of Mineworkers and Construction Union (Amcu): after years of obscurity, it made dramatic gains on the platinum belt in the 2010s, where it became the majority union (Botiveau 2017). The unions proved largely unable to organise or represent the masses of casual and outsourced workers, which formed a growing sector of the working class. Then Cosatu itself split in 2014–2015, as Numsa and the Food and Allied Workers Union (Fawu) left to join with other, mostly very small, unions to form a new South African Federation of Trade Unions (Saftu) two years later, in 2017: this claimed to have over 700 000 members.

It is not very surprising that the older enthusiasm for Cosatu faded in labour studies. Some moved from optimistic assessments of union projects and prospects (Von Holdt 1998; Buhlungu 2000), to much more pessimistic assessments of the unions (Buhlungu, Brookes and Wood 2008), the persistence of strike violence (Von Holdt 2010a), racial conflicts (Buhlungu 2010), sexism in unions (Tshoaedi 2013), and the role of state sector unions in perpetuating the shocking state government services to the poor (Von Holdt 2010b).

There was a growing emphasis on the fragmentation of the workforce in the context of outsourcing, deindustrialisation and mass unemployment, and the unions' apparent inability to represent the precarious or 'peripheral' workforce (Barchiesi and Kenny 2002; Van der Walt et al. 2003; Webster and Bischoff 2011). Running alongside this was growing interest in marginal groups like waste-pickers and street traders (Samson 2015), workers coping with long-term unemployment

(Nkhatau 2012; Sefalafala 2018), and workers' struggles outside of traditional unions (Dickinson 2016; Sinwell with Mbatha 2016).

There were two main exceptions to increasingly pessimistic views of the unions. First, there was (usually short-lived) excitement around what seemed to represent major ruptures with the past. For some, this centred on the so-called 'Numsa moment', in which the union rejected the ANC (and SACP), failed to win its position in Cosatu and was ousted (in 2015), co-founded Saftu (in 2017), and engaged in processes to create a new left pole, notably sponsoring the Socialist Revolutionary Workers Party (in 2018). Hope was also placed in bodies like Amcu and the workers' committees that emerged in mining, the Post Office and universities (Ness 2016). Second, there was a growing interest in examples of union renewal, often emphasising the need for unions to move beyond 'core' workers, especially towards non-waged workers (Webster, Britwum and Bhowmik 2017).

THE IMPRINT OF PAST EMPHASES

Against this backdrop, we can map out the broad patterns of what has been covered in studies of the modern labour movement in South Africa, and outline some new directions that could be taken. Before doing so, it is important to emphasise just how innovative, rich and path-breaking the new scholarship on South Africa was. This work was mainly done by local scholars rather than by Western scholars engaging from afar. While the work was influenced by approaches from abroad, like labour process theory (Braverman 1974) and the 'new' Thompsonian history, these were never simply imported wholesale. They were critically engaged and formed part of something new. It entailed a challenge to colonial histories and a transformation of Marxist-influenced approaches that rejected economism and grappled with gender and race, developing (along with Brazil and India), some of the most innovative labour studies in the so-called Global South, and influencing the Western academy itself with its development of ideas around internal colonialism, racial capitalism and social movement unionism (Webster 2004; Van der Linden 2007, 169–170; Seidman 2011; Iggers 2016, 243–244).

The trajectory of studies of the local labour movement has left a deep imprint. As indicated, these studies – both historical and sociological – were deeply shaped by the wave of unionism from the 1970s, focused on the Tuacc/Fosatu/ Cosatu lineage, with the focus on big blue-collar unions like Mawu/Numsa, NUM and Sactwu; in addition, the South African Commercial, Catering and Allied Workers Union (Saccawu), Nehawu and the South African Democratic Teachers Union (Sadtu) attracting growing interest (Amoako 2012, 2014).

The history of Cosatu was, in turn, represented as the latest phase in a history of progressive unions, traced back through Sactu (formed in 1953), the Council of Non-European Trade Unions (formed in 1941), the left-wing industrial unions affiliated to the multi-racial South African Trades and Labour Council (founded in 1930), and the Industrial and Commercial Workers' Union (ICU) formed in 1919.

When other unions were examined, the focus was on examples of what *not* to do: the exclusivist white unions that championed job colour bars, Afrikaner nationalist unions, and moderate unions like the Trade Union Council of South Africa (Tucsa), were all deemed to have been 'incorporated' by the racist state from 1924 (Davies 1979; O'Meara 1983). The argument was, roughly, that the statutory industrial relations system first established by the 1924 Industrial Conciliation Act allowed many coloured, Indian and white workers to have 'registered' unions with rights, access to dispute resolution and (in some cases) protected strikes. Most unions involved in the system, it was argued, became bureaucratic and moderate. White workers also made rapid gains through job reservation, and racist wage, welfare and educational systems. They were institutionally divided from black African workers, who were largely excluded from the Act[2] and faced with numerous other discriminatory and coercive measures, including substantial restrictions on strikes. Thus, the argument went, the white working class was severed from its own militant past – like the 1922 Rand Revolt, an armed insurrection – as well as its class comrades, becoming co-opted into the racial capitalist system.

The story of militant, left-wing unions provided a useable past and heroic lineage for the new unionism, featured prominently at the History Workshop's Open Days, in pamphlets by the Labour History Group (for example, Horn 1981) and in Lacom materials, and was also central to discussions of the lessons of past experiences in, for example, the Fosatu (1985) media.

While politically useful, the emphasis on a leftist, non-racial tradition could easily imply a neat organisational and political continuity. It is important to note that there is no simple line of descent between these unions, and that there were many ruptures. For example, while Tuacc and Fosatu always had ANC and Sactu activists, neither was founded, led nor notably influenced by either (Legassick 2008). Fosatu (1985) analyses, indeed, were openly critical of the Sactu tradition, and framed the new federation as a sharp break with it.

The reduction of union history to that of left-wing unions was also very misleading. The left-wing unions were not a majority of the South African labour movement before the end of the twentieth century. There was one (brief) exception: in the late 1920s, the ICU (briefly) reached 100 000 members in South Africa; adding this to the left-wing of the other main bodies – the Cape Federation of Labour and the South African Trades Union Congress – would have pushed the membership of the left unions to over 50 per cent of the total for the first and only time before the 1990s.

According to Fosatu's Chemical Workers Industrial Union, 'In the 50's and early 60's the major grouping of trade unions was SACTU' (CWIU 1984, 1). This was simply not true. Sactu was founded with just 32 000 members, and never exceeded 50 000. Meanwhile, there were 145 000 in the whites-only, pro-apartheid South African Confederation of Labour (Sacol), formed in 1957, and 183 400 in the moderate Tucsa, founded in 1954. The Federation of South African Labour Unions (Fedsal), founded in 1959, was around 24 000 in 1973 (Ulrich 2022, 15–16). At its launch, Fosatu was a fifth the size of Tucsa, and a third the size of Sacol (Byrne, Ulrich and van der Walt 2017, 257). In 1993, Cosatu accounted for less than half of union membership (Macun 2000, Table 3.1, 60, Table 3.3, 65), most in just three affiliates: NUM, Numsa and Sactwu (Von Holdt 1993, 19).

A related problem was a tendency to view the new unionism from the 1970s as merely about new, independent or unregistered *unions*. But older registered unions were key players. The Food and Canning Workers Union, formed in 1941 and part of Sactu before it collapsed as a functioning federation in the 1960s, was very active, also helping to found Fawu. Some used their positions in the moderate, multi-racial Tucsa to help new unions (Keal 2009). Tucsa's Western Province Motor Assembly Workers Union and its National Union of Motor Assembly and Rubber Workers of South Africa worked with Mawu, helped found Fosatu, and provided its first general secretary, Joe Foster. Samwu was co-founded by the Cape Town Municipal Workers Association which dated to the 1910s, providing over three-quarters of the founding members (Rudin 1996). The South African Society of Bank Officials, formerly of Tucsa, joined Cosatu in the 1990s (Moyo 2022). 'Registered' unions were never simply appendages of the state, or sweetheart formations – a point to which I will return when looking at white workers.

THE BIGGEST SINGLE EMPLOYER WAS NEVER CAPITAL

The focus on the militant unions, and specifically Tuacc/Fosatu/Cosatu, and on mainly black, usually blue-collar unions in the private sector, as well as the interest in Fordism and ISI, also meant there was little interest in the long history of state-sector unionism and the state as an employer, or in other workers' organisations other than unions. Such blind spots left substantial gaps in both our understanding of existing unions and federations, and of their lineages and traditions. This has been reinforced by the general decline in labour history itself, especially that dealing with unions.

The blind spots are obvious when we revisit how accounts of post-1973 unions discuss the labour law reforms that followed the Wiehahn Commission, appointed in 1977, which was tasked with examining labour legislation. Wiehahn recommended the removal of racial exclusions from labour laws like the Industrial Conciliation Act, as well as of statutory job reservation. (Contrary to popular belief, it was never illegal for black African workers to join unions, nor were bodies like the ICU or Sactu banned.) The commission simply proposed the removal of racist restrictions, so that all existing and future unions could register on equal terms, subject to equal regulation by the state.

The changes, soon made law, are still widely described in the literature as union rights being, finally, 'granted to all Africans' (Baskin 1991, 26–27). This is simply not true – it is an example of the how the blind spots have affected analyses.

First, laws passed in 'white' South Africa did not automatically apply to self-governing and 'independent' homelands. In 1970, homelands were formally exempted from key South African labour laws; most promulgated their own extremely draconian laws and ignored Wiehahn (Haysom and Khoza 1984).

Second, the post-Wiehahn reforms in 'white' South Africa retained the original Industrial Conciliation Act's exclusion, from the statutory industrial relations system, of employees in essential services and education including universities; of large parts of the civil service, government work and the state-owned corporations; and of all domestic and agricultural jobs. In 1972, only 600 000 of around 2.4 million coloured, Indian and white workers were covered by the Act (Du Toit 1976, 56, 78).

In short, a very large number of coloured, Indian and white workers never actually got union rights in 1924; and these sectoral and occupational exclusions were retained with the Wiehahn reforms from 1979, which were also not fully applicable to the homelands. This left many workers of all races – including many black Africans – still outside the statutory industrial relations system.[3] These substantial exclusions were only removed with the post-apartheid, Labour Relations Act in 1995. (This meant, interestingly, that academics – radical or otherwise – did not have full union rights before the democratic transition).

The focus on the new wave of unionism, initially concentrated in the private sector and on the big blue-collar unions in that sector, led to serious neglect of the role of the long history of unions in the state, of studies of the state as workplace including via labour process theory, and of the distinctive logic of state activity. Understanding the state on its own terms is still neglected in labour movement studies, where the state typically appears as an agent of violence, patronage, or just another big employer.

Here, it is essential to bear in mind that the South African state has been the single biggest employer, investor, spender and receiver of revenue in the country for nearly a century. The state was (and is) the single biggest economic actor in the country, commanding vast resources. The focus during the 1980s on big private conglomerates ('white monopoly capital') by Cosatu (1987) and academics (for example, Savage 1988) largely ignored the fact that, out of the ten largest centralised economic entities, three were state-owned enterprises – South African Railways and Harbours (at number one), Eskom (third) and Iscor (ninth); the state-controlled but privately owned Reserve Bank was sixth (Innes 1983, 176).

This pattern has not changed. In 2018, Eskom was the fourth largest Africa-based profit-making corporation; and if we combine all the Transnet (the successor to South African Railways and Harbours) divisions, that entity comes in tenth on the continent (Africa Report 2019). The Public Investment Corporation is Africa's biggest sovereign wealth fund and asset manager, responsible for 12.5 per cent of the capitalisation of the Johannesburg Securities Exchange (Van der Walt, Klerck and Helliker 2022). The state also owns over 25 per cent of all land, including 55 per cent in the economic hub provinces of Gauteng and the Western Cape (Rumney 2005, 405–406).

There is a case, then, for a more nuanced analysis of the working class within the state, and of the long and distinctive history of state-sector unionism. Unions were active in the state-run railways and rail workshops as early as 1903; the revolutionary Industrial Workers of the World organised the Johannesburg trams around 1910; the (coloured) Teachers' League of South Africa was founded in 1913, the (white) South African Association of Municipal Employees in 1917; the ICU was founded in 1919 on the state-run docks, and much of its early membership was within the state sector.

Vast swathes of workers in the state sector were excluded by the Industrial Conciliation Act and its successors, although parts of the civil service had very limited rights with the 1920 Public Service Act. 'Staff associations' managed to claw out some victories, but had little mobilising power. For example, the (initially white) Public Servants Association (PSA), founded in 1920, was recognised (Macun and Psoulis 2000, 95–96), while the (mainly coloured) Cape Town Municipal Workers Association was recognised by the Cape Town municipality from the 1940s (Rudin 1996).

There was, then, not only a very long-standing and substantial history of state-sector unionism, but also a mixture of union types in the state, with approaches ranging from the more confrontational Industrial Workers of the World and ICU through to the moderation of staff associations and unions like the PSA and many affiliates of Fedsal (Ulrich 2022). So, the history and traditions of these unions is important in its own right, for explaining why many of the older state sector unions have proved so resilient post-apartheid, and for explaining the politics and the context of the Cosatu state-sector unions (see below).

State-sector unionism is nothing new: nearly a third of union membership, and at least 36 unions and staff associations, were active in the state sector in the early 1970s, while the biggest single union in the country was a Sacol municipal union (Du Toit 1976, 78, 168, 170, 173–176).

Under apartheid, the state as employer preferred to work with more pliant bodies, like conservative black teachers' associations and mild-mannered white civil servants' bodies. Some parts of the state actively fostered new staff associations in the 1980s to forestall militant unions (Kiloh and Sibeko 2000, 99–100). The old government did not shy away from using extensive systems of patronage in the homelands, as well as in the core 'white' state, on ethnic and racial lines and to political loyalists (Posel 2000; Chipkin and Meny-Gibert 2012).

Moreover, without in any way suggesting a moral equivalence between the NP and the ANC, there are striking parallels in the nationalist states that each forged. These similarities include a steady ballooning of bureaucratic posts, high levels of ineffi- ciency, 'cadre deployment', patronage, racial loyalism, fractured decision-making and competing goals (Von Holdt 2010b; Maylam 2013). In this situation, there is a growing merger of the ruling party and the state apparatus, including capture of unelected senior posts in the bureaucracies and state industries, and the spill-over of factional battles within the ruling party into the state itself. Obviously, these have major implications for unions and industrial relations.

Since the late 1980s Cosatu's growth has centred on the state sector, which now provides a (slight) majority of Cosatu's membership. Analysts have noted that Cosatu's membership numbers in the state sector rose from 78 000 in 1991, to 921 702 in 2012, and suggested that unions like Nehawu and Sadtu have benefitted handsomely from legal reforms and ANC patronage, as well as contributing to serious problems in service delivery – such as prioritising teachers' wages over investments in school infrastructure (Maree and Bischoff 2017, Table 11.1, 194).

But such analyses would surely be enriched by a more historical and compar- ative approach, examining the evolution of state-sector unions and government relations in the old South Africa, the evolution of professional bodies into unions like Sadtu – a craft rather than an industrial union – and grappling with the resil- ience of pre-Cosatu and non-Cosatu state-sector unions (see below). Non-Cosatu unions are often mentioned, but are rarely studied in depth in work on state-based unions (Maree and Bischoff 2017).

Labour process studies, looking at the past and present of state-sector work – especially white-collar work – are also needed. Studies of the wave of unionism from the 1970s claimed, as noted, a close link between Fordism and mass industrial unionism. This was an important insight but also a serious simplification. Unskilled migrant workers were key to the Tuacc and Fosatu unions (Ulrich 2007; Forrest 2011). State employees in municipalities and on the docks were integral from 1973 onwards (Rudin 1996). Labour process explanations of unionism can be unduly deterministic (Alexander 2007). Crucially, however, they have been largely absent from work on state-sector (as well as white-collar) unionism. There is recent work on scientific management in the apartheid bureaucracy (Roos 2020) and on the labour process in post-apartheid municipal call centres (Magoqwana and Matatu 2012), but much remains to be done.

COSATU IN CONTEXT: OTHER FEDERATIONS, UNIONS AND HISTORIES

More attention, then, should be paid to the other union traditions, histories and formations. The rise of Cosatu did not entail the eclipse of the rest of labour, including in the state. Tucsa collapsed in 1987, but in 1993 there were eight union federations, 201 unions and 2 890 174 unionists (Macun 2000, Table 3.1, 60, Table 3.3, 65). Cosatu was just one, with 15 affiliates and 1 300 000 members (Von Holdt 1993, 19). In 1999, there were 20 staff organisations in the public service, representing almost 96 per cent of staff (Macun and Psoulis 2000, 101); just a quarter of these were in Cosatu.

Cosatu's predominance should therefore not be read back into the past: it took another decade before Cosatu reached its peak of 1 900 000 members – just on two-thirds of unionists – but a decade later, it was down again to 1 600 000 with the loss of Fawu and Numsa, and the rise of Amcu. This was below its 1996 figure of 1 743 172 (Macun 2000, Table 3.4, 66), and less than half of total union membership. While the 2015 split was shocking, Cosatu has never been anything near the whole labour movement, even post-apartheid.

Despite this, many studies assume that a discussion of Cosatu suffices as a discussion of unionism in South Africa. Most studies of unions in South Africa before 2014 barely mentioned non-Cosatu unions and, when they did so, tended to discuss them in passing or as a dying breed. Even today, interest in non-Cosatu unions centres on Numsa (formerly of Cosatu) and Amcu (a split from Cosatu's NUM), and on the General Industries Workers Union of South Africa (a split from the Chemical, Energy, Paper, Printing, Wood and Allied Workers Union (Ceppwawu) and a Saftu founder union) (Rees 2011).

The Federation of Unions of South Africa (Fedusa) was founded in 1997 by two existing federations centred in the state: the Federation of South African Labour Unions (Fedsal) and the Federation of Organisations Representing Civil Employees. Fedusa numbers have long hovered around 600 000, making it (before the formation of Saftu) the second biggest federation. Like Saftu, Fedusa initially grew mainly by attracting existing bodies. In the Fedusa case, this meant affiliations by older unions or amalgamations of pre-existing unions, such as the National Professional Teachers' Organisation of South Africa and the Independent Municipal and Allied Workers Union (Imatu), as well as several newer (often general) unions (Ulrich 2022).

These unions and federations sometimes get mentioned in studies of the labour movement (notable examples: Macun and Psoulis 2000; Bezuidenhout 2017), including their role in big state-sector strikes in 1999, 2004, 2007 and 2011 (Bekker and Van der Walt 2010; Ceruti 2011; Amoako 2012; Ulrich 2022). But few have been studied in detail. For example, the first history of Fedusa was written in 2022 (Ulrich 2022).

THE CHANGING WHITE WORKING CLASS

These other unions barely feature in discussions of union democracy, renewal or innovation, yet have shown a surprising ability to adapt and grow, not least among black workers (Ulrich 2022). Fedusa's largest affiliate, the PSA, has reached 235 000 members, comparing favourably to Nehawu's 280 000 at the time of writing. Imatu, formerly of Fedusa, competes with Samwu. Like the PSA, it brands itself (with some success) as an efficient, non-aligned, service-providing union, as opposed to the allegedly strike-prone Cosatu unions (Musi 2010; Nthinya 2014). This flexibility and reinvention seems at odds with the traditional characterisation of Fedusa in the literature as bureaucratic (Ulrich 2022), a label that also obscures that Fedusa, its affiliates and similar formations have tiny budgets and staffs compared to Cosatu, its affiliates and the bigger Saftu unions.

It is also impossible to understand such unions without understanding their connections to coloured, Indian and white workers. Many came from craft union, staff association, Fedsal and Tucsa backgrounds. What is remarkable is the extent to which they have been able to develop into non-racial unions from the 1980s. Generally speaking, these unions are more non-racial than the bigger Cosatu and Saftu unions, in the sense that they are far more racially diverse in composition. Even more notable is the case of two traditionally moderate unions with large white memberships that went over to Cosatu and Saftu – the South African Society of Bank Officials went to Cosatu in the 1990s, and the South African Policing Union became Saftu's third largest affiliate.

But we know little about the major realignment in the white working class, as well as the racial politics, that such processes must have entailed. We also know little about how the white working class was itself affected by fragmentation once the large concentrations of white workers in the state corporations and civil service came to an end, as affirmative action and downsizing were applied from the 1990s.

The white working class after 1948 largely disappeared from labour history research, perhaps reflecting an 'implicit assumption' that class analysis was 'no longer valid' for whites (Money and Van Zyl-Hermann 2020, 1–2). But white workers have consistently been a large part of the union movement, not least in the state sector where the white workforce was increasingly concentrated: by the late 1950s, half the workforce of Iscor, South African Railways and Harbours and Sasol was white, a situation that persisted to the early 1990s (Kiloh and Sibeko 2000, 37, 86; Freund 2019, 42, 92–93). (This in fact meant, somewhat ironically, that a growing part of the white working class lacked union rights as apartheid progressed.)

There is one major exception: there have been several major studies of Solidarity (Solidariteit), including an official history (Visser 2008, translated and updated as Visser 2016), a monograph (Van Zyl-Hermann 2021), and several papers (including by the aforementioned and Xaba 2018). This union originated with the Transvaal Miners Association founded in 1902, later the Mineworkers Union (MWU). The union played a major role in the 1922 Rand Revolt, which centred on the job colour bar. It was won over to Afrikaner nationalism in the 1930s and 1940s (Naudé 1969; O'Meara 1983), helped found Sacol, initially enjoyed direct access to the apartheid government but moved into opposition by the late 1960s (Visser 2008, 2016), and it opposed the Wiehahn reforms as an attack on white workers (Van Zyl-Hermann 2021). Aligning itself with the anti-NP white right in the 1980s, the union was in a disastrous state by the early 1990s.

In the 1990s, the MWU started to reinvent itself. It left Sacol in 1992, and expanded beyond mining – initially, into state industries. The old blue-collar leadership was replaced from 1997 by university graduates. It developed into a general union (thus the new name, Solidarity), and positioned itself as a voice for racial minorities, but above all Afrikaners, rather than the white working class as such (Visser 2008, 2016). For instance, it reinvented the Rand Revolt as an Afrikaner (and SACP) rebellion against British imperialism, rather than a class battle (Van Zyl-Hermann 2021, 256–261).

The union, which had fallen below 30 000 members by 1992, could claim 180 000 members in 2019. It has attracted attention both because of its active use of litigation against measures like affirmative action, its founding of AfriForum in 2006, and its creation of the Solidarity Movement. That includes a job placement agency, financial services, in-house lawyers, sophisticated media, a research unit, its own technical college and university, promotion of Afrikaans publishing and music, allied student and youth groups, and charity and self-help groups

(Visser 2008, 2016; Xaba 2018; Van Zyl-Hermann 2021). This has expanded the impact of the union far beyond its membership. AfriForum, for example, has a 'booming voice' and 'a strong influence on the broader white society' (Du Preez 2018).

Three final points can be made here. First, it is important not to assume that the history and politics of a given union stop at the borders of a state, or that state borders are the obvious unit of analysis – that is methodological nationalism. The MWU had branches in Zambia and Zimbabwe in the 1930s (Van der Walt 2007b), but this was not unique: for example, the ICU also organised in Swaziland (now Eswatini), Lesotho, Namibia, Zambia and Zimbabwe (Johnson, Nieftagodien and Van der Walt 2022), the South African Society of Bank Officials was active in Malawi, Namibia and Zimbabwe (Moyo 2022), and Sacol was active in Namibia (Du Toit 1976, 81–82). In the 1940s, the Southern African Labour Congress brought together white trade unions and labour parties from four countries (Money 2018). Sactu collapsed as a functioning federation in the 1960s, but it remained active in exile and underground movements and in the South African Allied Workers Union (Saawu), which merged into Cosatu. The story of militant, left-wing labour promoted by Fosatu and others was essentially that of a specifically South African working class (Byrne et al. 2017), with little space for these transnational dimensions.

Second, it is a mistake to assume that labour movements or the working class are naturally of the left, that left-wing unions represent the 'real' story of labour, that moderate unions are not authentic unions, or that conservative or right-wing influences are thus (in O'Meara's 1983 formulation) an 'assault' on unionism from without.

As indicated in earlier sections, as well as by the MWU/Solidarity case, such assumptions significantly distort our understanding of labour. Correcting this requires more than just looking at more unions; it requires appreciating the complexity of *all* unions.

For example, the ICU in 1920s Natal was increasingly influenced by Zulu nationalism and its key leader, A.W.G. Champion, later joined Inkatha (Marks 1986); many Durban 1973 strikers requested aid from the Zulu monarchy (Ulrich 2007); and former Fosatu workers helped form two labour bodies aligned to Zulu nationalism in the 1980s. While the United Workers' Union of South Africa is defunct, the National Sugar Refining and Allied Industries Union was, quite recently, 'the largest independent union in the sugar industry' (Hickel 2015, xii). Within Cosatu itself – formally a Marxist-Leninist body – conservative views on many issues are widespread (Buhlungu 2010; Tshoaedi 2013, 2017; Benya 2013; Sitas 2017; Gongqa 2019).

These non-leftist currents are not mere tools of the status quo; they are also not atavisms, but responses to the dislocations of today. The Natal ICU was seen as extremely dangerous, and faced ongoing repression. Solidarity is explicitly opposed to 'the form of capitalism that has emerged in recent years' (quoted in *South African Labour Bulletin* 2003, 30) and aspires to 'become a state within a state' (Van Zyl-Hermann 2021, 227). The National Sugar Refining and Allied Industries Union articulates a fundamental rejection of liberal modernity, rooted in rural traditionalism (Hickel 2015).

COSATU, BUT NOT ENTIRELY

There are also surprising gaps in what we know about Cosatu itself, and a major reason is that interest in labour history as a whole declined from the 1990s. The new wave of unionism that started in the 1970s is not exactly new any more. Cosatu and the National Council of Trade Unions are nearly 40 years old, and Fedusa nearly 30 years old. Cosatu, Fedusa and Saftu all have affiliates that have a continuous organisational history going back 80 years or more, like Samwu, the PSA and Fawu; even more recent unions like CWIU and Numsa can be traced to 1973, 40 years ago. Some unions that started as splinters are also surprisingly old: Amcu, for example, dates to 1998.

The focus on the Tuacc/Fosatu/Cosatu tradition has also meant that very little material is available on the National Council of Trade Unions, which was founded in 1986 as a rival to Cosatu and claimed (inaccurately) similar numbers at the time. It was part of a current of unions influenced by Black Consciousness, which have also largely been ignored with the exception of NUM, which later became ANC-aligned. The Young Christian Workers and liberation theology were also important in labour (Vally, Bofelo and Treat 2013; Forrest 2019), but have received little attention.

The emphasis on the Tuacc/FOSATU lineage also affects the study of Cosatu itself. Older unions like the Food and Canning Workers Union, the NUM, and Fosatu unions like CWIU and Mawu provided the bulk of Cosatu's founders. However, the new federation was also founded by bodies from other traditions like the (Western Cape) General Workers Union (Maree 1992), and the small so-called 'community unions' like Saawu which had direct ANC and Sactu links. The latter were extremely loosely organised, with weak shop-floor structures, and were unable to provide basic membership information at the unity talks and founding of Cosatu. Saawu – the largest – also suffered a split (Baskin 1991, 41, 50, 55). It had just over 25 000 members at the Cosatu founding, out of 460 000, up from 20 000 in the early 1980s (Baskin 1991, 55; Kiloh and Sibeko 2000, 76–77).

The Western Province General Workers Union tradition has been largely ignored (the key exception is Maree 1992), and no systematic history has been written of the 'populist' community unions, although the latter were key players and had an impact on Cosatu completely disproportionate to their numbers. Saawu was (partly) merged into Nehawu and the South African Railways and Harbour Workers Union (Sarhwu) as part of Cosatu's process of consolidating affiliates. There is some useful material on Saawu in the two official histories of Nehawu (Molete 1997; Hadebe and Bhengu 2021), and the semi-official history of Sarhwu (Kiloh and Sibeko 2000). Although Saawu in fact provided surprisingly few members to either union, it takes centre stage in these histories, linking both to Sactu and the ANC/SACP tradition. (Sarhwu, launched around 1985, also affirms this lineage by insisting it was the revival of a Sactu union of the same name, founded in 1936.)

Despite the traditional academic focus on Cosatu's NUM, Numsa and Sactwu, and the growing ongoing interest in Nehawu, Saccawu, Sadtu and Samwu, our knowledge of even these unions is very patchy. The lack of historical work on the unions limits our understanding of Cosatu itself.

NUM probably fares best of all, with numerous case studies, a three-volume semi-official history (Allen 2005) and a major new study (Botiveau 2017). The rise of Amcu also drew attention to issues in Cosatu unions, including NUM (Maree 2017), while NUM's important role (along with Nehawu and others) in the expulsion of Numsa attracted attention. There is a detailed history of Numsa and its predecessors like Mawu (Forrest 2011), which is promoted by the union, but this account ends in 2005. Work on Numsa centres on surveys, workplace case studies, and hopes for the 'Numsa moment' (Pillay 2015). Samwu and Sadtu also feature significantly in work on municipal restructuring and on post-apartheid schooling, respectively (Barchiesi 2007; Musi 2010; Letseka, Bantwini and King-McKenzie 2012), and a major study of Samwu's efforts to organise precarious workers has recently appeared (Ludwig 2019).

There is, on the plus side, relatively recent work on Fosatu, Saccawu, Sactwu and their predecessors (Lichtenstein 2014; Byrne et al. 2017; Kenny 2019; Neunsinger 2019) and on the Tuacc/Fosatu tradition (Ulrich 2007). A number of important honours and masters theses have also appeared on issues like union strategy (for example, Sebei 2019) and responses to immigrants (for example, Di Paola 2013; Gongqa 2019).

From the 1990s onwards, several unions have also produced their own official histories. Nehawu produced one in 1997 and another in 2021 (Molete 1997; Hadebe and Bhengu 2021). There are histories by the CWIU, which is now part of Ceppwawu (CWIU 1984; Rosenthal 1994), the Police and Prisons Civil Rights Union (Popcru) (Theledi 2015), and Sadtu (Kumalo and Skosana 2014), and a semi-official history of Saccawu (Forrest 2005). There are, sadly, several stalled projects, including one on Ceppwawu, but some new official histories are also in the works, like one for Samwu by Lawrence Ntuli.

Official histories are extremely valuable, and most include extensive interviews. They are framed by the parameters set by the unions, and have a tendency to emphasise achievements, official positions and leaders, rather than debates and controversies. Nonetheless they are an essential source.

Two other factors contribute to the gaps. First, there is very little left of the old milieu of the labour service organisations, popular publishers and non-governmental organisations that generated and publicised work on the history and politics of labour. Relations between unions and those seen as outsiders are, at present, sometimes a bit cool. This reflects a general trend, in which some sectors of the unions have labelled certain studies as unduly critical or factional (Satgar and Southall 2015), or have been reluctant to cooperate with researchers (Nthejane et al. 2017).

Second, the tradition of ordinary worker biographies and autobiographies has almost disappeared. Both *New Nation* and the union-aligned *South African Labour Bulletin* produced regular profiles (and obituaries) of union activists into the 1990s, while Mawu, Numsa, Lacom and the Natal Worker History Project published several book-length texts along the same lines (for example, Qabula 1989). While several of the latter were republished in recent years by Jacana (in its Hidden Voices series), backed by the National Institute for the Humanities and Social Sciences (with a notable omission: Lacom 1989a), there is little sign of new work in this vein. What is available, however, are several important biographies of former union leaders, like Neil Agget and Cyril Ramaphosa (Naidoo 2012; Butler 2013) and the memoirs of several others (Sibeko with Leeson 1996; Govender 2007; Naidoo 2010; Copelyn 2016; Craven 2016; Theron 2017).

CONCLUSION: SYNTHESES, COMPARISONS AND CONCEPTS

A more balanced understanding of the union movement would greatly complicate the narrative of a glorious rise from the 1970s into the 1980s that somehow crashed down into crisis from the 2000s. This is, in fact, a particular reading of the history of the Tuacc/Fosatu/Cosatu lineage, which ignores the incredible resilience and variety that unions have shown in South Africa over the last 140 years. It is also based on a 'binary division of South African time' that romanticises the earlier period (Botiveau 2017, 15). It downplays early tendencies towards intolerance and centralising power, including the murder of Fosatu 'workerists' by ANC-aligned militias, the subversion of union democracy by party cells (Copelyn 2016, 166–178), and Cosatu leaders Jay Naidoo and Cyril Ramaphosa signing off on a joint 1986 ANC/Cosatu/SACP statement announcing a partnership, without any mandate and in violation of the federation's unambiguous founding resolution that it 'shall not affiliate to any political tendency or organisation' (Cosatu 1985).

Furthermore, the greatly overused term 'crisis' does not adequately describe a union movement that remains remarkably stable in terms of absolute numbers, and a union density that (outside of the traditionally non-union sectors of agriculture and domestic work) remains one of the highest in the world despite union weaknesses (Van der Walt 2019; Visser 2019). Moreover, while there are serious challenges within the unions, survey evidence also indicates important strengths: for example, most Cosatu workers report regular elections (and recalls) of shop stewards and regular workplace meetings (Maree 2017, 149–157).

That said, we are not yet in a position to provide an alternative to the rise-and-fall narrative. While there are a number of overviews of the union movement, and numerous case studies and much data, as well as some wonderful new material, there is not enough material for a new general labour history of the country (the last was Lacom 1989b), or even a new history of Cosatu (the last was Baskin 1991). Even a more modest goal, such as a dictionary of labour biography, seems out of reach at present.

There is not enough 'old' labour history – institutional histories, emphasising formal developments, decisions, leaders and strikes – or 'new' Thompsonian-style labour history – emphasising the lived experience of ordinary workers and their making of unions. Other than Solidarity and NUM cooperatives (Philip 2018), we know very little about the non-union associational bodies generated by unions, such as choirs and cooperatives. Studies of union education have, happily, gained new momentum (Cooper and Hamilton 2020), although much remains to be done.

The ideological coordinates – and the intellectual and political life – of different sectors of the union movement clearly need more study. Analyses of union politics – notably of Cosatu, Saftu and Numsa – often operate at very general levels, examining union views on the ANC, union renewal, neo-liberalism, women, and so on. For example, much of the commentary on the 'Numsa moment' – both critical and laudatory – was based on official union statements and interviews with national leaders.

But formal statements, frozen at specific moments of time and largely issued by a few powerful offices and people are only a small, and partial, reflection of fractured larger labour milieus in which specific sets of ideas are deployed, reworked and contested, playing out in specific contexts and enabling and blocking different options. These deeper worlds underlie union declarations, debates and decisions, and co-exist with the mundane daily union work of negotiating wages, hours and retrenchments. Some work helps unpack these (Hickel 2015; Kenny 2019; Van-Zyl Hermann 2021) but much remains to be done.

It would also be a grave mistake to read ordinary members' consciousness from head-office documents and congress statements. Surveys consistently report that most Cosatu members know very little about the neo-liberal macro-economic policies that are condemned by union head offices and congresses (Maree 2017, 158–161). Marxist-inflected slogans and declarations co-exist with other influences in the union: in 2014, for example, almost 75 per cent of union members were church members (Sitas 2017, 45–46). Various nationalisms and related loyalties remain very potent in Cosatu and Saftu unions, and interact with both Marxist and religious influences in complex ways; nationalism is not restricted to Solidarity.

Another indication is that declining support for the ANC simply has not translated into support for a new left party, as many on the left, including in Saftu, supposed it would. Survey data reveals that in 2014, 30 per cent wanted Cosatu to be non-aligned, compared to 45 per cent favouring the Alliance and 8 per cent wanting a workers' party; 56 per cent 'Strongly agree/agree' that 'Workers cannot rely on political parties to protect their interests' (Cherry, Jikeka and Malope 2017, 92–94). Saftu is formally socialist and anti-ANC, and Numsa, with over 350 000 members, formally endorsed the Socialist Revolutionary Workers Party in 2019. The party got less than 25 000 votes, failing to win a single seat in parliament.

One of the major changes in South African elections is, instead, the consistent growth of a massive pool of people who – presumably disillusioned or disinterested – simply do not vote, and are often cynical when they do. While news cycles focus on politicians, over half the country has withdrawn from official politics altogether. This is partly obscured by the election system, which allocates seats by the proportion of votes won, enabling small parties with relatively tiny numbers of core supporters to seem to take major strides. The Economic Freedom Fighters (an ANC breakaway) and the Freedom Front Plus (overlapping with the Solidarity/AfriForum milieu) doubled their parliamentary seats in 2019 by winning 712 262 and 249 149 new votes respectively, a tiny fraction of the votes the ANC has lost, and a drop in the ocean of a voting-age population of around 37 million. The ANC's decline is not, in short, based primarily on voters shifting to new parties, but rather on current and former ANC supporters withdrawing altogether. How do we name and understand these complexities, including this anti-politics politics?

This brings me to the final point, which is that a more balanced examination of the labour movement, over time and across federations, unions and traditions, has some important theoretical implications. A growing number of studies (Bezuidenhout and Tshoaedi 2017) have debated whether Cosatu is still 'working class', on the grounds that the average member is now better paid and better educated, and that the proportion of members who are artisans, white-collar or state-sector workers has increased. But the grounds for such criteria to serve as markers of class are by no means clearly articulated. What level of income, or skill, moves individuals between classes, and why? Applying these to the past would, logically, also mean that a great deal of the union movement – dating back around 140 years – was never quite working-class either, since much of it was never in the mould of CWIU, NUM, Numsa or Sactwu.

A more systematic class analysis, critically engaging the Marxist-influenced labour scholarship of the 1970s to 1980s – but most especially the critiques of the structuralists (Saunders 1988; Bozzoli and Delius 1990) – would greatly enrich the discussion of Cosatu today, and perhaps address these issues. The study of the modern South African labour movement has, however, increasingly tended to centre on constructing mid-level concepts, often presented in tables, rather than engaging with larger theory. The tendency to eschew larger, more systematic theory is (as argued earlier) not new and maintains the eclectic tendency to simply add new concepts onto accreting layers of older ones rather than engage systematically in theoretical work.

As an example, studies of the modern labour movement have relied heavily on distinctions between 'economistic' or business unions (mainly concerned with bread-and-butter issues), 'political' unions allied with parties, and 'social movements' that engage in wider alliances. In turn, these were often mapped onto organisational types, with business unionism linked to bureaucratic, craft, white-collar and moderate (or right-wing) unions (and staff associations), and political and social movement unionism linked to mass, democratic, leftist (and national liberation or socialist) unions. New conceptual work has long followed a pattern of developing and expanding matrices of apparently contrasting types.

The problem is that these contrasts are often based on a fairly narrow range of cases and on neat distinctions. What are we to make of Solidarity, for example, which seems to meet almost every criterion for social movement unionism and, indeed, to fit that category rather better than today's Cosatu or Saftu – but which is on the right? Many unions that developed from the 1970s, including from the Tuacc/Fosatu tradition, today have far larger bureaucracies and budgets than the old 'bureaucratic' Tucsa unionism with which they were once so neatly contrasted.

Cosatu and the bigger Saftu unions now routinely offer a number of value-added services like funeral policies to attract members, and focus on 'economistic' issues – the distinction with, for example, Fedusa is not always sharp (Musi 2010). The main federations also do not neatly break down by union type, as Cosatu and Saftu, like Fedusa, have long had both industrial and craft-based affiliates. Saftu includes the South African Police Union, and Cosatu the Democratic Nursing Organisation of South Africa, Popcru and Sadtu, all based only on specific occupations; other workers in the self-same workplaces, like cleaners, are often left to Nehawu. Even the most moderate union is political, in the sense that it challenges by its very existence power relations at work; a union engages in a political act when it declares itself apolitical. Lastly, neither Popcru nor Sadtu, or for that matter Solidarity's earlier incarnation, MWU, conform to stereotypes that craft unions are economistic.

In short, a more holistic understanding of the history and contours of the modern South African labour movement can also force some rethinking of the core concepts that have been used in the field. There needs to be more systematic and large-scale theoretical work, as well as a broader research programme. Much has been done, but much still remains to be done.

ACKNOWLEDGEMENTS

This chapter is based on: Lucien van der Walt (2018) 'Fragmented Labour Movement, Fragmented Labour Studies: New Directions for Research and Theory,' presented at 'Taking Democracy Seriously: Reflecting on Trade Unions in the Last 20 Years and the Future of the Labour Movement in South Africa', University of the Witwatersrand, 6–7 September 2018; and Lucien van der Walt (2009) 'Nationalism, the State and the Fall (and Rise) of Labour History in the Wits History Workshop', 'Life after 30: Reflecting on 30 years of the History Workshop', University of the Witwatersrand, 3–5 April 2009.

NOTES

1   The Sached Trust was an independent body, formed 1959, that fostered black access to higher education (Nonyongo 1998).
2   'Pass-bearing' black Africans were specifically excluded, but the patchwork character of the pass law system before the mid-1950s created some loopholes.
3   This did not prevent employers of workers in the excluded categories or sectors from engaging with unions at their own discretion or in terms of laws like the Public Service Act (where applicable). However, without access to statutory bargaining councils and protected strikes, these workers tended to present their organisations as staff associations and/or professional bodies.

REFERENCES

Africa Report. 2019. 'Top 500 African Companies'. *Africa Report*, July–September 2019. 108: 83–97.

Alexander, Peter. 2007. 'History, Internationalism and Intellectuals: The Case of Harold Wolpe'. *Transformation*, 63 (1): 109–126.

Allen, V.L. 2005. *The History of Black Mineworkers in South Africa*. [Three volumes]. London: Merlin Press.

Amoako, Samuel. 2012. 'Cogs in the Wheel: Teacher Unions and Public Sector Strikes in Post-apartheid South Africa, 1999–2010'. *Labour, Capital and Society*, 45 (2): 84–110.

Amoako, Samuel. 2014. 'Teacher Unions in Political Transitions: The South African Democratic Teachers' Union (SADTU) and the Dying Days of Apartheid, 1990–1993'. *Journal of Asian and African Studies*, 49 (2): 148–163.

Andrews, Bill. [1941] 1977. *Class Struggles in South Africa*. Lusaka: South African Congress of Trade Unions.

Barchiesi, Franco. 2007. 'Privatisation and the Historical Trajectory of "Social Movement Unionism": A Case Study of Municipal Workers in Johannesburg, South Africa'. *International Labor and Working-Class History*, 71: 50–69.

Barchiesi, Franco and Bridget Kenny. 2002. 'From Workshop to Wasteland: De-industrialization and Fragmentation of the Black Working Class on the East Rand (South Africa), 1990–1999'. *International Review of Social History*, 47: 35–63.

Baskin, Jeremy. 1991. *Striking Back: A History of COSATU*. Johannesburg: Ravan Press.

Bekker, Ian and Lucien van der Walt. 2010. 'The 2010 Mass Strike in the State Sector, South Africa: Positive Achievements but Serious Problems'. *Social. History Online/Sozial. Geschichte Online*, 4: 138–152.

Bendix, Willy, ed. 1988. *South African Industrial Relations of the Eighties*. Cape Town: I.P.C.

Benya, Asanda. 2013. 'Gendered Labour: A Challenge to Labour as a Democratizing Force'. *Rethinking Development and Inequality*, 2: 47–62.

Bezuidenhout, Andries. 2017. 'Labour Beyond Cosatu, other Federations and Independent Unions'. In *Labour Beyond Cosatu: Mapping the Rupture in South Africa's Labour Landscape*, edited by Malehoko Tshoaedi and Andries Bezuidenhout, 217–234. Johannesburg: Wits University Press.

Bezuidenhout, Andries and Sakhela Buhlungu. 2011. 'From Compounded to Fragmented Labour: Mineworkers and the Demise of Compounds in South Africa'. *Antipode*, 43 (2): 237–263.

Bezuidenhout, Andries and Malehoko Tshoaedi, eds. 2017. *Labour Beyond Cosatu: Mapping the Rupture in South Africa's Labour Landscape*. Johannesburg: Wits University Press.

Bonner, Philip. 1978. 'The Decline of the ICU: A Case of Self-destruction'. In *Essays in Southern African Labour History*, edited by Edward Webster, 114–120. Johannesburg: Ravan Press.

Bonner, Philip. 1994. 'New Nation, New History: The History Workshop in South Africa, 1977–1994'. *The Journal of American History*, 81 (3): 977–985.

Bonner, Philip, Jonathan Hyslop and Lucien van der Walt. 2007. 'Rethinking Worlds of Labour: Southern African Labour History in International Context'. *African Studies*, 66 (2–3): 137–167.

Botiveau, Raphaël. 2017. *Organise or Die? Democracy and Leadership in South Africa's National Union of Mineworkers*. Johannesburg: Wits University Press.

Bozzoli, Belinda, 1983. 'Marxism, Feminism and South African Studies'. *Journal of Southern African Studies*, 9 (2): 139–171.

Bozzoli, Belinda and Peter Delius. 1990. 'Radical History and South African Society'. *Radical History Review*, 46–47: 13–45.

Braverman, Harry. 1974. *Labor and Monopoly Capital: The Degradation of Work in the Twentieth Century*. New York: Monthly Review Press.

Buhlungu, Sakhela. 2000. 'Trade Union Organization and Capacity in the 1990s: Continuities, Changes and Challenges for PPWAWU'. In *Trade Unions and Democratization in South Africa, 1985–1997*, edited by Glenn Adler and Edward Webster, 75–97. Houndmills, Basingstoke, Hampshire/New York: Macmillan and St. Martin's Press.

Buhlungu, Sakhela. 2010. A *Paradox of Victory: COSATU and the Democratic Transition in South Africa*. Pietermaritzburg: University of KwaZulu-Natal Press.

Buhlungu, Sakhela, Mick Brookes and Geoffrey Wood. 2008. 'Trade Unions and Democracy in South Africa: Union Organizational Challenges and Solidarities in a Time of Trans-formation'. *British Journal of Industrial Relations*, 46 (3): 439–468.

Bundy, Colin, ed. 1991. *The History of the South African Communist Party*. Cape Town: Department of Adult Education and Extra-Mural Studies, University of Cape Town.

Butler, Anthony. 2013. *Cyril Ramaphosa*. Johannesburg: Jacana.

Byrne, Sian, Nicole Ulrich and Lucien van der Walt. 2017. 'Red, Black and Gold: FOSATU, South African "Workerism", "Syndicalism" and the Nation'. In *The Unresolved National Question: Left Thought under Apartheid*, edited by Edward Webster and Karin Pampallis, 254–273. Johannesburg: Wits University Press.

Ceruti, Claire. 2011. 'The Hidden Element in the 2010 Public Sector Strike in South Africa'. *Review of African Political Economy*, 38 (127): 151–157.

Chemical Workers Industrial Union (CWIU). 1984. *A History of the Chemical Workers Industrial Union, 1974–1984*. Durban: CWIU.

Cherry, Janet, Nkosinathi Jikeka and Boitumelo Malope. 2017. 'The Politics of Alliance and the 2014 Elections'. In *Labour Beyond Cosatu: Mapping the Rupture in South Africa's Labour Landscape*, edited by Malehoko Tshoaedi and Andries Bezuidenhout, 85–110. Johannesburg: Wits University Press.

Chipkin, Ivor and Sarah Meny-Gibert. 2012. 'Why the Past Matters: Studying Public Administration in South Africa'. *Journal of Public Administration*, 47 (1): 102–112.

Cock, Jacklyn. 1980. 'Domestic Servants in the Political Economy of South Africa'. *Africa Perspective* (first series), 15: 42–53.

Cole, Peter. 2018. *Dockworker Power: Race and Activism in Durban and the San Francisco Bay Area*. Champaign, IL: University of Illinois Press.

Congress of South African Trade Unions (Cosatu). 1985. Minutes of the Inaugural Congress Held at the University of Natal, 29 November to 1 December 1985. Section on Political Policy (Annexure H). In Section 5.1, AH2373/Congress of South African Trade Unions (COSATU) collection, Historical Papers, University of the Witwatersrand.

Congress of South African Trade Unions (Cosatu). 1987. *Political Economy: South Africa in Crisis*. Johannesburg: Cosatu.

Congress of South African Trade Unions (Cosatu). 1997. *September Commission Report*. Johannesburg: Cosatu.

Cooper, David. 1991. 'Locating South Africa in the Third World: Comparative Perspectives on Patterns of Industrialisation and Political Trade Unionism in South America'. *Social Dynamics*, 17 (2): 1–40.

Cooper, Linda and Sheri Hamilton, eds. 2020. *Renewing Workers' Education: Towards a Radical, Alternative Vision*. Cape Town: HSRC Press.

Copelyn, Johnny. 2016. *Maverick Insider: A Struggle for Union Independence in a Time of National Liberation*. Johannesburg: Picador Africa.

Craven, Patrick. 2016. *The Battle for COSATU: An Insider's View*. Johannesburg: Bookstorm.

Davies, Robert. 1979. *Capital, State and White Labour in South Africa, 1900-60*. Brighton: Harvester.

Dickinson, David. 2016. 'Fighting their Own Battles: The *Mabarete* and the End of Labour Broking in the South African Post Office'. *Bargaining Indicators 2016*, 16: 23–38.

Di Paola, Miriam. 2013. 'A Labour Perspective on Xenophobia in South Africa: A Case Study of the Metals and Engineering Industry in Ekurhuleni'. Masters diss., University of the Witwatersrand.

Du Preez, Max. 2018. 'The Problem AfriForum is Causing the DA'. *News24*, 15 May 2018.

Du Toit, M.A. 1976. *South African Trade Unions*. Isando: MacGraw-Hill.

Federation of South African Trade Unions (Fosatu). 1985.'The Making of the Working Class: Part 15 – SACTU and the Congress Alliance'. *FOSATU Worker News*, October 1985.

Forman, Lionel. [1959] 1992. Chapters in the History of the March for Freedom. In *A Trumpet from the Housetops: The Selected Writings of Lionel Forman*, edited by Sadie Forman and André Odendaal, 1–98. Cape Town: David Philip.

Forrest, Kally. 2005. *Asijiki: A History of the South African Commercial Catering and Allied Workers Union (SACCAWU)*. Johannesburg: STE Publishers.

Forrest, Kally. 2011. *Metal that will not Bend: The National Union of Metalworkers of South Africa 1980–1995*. Johannesburg: Wits University Press.

Forrest, Kally. 2019. *Bonds of Justice: The Struggle for Oukasie*. Johannesburg: Jacana.

Freund, William. 2019. *Twentieth-Century South Africa: A Developmental History*. Cambridge: Cambridge University Press.

Gelb, Stephen, ed. 1991. *South Africa's Economic Crisis*. Cape Town and London, New Jersey: David Philip and Zed Books.

Gitsham, Ernest, and James F. Trembath. 1926. *A First Account of Labour Organisation in South Africa*. Durban: E.P. and Commercial Printing.

Godongwana, Enoch. 1992. 'Industrial Restructuring and the Social Contract: Reforming Capitalism or Building Blocks for Socialism?' *South African Labour Bulletin*, 16 (1): 20–23.

Gongqa, Nombulelo. 2019. 'South African Trade Union Responses to Xenophobia in Workplaces: The National Union of Mineworkers (NUM) and National Union of Metalworkers of South Africa (NUMSA)'. Masters diss., Rhodes University.

Govender, Pregs. 2007. *Love and Courage: A Story of Insubordination*. Johannesburg: Jacana.

Hadebe, Samukele and Sthembiso Bhengu. 2021. *In the Belly of the Beast: The History of NEHAWU*. Johannesburg: Chris Hani Institute and National Education, Health and Allied Workers Union (Nehawu).

Haysom, Nicholas and Modise Khoza. 1984. 'Trade Unions in the Homelands'. Carnegie Conference Paper number 100, Second Carnegie Inquiry into Poverty and Development in Southern Africa, Cape Town, 13–19 April.

Hickel, Jason. 2015. *Democracy as Death: The Moral Order of Anti-liberal Politics in South Africa*. Oakland, CA: University of California Press.

Horn, Pat. 1981. *The ICU*. Cape Town: Labour History Group.

Hyslop, Jonathan. 1992. 'Polar Night: Social Theory and the Crisis of Apartheid'. In *South African Review Six*, 171–185. Johannesburg: Ravan Press.

Iggers, Georg Gerson. 2016. 'The Role of Marxism in Sub-Saharan and South African Historiography'. In *Marxist Historiographies: A Global Perspective*, edited by Q. Edward Wang and Georg Gerson Iggers, 229–248. London and New York: Routledge.

Innes, Duncan. 1983. 'Monopoly Capitalism in South Africa'. *South African Review One*, edited by Glenn Moss, 171–183. Johannesburg: Ravan Press.

Johnson, David, Nieftagodien, Noor and Van der Walt, Lucien. 2022. 'Introduction'. In *Labour Struggles in Southern Africa, 1919–1939: New Perspectives on the Industrial and Commercial Workers' Union*, edited by David Johnson, Noor Nieftagodien and Lucien van der Walt, viii–xix. Cape Town: HSRC Press.

Jubber, Ken. 1983. 'Sociology and its Social Context: The Case of the Rise of Marxist Sociology in South Africa'. *Social Dynamics*, 9 (2): 50–63.

Jubber, Ken. 2006. 'Reflections on Canons, Compilations, Catalogues and Curricula in Relation to Sociology and Sociology in South Africa'. *South African Review of Sociology*, 37 (2): 321–342.

Keal, Hannah. 2009. ' "A Life's Work": Harriet Bolton and Durban's Trade Unions, 1944–1974', Masters diss., University of KwaZulu-Natal.

Kenny, Bridget. 2019. *Retail Worker Politics, Race and Consumption in South Africa: Shelved in the Service Economy*. London: Palgrave Macmillan.

Kiloh, Margaret and Archie Sibeko. 2000. *A Fighting Union: An Oral History of the South African Railway and Harbour Workers' Union, 1936–1998*. Johannesburg: Ravan Press.

Kumalo, Vusumuzi and Dineo Skosana. 2014. *A History of the South African Democratic Teachers Union (SADTU)*. Johannesburg: Sadtu.

Labour and Community Resources Project (Lacom). 1989a. *Comrade Moss*. Johannesburg: Learn and Teach Publications.

Labour and Community Resources Project (Lacom). 1989b. *Freedom! from Below: The Struggle for Trade Unions in South Africa*. Johannesburg: Skotaville.

Legassick, Martin. 2008. 'Debating the Revival of the Workers' Movement in the 1970s: The South African Democracy Education Trust and Post-Apartheid Patriotic History'. *Kronos*, 34 (1): 240–266.

Letseka, Moeketsi, Bongani Bantwini and Ethel King-McKenzie. 2012. 'Public-union Sector Politics and the Crisis of Education in South Africa'. *Creative Education*, 3 (7): 1197–1204.

Lewis, Jon. 1984. *Industrialisation and Trade Union Organisation in South Africa, 1924–55. The Rise and Fall of the South African Trades and Labour Council*. Cambridge: Cambridge University Press.

Lichtenstein, Alex. 2014. 'The "Red Card Union" vs. the "Blue Card Union": Post-Wiehahn Shop Floor Battles for Union Recognition in Natal's Textile Industry'. Paper presented to the Department of Historical Studies, University of Johannesburg, 18 March 2014.

Ludwig, Carmen. 2019. *Politics of Solidarity: Privatisation, Precarious Work and Labour in South Africa*. Frankfurt and New York: Campus Verlag.

Mabasa, Khewzi and Crispen Chinguno. 2018. 'Trade Union Organising in the Mining Sector: A Structural Perspective on Worker Insurgency and Shifting Union Strategies'. In *The Future of Mining in South Africa: Sunset or Sunrise?* edited by Salimah Valiani, 298–331. Johannesburg: Mapungubwe Institute for Strategic Reflection.

Macun, Ian. 2000. 'Growth, Structure and Power in the South African Union Movement'. In *Trade Unions and Democratization in South Africa, 1985–97*, edited by Glenn Adler and Edward Webster, 53–75. Houndmills, Basingstoke and New York: Macmillan and St. Martin's Press.

Macun, Ian and Christine Psoulis. 2000. 'Unions Inside the State: The Development of Unionism in the South African Public Service'. In *Public Service Labour Relations in a Democratic South Africa*, edited by Glenn Adler, 90–99. Johannesburg: Wits University Press.

Magoqwana, Babalwa and Sandra Matatu. 2012. 'Local Government Call Centres: Challenge or Opportunity for South African Labour?' In *Labour In The Global South: Challenges and Alternatives for Workers*, edited by Sarah Mosoetsa and Michelle Williams, 65–86. Geneva: International Labour Office.

Maree, Johann. 1992. 'Developing Trade Union Power and Democracy: The Rebirth of African Trade Unions in South Africa in the 1970s'. Unpublished manuscript.

Maree, Johann. 2017. 'Internal Democracy in COSATU: Achievements and Challenges'. In *Labour Beyond Cosatu: Mapping the Rupture in South Africa's Labour Landscape*, edited by Malehoko Tshoaedi and Andries Bezuidenhout, 191–216. Johannesburg: Wits University Press.

Maree, Johann and Christine Bischoff. 2017. 'Are COSATU's Public Sector Unions Too Powerful?' In *Labour Beyond Cosatu: Mapping the Rupture in South Africa's Labour Landscape*, edited by Malehoko Tshoaedi and Andries Bezuidenhout, 146–169. Johannesburg: Wits University Press.

Marks, Shula. 1986. *The Ambiguities of Dependence in South Africa: Class, Nationalism, and the State in Twentieth-century Natal*. Johannesburg: Ravan Press.

Maylam, Paul. 2013. 'Fragile Multi-class Alliances Compared: Some Unlikely Parallels between the National Party and the African National Congress'. In *New South African Review Three*, edited by John Daniel, Prishani Naidoo, Devan Pillay and Roger Southall, 61–75. Johannesburg: Wits University Press.

Meyer, Pieter. 1944. *Die Stryd van die Afrikanerwerker: Die Vooraand van ons Sosiale Vrywording*. Stellenbosch: Pro Ecclesia-Drukkery.

Moodie, Dunbar. 2016. 'Making Mincemeat out of Mutton-eaters: Social Origins of the NUM Decline on Platinum'. *Journal of Southern African Studies*, 42 (5): 841–856.

Molete, Martha. 1997. *NEHAWU History, the Unfinished Story: The History of the National Education, Health and Allied Workers Union, 1987–1997*. Johannesburg: Nehawu.

Money, Duncan (2018). 'Race and Class in the Postwar World: The Southern African Labour Congress'. *International Labor and Working-class History*, 94: 133–155.

Money, Duncan and Danelle van Zyl-Hermann. 2020. 'Introduction'. In *Rethinking White Societies in Southern Africa, 1930s–1990s*, edited by Duncan Money and Danelle van Zyl-Hermann, 1–22. Abingdon, Oxon: Routledge.

Mopeli, Tawana. 2021. 'A Workers' Association that Transitioned from a Fighting to an Infighting and Ultimately a Splintering Union: The Case of SATAWU'. Masters diss., University of the Witwatersrand.

Mosoetsa, Sarah. 2011. *Eating from One Pot: The Dynamics of Survival in Poor South African Households*. Johannesburg: Wits University Press.

Moyo, Wisdom Ntando. 2022. 'The 2019 SASBO Bank Workers' Strike in South Africa: Unpacking Labour Responses to the Fourth Industrial Revolution'. Masters diss., Rhodes University.

Musi, Mojalefa. 2010. 'Evaluating IMATU and SAMWU Policy Responses to IGoli 2002'. Masters diss., University of the Witwatersrand.

Naidoo, Beverley. 2012. *Death of an Idealist: In Search of Neil Aggett*. Johannesburg: Jonathan Ball.

Naidoo, Jay. 2010. *Fighting for Justice: A Lifetime of Political and Social Activism*. Johannesburg: Picador Africa.

Nasson, Bill. 1990. 'The Unity Movement: Its Legacy in Historical Consciousness'. *Radical History Review*, 1990 (46–47): 189–211.

Nattrass, Nicoli. 1991. 'Controversies about Capitalism and Apartheid in South Africa: An Economic Perspective'. *Journal of Southern African Studies*, 17 (4): 654–677.

Naudé, Louis. 1969. *Dr. A. Hertzog, die Nasionale Party en die Mynwerkers*. Pretoria: Nasionale Raad van Trustees.

Ness, Immanuel. 2016. *Southern Insurgency: The Coming of the Global Working Class*. London: Pluto Press.

Neunsinger, Silke. 2019. 'Translocal Activism and the Implementation of Equal Remuneration for Men and Women: The Case of the South African Textile Industry'. *International Review of Social History*, 64 (1): 37–72.

New Nation/History Workshop. 1989. *New Nation, New History, Volume 1*. Johannesburg: *New Nation* newspaper, History Workshop at the University of the Witwatersrand.

Nkhatau, Nthabiseng. 2012. 'Unemployment: A Challenge to Black Men's Sense of Hegemonic Masculinity'. Honours diss., Industrial Sociology and Labour Studies. University of Pretoria.

Nonyongo, Evelyn Pulane. 1998. 'The South African Committee for Higher Education (Sached) Trust'. In *Learner Support Services: Case Studies of DEASA Member Institutions*, edited by Evelyn Pulane Nonyongo and Alice Thandiwe Ngengebule, 116–129. Pretoria: University of South Africa.

Nthejane, Ntsehiseng, Sandla Nomvete, Boitumelo Malope and Bianca Tame. 2017. 'Research in a Highly Charged Environment: Taking Democracy Seriously, 2014'. In *Labour Beyond Cosatu: Mapping the Rupture in South Africa's Labour Landscape*, edited by Malehoko Tshoaedi and Andries Bezuidenhout, 18–36. Johannesburg: Wits University Press.

Nthinya, Neo. 2014. 'The Role of the Independent Municipal and Allied Trade Union (IMATU) in the Merger of the City of Tshwane and the Metsweding Municipalities (2010–2011)'. Masters diss., University of the Witwatersrand.

O'Meara, Dan. 1983. *Volkskapitalisme: Class, Capital and Ideology in the Development of Afrikaner Nationalism 1934–1983*. Cambridge: Cambridge University Press.

Philip, Kate. 2018. *Markets on the Margins: Mineworkers, Job Creation and Enterprise Development*. Woodbridge, Suffolk: James Currey.

Pillay, Devan. 2008. 'COSATU, the SACP and the ANC Post-Polokwane: Looking Left but does it Feel Right?' *Labour, Capital and Society*, 41 (2): 4–37.

Pillay, Devan. 2015. 'Half Full or Half Empty? The NUMSA Moments and the Prospects of Left Revitalisation'. In *New South African Review Five*, edited by Gilbert Khadiagala, Prishani Naidoo, Devan Pillay and Roger Southall, 48–62. Johannesburg: Wits University Press.

Posel, Deborah. 1983. 'Rethinking the "Race-Class debate" in South African Historiography'. *Social Dynamics*, 9 (1): 50–66.

Posel, Deborah. 1991. *The Making of Apartheid 1948–1961: Conflict and Compromise*. Oxford: Clarendon Press.

Posel, Deborah. 2000. 'Labour Relations and the Politics of Patronage: A Case Study of the Apartheid Civil Service'. In *Public Service Labour Relations in a Democratic South Africa*, edited by Glenn Adler, 41–61. Johannesburg: Wits University Press.

Qabula, Alfred Temba. 1989. *A Working Life, Cruel Beyond Belief*. Pinetown: Numsa.

Rees, Robin. 2011. 'Organising Labour Broker Workers: The Case of GIWUSA and SAMWU in Tshwane'. Masters diss., University of the Witwatersrand.

Roos, Neil. 2020. 'Social Engineering and Scientific Management: Some Reflections on the Apartheid Public Service and Historical Process'. In *Rethinking White Societies in Southern Africa, 1930s–1990s*, edited by Duncan Money and Danelle van Zyl-Hermann, 173–193. Abingdon, Oxon: Routledge.

Rosenthal, Tanya. 1994. *Struggle for Workers Rights: A History of the Chemical Workers and Industrial Union*. Durban: CWIU.

Rudin, Jeff. 1996. 'Ambivalent Identities: Coloured and Class in the Cape Town Municipal Workers' Association'. PhD diss., University of Warwick.

Rumney, Reg. 2005. 'Who Owns South Africa: An Analysis of State and Private Ownership Patterns'. In *State of the Nation: South Africa 2004–2005*, edited by John Daniel, Roger Southall and Jessica Lutchman, 401–422. Pretoria: HSRC Press.

Samson, Melanie. 2015. 'Accumulation by Dispossession and the Informal Economy: Struggles over Knowledge, Being and Waste at a Soweto Garbage Dump'. *Environment and Planning D: Society and Space*, 33 (5): 813–830.

Satgar, Vishwas and Roger Southall. 2015. *COSATU in Crisis: The Fragmentation of an African Trade Union Federation*. Midrand: KMM Review Publishing.

Saunders, Christopher. 1988. *The Making of the South African Past: Major Historians on Race and Class*. Cape Town and Johannesburg: David Philip.

Saunders, Christopher. 2007. 'Four Decades of South African Academic Historical Writing: A Personal Perspective'. In *History Making and Present Day Politics: The Meaning of Collective Memory in South Africa*, edited by Hans Erik Stolten, 280–291. Uppsala: Nordiska Afrikainstitutet.

Savage, Michael. 1988. 'An Anatomy of the South African Corporate Economy: Ownership, Control and the Interlocking Directorate'. In *South African Industrial Relations of the Eighties*, edited by Willy Bendix, 107–134. Cape Town: I.P.C.

Sebei, Mametlwe. 2019. 'The Response of the Labour Movement in South Africa towards the 2008/9 World Economic Crisis of Capitalism: A Marxist Critique of the Trade Union Perspectives and Strategies in the Great Recession'. Masters diss., University of the Witwatersrand.

Seekings, Jeremy. 2009. 'The Rise and Fall of the Weberian Analysis of Class in South Africa between 1949 and the Early 1970s'. *Journal of Southern African Studies*, 35 (4): 865–881.

Sefalafala, Thabang. 2010. 'Union Splits on the Mines: A Case Study of "Legal Voice" at Driefontein East Gold Mine, Carletonville, Gauteng'. Honours diss., University of the Witwatersrand.

Sefalafala, Thabang. 2018. 'Experiences of Wagelessness and the Meaning of Wage Work in the Free State Goldfields, South Africa'. In *To be at Home: House, Work, and Self in the Modern World*, edited by James Williams and Felicitas Hentschke, 56–61. Berlin: De Gruyter.

Seidman, Gay. 1994. *Manufacturing Militance: Workers' Movements in Brazil and South Africa, 1970–1985*. Berkeley, CA: University of California Press.

Seidman, Gay. 2011. 'Social Movement Unionism: From Description to Exhortation'. *South African Review of Sociology*, 42 (3): 94–102.

Sibeko, Archie with Joyce Leeson. 1996. *Freedom in our Lifetime*. North York, Ontario: Ontario Public Service Employees Union.

Silberbauer, Eitel Raymond. 1968. *Understanding and Motivating the Bantu Worker: A Productivity Book*. Johannesburg: Personnel Management Advisory Service.

Sinwell, Luke with Siphiwe Mbatha. 2016. *The Spirit of Marikana: The Rise of Insurgent Trade Unionism in South Africa*. London: Pluto Press.

Sitas, Ari. 2017. 'The Social Character of Labour Politics'. In *Labour Beyond Cosatu: Mapping the Rupture in South Africa's Labour Landscape*, edited by Malehoko Tshoaedi and Andries Bezuidenhout, 37–47. Johannesburg: Wits University Press.

Slater, Henry. 1976. 'Transitions in the Political Economy of South-Eastern Africa before 1840'. PhD thesis, University of Sussex.

South African Labour Bulletin. 2003. 'What has Happened to the White Worker? [interview with Flip Buys]'. *South African Labour Bulletin* 27 (4): 30–31.

Southall, Roger. 1985. 'Monopoly Capital and Industrial Unionism in the South African Motor Industry'. *Labour, Capital and Society*, 18 (2): 304–342.

Surtee, Sabera. 1999. 'Indian Teachers Challenge SADTU'. *South African Labour Bulletin*, 23 (2): 63–66.

Theledi, Nkosinathi. 2015. *Historical Background of POPCRU: 25 Years of POPCRU's Existence – A Reflection from Inception in 1989 until 2015*. Johannesburg: Porcupine Press.

Theron, Jan. 2017. *Solidarity Road: The Story of a Trade Union in the Ending of Apartheid*. Johannesburg: Jacana.

Tiley, Alan. 1974. *Bridging the Communication Gap between Black and White*. Cape Town Tafelberg.

Tshoaedi, Malehoko. 2013. 'Making Sense of Unionised Workers' Political Attitudes: The (Un)Representation of Women's Voices in COSATU'. In *COSATU'S Contested Legacy: South African Trade Unions in the Second Decade of Democracy*, edited by Sakhela Buhlungu and Malehoko Tshoaedi, 90–109. Leiden: Brill.

Tshoaedi, Malehoko. 2017. 'The Politics of Male Power and Privilege: Understanding Sexual Harassment in Post-apartheid Trade Unions'. In *Labour Beyond Cosatu: Mapping the Rupture in South Africa's Labour Landscape*, edited by Andries Bezuidenhout and Malehoko Tshoaedi, 129–145. Johannesburg: Wits University Press.

Toussaint [Rusty Bernstein]. 1983. 'A Trade Union is Not a Political Party: A Critique of the Speech "Where FOSATU Stands"'. *African Communist*, 93: 35–47.

Ulrich, Nicole. 2007. 'Only the Workers Can Free the Workers: The Origins of the Workers' Control Tradition and the Trade Union Advisory Coordinating Committee, 1970–1979'. Masters diss., University of the Witwatersrand.

Ulrich, Nicole. 2022. 'A History of FEDUSA'. Research report for the Federation of Unions of South Africa.

Vally, Salim, Mphutlane wa Bofelo and John Treat. 2013. 'Worker Education in South Africa: Lessons and Contradictions'. *McGill Journal of Education*, 48 (3): 469–490.

Van der Linden, Marcel. 2007. 'Labour History: The Old, the New and the Global'. *African Studies*, 66 (2–3): 169–180.

Van der Walt, Lucien. 2006. 'After 10 Years of GEAR: COSATU, the Zuma Trial and the Dead End of "Alliance" Politics'. *Zabalaza: A Southern African Journal of Revolutionary Anarchism* 7: 2–3.

Van der Walt, Lucien. 2007a. 'Anarchism and Revolutionary Syndicalism in South Africa, 1904–1921: Rethinking the History of Labour and the Left'. PhD diss., University of the Witwatersrand.

Van der Walt, Lucien, 2007b. 'The First Globalisation and Transnational Labour Activism in Southern Africa: White Labourism, the IWW and the ICU, 1904–1934'. *African Studies* 66 (2/3): 223–251.

Van der Walt, Lucien. 2019. 'Rebuilding the Workers' Movement for Counter-Power, Justice and Self-Management: A Contribution to the Debate'. *Amandla*, 63: 24–25.

Van der Walt, Lucien, Chris Bolsmann, Bernadetter Johnson and Lindsey Martin. 2003. 'Globalisation, the Market University and Support Service Outsourcing in South Africa: Class Struggle, Convergence and Difference, 1994–2001'. *Society in Transition* 34 (2): 272–294.

Van der Walt, Lucien, Gilton Klerck and Kirk Helliker. 2022. 'State Capitalism in Sub-Saharan Africa'. In *The Oxford Handbook of State Capitalism and the Firm*, edited by Alvaro Cuervo-Cazurra, Anna Grossman, Illya Okhamatovskiy, Pei Sun, Geoffrey Wood and Mike Wright, 545–578. Oxon: Oxford University Press.

Van Zyl-Hermann, Danelle. 2021. *Privileged Precariat: White Workers and South Africa's Long Transition to Majority Rule*. Cambridge: Cambridge University Press.

Visser, Jelle. 2019. *Trade Unions in the Balance*. ILO ACTRAV Working Paper. Geneva: ILO.

Visser, Wessel. 2008. *Van MWU tot Solidariteit: Geskiedenis van die Mynwerkersunie, 1902–2002*. Pretoria: Solidariteit.

Visser, Wessel. 2016. *A History of the South African Mine Workers, 1902–2014*. Lewiston, NY: The Edwin Mellen Press.

Von Holdt, Karl. 1993. 'Impressive Gains, Organisational Crisis'. *South African Labour Bulletin*, 17 (6): 14–22.

Von Holdt, Karl. 1998. 'COSATU's Vision: A Society Worth Living In'. *South African Labour Bulletin*, 22 (4): 7–13.

Von Holdt, Karl. 2003. *Transition from Below: Forging Trade Unionism and Workplace Change in South Africa*. Pietermartizburg: University of Natal Press.

Von Holdt, Karl. 2005. 'Political Transition and the Changing Workplace Order in a South African Steelworks'. In *Beyond the Apartheid Workplace: Studies in Transition*, edited by Edward Webster and Karl von Holdt, 45–71. Pietermaritzburg: University of KwaZulu-Natal Press.

Von Holdt, Karl. 2010a. 'Institutionalisation, Strike Violence and Local Moral Orders'. *Transformation*, 72 (1): 127–151.

Von Holdt, Karl. 2010b. 'Nationalism, Bureaucracy and the Developmental State: The South African Case'. *South African Review of Sociology*, 41 (10): 4–27.

Von Holdt, Karl and Edward Webster. 2005. 'Work Restructuring and the Crisis of Social Reproduction: A Southern Perspective'. In *Beyond the Apartheid Workplace: Studies in Transition*, edited by Edward Webster and Karl von Holdt, 1–20. Pietermaritzburg: University of KwaZulu-Natal Press.

Walker, Ivan and Ben Weinbren. 1961. *2000 Casualties: A History of the Trade Unions and the Labour Movement in South Africa*. Johannesburg: South African Trade Union Council.

Webster, Edward. 1985a. *Cast in a Racial Mould: Labour Process and Trade Unionism in the Foundries*. Johannesburg: Ravan Press.

Webster, Edward. 1985b. 'Competing Paradigms: Towards a Critical Sociology in Southern Africa'. *Social Dynamics* 11 (1): 44–48.

Webster, Edward. 2004. 'South African Labour Studies in a Global Perspective, 1973–2006'. *Labour, Capital and Society* 37: 258–282.

Webster, Edward and Glenn Adler. 2000. 'Introduction: Consolidating Democracy in a Liberalizing World – Trade Unions and Democratization in South Africa'. In *Trade Unions and Democratization in South Africa, 1985–97*, edited by Glenn Adler and Edward Webster, 1–19. Houndmills, Basingstoke and New York: Macmillan and St. Martin's Press.

Webster, Edward and Christine Bischoff. 2011. 'New Actors in Employment Relations in the Periphery: Closing the Representation Gap amongst Micro and Small Enterprises'. *Relations Industrielles/Industrial Relations Quarterly Review* 66 (1): 11–33.

Webster, Edward, Akua O. Britwum and Sharit Bhowmik, eds. 2017. *Crossing the Divide: Precarious Work and the Future of Labour*. Pietermaritzburg: University of KwaZulu-Natal Press.

Webster, Edward, Rob Lambert and Andries Bezuidenhout. 2008. *Grounding Globalization: Labour in the Age of Insecurity*. Oxford: Blackwell.

Xaba, Jantjie. 2018. 'Social Capital Unionism and Empowerment: Case Study of Solidarity Union'. Paper presented at 'Taking Democracy Seriously: Reflecting on Trade Unions in the Last 20 Years and the Future of the Labour Movement in South Africa', University of the Witwatersrand, 6–7 September 2018.

PART I

CHANGING SOLIDARITIES

2

Patriarchal Collusions and Women's Marginalisation in Mining Unions

Asanda-Jonas Benya

INTRODUCTION

Labour feminists have long criticised trade unions for embracing and reproducing a culture that valorises androcentric norms and logics, functioning as boys' clubs with 'brotherhood' solidarities that exclude or marginalise women (Colgan and Ledwith 1996; Franzway 2000; 2001; Munro 2001; Ledwith 2012; Acker 2012). Like their global counterparts, South African trade unions and federations, especially those organising in male-dominated workplaces, have also faced similar criticisms (Berger 1992; Orr, Daphne and Horton 1997; Tshoaedi and Hlela 2006). While much has been said about transforming unions and taking seriously women's struggles in workplaces, the recalcitrant masculine culture of unions remains. Women's experiences are still coloured by marginalisation, and they continue to be seen as 'outsiders inside' and as invaders.

Using data from participant observation where I worked full shifts underground for almost a year while living with mineworkers in their residences, and interviews conducted between 2008 and 2019 at a platinum mine in South Africa, I outline women's experiences in three mining unions: the United Association of South Africa (Uasa), the Association of Mineworkers and Construction Union (Amcu) and the National Union of Mineworkers (NUM). Being with workers daily allowed me not only to understand the lives of women miners, but the life of mineworkers generally. During my time as a participant research mineworker I also attended meetings, participated in strikes, and attended social and family events. This allowed me to be fully immersed in the miners' lives. In this chapter, I reflect on their responses to unionisation, their nominal membership in some unions and how they make sense of their marginal and outsider status. I categorise their responses and approaches to unionisation into four groups:

- the women's structure group, which included detached and disgruntled women who were officially members of NUM;
- the Uasa group, which was antagonistic and anti-union;
- the invisible and marginal Amcu group;
- and what I call the loners, who were despondent women disappointed with unions.

I explain what distinguishes them from each other and what they demonstrate about the workings of the 'patchwork quilt of patriarchies' and unwritten scripts of exclusion. Belinda Bozzoli (1983, 149) defines the 'patchwork quilt of patriarchies' as a 'system in which forms of patriarchy are sustained, modified and even entrenched in a variety of ways depending on the internal character of the system'.

What I demonstrate through interviews and my analysis is that unions as boys' clubs with brotherhood solidarities are not only complicit in the production of unequal power relations and gender inequity at work, but also perpetuate it within their own structures by reinforcing hetero-patriarchal norms and by neglecting women workers' interests. Alongside employers, and contrary to their goals, mining unions reproduce a culture that disempowers and side-lines women workers. Mining unions not only need to smash capitalism (a virtue unions have compromised on since the advent of democracy) and racism, but must also smash patriarchy both in workplaces and within their own structures. Unions must disrupt the traditional, sexist practices that treat women as outsiders in the workplace and in unions. The narrow shop-floor focus of traditional trade unions does not serve women members. To serve women, there needs to be a rupture from androcentricity, and unions have to appreciate the connection between pocketbook issues and women's day-to-day workplace struggles, or what Dorothy Cobble (2007) calls the 'sex of class'. I see this incorporation of women's issues as presenting unions with possibilities not only for inclusivity but also for numerical strength and political relevance in this current juncture in mining workplaces. That reckoning is critical for the future of the labour movement, as women are a permanent feature of work.

HISTORICAL OVERVIEW OF WOMEN'S ORGANISING IN SOUTH AFRICA

While the inclusion of women in mining unions is as recent as 2003, the participation of women in unions has a much longer history (Walker 1982; Tshoaedi and Hlela 2006; Tshoaedi 2008, 2017; Byrne and Orr 2015). From as early as the 1940s black women have been actively involved in the labour movement. They organised workers in the trenches and on the shop floor, and at the height of apartheid. As a result of women's participation in union activities, especially in the garment industry, in the 1940s and again in the 1970s unions won significant gains for working women (Carim 1980, 4, 11; Byrne and Orr 2015, 80–86). The gains included the right of African women to belong to registered unions, the right to a four-week paid holiday, unemployment insurance benefits, and a 44-hour working week instead of the 46 hours that African men endured (Carim 1980; Walker 1982). Women such as Emma Mashinini, Christina Okolo, Frances Baard, Maggie Magubane, Lydia Kompe, Johanna Cornelius, Lucy Mvubelo, Elizabeth Mafekingwere, Ray Alexander, Liz Abrahams, Viola Hashe, Anna Scheepers and many others were at the forefront of the labour movement (Walker 1982; Baard 1986; Ackermann, Draper and Mashinini 1991; Berger 1990; 1992; Kuumba 2001; Tshoaedi 2008; Strydom and Coetzer 2009, 2012).

From the 1980s, however, women's participation and prominence in unions shifted. Malehoko Tshoaedi's (2008) research shows that as trade unions gained recognition, and grew in number and influence, union positions became powerful and masculine, and women such as Emma Mashinini and Lydia Kompe were pushed away from leadership positions. Women were no longer at the forefront of labour activities until the 1990s when they worked as administrators and not as key decision-makers (Berger 1992, 288; Tshoaedi and Hlela 2006, 98). During this period and across all unions women faced overt discrimination and bias, with leadership positions dominated by men. Through women's struggles and resistance to male domination, some unions introduced formal and informal gender structures (Tshoaedi 2008, 2012b; Sihlali 2015, 44–48). Work on women in trade unions demonstrates the feminist struggles waged by women activists to challenge union leadership and to ensure the representation of women's interests in workers' struggles (Orr et al. 1997; Tshoaedi 2008, 2012a, 2012b).

CONTEMPORARY MINING UNIONS IN SOUTH AFRICA

The focus of this chapter is on mining unions, specifically in the platinum sector, which has the highest number of workers in the mining industry. According to a report released by the Minerals Council South Africa (2019, 16), in 2019 there were 460 015 workers in mining; of those 168 102 were in platinum, 92 916 were in gold, and 94 297 in coal. According to Salimah Valiani and Nesta Ndebele (2018), quoting the statistician general, in 2015 women employees constituted 14.7 per cent of the total mining workforce in platinum group metals (PGM). The Minerals Council (2020, 67) reports that there were 21 103 women employees in platinum, which is about 13 per cent of the PGM workforce; in gold there were 12 281 women (13 per cent) and in coal 13 828 women (15 per cent). At the mine where the research for this chapter was conducted, company records showed that women constituted 11 per cent of the workforce in 2019. My research shows that these women mainly worked as equipping helpers, store issuers, belt and cage attendants, loaders, and scraper winch and locomotive operators. Few worked as gang leaders, panel operators, miners or shift-boss supervisors, and none were rock drill operators. The rest were in above-ground occupations and worked as administrators, shift-boss assistants or what is commonly known as *pikininis*[1] in mining, environmental and surveyor helpers and ventilation officers.

Prior to 2012, most of these workers (mainly black Africans) were organised by the National Union of mineworkers. In 2011, for example, NUM membership stood at 308 628 and at 300 000 in 2012. In 2013 and 2014 NUM's membership numbers are hard to pin down, but as of 2018 they had gone down to 176 232, a decline of almost 40 per cent since the Marikana massacre in 2012 (Chinguno 2020, 74). Amcu, on the other hand, in 2013 won recognition rights in some of the biggest mines in the platinum belt, and has been on a steady rise in membership, with numbers reported at between 200 000 and 250 000. It has since become one of the dominant mining unions to organise in the platinum belt. White and coloured workers, on the other hand, have been historically organised by Solidarity and Uasa.

At the mine where this research was conducted, by 2017 only 5 per cent of workers were organised by NUM, a negligible number was organised by Uasa, 4–5 per cent who were mainly white and coloured workers were organised by Solidarity, and 80–90 per cent were organised by Amcu.

According to a union official in Rustenburg, until 2003 mining unions had no women in their membership or leadership. The only women in their staff complement worked as office administrators. With the inclusion of women in mining, mining unions had to adapt and organise women (Benya 2013).

While women are included in unions, their inclusion seems to be nominal and their interests continue to be on the periphery or ignored (Benya 2013, 55–57). Women are not only marginalised; they are not seen as *real* workers and therefore not represented *fully* as workers. Since women in unions are treated as outsiders and men are automatically insiders, this indicates a crisis of representation. The covert use of gender identity as an indicator for inclusion means that unions are ignoring (at best) or rejecting (at worst) the legal inclusion of women in the mining industry.

THE INCLUSION OF WOMEN IN MINING

From its inception, the South African mining industry was dominated by men (Breckenridge 1998, 675). With the exception of asbestos mines, women were excluded on the basis of their gender (McCulloch 2003, 424). The dominant heteronormative culture meant that mines utilised sexist myths and superstitions about women in mining as a basis for their exclusion. In their research on South African mines, Crispen Chinguno and Kwezi Mabasa (2018, 303) argue that the state ensured the exclusion of women in mines and its surrounding towns 'through heavily policed pass laws and influx control measures and prohibitions on freedom of association'. Such prohibitions meant that women were relegated to the social reproduction of the labour force as wives, mothers and care workers for the injured and old labourers who become useless to capital (Wolpe 1972, 434–435). In this context, mining unions' membership consisted exclusively of men.

South African mining legislation was only reviewed in the late 1990s up to the early 2000s, outlawing discrimination against women in mining, especially underground. That led to the promulgation in 2002 of the Mineral and Petroleum Resources Development Act and the Broad-Based Socio-Economic Empowerment Charter (known as the Mining Charter) (Republic of South Africa 2002, 2010), which were aligned to the principles of the country's constitution which espouses equality in the workplace and the broader society. Significantly, the Act and the Charter facilitated *some* gender and racial transformation in mining. For instance, the Charter required that women constitute at least 10 per cent of mine employees within five years from its implementation – that is, between 2004 and 2009.[2] The Charter also established a penalty for not complying with the requirement for inclusion of women (companies could lose their mining licences). These legislative shifts led to the opening up of mine work to women.

Women in mining entered the industry at the same time that women in unions affiliated to the Congress of South African Trade Unions (Cosatu) were actively demanding that unions prioritise the representation of women and gender issues within the unions and the workplace (Orr 2001). Those who joined NUM not only faced challenges around unions and the gender question in the post-apartheid union landscape, but also the added challenges of joining a union that had been exclusively organising men who questioned the legitimacy of women in mining.

While women have continued to join unions, their relations with unions have been marred by patriarchal and sexist attitudes. While for men, unions have served as a space of refuge and solidarity with fellow workers, women have experienced marginality and neglect, and even some abuse. This outsider status has contributed immensely to women's marginality and has limited their participation in trade union activities (Tshoaedi 2008, 2017). This does not mean, however, that there have been no victories for women in mining unions. In a paper on gendered labour (Benya 2013) I detail how NUM has challenged the gender wage gap and to some extent gender occupational segregation in the mines. What I demonstrate here, though, is that some of those gains have been lost in recent years, and that much work remains to be done.

CONCEPTIONS OF EXCLUSION WITHIN UNIONS

Oppression, exploitation, discrimination and exclusion in South African trade unions has been historically understood within the broader frames of state repression and authoritarian and racist workplaces. Unions have not focused on internal oppression and exploitation. Indeed, for almost a century, black unions have represented marginalised black workers and championed their rights. For these unions the logics and scripts of oppression, exploitation, exclusion, alienation and marginalisation during segregation and apartheid were relatively straightforward: black miners and their unions were on one side, and white miners, mining capital and the state were on the other side. Race and class were central in these exclusionary hierarchical wage-bar binaries. Black working-class men were at the bottom with low wages, and white workers were at the top. While black workers were systematically seen as cheap labour, white workers enjoyed decent working conditions and decent pay because of racial solidarities and racialised wage differences under segregation and apartheid legislation.

From colonialism through to apartheid, workplace hierarchies necessitated that unions organise along lines of class and race, neglecting the focus on gender. While solidarity around race and class were obvious, albeit exclusionary, explicit solidarity on the basis of gender was seen as divisive and dangerous. The consensus was that the enemy was outside union structures. Therefore, within unions there was very little inward-looking critical discourse about the ways in which unions might be furthering other forms of exclusion, alienation and marginalisation. Thus, the visible class and racial lines of inclusion and invisible gendered lines of exclusion continued unabated. This framing has for decades marked solidarities among black male workers. That solidarity is seen as under threat by the inclusion of the 'other' – that is, women. The inclusion of women in mining further illustrates feminist claims that capitalism, racism and patriarchy often converge to exploit and oppress black women, sometimes even more intensely than black men (Davis 2011, 229).

Women's presence in the mines, therefore, not only crystallises who is an imagined and welcomed mineworker but also who is not, despite official discourse. Their presence illuminates the taken-for-granted script of inclusion (and by extension the unwritten script of exclusion) which informs who unions imagine their membership to be and the focus of their mandate. That is, the written script of inclusion emphasises class and race with minimal reference to the gendered lines of exclusion. When we appreciate this historical frame, we are better placed to understand why women see themselves, and are also seen, as outsiders, and are therefore not recognised or given space to influence the agenda of mining unions.

THE SCRIPTS OF EXCLUSION DECODED

Drawing from the ethnographic research with women who work in underground conventional and mechanised platinum mines, I demonstrate how androcentrism is a norm and has mediated the experiences of women mineworkers. To do so, I outline four different but related ways in which women miners have experienced the 'collusion of patriarchies' within unions. While I emphasise the neglect of women by unions, I also want to stress that employers too are implicated in the neglect and cementation of the outsider status of women (see also Tshoaedi 2008, 163). Collective masculine sensibilities effectively render women outsiders, and the 'exclusive, inflexible, unfathomable strongholds of maleness and masculinity' of unions and employers holds the androcentric culture and system in place (Ledwith 2012: 189).[3] It is this solidarity between employers, male workers and union stewards that Bozzoli calls the 'patchwork quilt of patriarchies' – a system that operates to sustain and reproduce patriarchy (Bozzoli 1983, 149).

Group 1 – Women's structure group: experiences of neglect within NUM

Most of the women in this first group were NUM members, and a few were with Amcu. The women in NUM remarked that their union had become 'too political' and was more concerned with national party politics, specifically the ruling African National Congress (ANC), and as such cared less about bread-and-butter work-place issues. Women also argued that union leaders were using their positions to craft political and business careers for themselves, and were less concerned with the plight of workers. This confirms research conducted by Sian Byrne, Rob Rees and Liesl Orr (2015) and by Sarah Mosoetsa and Christine Bischoff (2015). Unionists were thus seen to be siding with both the ruling ANC and employers instead of workers.

Women used the Marikana case as an example of how NUM leaders were no longer prioritising workers' issues, but had closer relations with employers and the ANC. They expressed their disappointment at how the union had sided with employers and abandoned them during wage negotiations. Workers were further shocked by the union's refusal to condemn the Marikana massacre, which went against their historical role as advocates for workers' human rights. The NUM's actions and inactions during the Marikana strikes were read as a lack of care for workers (Botiveau 2017). While they retained their membership in NUM, these workers distanced themselves from the union, both emotionally and in terms of their participation. For them, the Marikana massacre demonstrated how a patch-work quilt of patriarchies operates for the benefit of union leaders, the police, employers and the ruling party, while workers starved with no representation. That women's issues did not figure prominently in NUM was another indicator that the union did not serve workers.

The close links between trade unions and political parties has a long history in South Africa, and indeed in most post-colonial states across Africa and Latin America (Beckman, Buhlungu and Sachikonye 2010). In South Africa the links between NUM and the ruling ANC go back to the very formation of NUM (Webster and Buhlungu 2004; Buhlungu 2006, 2010; Botiveau 2017). This relationship was further solidified in the Tripartite Alliance (comprising the ANC, Cosatu and the South African Communist Party) which was formalised after the democratisation of South Africa. It is thus a long-standing relationship with strong ties not only to NUM but to the labour movement generally.

The sentiments about focusing on political party leadership battles expressed by mineworkers in this research were, therefore, not surprising, considering the close association between the ANC and NUM (Buhlungu and Bezuidenhout 2008;

Chinguno and Mabasa 2018). The 'close proximity of NUM to the ANC has come with substantive costs to the union's legitimacy' (Chinguno and Mabasa 2018, 322; see also Ntswana 2014). The union's response to these assertions, however, was that their relationship with the ruling party should be seen as a victory and as a strategic relationship. It is meant to benefit NUM members and the broader working class by influencing the ANC, ensuring that workers have a voice in national policy issues (Sithethi, interview, 2012). However, in the course of this research, this view was contradicted by workers, who argued that the unions' proximity to the ANC and to employers was a distraction and that it eroded internal union democratic practices.

When asked about their attendance at and participation in NUM meetings, it appeared that very few of the women had attended union meetings. There they were not only a numerical minority, but their interests were hardly discussed and contributions barely acknowledged beyond their traditional feminine roles (see also Benya 2009). Instead of union meetings, the interviewees seemed to prefer women-only spaces. These spaces were usually organised for all women in the shafts and were not union-specific, even though they were usually led by women representatives from the majority union. Women's lack of participation in union meetings was not surprising, considering that they felt relegated to the margins by their union. Their views were consistent with those reflected in studies done both in South Africa and other parts of the world, where women form and use parallel spaces and forego or minimise their participation in union spaces because their issues are neglected in such spaces (Tshoaedi 2008; Britwum and Ledwith 2014, 5–10; Munakamwe 2014). Sian Byrne and Liesl Orr (2015, 82) in their survey of Cosatu unions note that 'women were more likely to participate in union meetings amongst the unions with 60 per cent or more women members … and least likely to participate in unions with 30 per cent or less women members', such as the mining unions or other unions in male-dominated industries.

Rather than negotiating terms of engagement with unions, this group of women detached themselves from union activities. This was their way of showing disgruntlement with trade unions, and not a show of indifference towards workers' issues. They continued to contend that trade unions were relevant, but that theirs was considered 'useless' for reasons around lack of representation, as described. Their disgruntlement with and detachment from unions, therefore, stems from exclusionary practices that reinforce the patchwork quilt of patriarchies within union spaces. It also stems from their experiences of unions not centring women's issues, not making significant attempts to make sure that women feel safe during strikes, and not meaningfully and earnestly integrating women into their main structures. Some interviewees argued that it stemmed from the fact that unions have done little to eliminate gender disparities that disproportionately affect women in the workplace (see also Franzway 2000, 2001). This detachment should be read not as disinterest or a sign of being apolitical, but as a protest against and rejection of marginality, and a 'quiet statement' or fight for spaces that recognise their needs and interests.

Group 2 – The Uasa group: non-emphasis on strike participation as an expression of care

Unlike the group of women who viewed unions as relevant even though ineffective due to their focus on party politics, the second group of women viewed traditional unions as irrelevant, no longer serving workers, and therefore useless. As such, these women joined Uasa, which is an affiliate of Federation of Unions of South Africa (Fedusa).[4] They do not consider Uasa to be a 'real union' but an *association* which does more than trade unions do. According to these workers, Uasa represents them not only at work, but outside of work as well: 'If you are in trouble ... they can give you a lawyer, so it's not a union...' (Focus group discussion, Rustenburg, July 2012).

In a model that Bezuidenhout (2017) has called economic unionism, union members received other benefits as well. For example, workers who were Uasa members talked about maternity benefits. In three focus group discussions, Uasa members who had been pregnant claimed that they had received R1 000 after their return from maternity leave and upon producing a birth certificate for their newborn child. Through their Uasa membership they could also enjoy weekends away at lodges or day trips to Sun City at discounted rates, something they would struggle to afford without the Uasa-negotiated discounts. One participant, Angela, added that during her annual leave she went to Gqeberha (formerly Port Elizabeth) with her friends who are nurses: 'It was my first time going so far ... I had never been to PE' (Angela, interview, August 2012). According to her, the bus ticket was 'cheap' because she had a discount: 'They send us SMSs to tell us about discounts for lodges ... for the bus, you pay less'. Angela mentioned other Uasa benefits as well: 'You can get a (bank) loan ... Uasa does not just represent you at work ... Uasa also gives lawyers in case you get arrested' (Angela, interview, August 2012; Focus group discussion, August 2012). Other benefits women talked about were pregnancy and maternity benefits, and car deals with Bidvest McCarthy. Workers also revealed that through Uasa they had access to burial institutions like Avbob. One interviewee, Dimpho, commented that 'when you join Uasa you also get a funeral plan ... like when a relative you've registered dies, you get money ... R3 000 for each person' (Dimpho, interview, August 2012). Uasa not only gave them access to the benefits mentioned above; the women also spoke of their aspirations to a different lifestyle, one they believed was better than what NUM and Amcu offered. These benefits were presented as evidence that Uasa cared for its members.

Consistent with the 'ethic of care' evoked above, workers also stressed the different expectations Uasa has of them during strikes. They remarked, 'Uasa does not expect us to join strikes'; instead Uasa sends text messages 'telling us not to come [to work]', said Gontse, one of the interviewees (Gontse, interview, August 2012; focus group discussion, August 2012). Minnie, another worker, said Uasa 'cares about us ... when there is a strike they send us WhatsApp messages to say we must not come to work' (Minnie, interview, August 2012; Focus group discussion, August 2012). The reluctance of Uasa to participate in strikes is old; it was also noted by Gwede Mantashe (2009, 50), who was at that time the NUM General Secretary, when he said that for years UASA had 'never disrupted production by disturbance or strike'. Women read Uasa's non-participation in strikes as an expression of care, as opposed to what they saw as disregard for women's safety by other unions that insisted on women joining violent strike action.

While reports of sexual harassment in mining were rampant and cut across unions, occupations and locations of work, women's responses differed from union to union. The majority of Uasa members interviewed seemed to have experiences of at least being listened to, even though nothing was done. NUM and Amcu members, on the other hand, shared experiences of not being taken seriously, being advised against escalating sexual harassment incidents, and to see them as 'appreciation' rather than harassment and being sexualised by union officials (see also Tshoaedi 2017). While the denial and concealment of sexual harassment is pervasive – another strategy that sustains the patchwork quilt of patriarchies – and is as common in union structures as it is in workplaces (Byrne and Orr 2015, 86), Uasa seems to have a somewhat different approach. Instead of denying the existence of sexual harassment, they listened, even though they did not act on it, women argued.

In the handling of sexual harassment by all unions, the conspiracy of silence continued to be the standard response. In other words, the 'patchwork quilt of patriarchies' or the 'collusion of patriarchies' still prevailed. Union leaders, employers, union members and workers generally were involved in this 'conspiracy'. According to interviewees, sexual harassment was only taken seriously when there were issues at stake other than the well-being of the harassed woman. In a study by Byrne and Orr (2015, 86) the prevalence of sexual harassment committed by union leaders was even more pronounced than that by management. Men generally, regardless of their positions or occupations, were implicated, but to varying degrees. Sexual harassment was not only prevalent in trade unions, but in federations such as Cosatu. According to

Tshoaedi (2017), it is widespread inside Cosatu and at times swept under the carpet through the lack of honest debate about it, indifference and even leaders' failure to hold those accused accountable. In light of all this, the provision of lawyers by Uasa presented an avenue women could pursue when confronted with sexual harassment. This possibility seemed significant for women workers as an avenue for redress.

Unlike the first group, which was disgruntled and detached but continued to view unions as relevant though useless, this group held antagonistic and anti-union sentiments but were not apolitical. Like the first group, they felt mistreated inside traditional trade unions – ignored at best, marginalised and oppressed at worst – and effectively treated as outsiders who needed to be put in their place. Within Uasa, however, they felt welcomed and provided for by the union. Women were not only detached from unions but were disinterested in unions in their current configuration, and indifferent to unions since they saw them as not serving their interests but rather the interests of those whom the unions deemed to be legitimate members.

Group 3 – The Amcu group: victories, violence and vulnerability

The third group of women were mainly Amcu members and saw the critical role that could be played by unions if they were held accountable. While they were optimistic about Amcu representing them as workers, they remained pessimistic about their representation as women. Some went so far as to liken Amcu to an abusive but useful and much-needed spouse.

As already indicated, women in this group were mainly Amcu members who had lost all faith in NUM. They were hopeful, however, about Amcu and saw it as responsive to workers generally, even though not so responsive to women. They remained critical of Amcu's gender-blind approach to workplace issues and of the union's adoption of NUM structures instead of creatively thinking about bringing women to the centre. Despite these critiques, these women remained hopeful about Amcu in the Marikana moment (2012–2014), and especially as Amcu was winning major victories in the platinum industry. Therefore, they moved between optimism and pessimism when it came to Amcu.

In informal group discussion, Tshire noted:

> We have to join [Amcu]. What can we do, we don't have a choice ... We know that they [Amcu leaders] will do the same thing [that NUM did] ... They are still new now, but they are going to change and be like the NUM ... It's the same people, these people ... Yes they are Amcu, but it's the same leaders [who led NUM]. (Focus group discussion, March 2012)

The respondents understood that Amcu's leaders and most of its active members were once members and leaders in the same NUM that the women had rejected. This was often used as a rationale for giving the union their provisional trust despite their expectation that their leadership might turn on workers, as they perceived NUM to have done in Marikana. In previous work, borrowing from Spivak (1993, 60), I have described this position as an 'impossible no' position. This is when one is unable to reject a structure that one intimately inhabits, even though one may continue to critique it. This is a paradox that women, forced to operate within the patchwork quilt of patriarchies, have to traverse.

In interviews and focus group discussions, women in the Amcu group made it clear that they were not optimistic that unions would be responsive in the long term, especially to women. Vicky stated:

> We have to join them and ... change them ... You think they will change if we don't attend? No, I can tell you now, they won't; they will be like that forever and we will stay here complaining forever ... So it is better if we go and join Amcu and change it, and fight to change it for ourselves as women. (Vicky, interview, October 2012)

These women, therefore, were pragmatic in their shifts between optimism and pessimism. In their pessimism, some had resigned themselves to not receiving assistance from the union, both as women and as workers. To address women's issues, this group of women, similar to the ones above, participated in structures that brought together women from all trade unions. What they all had in common was a belief that they needed unions even though they felt abused and neglected by them and found solace in women's structures.

Despite the fact that all workers were invited to Amcu meetings and even forced to attend, through barring of buses and taxis from taking workers to their hostels or taxi ranks after work, they still talked about Amcu meetings as only really welcoming men and their viewpoints and not women. Women felt that the space for them to participate was not open. Their role was to attend and endorse without engaging, especially if they held different views. Women thus concluded that, like lekgotlas, Amcu meetings were geared towards the interests of men. Women should be satisfied with attending or giving reports, but should not engage directly.

Like the disgruntled 'women's structure group' (Group 1), at union meetings, women in this group experienced intimidation. However, instead of detaching, as the first group did, they made themselves 'invisible' at meetings. They learned the art of invisibility, even though emotionally still invested, rather than risk being heckled for asking the 'wrong' questions. Even though invisible in terms of participation, some of them still insisted that women had to attend meetings to at least hear what was happening and to ensure that they were in good standing with the union in case they encountered problems at work. Others, however, only attended union meetings when forced to do so.

The women in the Amcu group were concerned with the union's dominant focus on wages to the neglect of other equally important workplace concerns, especially those affecting women. The lack of representation of or focus on women and their marginality within Amcu was articulated in many ways, including making references to the exclusively male leadership of the union at national, branch and shaft levels.

While the Amcu group of women did not willingly attend union meetings, they did willingly attend women's shaft meetings. They argued that these were the only meetings that catered to their needs. They saw these meetings as the only ones where they could freely talk about women-specific interests and grievances such as their challenges as mothers working in mining, pregnancy and breastfeeding while working underground, balancing family obligations with early mine shifts, menstruating while working in sections that had no useable toilets underground, and how these issues affected their productivity at work. For example, in focus group discussions, some of the women remarked that pregnancy or choosing to breastfeed was not only a reproductive matter, but also a financial issue. When women choose to breastfeed after giving birth, they are effectively choosing to forgo their income, as they are not allowed back underground while breastfeeding. These women-only meetings and spaces were stigmatised by men and the union structures, and used to justify the widely peddled notion that women are lazy.

The majority of women in this Amcu group, whether they attended union meetings or not, had trepidations about going on strike. Like the first group – the women's structure group – the violent nature of strikes was often cited as a reason for non-participation; during focus group discussions some women also cited intimidation. They remarked that the union, while aware of violence during strikes, did not discourage its use as a means of achieving their goal – threatening dissenters and scaring off scab labourers. Capturing the mood at strikes and the vulnerability of women, Ntate Ras (Interview, March 2012), for example, said, 'When we are striking, we do not have friends; our friends are those participating ... those who are on our side, not against us'. He went on to call those who did not participate in strikes and those who held different views as *amagundwane* (rats). One woman asked in discussions, 'Do you think they [unions and men] care about us? No, they see all women as *amagundwane*' (Focus group discussion, July 2012). The fear of violence during strikes was justifiable for most women because difference and disagreeing were often seen as betrayal. For women, difference did not have to be spoken; their existence as women in a predominantly male space rendered them 'different', thus untrustworthy, and therefore outsiders. Women occupied an ambivalent position, and one that could easily render them targets of violence should it break out.

Violence during strikes and violence against women generally were seen as synonymous. In three different focus group discussions women remarked that during strikes 'workers [men] … do not listen' and that there are 'no rules at strikes'. Another woman asked, 'Who will protect you if they do something to you? There are no laws or sexual harassment policies when they [men] are striking'. She went on to say, 'They can do as they please to you' (Focus group discussion, July 2012). These sentiments pointed to the fear and vulnerability women felt while on strike. In focus group discussions women talked at length about a video of a woman believed to be a scab labourer who was stripped naked during a strike. They believed that this video, which circulated among mineworkers in 2012, was meant to instil fear, put them in their place and 'teach women a lesson' should they betray the cause or not toe the line.

One interviewee, Mama Mavis, alluded not only to threats but actual violence that she had witnessed during strikes and how it also lingered in the air at union meetings. She argued that 'as a mother' who has children to take care of, the violence did not sit well with her. She asked, 'Who would take care of my children if I get killed or injured in their strikes?' (Mama Mavis, interview, June 2012). The violence, which has a long history in South African labour and social movements (Von Holdt 2013, 592–594), and particularly in the mines (Chinguno 2013, 640–641), is associated with mining masculinity and mobilised by men to advance power. This also contributed to women's lack of participation in union activities.

This invisibility in union activities and disinterest in strikes, then, should not be read as a sign of being apolitical, but as a negotiation of the vulnerability felt by women. Unlike in Mosoetsa and Bischoff (2015, 31), where women did not join unions because they were apolitical, the Amcu group recognises injustices against women at work. But it is their lack of faith in union structures, and in the avenues through which strike grievances such as violence targeting them would be addressed, that concerns them. This 'disinterest' needs to be read alongside the gender-based violence trends in South Africa and especially in masculine spaces. These women are political. They see the link between the political and the personal, the pocketbook and breastfeeding and/or pregnancy, hence they attend meetings organised by women's structures. To see them as apolitical or ignorant of worker politics is to dismiss their demands and disregard their worker consciousness.

Group 4 – The 'loners' group: union irrelevance and growing antipathy

While the three groups previously discussed claimed to be affiliated to some union or association, 'the loners group' of women saw all unions, including Uasa, as useless and only relevant for some workers. The majority of them were nominal members of either NUM or Amcu and did not proclaim their membership as genuine, but as required by the mine. Most of them were at the top of the underground occupational hierarchy and were thus paid better than most workers. The demands that unions, even the most 'successful' one (Amcu in 2013 when this interview took place), made on behalf of workers did not make a significant change in their earnings. Therefore, while union demands in 2012 of R9 000 and R12 500 a month were seen as radical, these women (mostly miners) were already earning close to that, and even more than that after production bonuses (payslips were shown to the researcher to corroborate this claim). This is why they felt that unions were largely irrelevant, although they realised that unions were needed by *some* workers to demand higher wages.

The loners' group participated in neither union meetings nor women's structures. They only attended union meetings if shop stewards held up the cage and prevented them from going underground, or forcibly removed workers from taxis and shut down the taxi rank. They distanced themselves from union activities, marking them irrelevant. Similarly, women's meetings were seen as 'awkward' at best and 'useless' at worst. Katlego, an interviewee who was a miner, said she disliked that these women-only meetings were explicitly and exclusively for women, and consequently distanced herself from these structures and their activities (Katlego, interview, October and November 2012).

Across the different shafts I worked at, women's meetings were framed by women, men, union leaders and management as complaints meetings. Meetings called by men, on the other hand, were seen as legitimate and constructive, 'dealing with work ... worker issues ... and money'. To justify the lack of interest in women's structures, the 'loner' women often said that women go to these meetings to 'complain', 'to cry' or 'talk ... about toilet sprays and mirrors' – language used by men unionists. Katlego (Interview, November 2012) said, 'I need to drill and blast; I cannot waste time with them [women] ... I'm a miner at work, not a woman'. Reports of discomfort with women-only structures and spaces is common in scholarship that looks at women in masculine workplaces. In this scholarship some women report feeling awkward attending meetings called only for women (Martin 2003; Benya 2009; Rhoton 2011). The disregard for women's structures, then, was based on their being stigmatised, seen as spaces for lazy women and ineffective in addressing substantial workplace issues.

This group's response towards women's structures was a way of 'discursive separation or dissociating from other women' (Rhoton 2011, 700).

On the other hand, the antipathy towards unions was usually due to experiences of being let down by the union, in addition to union wage demands falling short of expectations. Shado, for example, recounted a story of how the union failed her. She considered the union and women's structure as 'useless' and 'powerless' and she justified this by recalling a fatal accident in her stope in her absence where two rock drill operators died. Because she was the responsible miner, she was charged with their deaths, even though the incident had taken place in her absence. She argued that the trauma of the deaths of the drill operators and the blame directed at her by management and union officials made her realise that she was alone at work and only she could represent her interests, not a union or a women's structure. She said that 'the union did nothing except to emphasise that [I] should not be a miner in the first place', because she was a woman. She argued that the union was 'useless and didn't assist me when I had a case, and when I was accused of killing two of my rock drill operators underground' (Shado, interview, November 2012). She rhetorically asked, what then could she need the union for? While Shado felt betrayed by her union, other women in this group also saw no use for a union. Their relationships with unions ranged from apathy to antagonism.

CONCLUSION: THE ARCHITECTURAL PLAN OF RESPONSIVE UNIONS AND EMANCIPATORY POSSIBILITIES

The four groups demonstrate that unions have a long way to go to rid themselves of patriarchal impulses embedded in their culture and embodied by their members, and to disrupt the patriarchal collusion that perpetuates women's marginality. The crisis facing the labour movement is not only that of capitalism and its attending consequences, but also a crisis of masculinity that has been normalised, a crisis of resistance tools, tactics, strategies and structures that labour has relied on in the fight against domination and exploitation of all workers, especially women. An alternative inclusive culture needs to re-emerge. Such a culture needs to appreciate, in practice, the connectedness of struggles and the links between class, race and gender. The four groups demonstrate how the 'patchwork quilt of patriarchies', buttressed by capitalism and racism, operate to reinforce women's marginality. What then does it mean to imagine alternatives for worker representation?

The call here is to radically reimagine unions and rewrite parts of the current script, rather than simply including women. Instead of reinforcing the 'exclusive brotherhood' of unions, and turning a blind eye to the durability and normalisation of masculinity in mining unions, and thus entrenching patriarchy and naturalising masculine exclusivity in mining, a future script that radically reimagines political responsiveness should be written. If indeed all structures that go through crisis already have the seeds for new structures embedded within their current configuration, then unions need to pay attention to those seeds; this would enable the formation of new structures that women are demanding. Sarah Mosoetsa and Christine Bischoff (2015, 31–32) recommend that unions use this moment to urgently and creatively think of new strategies and to revitalise old (radical) ones. In addition to the above, I am suggesting that unions also re-examine the very ethos and foundations of unionism to reflect the current conjuncture, or risk becoming irrelevant. A radical ethic of care and taking seriously issues affecting women needs to be brought into the fold. Such an approach will open up numerous emancipatory possibilities for workers, and for organising women mineworkers in particular.

NOTES

1   *Pikinini* means 'small boy' or 'baas [boss] boy'. It is a derogatory term and was largely a feature of colonialism and the apartheid workplace order. *Pikinini* is now used to include women doing auxiliary work.

2   The Mining Charter was developed in 2002, but came into real force and official implementation by mining houses in 2004; hence all mining documents use 2004–2009. After the Charter was promulgated, the understanding was that mining houses needed to do some work internally to ready their male workers for the presence of women miners, to build change houses, negotiate gender-sensitive policies and start introducing women. Two years were allowed for that kind of work, and thus 2004 was the official starting date of implementation. The Mining Charter was gazetted in 2010, and amended in 2018.

3   While I do not draw much from international literature here, I am aware of it and that the struggles women face, especially in male-dominated unions, are similar across the world. See Milkman 1982, 2013; Cobble 1988, 1991, 2007; Ledwith et al. 1990; Colgan and Ledwith 1996; Franzway 2000; Venkata Ratnam and Jain 2002; Britwum 2010; Cooper 2012.

4   On its website, Fedusa describes itself as an organisation that brings together 'employees' from different backgrounds 'for a much stronger, party-politically independent, non-racial and stable trade union federation with unions who can advance the interest of the employees and of the economy of South Africa in an independent and responsible manner' (http://www.fedusa.org.za, accessed 9 May 2023).

REFERENCES

Acker, Joan. 2012. 'Gendered Organisations and Intersectionality: Problems and Possibilities'. *Equality, Diversity and Inclusion: An International Journal* 31 (3): 214–224.

Ackermann, Denise, Jonathan Draper and Emma Mashinini. 1991. *Women Hold Up Half the Sky: Women in the Church in Southern Africa*. Pietermaritzburg: Cluster Publications.

Baard, Frances. 1986. *My Spirit is not Banned*. Harare: Zimbabwe Publishing House.

Beckman, Björn, Sakhela Buhlungu and Lloyd Sachikonye. 2010. *Trade Unions and Party Politics: Labour Movements in Africa*. Pretoria: HSRC Press.

Benya, Asanda. 2009. 'Women in Mining: A Challenge to the Occupational Culture in Mines'. Masters diss., University of the Witwatersrand.

Benya, Asanda. 2013. 'Gendered Labour: A Challenge to Labour as a Democratizing Force'. *Rethinking Development and Inequality* 2 (1): 47–62.

Berger, Iris. 1990. Gender, Race, and Political Empowerment: South African Canning Workers, 1940–1960. *Gender & Society* 4 (3): 398–420.

Berger, Iris. 1992. *Threads of Solidarity: Women in South African Industry, 1900–1980*. Bloomington, IN: Indiana University Press.

Bezuidenhout, Andries. 2017. 'Labour Beyond Cosatu, other Federations and Independent Unions'. In *Labour Beyond Cosatu: Mapping the Rupture in South Africa's Political Landscape*, edited by Andries Bezuidenhout and Malehoko Tshoaedi, 217–234. Johannesburg: Wits University Press.

Botiveau, Raphaël. 2017. *Organise or Die?: Democracy and Leadership in South Africa's National Union of Mineworkers*. Johannesburg: Wits University Press.

Bozzoli, Belinda. 1983. 'Marxism, Feminism and South African Studies'. *Journal of Southern African Studies* 9 (2): 139–171.

Breckenridge, Keith. 1998. 'The Allure of Violence: Men, Race and Masculinity on the South African Goldmines, 1900–1950'. *Journal of Southern African Studies* 24 (4): 669–693.

Britwum, Akua O. 2010. 'Union Democracy and the Challenge of Globalisation to Organised Labour in Ghana'. Doctoral diss., Maastricht University.

Britwum, Akua O. and Sue Ledwith, eds. 2014. *Visibility and Voice for Union Women: Country Case Studies from Global Labour University Researchers*. Munich: Rainer Hampp Verlag.

Buhlungu, Sakhela, ed. 2006. *Trade Unions and Democracy: Cosatu Workers' Political Attitudes in South Africa*. Pretoria: HSRC Press.

Buhlungu, Sakhela. 2010. *A Paradox of Victory: COSATU and the Democratic Transformation in South Africa*. Pietermaritzburg: University of KwaZulu-Natal Press.

Buhlungu, Sakhela and Andries Bezuidenhout. 2008. 'Union Solidarity under Stress: The Case of the National Union of Mineworkers in South Africa'. *Labor Studies Journal* 33 (3): 262–287.

Byrne, Sian and Liesl Orr. 2015. 'A Woman's Place is in her Union: Reflections on Women, Gender Struggles and Trade Unions in COSATU's Past and Present'. In *COSATU Workers' Surveys of 2006 and 2012: What Do They Tell Us?* edited by Debbie Budlender and Liesl Orr, 79–96. Johannesburg: Naledi.

Byrne, Sian, Rob Rees and Liesl Orr. 2015. 'Internal Democracy and Worker Control in COSATU: The Importance of Rank and File Participation'. In *COSATU Workers' Surveys of 2006 and 2012: What Do They Tell Us?* edited by Debbie Budlender and Liesl Orr, 57–78. Johannesburg: Naledi.

Carim, Shirene Fradet. 1980. 'The Role of Women in the South African Trade Union Movement'. Pamphlet. United Nations, Unit on Apartheid, Department of Political and Security Council Affairs. 1-17. http://psimg.jstor.org/fsi/img/pdf/t0/10.5555/al.sff.document.nuun1980_09_final.pdf. Accessed 11 June 2021.

Chinguno, Crispen. 2013. 'Marikana: Fragmentation, Precariousness, Strike Violence and Solidarity'. *Review of African Political Economy* 40 (138): 639–646.

Chinguno, Crispen. 2020. 'The Marikana Paradox: Gaining the Remuneration but Losing the Union'. In *Marikana Unresolved: Massacre, Culpability and Consequences*, edited by Mia Swart and Ylva Robny-Gumede, 67–86. Cape Town: UCT Press.

Chinguno, Crispen and Khwezi Mabasa. 2018. 'Trade Union Organising in the Mining Sector: A Structural Perspective on Worker Insurgency and Shifting Union Strategies'. In *The Future of Mining in South Africa: Sunset or Sunrise?* edited by Salimah Valiani, 298–334. Johannesburg: Mapungubwe Institute for Strategic Reflection.

Cobble, Dorothy. 1988. '"Practical Women": Waitress Unionists and the Controversies over Gender Roles in the Food Service Industry, 1900–1980'. *Labor History* 29 (1): 5–31.

Cobble, Dorothy. 1991. *Dishing it Out: Waitresses and their Unions in the Twentieth Century.* Champaign, IL.: University of Illinois Press.

Cobble, Dorothy. 2007. *The Sex of Class: Women Transforming American Labor.* Ithaca, NY: Cornell University Press.

Colgan, Fiona and Sue Ledwith. 1996. 'Sisters Organising – Women and their Trade Unions'. In *Women in Organisations*, edited by Fiona Colgan and Sue Ledwith, 152–185. London: Palgrave.

Cooper, Rae. 2012. 'The Gender Gap in Union Leadership in Australia: A Qualitative Study'. *Journal of Industrial Relations* 54 (2): 131–146.

Davis, Angela Y. 2011. *Women, Race and Class.* New York: Vintage.

Franzway, Suzanne. 2000. 'Women Working in a Greedy Institution: Commitment and Emotional Labour in the Union Movement'. *Gender, Work and Organization* 7 (4): 258–268.

Franzway, Suzanne. 2001. *Sexual Politics and Greedy Institutions: Union Women, Commitments and Conflicts in Public and Private.* Annandale, NSW: Pluto Press Australia.

Kuumba, M. Bahati. 2001. *Gender and Social Movements.* Oxford: Altamira.

Ledwith, Sue. 2012. 'Gender Politics in Trade Unions: The Representation of Women, between Exclusion and Inclusion'. *Transfer: European Review of Labour and Research* 18 (2): 185–199.

Ledwith, Sue, Fiona Colgan, Paul Joyce and Mike Hayes. 1990. 'The Making of Women Trade Union Leaders'. *Industrial Relations Journal* 21 (2): 112–125.

Mantashe, Gwede. 2009. 'The Decline of the Mining Industry and the Response of the Mining Unions'. Masters diss., University of the Witwatersrand.

Martin, Patricia Yancey. 2003. '"Said and Done" versus "Saying and Doing" Gendering Practices, Practicing Gender at Work'. *Gender and Society* 17 (3): 342–366.

McCulloch, Jock. 2003. 'Women Mining Asbestos in South Africa 1893–1980'. *Journal of Southern African Studies* 29 (2): 413–432.

Milkman, Ruth. 1982. 'Redefining "Women's Work": The Sexual Division of Labor in the Auto Industry during World War II'. *Feminist Studies* 8 (2): 337–372.

Milkman, Ruth. 2013. *Women, Work and Protest: A Century of US Women's Labor History.* London: Routledge.

Minerals Council South Africa. 2019. *Facts and Figures, 2019.* https://www.mineralscouncil. org.za/industry-news/publications/facts-and-figures/send/17-facts-and-figures/1250-facts-and-figures-2019. Accessed 7 March 2021.

Minerals Council South Africa. 2020. *Facts and Figures, 2020.* https://www.mineralscouncil. org.za/industry-news/publications/facts-and-figures/send/17-facts-and-figures/1366-facts-and-figures-2020-pocketbook. Accessed: 7 March 2021.

Mosoetsa, Sarah and Christine Bischoff. 2015. 'Organising the Unorganised: Challenges and Possibilities for Bridging the Representation Gap in South Africa'. In *COSATU Workers' Surveys of 2006 and 2012: What Do They Tell Us?*, edited by Debbie Budlender and Liesl Orr, 27–44. Johannesburg: Naledi.

Munakamwe, Janet. 2014. 'Women in the South African Trade Union Movement'. In *Visibility and Voice for Union Women: Country Case Studies from Global Labour University Researchers*, edited by Akua O. Britwum and Sue Ledwith, 158–179. Munich: Rainer Hampp Verlag.

Munro, Anne. 2001. 'A Feminist Trade Union Agenda? The Continued Significance of Class, Gender and Race'. *Gender, Work & Organization* 8 (4): 454–471.

Ntswana, Nyonde. 2014. 'The Politics of Workers Control in South Africa's Platinum Mines: Do Workers' Committees in the Platinum Mining Industry Represent a Practice of Renewing Worker Control?' Masters diss., University of the Witwatersrand.

Orr, Liesl. 2001. Women's Work and Globalisation Trends: The South African Picture. *Agenda* 16 (48): 31–37.

Orr, Liesl, Jeremy Daphne and Claire Horton. 1997. COSATU Congress: Did Women Reject the Quota?' *Agenda* 13 (35): 24–29.

Republic of South Africa. 2002. Mineral and Petroleum Resources Development Act No. 28 of 2002. *Government Gazette* No. 23922, 10 October 2002. https://www.gov.za/sites/default/files/gcis_document/201409/a28-02ocr.pdf. Accessed 10 May 2023.

Republic of South Africa. 2010. Broad-based Socio-economic Empowerment Charter (Mining Charter 2002). *Government Gazette* No. 33573 of 20 September 2010. https://static.pmg.org.za/docs/101110gazette_0.pdf. Accessed 19 July 2012.

Rhoton, Laura. A. 2011. 'Distancing as a Gendered Barrier: Understanding Women Scientists' Gender Practices'. *Gender and Society* 25 (6): 696–716.

Sihlali, Nokwanda. 2015. 'Women in Trade Unions and Gender Transformation: A Case Study of the National Union of Metal Workers of South Africa (NUMSA)'. Masters diss., University of the Witwatersrand.

Spivak, Gayatri Chakravorty. 1993. *Outside in the Teaching Machine*. New York: Routledge.

Strydom, Irene and Pieter Coetzer. 2009. 'Anna Scheepers' Struggle for the Recognition of the Dignity of Labour for All Workers and for the Equality of Women in All Spheres'. *Journal for Contemporary History* 34 (3): 17–31.

Strydom, Irene and Pieter Coetzer. 2012. 'Lucy Mvubelo's Role in the South African Trade Unions, 1960–1974'. *Journal for Contemporary History* 37 (1): 20–44.

Tshoaedi, Malehoko. 2008. 'Roots of Women's Union Activism: South Africa 1973–2003'. PhD diss., Leiden University.

Tshoaedi, Malehoko. 2012a. '(En)gendering the Transition in South Africa: The Role of COSATU Women Activists'. *Transformation: Critical Perspectives on Southern Africa* 78: 1–26.

Tshoaedi, Malehoko. 2012b. 'Women in the Forefront of Workplace Struggles in South Africa: From Invisibility to Mobilization'. *Labour, Capital and Society/Travail, Capital et Société* 45 (2): 58–83.

Tshoaedi, Malehoko. 2017. 'The Politics of Male Power and Privilege in Trade Unions: Understanding Sexual Harassment in COSATU'. In *Labour Beyond Cosatu: Mapping the Rupture in South Africa's Labour Landscape*, edited by Andries Bezuidenhout and Malehoko Tshoaedi, 129–145. Johannesburg: Wits University Press.

Tshoaedi, Malehoko and Hlengiwe Hlela. 2006. 'The Marginalisation of Women Unionists during South Africa's Democratic Transition'. In *Trade Unions and Democracy: COSATU Workers' Political Attitudes in South Africa*, edited by Sakhela Buhlungu, 97–114. Cape Town: HSRC Press.

Valiani, Salimah and Nesta Ndebele. 2018. 'A Feminist Perspective on Women and Mining in South Africa'. In *The Future of Mining in South Africa: Sunset or Sunrise?*, edited by Salimah Valiani, 266–297. Johannesburg: Mapungubwe Institute for Strategic Reflection.

Venkata Ratnam, C.S. and Harish C. Jain. 2002. 'Women in Trade Unions in India'. *International Journal of Manpower* 23 (3): 277–292.

Von Holdt, Karl. 2013. 'South Africa: The Transition to Violent Democracy'. *Review of African Political Economy* 40 (138): 589–604.

Walker, Cheryl. 1982. *Women and Resistance in South Africa*. Johannesburg: Monthly Review Press.

Webster, Edward and Sakhela Buhlungu. 2004. 'Between Marginalisation and Revitalisation? The State of Trade Unionism in South Africa'. *Review of African Political Economy* 31 (100): 229–245.

Wolpe, Harold. 1972. 'Capitalism and Cheap Labour-power in South Africa: From Segregation to Apartheid'. *Economy and Society* 1 (4): 425–456.

INTERVIEWS AND FOCUS GROUP DISCUSSIONS

Focus group discussion, Rustenburg, March 2012.
Focus group discussion, Rustenburg, July, 2012.
Focus group discussion, Rustenburg, August 2012.
Angela, Engineer Assistant (*pikinini*), Rustenburg, August 2012.
Dimpho, Shift Boss Assistant (*pikinini*), Rustenburg, August 2012.
Gontse, Shift Boss Assistant (*pikinini*), Rustenburg, August 2012.
Katlego, Miner, Rustenburg, October and November 2012.
Mama Mavis, Store Issuer, June 2012.
Minnie, Shaft Ventilation Officer's Assistant (*pikinini*) Rustenburg, July and August 2012.
Ntate Ras, Rock Drill Operator, Rustenburg, March 2012.
Shado, Miner, Rustenburg, November 2012.
Sithethi, Regional Coordinator, Rustenburg, 2012.
Vicky, Shift Boss Assistant (*pikinini*), Rustenburg, October 2012.

3

Youth, Trade Unions and the Challenges of Employment

Christine Bischoff

INTRODUCTION

In post-apartheid South Africa, high youth unemployment is a national emergency. Young people are more subject to working poverty and are inclined to lose their jobs during crises. In South Africa, young people struggle to find employment, and they face the greatest risk of losing employment during a pandemic (Espi, Leibbrandt and Rancchod 2021). As South Africa headed to its sixth national democratic elections in May 2019, the key political parties contesting the election promised that youth unemployment would be dealt with, and many parties pledged to create more jobs. The South African government has struggled to put the unemployed into jobs, most especially the youth.

Globally youth unemployment is receiving more attention as young people's engagement in the labour market is declining. The International Labour Organization (ILO 2020) estimates that currently there are 429 million young workers globally. However, between 1999 and 2019, the total number of youth in the labour force had decreased from 568 million to 497 million; presently the global youth unemployment rate is 13.6 per cent. It is estimated that a fifth of young people globally are not gaining labour market experience, earning an income from working, or improving their education and skills. They are not in employment, education or training (NEET). Young workers also face high rates of poverty and are found in non-standard, informal and less secure types of employment (ILO 2020). Many young people in developing economies commence their labour market attachment as unpaid workers contributing to family work before moving on to work on their own. In the era of work becoming increasingly flexible and precarious, coupled with rapid technological change in the workplace, the predicted rise in economic inequality, insecure forms of employment and inadequate job opportunities has the potential to negatively impact the well-being of future generations. The unemployment rate in the Brics countries – Brazil, Russia, India, China and South Africa – was estimated at 6.7 per cent in 2020. About 28.4 per cent of the youth labour force was underutilised, which means that they were either unemployed or in the potential labour force (ILO 2020). The key factor in establishing who to count as unemployed is that the person has to be actively looking for employment and so they are part of the potential labour force. As noted, among the Brics countries, youth unemployment rates are highest in South Africa, but the rate in Brazil has increased, while the other three countries remain at the global average (ILO 2018).

Observing the South African labour market, in the second quarter of 2021 (April to June), there were 4.7 million unemployed youth. The official unemployment rate (or the narrow definition of unemployment)[1] for youth in the 15 to 24 age category was 64.4 per cent, and for youth in the 25 to 34 age category it was 43.9 per cent. Under the expanded definition of unemployment, the jobless rate was 74.8 per cent for the youth aged 15 to 24 (up by 20.6 per cent, from 54.2 per cent in 2008) and 52.3 per cent for youth aged 25 to 34 in 2021 (up by 19.4 per cent, from 32.9 per cent in 2008) (Stats SA 2021). Thus the youth are a significant part of the unemployed, they have become discouraged from taking part in the labour market, and they are also not in employment, education or training (Stats 2021). To summarise, almost one in two young people aged 15 to 34 years of age in the labour force are without a job and about a quarter (24.4 per cent) have jobs (Stats 2021).

The trade union movement has referred to the unemployment crisis in South Africa as a 'ticking time bomb', a warning that has been linked to increasing involvement of the youth in service delivery protests in various communities. The dangers of such a high unemployment rate among youth were recently noted during the July 2021 unrest in KwaZulu-Natal and Gauteng. The unrest resulted in 374 deaths. The economic impact is estimated at more than R50 billion. The July unrest, although politically motivated, reflected the frustrations and desperation of the unemployed, mostly the youth in working-class communities.

The lack of work at the early stages of one's working life has long-term implications, not only for individuals personally but for society as a whole. For society, youth unemployment means the risk of losing potential young talent and skills that may contribute not only to growing the economy, but also to diversifying it through new ventures and technologies. The personal consequences of long-term unemployment include low self-esteem and depression, which in turn affect the employability of youth (Graham and Mlatsheni 2015, 53).

Little attention has been paid to the youth in South African labour studies. Scholarly analysis of Congress of South African Trade Unions (Cosatu) members has not looked, in depth, at the reasons for the lack of youth representation among Cosatu affiliates (Bezuidenhout and Tshoaedi 2017). This chapter seeks to address that gap. In addition, this chapter provides details on trade union membership rates among employed youth. Labour market information plays a crucial part in understanding the lack of youth participation in trade unions, and this in turn can be used by the South African labour movement to close the representational gap among employed youth. Evidence of where trade unions elsewhere have responded to the challenges of organising youth is also discussed, as there has been a decline in trade union membership among youth globally.

THE IMPACT OF UNEQUAL EDUCATIONAL OPPORTUNITIES ON YOUTH UNEMPLOYMENT

The definition of youth varies across different countries and is dependent on the country's cultural, institutional and socio-political issues (Van Aardt 2012). According to South Africa's National Youth Policy, youth are those who fall into the 14 to 34 age group. The Basic Conditions of Employment Act (No. 75 of 1997) states that only people aged 15 years old or above may legally participate in the labour market in South Africa. Unemployment patterns in South Africa continue to reflect the apartheid legacy of exclusion and marginalisation of African and coloured people. Youth unemployment rates are higher among black African (38.6 per cent) and coloured (25.9 per cent) youth. Among Indian (17 per cent) and white (10 per cent) youth, unemployment rates are relatively lower (Stats SA 2022). These differences in employment rates are also shaped by the differences in educational opportunities, which are still influenced by racial disparities in terms of access to quality education. Statistics from the Department of Basic Education show that the percentage of youth completing Grade 12 is estimated at

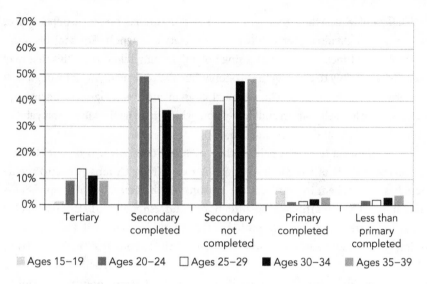

Figure 3.1: Highest educational level of unemployed youth, 2021 (%)
Source: Statistics South Africa (2021)

51.6 per cent and 52.5 per cent for black African and coloured youth respectively. For Indians and whites it is 81.9 per cent and 81.1 per cent (BusinessTech 2020). The crisis in the South African education system contributes to the youth unemployment crisis. It is estimated that 39.1 per cent of the unemployed have less than a matric qualification and that 36.6 per cent of the unemployed do have a matric qualification.

Figure 3.1 shows that, as at 2021, more unemployed youth aged between 15 and 34 years of age have completed their secondary schooling than those who have not. The exception is the 30 to 34 years of age group, where more (47.4 per cent) have not completed their secondary schooling compared to those who have (36.3 per cent). Very few youth who are unemployed have a tertiary qualification. As concerning as the graduate unemployment rate for the youth is – 11 per cent in 2021 – it is still clear from Figure 3.1 that the bulk of unemployed youth are those who have either had some secondary schooling or who have completed their secondary schooling. Thus the unemployed youth tend not to be educated beyond the Grade 12 or matric level.

The low levels of education among youth have implications for productivity levels and economic growth (Graham and Mlatsheni 2015). This is even more concerning in the context of the Fourth Industrial Revolution, which requires an educated and highly skilled workforce.

In other words, the structural change observed in labour demand trends is the shift towards high-skilled workers (Oluwajodu et al. 2015; Wood and Bischoff 2021). Studies have established that South Africa has a profound mismatch between educational achievements and job requirements, resulting in a serious skills shortage in the country (Mncayi and Dunga 2016). Young people's limited access to suitable education and training jeopardises their chances in the labour market. Unemployment is structural in the sense that if those available for work happen to be poorly educated workers, which is the bulk of the supply of labour, they struggle to find employment, as there is insufficient demand for low-skilled labour. It has become necessary for the already skilled to keep up with the demands of the world of work, especially with the expansion of information technology (IT), artificial intelligence (AI) and robotics. The South African labour market is characterised by a shortage of job opportunities, as economic growth is sluggish and under-qualification is more the case than over-qualification (DHET 2019).

LABOUR MARKET INTERVENTIONS AIMED AT ADDRESSING YOUTH UNEMPLOYMENT

In order to 'up-skill' the labour force, the South African government passed the Skills Development Act (No. 97 of 1998) (SDA). The SDA aimed to advance the skills of the South African workforce, boost investment in education and training in the labour market, persuade employers to offer opportunities for learning to their employees, and remedy inequality in employment opportunities. The National Skills Authority was initiated to guide the Minister of Labour on the construction and application of skills policy. The Sector Education and Training Authorities were created to apply policy at the sector level and to create learnerships to assist in nurturing the skills base in their sectors. The third phase of the National Skills Development Strategy wrapped up at the end of March 2020. This paved the way for the National Skills Development Plan (NSDP) 2030, which took effect from April 2020. The National Skills Fund, established in 1999, provides funding for skills development initiatives as identified by NSDP 2030.

As noted, South African youth unemployment is considerably higher than in other developing countries, and many young people battle to find their first job. There have been a number of interventions to address this challenge. The Umsobomvu Youth Fund was set up in 2001 to create opportunities for youth in entrepreneurship and job creation. In 2005, the National Youth Commission merged with the Umsobomvu Youth Fund to work on youth development. In 2008, the National Youth Development Agency (NYDA) was created to address the hardships that youth encounter. On offer is training for youth such as how to perform in interviews, as well as grants for young entrepreneurs. Recently, the NYDA in conjunction with the Department of Small Business Development has made grant funding and business support available to 1 000 young entrepreneurs (Global Entrepreneur Monitor Report 2020).

The South African government introduced the Employment Tax Incentive (ETI) in 2014 to persuade employers to employ young and less-experienced work-seekers by lowering the expense of hiring them via a cost-sharing mechanism with the government. Specifically, employers are encouraged to recruit young people between the ages of 19 and 29 years; these are generally the less-experienced workers. The incentive allows the employer to reduce the amount of pay-as-you-earn (PAYE) tax that is required by the South African Revenue Service by the amount of the ETI, and it can be claimed for a maximum of 24 months for any one employee. Cosatu objected to the ETI because it did not exclude labour broking companies and outsourced service providers as well as firms not supporting decent work and fair labour practices. It was also feared that the ETI would lead to older workers being ousted and that it would act as a restraint on wages (Cosatu 2016). However, a 2014 survey found that most Cosatu workers did not know what the ETI was (Bischoff and Tame 2017).

The Federation of Unions of South Africa (Fedusa) supported the ETI and internships for youth, arguing that it counted as valuable work experience for youth, who needed this exposure to improve their future career prospects. Those who participate in the scheme earn between R2 000 and R4 000 per month, and the uptake is largest in the trade, financial and business services sectors (National Treasury 2016). The government has recently extended the ETI scheme until 28 February 2029.

In 2018, President Cyril Ramaphosa introduced the Youth Employment Service (YES); its intention was to provide employment to the approximately one million unemployed South African youth. The initiative is a one-year work experience programme designed to assist youth with business development, skills training and employment opportunities. YES is the largest private-sector funded jobs impact programme in the country, and has worked with 1 700 private companies and implementation partners to support almost 70 000 young people. YES has also partnered with several other organisations – the Harambee Youth Employment Accelerator (which is a not-for-profit social enterprise tackling global youth unemployment, working with over 1.5 million youth in South Africa); the Jobs Fund (which was launched in 2011 by the National Treasury to address the unemployment challenge in South Africa by funding projects that stimulate new models that boost employment creation); and the Presidential Youth Employment Intervention (a multi-sector action plan aimed at addressing youth unemployment) (Naidoo 2021).

In 2019, an amendment to the Broad-Based Black Economic Empowerment (B-BBEE) codes of good practice made it possible for companies to improve their scorecards between one and two levels by investing in youth work experience through YES (*City Press* 2019).

Job creation via the Expanded Public Works Programme (EPWP) for the almost nine million young people who are not in employment, education or training is also an opportunity that offers direct relief to households. This public employment programme is an opportunity to alleviate youth unemployment and to equip young people with short-term work experience, skills and more extensive social networks. However, research has shown that the EPWP has not lightened the youth unemployment burden, nor is it placed to link young people to longer-term work options (Duncan-Williams, Da Costa and Kempken 2021). Added to this, the bulk of EPWP participants do not have a matric (73.7 per cent in 2018) (Ngoma 2020).

In October 2018, South Africa hosted a Jobs Summit to advance job creation, as promised by the newly appointed President Ramaphosa's inaugural State of the Nation speech earlier in the year. Together government, the business community and labour organisations worked to develop a common approach and to improve coordination among stakeholders. The Presidential Working Committee on the Jobs Summit was set up to implement the commitments made at the summit. It met regularly to track progress on the job-creation commitments (there would be 275 000 jobs created per annum, it was predicted) and to curtail job losses in various sectors (by reviving the training layoff scheme) (SA News 2021). Even though the Presidential Jobs Summit was meant to be inclusive and broad, unemployed and precariously employed South Africans were not represented in the forum at all. The Assembly of the Unemployed was set up as a response to this initiative (Alternative Information and Development Centre 2020). By 2020, President Ramaphosa had stopped hosting the Jobs Summit.

In response to Covid-19's effect on jobs and livelihoods and as part of the Economic Reconstruction and Recovery Plan (ERRP) as announced by President Ramaphosa in October 2020, Phase II of the Presidential Youth Employment

Initiative was implemented in November 2021. This is meant to serve as a mass public employment intervention that aims to skill the youth, using public schools as a channel through which they can gain skills. Under the auspices of the Department of Basic Education, the Basic Education Employment Initiative claims to have created approximately 287 000 employment opportunities for youth between the ages of 18 and 35 years in about 26 000 public schools. Young people work in positions such as education assistants for a period of five months at the minimum wage (which in 2022 was approximately R3 800 per month). Survey results suggest that the experience has been helpful for the schools and for the households of the young people (Duncan-Williams, Da Costa and Kempken 2021).

The National Youth Policy 2020–2030 was approved in October 2020 by the Department of Women, Youth and Persons with Disabilities to strengthen youth development during and after the Covid-19 pandemic. The policy has an integrated Youth Development Strategy which was developed by the NYDA. The strategy has five pillars, namely quality education skills, economic transformation, entrepreneurship and job creation, mental health, and the promotion of physical health; it also considers issues of pandemics, social cohesion and nation-building. The policy stresses the need for key players to intensify their commitment to youth development as a priority (SA News 2021).

In June 2021, President Ramaphosa announced that the National Pathway Management Network would be set up. It is a partnership between the NYDA, Harambee Youth Employment Accelerator, Department of Science and Innovation, Department of Employment and Labour, Department of Higher Education and Training, Department of Small Business Development and the Youth Employment Service (Mahlangu 2021). The various government institutions and social partners are tasked with providing opportunities for young people by coordinating, accelerating and enhancing all the current programmes and thus clearing the pathways to learning and employment for the youth.

Figure 3.2 illustrates the unemployment rate for South African youth in the 15 to 34 age category from 2008 to 2021. It demonstrates that in spite of the above-mentioned initiatives, youth unemployment has remained high.

Figure 3.2 clearly shows that that the youth unemployment rate has increased over the thirteen-year period. In 2008, the rate was 31.1 per cent, by 2019 it was 42 per cent and in 2021 it was 48 per cent. Enormous obstacles face the youth when they attempt to enter the labour market. Not only are they inexperienced, but the length of time they have been unemployed is a major factor that challenges this group when seeking employment. The next section looks at labour market data on unemployed youth in more detail.

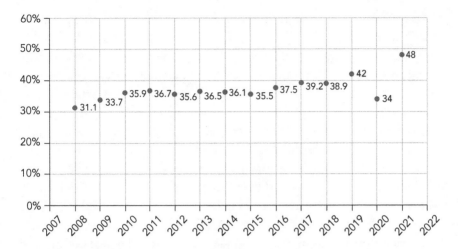

Figure 3.2: Youth unemployment rate, 2008 to 2021 (%)

Source: Statistics South Africa (2021)

SOUTH AFRICAN YOUTH NOT IN EMPLOYMENT, EDUCATION OR TRAINING

It is estimated that before the Covid-19 pandemic, 230 000 learners aged 7 to 17 years dropped out of school annually in South Africa; during the pandemic this increased dramatically as about 750 000 children dropped out of school, and many of the young learners have not returned to schooling (Damons 2021). In 2021, 897 163 candidates registered for the National Senior Certificate examination, and 537 687 candidates passed. Those who failed to obtain the qualification became unemployed; some attempted to enter the labour market or enrol for the second-chance matric programme. Those who obtained the qualification might also remain unemployed, or they might access the labour market or participate in public or private post-school training.

The NEET cohort is divided into two categories. The first part of the cohort comprises Inactive NEET – people who are not in employment, education or training, and not looking for work. The second category comprises the Unemployed NEET – people who are not in employment, education or training but are seeking employment and are free to start work. Persons are grouped into the Inactive NEET if they are too young, too old, retired, a homemaker, have health issues, or are discouraged work-seekers. The NEET rate is determined by dividing the number of persons in an age group who are NEET by the total working-age population in the same age group.

There has been an increase in the number of Unemployed NEET because of the Covid-19 pandemic. Indeed, Statistics South Africa (Stats SA) reported that 2.2 million people lost their jobs during the first three months of 2020, during South Africa's first lockdown, and two million more people entered the NEET. Of the youth who lost their jobs during the first national lockdown from March 2020, those who had higher educational qualifications found other jobs. That is, between February and October 2020, the employment of young people who held more than a matric certificate grew from 42 per cent to 46 per cent. For youth without a matric, their employment rate decreased from 28 per cent to 23 per cent, and 17 per cent of the youth who were put out of work between February and April 2020 did not return to employment. Low education and skills levels thus increase the risk of a person being part of the Unemployed NEET. Indeed, approximately 59 per cent of people aged 15 to 60 who were Unemployed NEET in 2020 had less than a matric as their highest educational qualification; this was followed by those who were in possession of a matric (about 34 per cent). People who had a tertiary qualification only constituted seven per cent of the Unemployed NEET (Smit 2021).

As of 2021, 18.1 million people aged 15 to 64 were Unemployed NEET, which was 46 per cent of the working population (39.6 million). There were 3.3 million (32.4 per cent) young people aged 15 to 24 who were Unemployed NEET and 5.7 million (56 per cent) young people aged 25 to 34 who were Unemployed NEET (Stats 2021); all in all, a total of 9 million youth are Unemployed NEET. Therefore, over half (51 per cent) of the Unemployed NEET are made up of the youth – that is, more than four in ten young people between the ages of 15 and 34 were not in employment, education or training in 2021. From 2013 to 2021, the actual Unemployed NEET rate has remained the highest among youth aged 25 to 34 years. The youth Unemployed NEETs are generally found in geographically and economically marginal provinces and in small towns (Ngoma 2020). This further illustrates the youth's marginalisation in education and training and in the labour market, which in turn makes them more dependent on the small number of people who are in employment.

Unemployment, even by its narrow definition, has increased in general, and particularly for the youth. With the devastation wrought by the Covid-19 pandemic, South Africa is in a phase of reconstruction and development as it faces a serious human development crisis. The challenge in South Africa currently is to develop strategies to promote job-intensive economic growth (Mlatsheni and Graham 2021). Figure 3.3 provides information on the last time that unemployed youth worked, and how long they have been out of work as of June 2021.

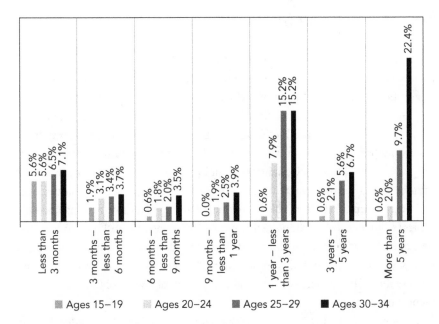

Figure 3.3: Last time unemployed youth worked, 2021 (%)

Source: Statistics South Africa (2021)

Figure 3.3 shows that 5.6 per cent of youth in the 15 to 19 age group last worked less than three months ago. However, as age increases, the length of time that youth have been out of work increases, too. That is, most youth in the 20 to 24 age group (7.9 per cent) and in the 25 to 29 age group (15.2 per cent) said that they last worked one year to three years ago. Most youth in the 30 to 34 age group (22.4 per cent) said that they last worked more than five years ago. This illustrates the argument that youth unemployment remains engrained in the structural dynamics of a labour market that positions young people at the margins of the economy (Mlatsheni and Graham 2021).

Added to the fact that most of the unemployed youth in South Africa do not have an education beyond matric, most have not worked before. For those who have worked, they have not worked for some years. Youth who only have a National Senior Certificate (matric) qualification remain inhibited by labour market entry requirements such as skills acquired through higher education. To address youth unemployment, issues such as adequate resourcing of schools, the provision of a quality education and scholars who drop out before completing Grade 12 need to be remedied. It is important to pay attention to the NEET rate as it is a significant labour market indicator for youth (DHET 2017).

EMPLOYABILITY AND THE YOUTH

There is no universal definition of employability; its definition is subject to society's cultural norms, levels of economic development and employer norms. In addition to this, the concept has changed due to the global decline in lifelong employment and the enlargement of the services economy. Lifelong employability is the ability to be productive and to be in jobs that are rewarding during a working life, and to possess up-to-date skills and capabilities (Marock 2008). Employability skills are the qualities of employees, aside from their technical ability, that employers most value. These skills comprise: reading, basic mathematical and other essential skills; problem-solving, planning, decision-making and other critical higher-order thinking skills; reliability, a positive outlook, cooperativeness and similar emotional skills and characteristics (Marock 2008). In addition to this, the responsibility of employment rests with individuals, and they have to possess the ability to access and sustain employment and to obtain new employment if necessary.

Employability is also about how companies and other stakeholders support employment, as well as how the larger economic and educational circumstances influence the conditions and opportunities for employment. In the second quarter of 2021, there were 14 942 000 people in employment; of these, 5 047 000 youth were in employment (Stats 2021).

Figure 3.4 looks at the employment status of youth between 2008 and 2021, in order to identify changes over the last 13 years.

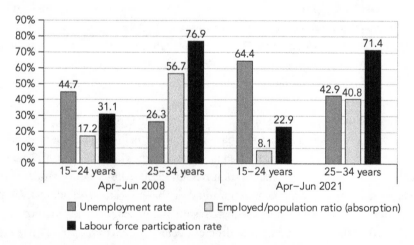

Figure 3.4: Youth and employment status, 2008 and 2021 (%)

Source: Statistics South Africa (2021)

The employed/population ratio for youth in the 15 to 24 age group dropped by 9.1 per cent (from 17.2 per cent in 2008 to 8.1 per cent in 2021). For the 25 to 34 age group it dropped by 15.9 per cent (from 56.7 per cent in 2008 to 40.8 per cent in 2021). The labour force participation rate – the proportion of the working-age population that is employed – for youth in the 15 to 24 age group dropped by 8.2 per cent (from 31.1 per cent in 2008 to 22.9 per cent in 2021). For youth in the 25 to 34 age group, it dropped by 5.5 per cent (from 76.9 per cent in 2008 to 71.4 per cent in 2021). These figures illustrate the labour market's increasing inability to absorb youth, mostly due to the Covid-19 pandemic and slow economic growth.

At an aggregate level, the highest educational qualification among employed youth is the National Senior Certificate qualification (secondary schooling completed), at 17.7 per cent in 2021. However, this is followed by those who have not completed their secondary schooling (14.8 per cent) and then by those who have a tertiary qualification (14.3 per cent) (Stats 2021). The employed youth comprise those who have completed their secondary schooling and those who have not completed their secondary schooling (32.5 per cent), followed by those who have a tertiary qualification (14.3 per cent). Figure 3.5 illustrates the highest educational level completed by employed youth in 2021, by age category. According to Figure 3.5, more employed youth in the 15 to 19 age category have not completed their secondary schooling (59.5 per cent),

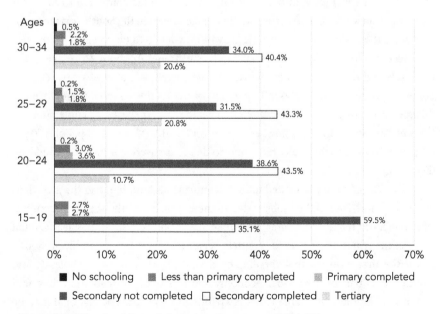

Figure 3.5: Employed youth by education status, 2021 (%)
Source: Statistics South Africa (2021)

more employed youth in the 20 to 24 age category have completed their secondary schooling (43.5 per cent), more youth in the 25 to 29 age category have completed their secondary schooling (43.3 per cent) and more youth in the 30 to 34 age category have completed their secondary schooling (40.4 per cent). Indeed, the largest proportion of youth employed have at least a matriculation certificate (DHET 2019).

The possession of a higher-level qualification has a positive influence on one's labour market chances, especially for an emerging industrialised country like South Africa. The employment path in post-apartheid South Africa is marked by a shift towards a service-oriented economy, and the demand for skills is shaped by structural changes in the economy. The Accelerated and Shared Growth Initiative for South Africa has singled out skills shortages as one of the main barriers to growth in South Africa. However, the intensity of skills shortages and surpluses differs between sectors. The skills profile for employment in shortage occupations includes sophisticated problem-solving and social skills; knowledge shortages exist in computers and electronics, administration and management, and clerical knowledge. The skills planning challenge is to efficiently match supply and demand in the private and public sectors while tackling past structural inequalities of gender and race as well as spatial location (DHET 2019). The kind of tertiary qualification is also critical in securing employment.

At an aggregate level, most of the employed youth across the 15 to 34 age category (38.1 per cent) work in the wholesale and retail trade compared to the other industries (Stats 2021). A structural shift has taken place in the South African economy since the early 1990s. Economic growth now tends to be powered by the tertiary sector, which includes wholesale and retail trade. At about 15 per cent, the wholesale and retail sector is the fourth biggest contributor to South Africa's gross domestic product (GDP); about 21 per cent of the total workforce is employed in this sector, making it the sector that employs the largest share of people after the Community, Social and Personal Services sector (DHET 2019). Most people (70 per cent) in jobs in the wholesale, retail and trade sectors were consistently employed there (Ingle and Mlatsheni 2017).

Skills intensification is located in manufacturing and mining, and the growth in low-skilled and semi-skilled jobs is due to the expansion of the services economy, which includes retail, restaurants, and finance and business services. Clearly, retail is one of the easiest industries for youth to access (*Business Day* 2018). Even though this is the first industry that the employed youth find accessible, wholesale and retail trade is part of the service economy and it is marked by low-pay, low-skill and precarious jobs, which the Covid-19 pandemic exposed. The National Income Dynamics Study – Coronavirus Rapid Mobile Survey (NIDS–CRAM) reported a large decrease in employment during the initial period of lockdown, from the end of March to the end of April 2020. The loss of jobs was not evenly distributed among the different groups; the most vulnerable groups, such as youth and the less educated, were disproportionately negatively affected (Ranchhod and Daniels 2021).

At an aggregate level, most youth are employed as elementary workers (27 per cent) followed by those who are employed as service workers, shop workers and market sales workers (19 per cent). What this data indicates is that the labour market is becoming more crowded with matriculants who are in competition with each other. The jobs they undertake often involve low-skilled or semi-skilled work that is not easy to automate, such as cashiers in the retail and wholesale industries. This means that there is an alignment of low skills and jobs that require this skill set. It is also these workers who are most vulnerable to developments in technology and the Fourth Industrial Revolution.

Labour force data show that youth with a National Senior Certificate qualification receive minimal training and are easily absorbed into non-career paths marked by low skills, which are becoming significant features of youth employment in South Africa. As income inequality is driven by wage inequality, wage data has shown that a new phenomenon is the rise of individuals in the middle of the wage distribution whose earnings are declining. These workers include those employed in the retail industry, where young workers are concentrated (Bhorat 2019). The retail industry does not pay well, and about 40 per cent of workers earn below the minimum wage.[2] The low wages could serve as an incentive for young retail workers to join a trade union in the hopes of improving their wages in addition to the various challenges that young workers face such as gender, race and age discrimination, from which trade unions could protect them. Yet, of the youth who are employed a large proportion do not belong to a trade union, and this is discussed in the next section.

YOUTH IN TRADE UNIONS, GLOBALLY AND IN SOUTH AFRICA

Union membership has declined globally. According to the European Trade Union Confederation (ETUC 2021), trade unions in Europe are in crisis; in 27 out of 31 European countries, trade union membership has declined. It is expected that within the next ten years, unions in Europe will lose more than 11 million members. Additionally, the median age of trade union members has increased; members now tend to be in their mid-40s and early 50s (ETUC 2021). Many European trade unions depend on attracting young workers in order to be viable. For example, trade unions have decreased their subscription rates for young trade unionists, have launched youth or student sections to advance higher rates of participation in union affairs, and have endeavoured to cultivate more input from young members on the development of union policy. The ETUC encourages trade unions to set up youth structures, such as a Youth Committee that will become a permanent structure for young trade union activists, and to create ways for young people to meaningfully participate in the trade union, to systematically work on youth topics and to build capacity of the youth in trade unions. The Youth Committee would have its own statute and mandate (anchored in the statute of the trade union but autonomous from it), to empower young members to discuss the topics relevant to them. The Youth Committee would function as part of a network to recruit young workers using current communication and digital tools that appeal to young workers such as social media and podcasts, The policies that trade unions could devise that pertain to the challenges faced by young people in the labour market include apprenticeships, youth unemployment, precarious work and discrimination based on age and other grounds, to name a few. Clearly the youth is not a homogeneous group, but age is critical to thinking through social inequalities: 'chronological age is one of those key markers – like race and gender – that greatly influence how a person is treated' (Crawford 2006, 27). The kinds of topics that trade unions could address to attract young workers include the environment, migration, gender and racial equality, LGBTQI+ and non-standard forms of employment, among others, as well as involving young trade union members in collective bargaining and social dialogue (ETUC 2021).

The trade union density rate in South Africa is 29 per cent (OECD and AIAS 2021). According to Cloete (2021), in South Africa currently only one in four employed workers (around 23 per cent) are trade union members; thus 77 per cent of employed workers do not belong to a union. Neither are many employed youth organised into trade unions (Mosoetsa and Bischoff 2015). This means that it is employers who are determining the conditions of employment and wages for the unorganised workers. Figure 3.6 looks at whether employed youth are trade union members.

Figure 3.6 shows that most of the employed youth across age categories are not trade union members. Trade union membership is lowest for those in the 15 to 19 age group (5.4 per cent) and highest for those in the 30 to 34 age group (24.2 per cent). Trade union membership is concentrated among older workers in the workplace; overall, only one in four South Africans who are part of the workforce opt to join trade unions (Mosoetsa and Bischoff 2015). Studies of low trade union membership among youth focus on their reasons for not joining trade unions. These reasons include the youth not being aware of what unions do and how they function, trade unions not being pertinent to workplaces where there is little risk of injury or where safety practices are in place, where working conditions are good, and where youth experience job security (Kahmann 2002).

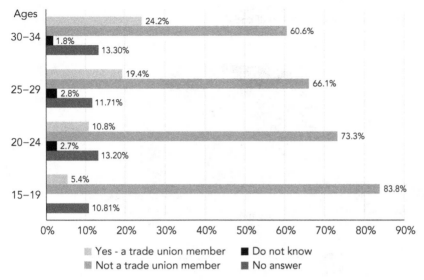

Figure 3.6: Employed youth, by trade union membership, 2021 (%)

Source: Statistics South Africa (2021)

Figure 3.7 shows the percentage of employed youth in various industries who *were not* trade union members in 2021:

- 47.9 per cent of youth in the wholesale and retail trade industry
- 45.2 per cent of youth in the construction industry
- 42.3 per cent of youth who were service, shop and market sales workers
- 37.9 percent of the youth who were elementary workers
- 63.6 per cent of the youth who were skilled agricultural and fishery workers (Stats 2021).

It must be noted that all workers in the wholesale and retail sector are covered by a sectoral determination as set by the Department of Employment and Labour. This covers minimum wages, working hours, number of leave days and termination rules, and therefore establishes the basic conditions of employment for employees in the sector. The low trade union membership rates among those employed in this sector can be attributed to this sectoral determination, but also to the fact that the trade unions are not organising these workers at their workplaces. There is also a representation gap among formal sector workers who have employment and income security, a gap which is typically more a feature among those who are casualised, part-time or in temporary employment relationships due to retrenchments and the desire to cut labour costs (Webster and Bischoff 2011).

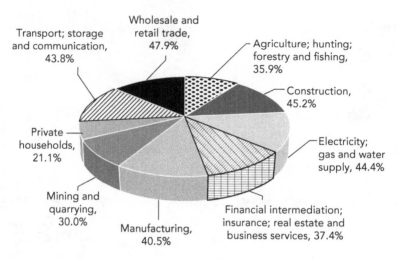

Figure 3.7: Employed youth, by trade union membership and industry, 2021 (%)

Source: Statistics South Africa (2021)

Many young workers are employed in the wholesale and retail trade industry, and this is the sector where job growth continues to take place. Young workers are well aware of the issues in their workplaces, but many do not know how trade unions could help them, or think that trade unions are irrelevant or too politicised (Mthethwa 2019). The National Labour and Economic Development Institute carried out two surveys of workers in South African workplaces, both organised and non-organised, in 2006 and 2012. The data indicated that more than half of non-organised workers (53 per cent) were under the age of 35 years. That is, young workers are under-represented among union members (Mosoetsa and Bischoff 2015).

Trade unions have historically battled to recruit younger workers into their ranks, but the data presented here shows that the young, unorganised workers are in permanent forms of employment in workplaces that are easy to reach. To recruit these young workers, trade unions need to devise new methods of recruitment that will appeal to the youth (and not use mass meetings, for example). Trade unions need to take advantage of online communication tools. There were restrictions on travel and movement due to the Covid-19 pandemic, yet there has been uneven uptake of online communication tools such as WhatsApp by the labour movement (Elsely 2020). This needs to be addressed.

During the Covid-19 lockdown in 2020, food retailing supermarkets were expected to provide services, yet the retail workers were not officially regarded as frontline workers. In addition to this, the retailers did very little about the safety and well-being of their employees, such as providing adequate personal protective equipment (Saccawu Media Unit 2020). There are new challenges in the workplace due to the Covid-19 pandemic, and this requires shop stewards to be more attentive and efficient across all sectors. In workplaces, shop stewards need to be more acquainted with the various Occupational Health and Safety guidelines and directions so that they can assess whether employers have set up a safe and conducive workplace in the current Covid-19 pandemic (Mulaisi 2021). Apart from health and safety, and in an effort to improve their organisational capacities and efficiencies, trade unions need to take advantage of the opportunities that arose during the Covid-19 pandemic to build their capacity in other areas such as wage negotiations and skills development among the young, unorganised workers, which could entice them to become trade union members.

CONCLUSION

This chapter has shown that South Africa's youth unemployment rate has increased despite various interventions to thwart the lack of jobs, such as the youth wage subsidy programme and the Employment Tax Incentive, which have not led to a statistically significant increase in youth employment. A large constituency of the youth lack the necessary education, skills and experience, and therefore are more vulnerable to unemployment than any other age group. Where youth are employed, they are often found in low-skilled and semi-skilled jobs in the labour market. The most common sector for youth who are regularly employed is the wholesale and retail trade sector. Even though a higher level of education can play a significant role in South Africa in addressing the challenge of securing employment, the highest qualification that most youth hold is a matric certificate. Unemployment is greatest for those who left school before they matriculated, and is lowest among those with a higher educational qualification. Even if the youth acquired skills, youth unemployment would remain at its current trajectory as South Africa is characterised by jobless growth. The decline in trade union membership signifies that unions are struggling to attract more members, and trade union density is particularly low among employed youth. The Covid-19 pandemic has highlighted the importance of workers, especially those at the forefront. The challenges noted in changing the dynamics of racialised access to quality education in South Africa indicate that the majority of those who are affected by youth unemployment remain working-class black African and coloured persons. Although most youth do not regard trade unions as useful or relevant, trade unions need to put in place effective measures to mobilise this group of workers. Trade unions remain the best organisations to protect the interests of all workers. But more importantly, the future of work globally and in South Africa shows increases in precarious work with poor wages and working conditions. The shift in technology, including the rise of artificial intelligence, information technology and robotics, has major consequences for the working class, and trade union organisation and mobilisation is required to ensure the protection of workers in this next phase of capitalist expansion.

NOTES

1 According to Statistics South Africa, the narrow (or official) definition of unemployment includes individuals who did not work during the seven days before they were interviewed but wanted to work and were able to start work within a week of the interview, and had actively looked for work or were self-employed in the four weeks prior to the interview. Under the expanded definition of unemployment, they had not looked for work for four weeks before the interview.

2 Employment and Labour Minister Minister Thulas Nxesi announced the 2022 national minimum wage for each ordinary hour worked has been increased from R21.69 to R23.19 for the year 2022, with effect from 1 March 2022 (Republic of South Africa 2022).

REFERENCES

Alternative Information and Development Centre (AIDC). 2020. 'The Real Jobs Summit: A Long Journey to Economic and Political Freedom'. *AIDC*, 5 May 2020. https://aidc. org.za/the-real-jobs-summit-a-long-journey-to-economic-and-political-freedom. Accessed 20 May 2020.

Bezuidenhout, Andries and Malehoko Tshoaedi. 2017. *Labour Beyond Cosatu: Mapping the Rupture in South Africa's Labour Landscape*. Johannesburg: Wits University Press.

Bhorat, Haroon. 2019. 'SA's Missing Middle'. *Business Live*, 24 October 2019. https://www. businesslive.co.za/fm/opinion/on-my-mind/2019-06-27-haroon-bhorat-sas-missing-middle. Accessed 20 May 2020.

Bischoff, Christine and Bianca Tame. 2017. 'Labour Aristocracy or Marginal Elite? Cosatu Members' Income, Other Sources of Livelihood and Household Support'. In *Labour Beyond Cosatu: Mapping the Rupture in South Africa's Labour Landscape*, edited by Andries Bezuidenhout and Malehoko Tshoaedi, 48–61. Johannesburg: Wits University Press.

Business Day. 2018. 'SA's Hardest Workers are in Mining and Retail, Says OECD'. *Business Live*, 17 April 2019. https://www.businesslive.co.za/bd/national/labour/2018-05-22-sas-hardest-workers-are-in-mining-and-retail-says-oecd.

BusinessTech. 2020. 'This is the School Drop Out Rate in South Africa'. *BusinessTech*, 6 October 2020. https://businesstech.co.za/news/government/438509/this-is-the-school-drop-out-rate-in-south-africa.

City Press. 2019. 'Invest in Youth Employment – For Your Business and BEE Scorecard'. *City Press*, 4 April 2019. https://www.news24.com/citypress/business/invest-in-youth-employment-for-your-business-and-bee-scorecard-20190404. Accessed 20 May 2020.

Cloete, Karl. 2021. 'Labour Pains: Trade Union Membership has Declined Badly and Bosses are Calling the Shots'. *Daily Maverick*, 2 March 2021. https://www.dailymaverick.co.za/opinionista/2021-03-02-labour-pains-trade-union-membership-has-declined-badly-and-bosses-are-calling-the-shots. Accessed 19 January 2022.

Congress of South African Trade Unions (Cosatu). 2016. 'Submission by Cosatu on the Employment Tax Incentive Submitted to the Standing Committee on Finance, Parliament, Republic of South Africa'. Johannesburg: Cosatu.

Crawford, Kate. 2006. *Adult Themes: Rewriting the Rules of Adulthood*. Sydney: Pan Macmillan Australia.

Damons, Marecia. 2021. 'School Attendance is at the Lowest it has been in 20 Years'. *GroundUp*, 9 July 2021. https://www.groundup.org.za/article/many-750000-children-have-dropped-out-school-during-pandemic. Accessed 23 January 2023.

Department of Higher Education and Training (DHET). 2017. '2016 Fact sheet on "NEETs" (Persons who are Not in Employment, Education or Training)'. Pretoria: DHET.

Department of Higher Education and Training (DHET). 2019. 'Skills Supply and Demand in South Africa'. Pretoria: DHET.

Duncan-Williams, Kristl, Beverly da Costa and Erica Kempken. 2021. 'Four Lessons from Youth Work Initiative'. *Mail and Guardian*, 10 October 2021. https://mg.co.za/education/2021-10-10-four-lessons-from-youth-work-initiative.

Elsely, Trenton. 2020. 'How are African Trade Unions Responding to Covid-19 Pandemic? 10 Key Points in a New Report'. *Labour Research Service*, 24 January 2020. https://www.lrs.org.za/2020/06/01/how-are-african-trade-unions-responding-to-covid-19-pandemic-10-key-points-in-a-new-report.

Espi, Gabriel, Murray Leibbrandt and Vimal Ranchhod. 2021. 'Employment Dynamics in South Africa during the Covid-19 Era: An Update Covering the Second Wave'. *National Income Dynamics Study (NIDS) – Coronavirus Rapid Mobile Survey (CRAM)*, 4 May 2021. Cape Town: Southern Africa Labour and Development Research Unit.

European Trade Union Confederation (ETUC). 2021. 'Recommendations for Engaging Young People in Trade Unions'. 8 March 2021. https://www.etuc.org/en/publication/engaging-young-people-trade-unions.

Global Entrepreneur Monitor Report. 2020. *Global Report*. London: Global Entrepreneurship Research Association.

Graham, Lauren and Cecil Mlatsheni. 2015. 'Youth Unemployment in South Africa: Understanding the Challenge and Working on Solutions'. *South African Child Gauge* 2: 51–59.

Ingle, Kim and Cecil Mlatsheni. 2017. *The Extent of Churn in the South African Youth Labour Market: Evidence from NIDS 2008–2015*. SALDRU Working Paper Number 201/NIDS Discussion Paper 2016/17. Cape Town: The Southern Africa Labour and Development Research Unit.

International Labour Organization (ILO) 2018. *Youth Employment*. BRICS Briefs Series. Geneva: International Labour Office.

International Labour Organization (ILO). 2020. *Global Employment Trends for Youth 2020: Technology and the Future of Jobs*. Geneva: International Labour Office.

Kahmann, Marcus. 2002. 'Trade Unions and Young People: Challenges of the Changing Age Composition of Unions'. Discussion and Working Paper 2002.02.02. Brussels: The European Trade Union Institute.

Mahlangu, Bongani. 2021. 'President Ramaphosa is Right that Youth Unemployment is a Crisis, but his Analysis is Wrong'. *Daily Maverick*, 20 October 2021. https://www.dailymaverick.co.za/opinionista/2021-10-20-president-ramaphosa-is-right-that-youth-unemployment-is-a-crisis-but-his-analysis-is-wrong.

Marock, Carmel. 2008. *Grappling with Youth Employability in South Africa*. Employment Growth and Development Initiative: Human Sciences Research Council. Pretoria: Human Sciences Research Council.

Mlatsheni, Cecil and Lauren Graham. 2021. 'Young People and Women Bear the Brunt of South Africa's Worrying Jobless Rate'. *The Conversation*, 7 September 2021. https://the-conversation.com/young-people-and-women-bear-the-brunt-of-south-africas-worry-ing-jobless-rate-167003.

Mncayi, Precious and Steven Henry Dunga. 2016. 'Career Choice and Unemployment Length: A Study of Graduates from a South African University'. *Industry and Higher Education* 30 (6): 413–423.

Mosoetsa, Sarah and Christine Bischoff. 2015. 'Organising the Unorganised'. In *The Cosatu Workers Survey of 2006 and 2012: What Do they Tell Us?*, edited by Debbie Budlender and Liesl Orr, 27–44. Johannesburg: Naledi.

Mthethwa, George. 2019. 'What Have We Learned About Trade Union Organising in Chang-ing Workplaces?' *Labour Research Service*, 24 January 2019. https://www.lrs.org.za/2020/02/26/what-have-we-learned-about-trade-union-organising-in-changing-workplaces-2.

Mulaisi, Lebogang. 2021. 'How to Become an Effective Shop Steward During the Covid-19 Crisis'. *Labour Research Service*, 24 January 2021. https://www.lrs.org.za/2021/02/01/how-to-become-an-effective-shop-steward-during-the-covid-19-crisis.

Naidoo, Ravi. 2021. 'South Africa's Youth Unemployment Crisis: The Clock is Ticking, and it's Five Minutes to Midnight'. *The Daily Maverick*, 5 December 2021. https://www.dai-lymaverick.co.za/opinionista/2021-12-05-south-africas-youth-unemployment-crisis-the-clock-is-ticking-and-its-five-minutes-to-midnight.

National Treasury. 2016. *Employment Tax Incentive Descriptive Report*. Pretoria: National Treasury.

Ngoma, Amuzweni. 2020. 'A Net to Catch the NEETs'. *Mail and Guardian*, 21 August 2020. https://mg.co.za/opinion/2020-08-21-a-net-to-catch-the-neets.

Organisation for Economic Co-operation and Development (OECD) and Amster-dam Advanced Institute for Advanced Labour Studies (AIAS). 2021. 'South Africa: Main Indicators and Characteristics of Collective Bargaining'. In *Institutional Charac-teristics of Trade Unions, Wage Setting, State Intervention and Social Pacts*. Paris: OECD Publishing. Accessed 10 May 2023. https://www.oecd.org/employment/collective-bar-gaining-database-southafrica.pdf.

Oluwajodu, Faith, Derek Blaauw, Lorraine Greyling and Ewert Kleynhans. 2015. 'Graduate Unemployment in South Africa: Perspectives from the Banking Sector'. *SA Journal of Human Resource Management/SA Tydskrif vir Menslikehulpbronbestuur* 13 (1): 1–9.

Ranchhod, Vimal and Reza Daniels. 2021. *Labour Market Dynamics in South Africa in the Time of Covid-19: Evidence from Wave 1 of the NIDS-CRAM Survey'*, 1–24. Report 9. National Income Dynamics Study – Coronavirus Rapid Mobile Survey (NIDS-CRAM): 1-24. Cape Town: The Southern Africa Labour and Development Research Unit.

Republic of South Africa. 2022. 'Minister Thulas Nxesi Announces 2022 National Minimum Wage Increases'. 8 February 2022. https://www.gov.za/speeches/minister-thulas-nxesi-announces-2022-national-minimum-wage-increases-8-feb-2022-0000. Accessed 10 May 2023.

Saccawu Media Unit. 2020. 'Fighting Back against Employers' Onslaught on our Members, Using Covid-19 and National Lockdown as an Excuse. SACCAWU, 21 April 2020. https://saccawu.org.za/fighting-back-against-employers-onslaught-on-our-members. Accessed 20 January 2021.

Smit, Sarah. 2021. 'Startling Bounce-Back for SA's Labour Market – Nids-Cram Survey'. *Mail and Guardian*, 17 February 2021. Accessed 20 February 2022 https://mg.co.za/business/2021-02-17-startling-bounce-back-for-sas-labour-market-nids-cram-survey. Accessed 20 February 2022.

South African Government News Agency (SA News). 2021. 'Tackling Youth Unemployment'. *SA News*, 28 June 2021. https://www.sanews.gov.za/features-south-africa/tackling-youth-unemployment. Accessed 20 February 2022.

Statistics South Africa (Stats SA). 2021. *Labour Force Survey for April to June 2021, Quarter 2*. Pretoria: Stats SA.

Statistics South Africa (Stats SA). 2022. *Quarterly Employment Survey, Quarter 1*. Pretoria: Statistics South Africa.

Van Aardt, Isa. 2012. 'A Review of Youth Unemployment in South Africa, 2004 to 2011'. *South African Journal of Labour Relations* 36 (1): 54–68.

Webster, Edward and Christine Bischoff. 2011. 'New Actors in Employment Relations in the Periphery: Closing the Representation Gap amongst Micro and Small Enterprises'. *Industrial Relations/Relations Industrielle*, 66 (1).

Wood, Geoffrey and Christine Bischoff. 2021. 'Human Resources Management in South Africa: Context, Issues and Trends'. In *Towards a Human-Centred Agenda: Human Resource Management in the BRICS Countries in the Face of Global Challenges*, edited by Nikolai Rogovsky and Fang-Lee Cooke, 139–172. Geneva: ILO.

4

Community Health Care Workers in Gauteng: Volunteerism as a Band-Aid for Unemployment

Nomkhosi Xulu-Gama and Aisha Lorgat

INTRODUCTION

The fieldwork on which this chapter is based is part of a research project that looks at the relationship between worker education and household livelihoods. While such an approach is rare, the larger study focuses on this relationship because households are seen to be responding to the (un)employment crisis in various ways. Furthermore, exploring the role of worker education in these responses can provide unique insights into household livelihoods. This chapter looks specifically at community health workers (CHWs) and the role that they play in providing primary health-care services to households and communities under difficult and constrained circumstances. In particular, the chapter considers the precarious employment conditions under which CHWs operate, and posits that this is indicative of one new form that the future of work is taking – one in which volunteerism serves as a temporary and insecure means of employment creation. Sarah Mosoetsa (2011) suggests that households use social resources such as networks, alliances and informal associations to deal with crises. The household is an institution that bears the brunt when other institutions fail to do what is expected. It is seen as the major source for sharing resources like housing, income and psychosocial support.

Mosoetsa (2011) argues that households are now not only sites for reproduction but also sites for production. She states that households used to rely on political parties and trade unions, but these institutions have also been in decline. However, it seems that Expanded Public Works Programmes (EPWPs) are bringing back the relevance of political parties in assisting community members in times of unemployment. Mondli Hlatshwayo (2017) found that most people who access the opportunity of working in the EPWP are those with an African National Congress (ANC) affiliation, in one way or another. The work done by Hlatshwayo (2017) reveals what he regards as localised cadre deployment in the context of EPWP work. Community activism and having a network in the community have been seen as points that allow alignment with employment opportunities.

Although households have had to take on most of the burden, this does not mean they are strong enough or stable enough to do so effectively. Instead, Mosoetsa (2011) refers to them as having fragile stability, with a great deal of gender and generational conflict, among others. On the same note, Mosoetsa (2011) highlights the importance of unpaid work done by women as important not only for the household but for the broader economy as well. She further argues that households and the community at large feel betrayed by unions, which often do not seem to have the best interests of their workers at heart. Religious (spiritual) organisations are the ones who have come to play a bigger role for households in times of trouble.

As a result, this chapter focuses on 'volunteerism' as a band-aid for the lack of job prospects in a context that is shaped by the neo-liberal economic trajectory adopted by the South African state. South Africa has high and unsustainable levels of structural unemployment, which affects African young people disproportionately. Various stimulus mechanisms and policy prescriptions have failed to significantly address this unemployment crisis, and instead government has recognised that EPWPs (including community health work under the Community Work Programme [CWP]) serve a purpose in absorbing, at least temporarily and under relatively poor conditions, some of those unemployed persons. Additionally, scholarship of work in society, broadly covered by the discipline of industrial sociology, has largely ignored the connections between work and welfare. As this chapter shows, EPWPs provide important work opportunities for vulnerable individuals, but have also become an essential part of service delivery in an overstretched health and welfare system. Themba Masondo's (2018, 24) work also highlights this dimension of the CWP which has developed 'additional social multipliers' that 'resolve local social challenges ... by focusing the CWP on the massive community care deficits, environmental degradation, crime and by building a sense of solidarity among the CWP participants'. Community health-care workers are especially illustrative of this as they have become an essential part of primary healthcare provision.

Nevertheless, we argue that the EPWP (as illustrated in this paper by the experiences of community healthcare workers) is essentially akin to sticking a band-aid on a gaping and festering wound, a very small and limited intervention to address a very big and all-encompassing problem, with very limited and questionable success (Van der Westhuizen 2015; Pretorius 2019). In doing so, the chapter considers the blurring of distinctions between workplace and home, and workplace and community. In considering these shifting work dynamics, we also highlight gendered relations, since these emerged as a dominant focus of our research participants.

METHODOLOGY

We wrote this chapter using data that was collected from a focus group discussion with vulnerable workers in Johannesburg. We broadly define vulnerable workers as anyone who is selling their labour and its reproductive extension, whether directly as a wage-earner or indirectly in the reproductive sphere. These included volunteers, unemployed persons, casually employed persons, students and community activists. The general approach adopted is that there should be some linkages between community struggles and workers' struggles. Community health workers made up the majority of participants. The main issue we explored was the perceived relationship between worker education and household livelihoods.

Having CHWs as the majority of participants influenced the discussion in a particular direction. We had 17 participants, 4 males and 13 females. Their ages ranged between 21 and 53 years. The session was transcribed and translated into English by two members of the research team, who also facilitated the focus group discussion. Individuals were asked to voluntarily fill in informed consent forms as well as biographical data forms. These were collected at the end of the focus group discussion. Participants were given a R300 stipend for taking a day off their commitments to attend the focus group discussion. The decision to provide these stipends was taken because the participants were expected to take time off work to participate, and it was felt that they should not have to suffer loss of income as a result.

LITERATURE REVIEW

Almost every study we have looked at explicitly identified several limitations or challenges affecting the success of EPWP or CHW programmes. These included lack of ongoing training, lack of supervision and limited support (Nxumalo, Goudge and Thomas 2013; Austin-Evelyn et al. 2017; Nxumalo, Goudge and Manderson 2016; Wilford et al. 2018). Unlike others, Nxumalo et al. (2016) strongly posit that the achievements of the CHW programmes were limited as a result of such factors. However, Masondo (2018) focuses on the potential of the CWP to promote livelihoods. While he also looks at limitations, his conclusions are that the CWP offers ongoing and predictable income, has the potential to become a vehicle for livelihoods promotion, and has shown potential to generate community development multipliers.

Regarding the EPWP, the study by Bonguyise Khanyile (2008), although focused more on infrastructural projects and not on the programme as a whole, concludes that the jobs created are not sustainable because worker training takes less than six months and is not accredited. However, Khanyile does recognise that these short-term employment prospects bring hope for job creation. He mentions that most of the people who benefit from the EPWP are those who might have access to one of the many social grants distributed by government to qualifying recipients. EPWPs will not solve the unemployment problem, but they should be seen as one of many short- to medium-term interventions aimed at poverty alleviation (poverty being associated with unemployment). While they are complementary to social grants, EPWPs should never be seen as an alternative. EPWPs are also criticised for 'make-work' programmes, such as making people dig holes and then filling them in, just so that they are working (Van der Westhuizen 2015). Furthermore, most of the EPWP workers are paid below the minimum wage. He concludes that more effective monitoring and evaluation systems should be put in place to improve the lives of people.

Hlatshwayo (2017) documents the perspectives of the EPWP beneficiaries, as he believes that scholars often write about the EPWP but rarely provide qualitative data relating to the views and experiences of the people who work in these programmes. According to Hlatshwayo (2017), the workers expressed appreciation for the opportunity to work and earn an income. This enabled them to meet some of their family's needs and to deal with other challenges. The income received from the EPWP was also used to supplement the already existing household or even individual income, such as social grants or selling recycled waste. However, three of their top concerns were the low pay, the contractual nature of jobs and poor working conditions. Although the pay is very low, the beneficiaries said it made a big difference in their lives, including the ability to extend the government-funded housing in which they live.

Hlatshwayo (2017) reveals issues of safety and security on the job, and it is clear that different projects have different provisions for the safety and security of workers. Some projects provide safety equipment and clothing while others do not. The different projects also showed a variation in the number of days worked per week as well as the intensity of the work. These non-standardised practices were also noted in comparative studies of different CHW programmes (Nxumalo 2013; Vetten 2015; Nxumalo et al. 2016).

The CHW programme was established in 2004 and integrated into the Public Works Programme under the home and community-based care initiative in the first phase, and then extended formally under Phase 2 of the social sector EPWP in 2009. This served to improve primary health care provision in South Africa in line with the 1978 Alma-Ata Declaration (World Health Organisation 1978), and more especially to assist with the care of people living with HIV/AIDS and tuberculosis (Nxumalo 2013; Parenzee and Budlender 2015). 'This strategy also addressed the aim of improving the support and career opportunities for the volunteer workforce within the health sector' (Nxumalo 2013, 75). Importantly, the social sector EPWPs,[1] which 'tend to focus primarily on work responsibilities that women have traditionally fulfilled' (Parenzee and Budlender 2015, 2) were envisioned as a way of bringing more women into the EPWPs in order to meet the stipulated gender, youth and disability targets.[2]

The limited resources to care for people living with HIV/AIDS created an urgent need for community home-based care. The primary focus of the community home-based care workers was Directly Observed Treatment Surveillance, which targeted people living with HIV/AIDS and those with tuberculosis. Katinka de Wet (2012) argues that over the years, South Africa has made great strides with the remuneration of so-called voluntary home-based care work, and the issuing of titles and job descriptions as well as a new name, CHW. Their pay is not a salary but a stipend, which tends to be irregular and unsystematic. However, the ascribed 'voluntary' nature of the work is both problematic and disputed. Hlatshwayo (2017) details how people are generally recruited into these positions, and De Wet (2012) notes the vulnerability of those targeted to become volunteers: they tend to be those affected by unemployment, poverty and HIV/AIDS, and black women in particular.

The sad part of this 'voluntary' rhetoric is that the people who are targeted to become CHWs are faced with the same kind of health and financial problems that their patients encounter (Parenzee 2015). De Wet also cautions that it is incorrect to assume that those without money or with little money have a lot of time on their hands to do voluntary work (Berner and Philips cited in De Wet 2012, 115). She further argues that household chores are already mainly carried out by women and young girls – the very same group targeted by the CHW programme – and it is also a well-known fact that the responsibility for taking care of those who are sick within households lies primarily with women and young girls. Nxumalo's (2013) research shows that different programmes use different titles, and some distinguish between unpaid 'volunteers' and paid 'CHWs' on the basis of training (or the lack thereof).[3] However, as a general note, she states that with regard to primary healthcare interventions, 'it is important to keep in mind that their implementation efforts have relied on community volunteers, whether as part of a state programme or an independent NGO [non-governmental organisation]' (Nxumalo 2013, 19).

In their recent work, Nxumalo et al. (2016) also draw our attention to the limited capacity of the CHWs, which they argue compromises community trust and quality of care provided to people. They also note that the CHWs often have to deal with repercussions of the inadequate treatment that patients received from formal health facilities.

While CHW programmes play a crucial role in helping households overcome barriers to care, such programmes often fail because of insufficient skills or lack of support (Nxumalo et al. 2013). Ineffective district health systems are sometimes seen as reasons for the failure of these programmes. Nxumalo et al. (2013) found that there was very limited ongoing training with no opportunity for internal career progression. In one of the case study areas, these authors found that CHWs did not only undergo health training, but also worked with other service providers like police, social development and other agencies to help them address the multifaceted nature of their work. Lack of supervision is identified by various researchers as a major challenge for the CHWs in carrying out their duties (Nxumalo et al. 2013; Nxumalo et al. 2016; Austin-Evelyn et al. 2017). Nxumalo et al. (2013) also found that continuous investment in training and support for the CHWs did not only increase their confidence in doing their work, as outlined by other researchers, but also increased their commitment to the programme.

Nxumalo and her colleagues note:

> In 2016, CHWs are recognized by the post-apartheid government as partners in the health system, and many are incorporated as government employees, paid directly by the state and managed by government health facility managers and/or nurses. Others are formally employed by the local community based organisations or international non-governmental organisations (Nxumalo, Goudge and Manderson 2016, 62).

As we will show later, this positioning of CHWs as 'partners' and 'employees' is contentious from the perspective of CHWs themselves. Furthermore, as Van der Westhuizen (2015, 12) points out, the EPWPs tend to have a labour-replacing effect rather than a job-creating one, in that insecure, low-paying jobs are created instead of secure, permanent ones.

The work of Katherine Austin-Evelyn and her colleagues (2017) shows the strong levels of commitment the CHWs have to their work, regardless of the ever-present challenges. They expressed a specific interest in continuing to work for the organisation for quite some time. While most CHWs were unhappy with the lack of supervision, several of the participants of this study showed an understanding that the nurses (who serve as supervisors) were also under-resourced and over-stretched. Austin-Evelyn et al. (2017) show that the services of the CHWs and the expectations of the community members did not balance. The community expected more than was provided, with the CHWs claiming that they were expected to have a solution for every problem. CHWs were also expected to bring medication to community members so that they would not have to go to the clinic.

Community members did not like to go to the clinics because there was no (or inadequate) care and sometimes clinics were too far away and difficult to get to. This was especially difficult for elderly and infirm patients. They would spend a lot of time going to the clinic and waiting, only to spend a few minutes with a nurse. This was unlike the care offered by the CHWs, who came to their homes and spent more time attending to their needs and answering their questions. The 'prisoner of love' framework outlined by Paula England (2005) is particularly instructive in understanding the possible motivations of CHWs and why they are willing to provide such committed levels of care, despite the low pay and often poor working conditions they experience. The framework posits that altruistic instincts and the intrinsic fulfilment gained by engaging in care work are what lead to workers being willing to accept low pay for their labour. The term 'prisoner of love' was first used by Nancy Folbre and describes a situation in care work in which a 'kind of emotional hostage effect occurs' where 'emotional bonds put care workers in a vulnerable position, discouraging them from demanding higher wages or changes in working conditions that might have adverse effects on care recipients' (England 2005, 390).

FINDINGS AND ANALYSIS

In this section, we will present the narratives that were gathered from the focus group held with community health workers (CHI 2018). We believe it is important to highlight the workers' experiences in their own words, and to recognise and valorise their own interpretations and analyses.

Background of participants

Most of the research participants were unmarried, had children and lived in a township with their parent(s), siblings and their children. Some had matric and others did not. Most of them had personal experience of having taken care of a family member before becoming a CHW. This was an important identifier for many participants. This personal experience was mentioned as a primary influence in their decision to take up this work. The paths taken by participants into community health work varied, with some being introduced through networks and working with NGOs.

> I am a chairperson in the Community Child Workers' Forum, where we tackle the challenges of the community workers who are being exploited by the Department of Health, because they are using us as service providers but they are treating us as employees. So, we are tackling the struggle at the workplace. There is a division and a link between the community and the clinic, so we need to advocate for the community. We speak for the community at the clinics because sometimes the sisters [professional nurses] don't treat the patients in a right manner. They treat them badly. Sometimes you find a patient saying that they have been chased away from the clinic. And when you ask why, you don't even get a clear response as to why they were chased away. Sometimes there are migrant people who do not have passports. So, you find that they chase them away because they do not have passports, so we are the link between the Department of Health with the community. (Participant 3)

While most worked as CHWs, the group as a whole was very aware of their activist identities. Almost all of them were members of other grassroots organisations and also served on committees focusing variously on gender and labour issues; they also assisted with projects, such as community gardens.

> We do household registrations, screenings and find chronic diseases or any problems in that household. We do referrals; that is if one needs Home Affairs, we refer them to Home Affairs or police station, or wherever a person will get help from. (Participant 2)

Although training is received, much is learned on the job. Roles and responsibilities of the CHWs as identified by participants include: health education and promotion, advocacy, household registrations, referrals (in terms of identifying the needs and agencies that are best placed to assist), directly observed treatment surveillance, screenings (for chronic diseases), HIV/AIDS counselling and testing.

'I did that thing because of passion' – various feelings associated with being a CHW

> When I did the Community Health Care, I saw that these grannies need help; they need someone who will advocate for them. They just need some-one to sit with them and they can relate stories from the past. (Participant 3)
>
> I went there knowing that there is no pay. Now I have been doing this for nine years. I have been doing it all these years because of passion, but even the love I have for this thing will eventually get finished. (Participant 10)
>
> I don't see myself focusing on something else, other than community health care work … Even if a person has a problem that they have to take their medication and there is no food, this forces me that whatever I am eating in my house, I have to share with them so that they can be able to go take their medication. (Participant 5)

Multiple participants expressed frustration with their status as volunteers, a status that continues for years and results in what we have termed a cadre of 'permanent volunteers'. They note that they have worked for years, in some cases initially with-out pay, followed by a small stipend that remains below minimum wage thresholds. They are never given any substantive recognition for the essential role they play in primary healthcare provision, especially to poor and vulnerable communities.

Sometimes they have to take their own food and give it to their patients so that they can take medication. Nxumalo et al. (2016, 65) note that while the clinic provided medication and the services of the CHWs, it did not provide food. Most patients knew that taking medication without food was wrong, and that often resulted in them not taking essential medication. Some even argued that 'those tab-lets make you terribly hungry' (Nxumalo et al. 2016, 65).

> I started in an NGO. We were not getting anything except for sandwiches and juice. So, it's not about that. I went there in order to get money. I did not think of that but there are things which were on my mind. Sometimes you need money to go do that certificate and you find that you don't even

have the money to do that certificate. ... I think it took me two years or one year and a half before we could get a stipend. At that time the stipend was R250 but I did not lose hope. ... Being able to help the community, if the government were able to help as much as we do, I think that we would be having a beautiful South Africa ... but they are not doing their job. (Participant 6)

CHWs all expressed a belief in the good that they did, that their work benefitted their communities and society in general. There was a sense of great pride in being able to help. Many stated explicitly that they were doing this because of passion for the work. They saw themselves as agents of change, especially regarding the treatment of vulnerable people in their communities. Many also evidenced a sense of confidence that was likely tied to the skills and experience acquired, although this link was not explicitly made.

However, despite their passion for the work, many felt exploited, overworked and underpaid. There was a great deal of emotional labour that came into play in their day-to-day activities that was not given adequate recognition. In addition, they felt that they did many other people's jobs, basically filling in for others in order to ensure that basic services were delivered to community members and that they were able to access things like social grants. Job descriptions were non-existent and there seemed to be no boundaries to the work they were expected to do. This led to frustration on the part of CHWs, exacerbated by what they perceived as, and existing literature suggests is, an unsupportive government.

'Our job is really risky because they do not tell us of our boundaries' – CHW challenges

In the NGO that we worked for, we were promised that we would be taken to school and we would become nurses. But then, because of our government, who never fulfilled the things that he [sic] promised, things changed. And we ended up doing healthcare. And we were learning on the job; we were never given a manual of how do you take care of a patient. How do you educate? We would have in-service training of three days. They would tell us how to secure. How do you help a person take their medication? But how a person feels inside, how a person is mentally, emotionally and physically and how the family is dealing with all that? They did not teach us that. We had to learn ourselves. (Participant 3)

While CHWs knock off at 2 pm, sometimes what they need to do is not done by 2 pm. Sometimes, although their work had officially ended for the day, patients would follow them to their homes after work hours when they needed particular assistance. The practicality of their jobs does not have boundaries as they engage in nursing work, social work and assist with service delivery issues (as they sometimes deal with water and electricity problems). It angers them to realise that they have to do basically everything that affects a household, because they know that there are supposed to be different people from the various government departments who should be dealing with these issues. This points to distinct similarities with a study done by Bezuidenhout and Fakier (2016), looking at contract cleaning staff, where they state that 'these struggles call into question the very definition of a work*place*' [original emphasis]. They show that, like CHWs, outsourcing services reintroduce aspects of the 'apartheid workplace regime, such as job insecurity, low pay, and a lack of benefits. In a nutshell, cheap labor is being reproduced under new conditions as the burden of reproduction shifts onto households and communities in both urban and rural areas' (Bezuidenhout and Fakier 2006, 479).

According to Hlatshwayo (2017), EPWP beneficiaries complained that they work harder than some government or permanently employed people who work in the same geographic area, but they get paid much less and with no benefits. Hlatshwayo further added that in the past these EPWP jobs were performed by permanent workers who had benefits and were employed by municipalities.

> Now we just finished being trained for HIV counselling and testing. Now we must do HIV counselling and testing at the household ... we must do it at the household. We must check the medication, if they take it properly; if they do not take it properly, we need to educate. Also, we need to do direct observation treatment for patients who are suffering from TB [tuberculosis], make sure that the person takes medication and does not spread the disease. (Participant 3)

The above case is similar to the international experience pointed out by Abimbola Olaniran et al. (2017), where job descriptions are fluid and ever-changing. CHWs are not consulted but are expected to provide effective counselling and testing in support of public primary healthcare policy.

> We once had a patient who was being abused by their child. We had to go out to the social workers, and when we came back, when they returned the report to the social workers, we were also at risk, because we were seen as the cause of the family fights. Our job is really risky because they do not tell us of our boundaries. (Participant 6)

In certain situations, CHWs risk being seen by the community or the patient's family members as troublemakers when they intervene in a conflicted family by bringing in the South African Police Service or social workers. People might seek personal revenge on CHWs who report their wrongdoing, whether it is abuse (of children or the elderly, for example) or other types of behaviour with potential social and legal repercussions. Van Rie et al. (2018, 739) cautions that attention should be given to the protection of CHWs when providing care to households, given the high levels of violence in poor urban communities. This research emphasises that the CHWs provide considerable support to households, while not receiving that support themselves.

'They remind you that you are a volunteer' – what happens when there are no jobs?

> Because even the jobs we have are temporary jobs. There are no jobs which are sustainable. We as CHWs are exploited every time. We are treated as permanent workers, they want you at work at 8 am and there is no knock-off time. They want the reports; they want statistics; they want everything. But whatever rights that you want as a CHW, you do not get. When you begin to tell them that you want increment, they remind you that you are a volunteer. We had to force the Department of Health in Gauteng for an increment. We were getting a salary of R500 when we started this thing and we had to force the department up to a point where we were earning R1 263. … And even now we have not reached the minimum wage. We are now getting R2 600 which is still not a living wage. (Participant 3)

South Africa has an extremely high unemployment rate[4] when compared to other countries at a similar level of economic development. This was exacerbated by the lockdown measures during the Covid-19 pandemic. Statistics South Africa (2020) estimates that 2.2 million workers lost their jobs under the hard lockdown that was implemented in early 2020. Furthermore, it is projected that globally, many jobs will be lost as a result of massive changes to labour markets that are ascribed to the so-called Fourth Industrial Revolution. When there are no jobs, people become desperate and tend to believe anything that will give them some hope.

In the meantime, people find various ways of eking out livelihoods, as will be shown in the next section. Finding 'work', however, is still a goal for the participants, with the idea that having a job, even as a volunteer, is a source of pride and passion.

They also see it as having the potential to provide more secure future employment opportunities. This engagement made it clear to us as researchers that any job, even with inadequate or no remuneration, is one form the future of work is taking.

It is important to note, though, that these workers do not simply accept their exploitation, but have taken steps to address the challenges they face. The participants indicated that they had formed a collective and chose representatives to take forward their issues with management. This is supported by the action taken by Lawyers for Human Rights representing over 9 000 CHWs who have been employed on recurring fixed-term contracts with the Gauteng Department of Health for five years. This was deemed a violation of the Labour Relations Act, in terms of provisions of Section 198B(4),[5] which led to a ruling in their favour by the arbitrator (Karibu Staff 2018; Lehulere 2018).

'We have to find cheaper ways' – survival strategies

The CHWs spoke about having to migrate from the townships to live in the city, to make it easier to look for employment opportunities. This would also make it easy to travel to work once they found piece jobs. In the city they have to pay rent and share accommodation in order to reduce costs. At the same time, living in a township in a family house also makes them feel like they are renting; they call it *siyakhokha* which means 'we are paying'. The municipal bills are unaffordable and they are continuously rising in prices. Their argument is that the bill does not care if there is someone who is employed in that household or not. Being categorised as 'indigent' also does not help.

> Where one buys clothes changes, so instead of going to a mall to buy at Mr Price and all those other stores like PEP, which are considered the cheapest, we go downtown and we go to *dunusa*[6] and we buy R5 or R10 items, so those items you go back and wash them and wear them. Like this dress I am wearing was R10. Because clothing is a necessity and you can't cut down on necessities; you can't really walk around naked. ... And we also benefit from that kind of a black market. So, our strategies are heavily dense in engaging the black market – the black market not only for clothing but for food as well; we know exactly when to go and get certain items cheaper than you would get them at Pick 'n Pay, even Shoprite and Boxers as well. We know that buying in bulk saves us money and time compared to buying every month. ... when you try to think transport, because the taxis are going up, for example, I come from West Rand in Randfontein, so for me instead of using a taxi

it's going to cost me R26 from Joburg to Randfontein in town and not even getting home. I would rather take the train because the train is going to cost me R8. So, I am able to look at alternative transport which [is] cheaper … Are we able to eat as a collective instead of us cooking individually or cook together because that saves the ingredients that we have … instead of eating four times a day, as much as we would like to, we would rather eat twice, and those two meals a day are large meals. (Participant 13)

I like the question of the household strategies. I am talking from a black woman's perspective. I am a mother. Then I decide to sell liquor. You know, after two weeks, especially in the township, the police will come and harass me. They will want me to comply with the by-laws. … I want to save money so that my children can be able to get educated … You don't even know what by-laws mean. (Participant 17)

There are various survival strategies that people engage in, when they have little income available to them. These include buying from extremely cheap downtown street traders, engaging in black market transactions, buying in bulk as well as buying collectively with others, buying items that are close to expiry (and marked down), making alternative transport arrangements, participating in stokvels and community saving schemes, and using loan sharks. Some of the strategies require collective support, such as cooking and eating together, getting lifts from friends and *umholiswano*.[7]

In a township, selling liquor is one effective way for poor people to survive, especially for women, although this means not abiding by the municipal by-laws and being subjected to police harassment. In addition, living in a shack is understood to mean that you do not pay municipal bills. Many people rely on loan sharks to make ends meet. They borrow money with an intention and plan to regenerate money in one way or the other, but things do not always play out the way they plan.

Additional income-generating strategies like selling foodstuffs are negatively affected by their commitment as CHWs. They put in too many hours of community work at the expense of their own small private businesses. A few gave specific examples: one was selling atchar and others bought a machine in order to make fried chips, and both businesses failed dismally. Another reason for the failure of their business ventures was that they felt they lacked business management skills and small business support.

Government is seen as failing the people in many ways (lack of job opportunities; poor education options for children; restrictive by-laws for hawkers). Government was also criticised for not providing effective support to the CHWs, and as being the cause of the many challenges that they face in their work.

'Which labour is more important? Which labour do we pay for?' – gender dynamics

So when we think about work we shouldn't think about it from one point of view. Women experience work differently and they experience labour differently. Women naturally have different burdens and one of them is the burden of the family and the dependency that the family has on the woman ... And it goes into the conversation that which labour is more important? Which labour do we pay for? Do we not see the whole thing of a woman doing the work of cooking and cleaning and taking care of the children as work? Do we just think that it is just natural, she must just naturally do it? And therefore we want to scrutinise and say women don't want to work because they don't have the time or they are physically unable to do it or find any source of income outside of the household. I think when we think of labour and how it is structured in society we need to find a way to accommodate the children into work. A lot of the women don't go [to work] because they can't leave their children at home ... Women who have children are in a disadvantaged position of ever finding any form of stable income because the burden of the family lies on her. (Participant 16)

The problem is that *I think domestication is the highest form of slavery* [emphasis added] because at the time when I am mopping, I can't be reading a book. Because I am busy mopping the whole day so who is going to read my books? This thing of domestication is a problem and I do not even know who will marry me. (Participant 2)

I am also teaching myself ... that when I have a family, how will I take care of them? It starts from the relationship before marriage and if he can't take care of you now before marriage, forget about it. We need to accept that there is a girlfriend allowance. (Participant 5)

Our research indicated that men and women had different ideas of what women should be expected to do when there were no jobs. This perspective of a gendered division of labour is also apparent in how EPWPs are conceptualised and implemented. Parenzee (2015) asserts that EPWPs serve to undermine gender equality. For example, participants felt that women who are without a job could do laundry for others and get paid for doing so. Others felt that members of the household could support each other and be paid back either in kind, through bartering of time and other resources, or in cash. Some participants demonstrated an idea of shifting from traditional understandings of how a family works and supports each other.

For example, one participant looked after her sister's child and her sister paid her the money she would otherwise be paying a nanny.

Van Rie et al. (2018, 739) suggest that policy-makers need to find ways to effectively engage men in community-based care and to include efforts that promote a healthy lifestyle. The need for this was supported by the experiences of those participants who felt that men have difficulty dealing with unemployment. Men often become abusive; they misuse the little money that is available; and they make claims on the children's social grants.

CONCLUSION

This paper has explored the question of what happens when there are no jobs to be had, and it does so by focusing on community health workers. South Africa has an extremely high unemployment rate, especially when using the expanded definition, and the outlook for significant improvement is bleak. Considering this reality, many people are forced to adopt various strategies in order to support their households and those dependent on them. As has been shown, many people try to engage in informal economic activities such as brewing and selling liquor or food, but as Van der Westhuizen (2015, 26) highlights, EPWPs 'do not provide a bridge into the formal economy for the economically and socially excluded, of whom the majority are women. Rather it relegates poor people and especially women to temporary jobs'.

What made the CHWs complain bitterly was not only working extended hours and being underpaid, as well as having a job description that was constantly being amended, with the latest change being the addition of HIV/AIDS counselling and testing responsibilities at the household level. A large focus of their dissatisfaction was the perception that they were finding themselves doing the jobs of many different people from various municipal, provincial and local departments – including the Department of Social Development, Department of Health and the South African Police Service – who were employed permanently and earning a salary from those positions but not doing their jobs. CHWs felt that those jobs were left for them to do as they were working on the ground with the people, while the permanent employees sat in their offices and did nothing.

Survival strategies in a context of little or no work include volunteerism, solidarity, black market resources, and deploying persistence of and resistance to gendered relations and divisions of labour. Volunteerism in the sense in which it is used for CHWs is a way to support primary healthcare interventions by using the rhetoric of *ubuntu*[8] and building the nation. Shifting the responsibility of care to communities and households takes pressure off the government to allocate the greater resources that would be required by properly trained and remunerated health workers. These kinds of pragmatic, some might say cynical, calculations become necessary when the state is constrained by neo-liberal economic imperatives and limited resources. Despite these structural factors, the CHWs continue to show agency and have continued to struggle to improve their conditions. CHWs in Gauteng, led by one of our participants and with legal support provided by Lawyers for Human Rights, have won a significant victory through arbitration in the Public Health and Social Development Sectoral Bargaining Council to have their status recognised as permanent workers (Karibu Staff 2018; Lehulere 2018).

NOTES

1   The social sector EPWPs include Home/Community Based Care, Early Childhood Development, and Community Health Workers.

2   Initially the gender target was 60 per cent women, but that was dropped to 45 per cent and then raised to 55 per cent (Van der Westhuizen 2015). The other targets were 40 per cent youth and 2 per cent people with disabilities.

3   'At the time of data collection ... three CHWs were considered to be volunteers because they had not as yet undergone the standard national training course for CHWs known as the 69-day training course ... Although not formal policy, the organisation devised this to differentiate between the CHWs who were formally trained and practicing and those who were not trained and therefore not formally providing services. The volunteers only received a stipend after completing the 69-day training, when they would be able to provide services in their community. During the volunteering period, they would be paired with the more experienced CHWs to give them the opportunity to observe' (Nxumalo 2013, 153). Some of these 'volunteers', moreover, had been in this position for at least two years.

4   The official unemployment rate was 27.5 per cent in the third quarter of 2018 (Stats SA 2018).

5   This section sets out the circumstances under which lower-paid workers can be employed on fixed-term contracts.

6   *Dunusa* are cheap informal clothing sellers. Technically the term refers to having to bend over and dig through a pile of clothing tossed on the ground.

7   *Umholiswano* is an extension of the stokvel concept whereby the distribution of money is rotated on a monthly basis.

8   Ubuntu is a philosophy that posits that a person is a person through other people. In other words, it valorises our roles as human beings in relation to others.

REFERENCES

Austin-Evelyn, Katherine, Miriam Rabkin, Tonderayi Macheka, Anthony Mutiti, Judith Mwansa-Kambafwile, Thomas Dlamini and Wafaa M. El-Sadr. 2017. 'Community Health Worker Perspectives on a New Primary Health Care Initiative in the Eastern Cape of South Africa'. *PLoS ONE* 12 (3): 1–13.

Bezuidenhout, Andries and Khayaat Fakier. 2006. 'Maria's Burden: Contract Cleaning and the Crisis of Social Reproduction in Post-apartheid South Africa'. *Antipode* 38 (3): 462–485.

Chris Hani Institute (CHI). 2018. 'Household Livelihoods and Worker Education'. Focus Group Discussion, unpublished transcript, 4 October 2018. Johannesburg: CHI.

De Wet, Katinka. 2012. 'Redefining Volunteerism: The Rhetoric of Community Home-based Care in (the Not So New) South Africa'. *Community Development Journal* 47 (1): 111–125.

England, Paula. 2005. 'Emerging Theories of Care Work'. *Annual Review of Sociology* 31: 381–399.

Hlatshwayo, Mondli. 2017. 'The Expanded Public Works Programme: Perspectives of Direct Beneficiaries'. *The Journal for Transdisciplinary Research in Southern Africa* 13 (1): 1–8.

Karibu Staff. 2018. 'Forum Wins Permanent Status for CHWs in Gauteng'. *Karibu – A Working Class Newspaper*, 28 September 2018. https://karibu.org.za/forum-wins-permanent-status-for-chws-in-gauteng. Accessed 20 February 2019.

Khanyile, Bonguyise K. 2008. 'A Study of the Impact of Expanded Public Works Programme on Job Creation in the Zululand District Municipality'. MA diss., University of KwaZulu-Natal.

Lehulere, Oupa. 2018. 'Another Milestone in the CHWs' Struggle for Recognition'. *Karibu – A Working Class Newspaper*, 25 September 2018. https://karibu.org.za/another-milestone-in-the-chws-struggle-for-recognition. Accessed 20 February 2019.

Masondo, Themba. 2018. 'Protecting and Promoting Livelihoods of the Excluded through the Community Work Programme: A Comparative Case Study of Munsieville and Bekkersdal'. PhD diss., University of the Witwatersrand.

Mosoetsa, Sarah. 2011. *Eating from One Pot: The Dynamics of Survival in Poor South African Households*. Johannesburg: Wits University Press.

Nxumalo, Lynette N. 2013. 'Community Health Workers, Community Participation and Community Level Inter-Sectoral Action: The Challenges of Implementing Primary Healthcare Outreach Services'. PhD diss., University of the Witwatersrand.

Nxumalo, Nonhlanhla, Jane Goudge and Lenore Manderson. 2016. 'Community Health Workers, Recipients' Experiences and Constraints to Care in South Africa – A Pathway to Trust'. *AIDS Care* 28 (4): 61–71.

Nxumalo, Nonhlanhla, Jane Goudge and Liz Thomas. 2013. 'Outreach Services to Improve Access to Health Care in South Africa: Lessons from Three Community Health Worker Programmes'. *Global Health Action* 6 (1). DOI: 10.3402/gha.v6i0.19283.

Olaniran, Abimbola, Helen Smith, Regine Unkels, Sarah Bar-Zeev and Nynke van den Broek. 2017. 'Who is a Community Worker? A Systematic Review of Definitions'. *Global Health Action* 10 (1): 1–12.

Parenzee, Penny. 2015. 'Early Childhood Care and the EPWP: What is the Value-add and Implications for Poor Women and their Families'. In *Who Cares? South Africa's Expanded Public Works Programme in the Social Sector and its Impact on Women*, edited by Penny Parenzee and Debbie Budlender, 35–59. Cape Town: Heinrich Böll Stiftung.

Parenzee, Penny and Debbie Budlender. 2015. 'Introduction: A Gender Perspective on South Africa's Expanded Public Works Programme'. In *Who Cares? South Africa's Expanded Public Works Programme in the Social Sector and its Impact on Women*, edited by Penny Parenzee and Debbie Budlender, 1–10. Cape Town: Heinrich Böll Stiftung.

Pretorius, Liesl. 2019. 'Promise Check: 5 Million Work Opportunities instead of 6 Million for ANC?' *City Press*, 28 January 2019. https://www.news24.com/citypress/news/promise-check-5-million-work-opportunities-instead-of-6-million-for-anc-20190128. Accessed 20 February 2019.

Statistics South Africa (Stats SA). 2018. 'Quarterly Labour Force Survey Quarter 3, 2018'. https://www.statssa.gov.za/publications/P0211/P02113rdQuarter2018.pdf. Accessed 11 May 2023.

Statistics South Africa (Stats SA). 2020. 'Quarterly Labour Force Survey Quarter 2, 2020'. https://www.statssa.gov.za/publications/P0211/P02112ndQuarter2020.pdf. Accessed 31 January 2023.

Van der Westhuizen, Christi. 2015. 'Setting the Scene: Public Works Employment from the RDP to the NDP'. In *Who Cares? South Africa's Expanded Public Works Programme in the Social Sector and its Impact on Women*, edited by Penny Parenzee and Debbie Budlender, 11–34. Cape Town: Heinrich Böll Stiftung.

Van Rie, Annelies, Nora S. West, Sheree R. Schwartz, L. Mutunga, Colleen F. Hanrahan, Jabulani Ncayiyana and Jean Bassett. 2018. 'The Unmet Needs and Health Priorities of the Urban Poor: Generating the Evidence Base for Urban Community Health Worker Programme in South Africa'. *South African Medical Journal* 108 (9): 734–740.

Vetten, Lisa. 2015. 'Who Cares? Post-rape Services and the Expanded Public Works Programme in South Africa'. In *Who Cares? South Africa's Expanded Public Works Programme in the Social Sector and its Impact on Women*, edited by Penny Parenzee and Debbie Budlender, 60–77. Cape Town: Heinrich Böll Stiftung.

Wilford, Aurene, Sifiso Phakathi, Lyn Haskins, Ngwalisa A. Jama, Ntokozo Mntambo and Christiane Horwood. 2018. 'Exploring the Care Provided to Mothers and Children by Community Health Workers in South Africa: Missed Opportunities to Provide Comprehensive Care'. *BMC Public Health* 18 (171): 2–10.

World Health Organization. 1978. 'Report of the International Conference on Primary Health Care, Alma-Ata, USSR, 6-12 September 1978'. Geneva: World Health Organization. https://www.who.int/publications/i/item/9241800011. Accessed 10 May 2023.

PART II

TECHNOLOGY AND WORK

5

Trade Unions, Technology and Skills

Siphelo Ngcwangu

INTRODUCTION

The skills issue has historically been central to the formation of the trade union movement in South Africa and has been informed by racial divisions within the broader society. The history of the skills question in South Africa is a history of exclusion and inclusion shaped by political developments during specific periods of South African history. According to Gerald Kraak (1993), the predominantly African trade unions which emerged in the 1970s and 1980s did so alongside an established trade union movement which represented largely skilled white, coloured and Indian workers who were often hostile to the new unions.

In a context of sanctions that affected the South African apartheid economy during the 1980s, the Congress of South African Trade Unions (Cosatu) commissioned several studies under the Industrial Strategy Project to investigate ways of improving the country's manufacturing performance. The skills question arose within the unions during this period of various attempts at seeking to rebuild the economy while enhancing the skills of workers and the broader population.

The labour movement had conceptualised South Africa's post-apartheid skills development dispensation since the early 1990s, and embarked on various initiatives to strengthen its capacity to engage on matters of economic restructuring. These include Cosatu's Economic Trends Research Group, Numsa's Vocational Training Project and its Research and Development Groups which sought to articulate a vision for industrial, economic and skills training policies. As Bhabhali ka Maphikela Nhlapho (2019, 58) states, 'in our country it was the labour unions that sought the change in skills-development processes and advised the new democratic government that it needs to depart from the practices of the apartheid state'.

The skills debate is rooted in the larger political and ideological contestations about the ideology of competitiveness and the future of struggle in the unions. Numsa's adoption of skills-based grading systems was heavily contested within unions, and was seen to be a departure from ideas of emancipatory education that had formed part of the popular vision of trade unions for a post-apartheid skills development dispensation (Kodisang 2018). This departure was influenced largely by the changing global balance of forces and the influence of a small group of intellectuals within the unions.

The so-called Fourth Industrial Revolution, according to Klaus Schwab (2016, 37), builds on the third industrial revolution by introducing artificial intelligence – that is, software technologies that make computers or robots perform tasks similarly to or better than human beings. This is anticipated to cause more upheaval than previous industrial revolutions as it will have more speed, breadth and depth. Its impact on workplaces is often presented as novel or recent, yet workers have grappled with such changes over various periods in history, as they are manifestations of ways in which capital seeks to maximise profits by extracting value through minimising labour costs. Any discussion of the future of labour must consider the concrete changes that are occurring within workplaces as a central component of responding to the larger politics of skills development, new technologies and the future of the labour movement. To elaborate on this discussion the chapter covers the following areas: (1) a theoretical understanding of skills, trade unions and technology; (2) workplace changes and technological restructuring; and (3) trade union responses.

SKILLS, TRADE UNIONS AND TECHNOLOGY:
A THEORETICAL UNDERSTANDING

There is a constant struggle to build a consensus around the definition of the terms skill and work, leading to a tendency to fetishise technical skill. Chris Warhurst, Ian Grugulis and Ewart Keep (2004, 5) argue that there is some consensus around the concept of skill which is based on three overriding principles:

1. Skill includes internalised capacities resident in the individual worker.
2. Skill includes job design, divisions of labour, technology and control.
3. Skill is socially constructed.

In the South African context Eddie Webster and Jean Leger (1992) emphasise the importance of reconceptualising skills formation, taking into consideration the racial divisions of labour in the workplace arising out of the historical monopolisation of skilled labour by white workers. White workers dominated skilled trades, while black workers generally performed semi-skilled and unskilled work. This resulted in a call for recognition of prior learning to be a central focus of skills formation, and to be addressed by the trade union movement as a matter closely linked to wages and grading.

In the context of changes in the South African labour market and the rise of insecurity both in the labour market and in society, I would suggest that there is a fourth dimension of defining skill: this should embrace a realisation of economic activities that occur outside of formal employment. These activities may range from self-sustaining livelihood activity to entrepreneurial activity and informal ways of making a living.[1]

The study of skills within the sub-disciplines of sociology of work and labour studies has emerged largely from studies of the labour process. Historically these studies were influenced by the Marxian tradition, which seeks to understand the relationship between changes in the labour process and ways in which machinery and technology affect the formation of skills within organisations and society (Edwards 1979; Littler 1982; Burawoy 1985; Adler 2004). At the core of sociological studies of skills is an understanding of how capital transforms the labour process and undermines the power of skilled workers to exercise control over their work processes. In the late nineteenth century and the twentieth century, skill implied a certain degree of autonomy and control over work. This meant that skilled artisans, for example, also had control over their tools and the basic machinery that they used for working. The advent of technology and the separation of the worker from the product through distribution and sales systems means that the power of the skilled worker has been in decline.

Marx's contribution to our study of the labour process arises out of his seminal study of capital, in which he distinguishes between variable capital (invested in labour costs) and constant capital (investment in acquiring machinery). In relation to the development of manufacturing, Marx argued:

> In every craft it seizes, manufacture creates a class of so-called unskilled labourers, a class strictly excluded by the nature of handicraft industry. If it develops a one-sided speciality to perfection, at the expense of the whole of a man's working capacity, it also begins to make a speciality of the absence of all development. Alongside the gradations of the hierarchy, there appears the simple separation of workers into skilled and unskilled. (Marx, [1867] 1976: 470)

This is the sense in which Marx defines capital as manifesting in both a social form in broad society and a technical form in the organisation of work.

Harry Braverman (1974) is credited for resurrecting the work of Marx on the labour process. The main theme in Braverman's work that shaped the study of skills is his notion of capitalism's logic of *deskilling*, which manifested through Taylorism. However, there are contestations over the Marxian approach to skills and the labour process among scholars of the sociology of work and labour. For instance, Webster (1985) maintains that Braverman ignores the new bargaining power conferred on unskilled and semi-skilled workers when mechanisation replaces craft skill:

> Our hypothesis then is that while machine technology undermines the craft unions' bargaining leverage, leading to real subordination and relative surplus value, it also transforms unskilled labour into semi-skilled labour. By increasing the proportion of workers strategically involved in the mechanized production process it increases the bargaining power of a large section of the workforce. The new semi-skilled workforce now represents a threat to the deskilled workers who either try to recruit them or redraw the boundaries to exclude them. (Webster 1985, 14)

Machinery that is highly computerised has gradually eradicated the power of the skilled categories of workers. As Mondli Hlatshwayo states:

> Technology plays an important role in the labour process because it can increase the pace of work, lead to unemployment, result in changes in the definition of skills and give rise to changes in the composition of the work force.

The discovery of micro-electronics has played a bigger role in monitoring workers and production processes. (Hlatshwayo 2013, 60)

Technology, therefore, can never be seen as neutral; it is in fact inserted as part of an ideological package by capital to exercise control and to consolidate its power over workers in the context of production.

The so-called Fourth Industrial Revolution is one of the more recent attempts at explaining how disruptive new technologies will result in alienation of workers from the production process and increase capital's ability to limit the use of human labour in work processes. What is interesting is that the deployment of artificial intelligence and robotics (which are core components of the Fourth Industrial Revolution) is likely to have an impact on workers across skills category levels, from the 'low-skilled' to the 'high-skilled' professional strata. Randall Collins argues:

Until the 1980s or 90s, mechanization chiefly displaced manual labour. In the most recent wave of technology, we now have the displacement of administrative labour, the downsizing of the middle class. Information technology is the technology of communications, and it has launched the second great era of the contraction of work, the displacement of communicative labour, which is what middle-class employees do. Mechanization is now joined by robotization and electronicization – an ugly and ungainly term to add to our vocabulary of ugly terms dictating our long-term future. (Collins 2013, 3)

The transformation of clerical and office work involves the codification and translation of knowledge work into working knowledge. Phillip Brown, Hugh Lauder and David Ashton (2011) argue that if the twentieth century was defined by *mechanical Taylorism*, the twenty-first century will be defined by *digital Taylorism*.

This involves translating knowledge work of managers, professionals, and technicians into working knowledge by capturing, codifying, and digitalising their work in software packages, templates, and prescripts that can be transferred and manipulated by others regardless of location. It is being applied to offices as well as factories and to services as well as manufacturing. (Brown et al. 2011, 72)

The trends that are taking shape in the modern capitalist labour market will have a strong bearing on how the future of labour is configured, as well as how the erosion of skilled workers affects the bargaining power of unions.

123

WORKPLACE CHANGES AND TECHNOLOGICAL RESTRUCTURING

There is a sense within the South African skills development research community that skills research should focus on the domain of 'work itself', given that over the period of South Africa's political transition, more focus was placed on the policy terrain (Kruss and Wildschut 2019). This has meant that most skills research involves large-scale statistical aggregations and/or inference based on employer information about the nature of skills requirements. Some qualitative research focuses on stakeholders such as managers and government officials, but does not investigate the plants themselves (Kraak 2008; Akoojee 2012; Lundall 2017). This has resulted in a power imbalance within the debate about skills. The site of production (the micro level) is critical if we are to understand the skills issue in its entirety.

By 2017 the automotive sector in South Africa was the largest manufacturing sector, contributing 7.5 per cent to the country's gross domestic product and 12 per cent of all manufacturing exports. While the sector undertakes very limited product innovation locally, it remains a key role player and global leader in vehicle manufacturing. Most of the sector is owned by multinational corporations, incorporating South Africa into the global automotive market (Wildschut and Meyer 2019, 35). The automotive assembly sector receives significant support from the state through the Automotive Production and Development Programme which, in 2013, replaced the Motor Industry Development Programme. The industry employs 112 000 workers, but the South African Automotive Masterplan (SAAM) projects that the industry could employ 224 000 workers by 2035 if a 60 per cent productivity level increase is achieved (SAAM 2018, 20).

This section discusses three aspects of the production process that are related to skills and workplace restructuring. These are intended to illustrate the nature of changes that occur in highly technologically integrated plants, resulting in uneven consequences for workers.

Impact of technological changes and work restructuring on skills development

Technical innovation is inherently contradictory in nature. On the one hand, it is progressive because it increases productivity and takes society to new levels of development. At the same time, however, it is disruptive in that it leads to higher unemployment by replacing existing workers. The auto industry is at the cutting edge of this technological development. A former Numsa leader describes the extent of technological changes he has seen in automotive assembly plants around the world:

> I went to a GM [General Motors] plant in Oshawa [Ontario, Canada]; they are doing more cars now. Every 58 seconds you will get a car coming out. At the time that plant was producing more cars per annum than South Africa's seven plants. It will tell you the body of the car, the robots are running around these workers and it doesn't make any mistake; when that car comes up, down with six, when that car comes down, this robot knows which; there are the five robots there roaming, the rightful robot will run and that car is on the move as it goes to the right seats and the right colour then come down. The worker sits there and mark this and the other guy goes to check the seat. (Former Numsa leader 2, interview, 2012)

Viewed as a whole, the usage of technology in production has intensified and has had negative consequences for employment numbers, especially in the assembly segments of automotive plants. A worker in one of the plants argued that it makes no difference that some workers have degrees and diplomas because the machines are already programmed to do the work and therefore matric-level education is sufficient.

> Someone with a matric should be able to survive in our workplace. It does not make much of a difference that some people have diplomas. Machine has been programmed to work in a certain way. In Japan plants the robot can fit the door and measure the gaps; it means less worries about quality. (Anonymous 4, interview, 2013)

A Numsa shop steward stated that the increase in the deployment of technology, specifically in the body shop, had resulted in a significant shedding of jobs over a five-year period (between 2008 and 2013). This is the effect of so called 'line rebalancing', which is a lean production philosophy that is based on cost reduction and job rotation. Ultimately, even workers with skills are affected:

> Automation is flooding the sector and jobs are being shed. In [the] body shop, currently 100 people work there, while five years ago there were 500 or so workers. This term *line rebalancing* is lean manufacturing ... more production with fewer workers. In [the] US and Germany, it has been fought but cannot be avoided. Many members are affected negatively health-wise. (Anonymous 2, interview, 2013)

The impact of work restructuring because of technological changes is mainly on the reduction of costs through head-count reduction. The technology enhances output through advanced production methods and appropriates into technology the cognitive ability to problem-solve. So, when some workers view the introduction of robots with trepidation, they are responding to a concrete situation based on their observation of the reduction of staff in their environment.

With the advent and promotion of the so-called Fourth Industrial Revolution under capitalist conditions, the unions would do well to heed the questions posed by Phindile Kunene and Simone Cupido:

> Should unions bargain over the pace and process of introduction and use sector agreements more consciously to shape this "Fourth Industrial Revolution"? Can unions use this as a platform to build alliances beyond the shop floor? Have unions in South Africa been reactive or proactive in dealing with technology? Is there room for resistance or is the outcome a foregone conclusion? These questions do not only shift the discourse from one led by the global economic and political elite – the "Davos class" and its technicist narrative – they also present possibilities to imagine strategies for labour in the age of intensified automation (Kunene and Cupido 2019, 42)

Management's attitudes to training

Some workers drew a distinction between the attitudes of production-level management and senior management up to boardroom level. Clearly companies should see training as an investment in staff development for their own productivity, but also for the future well-being of the individual workers beyond the workplace. However, training remains among the major costs that are reduced when companies undergo restructuring or cost reductions. The cost factor is often stated as a big problem when it comes to pursuing apprenticeships instead of learnerships. Citing an example from the automotive industry, one training manager stated:

> Skills are a bit of a difficult issue or dilemma in the sense that employers are expected to train people due to the requirements and scarcity. But the problem is, funding is insufficient because employers do not have the resources to train those people, particularly the youth. Learnerships, I have doubts, but we need more apprenticeships, but they are more expensive.

> Problem is that employers are expected to take a person full time for an apprenticeship programme, sometimes about four years, in which some even drop out. The other problem is that some learners are doing skills development for the sake of a stipend. Some are not really interested in these programmes. The yearly cycle of a learnership is also a problem because there is not sufficient time for "hands on" learning for the students. The learnership is also more theoretical and very classroom based; it's not the 30/70 per cent split that is on the legislation. (Auto sector training executive, interview, 2013)

At the core of the negative characterisation of managements' attitude to training is the division of labour and who controls work:

> What is new and distinctive about this detailed division of labour is not the breaking down of a production process into its component parts, but who controls the organisation of work. Earlier generations of craft workers had divided work up, but they had still controlled the work. (Foley 1999, 190)

One training supervisor defined the problem as that of a 'delink' between management and training:

> There is maybe a delink between training and management because the management of this company – they see training as nothing, as not important if I must put it that way, specifically at the management level in the production. But at the highest level, obviously they must comply with what the law [says] they need to do there, and there they are supportive because they are issuing out the company's funds, even if they are reclaiming from the Sector Education and Training Authority [Seta]. (Anonymous 1, interview, 2013)

Management's pressure to reach targets and performance goals invariably affects time allocated for training. This is not uncommon in many places, as meeting targets through efficiencies and optimisation is central to the overall output of companies against which managers are measured, resulting in the phenomenon of management by stress. Franco Barchiesi (1998) profoundly argues that the introduction of methods of flexible manufacturing in the South African automobile industry shows that the implementation of 'lean production' cannot be mechanically derived from any 'model' but is instead shaped by local contingencies, internal unevenness, contradictions, and contestation. These principally revolve around the meanings and boundaries of worker 'involvement' and 'commitment' to production, which are regarded as crucial in managerial strategies. In particular, the meanings attached by workers to changing productive configurations are in response to a multiplicity of determinants of the regulatory ideas that articulate their subjectivity, be they linked to the search for security and stability, the maintenance of pride and autonomy on the job, or wage levels compatible with the survival of the family (Barchiesi 1998, 129).

The logistics revolution

Edna Bonacich and Jake Wilson (2008) give prominence to the term 'logistics revolution'. They note that the logistics revolution has 'arisen in response to a chronic problem of the capitalist system, namely, the disjuncture between production and distribution, or supply and demand' (Bonacich and Wilson 2008, 4). The basis of the logistics revolution can be found in the changing balance of power between manufacturers and retailers, and the associated shift from 'push' to 'pull' production. This is driven mainly by specific customer demands which require specialisation rather than 'massification'. Carlotta Benvegnù and colleagues (2019) define logistics as not only a matter of the circulation of commodities but also of production of spatiality, contributing to the transformation of geographies and influencing a wide range of different fields: from the planning of urban spaces to the mobility regimes governing migration, passing through multiple transnational assemblages of workers.

The implications of the logistics revolution for workers in production and skills development is significant. This is especially so given that the balance of power that rests with producers in a pull model of logistics management eventually has an impact on the structure of assembly in the plant, thereby also increasing the 'flexibilisation' discourse. Most auto assemblers use the Japanese model of *kanban* for materials sourcing, both internally and externally. They model their entire logistics and distribution value chain through just-in-time delivery, which is a central feature of lean production. According to a human resources executive in the auto sector:

> There is a level of specialisation in the organisation. Even if you have an engineering degree you will only use it in focused areas of your work. Logistics has also become more of a science than what it used to be. Efficiencies and the entire value chain system is driven now by the availability of materials. (Auto sector human resources executive, interview, 2013)

Lean production is strongly underpinned by a philosophy of elimination of waste and cost reduction. One training supervisor characterises the just-in-time system in the following way:

> By just-in-time they mean that the parts must arrive by the time we need them, because if you have many parts lying around the company which we would use next year, they might be damaged and then it's more cost. We cannot use them any more, and then they need again the storage to store them, and then to have the storage you need people to manage that store, so just-in-time. We find that maybe it's cost-saving because immediately if the part is from the harbour or whatever it goes straight to the line, from the container straight to the line, immediately. [If] it delays, obviously the car will go out incomplete from the line. (Anonymous 3, interview, 2013)

Logistics controlling, then, has a direct influence on the nature of training for workers. What we see emerging is a direct link between production control and materials handling. The point is that production control rests largely with warehousing and logistics, an issue that is usually not accounted for in research on skills. It is taken for granted that production operates almost on its own or in isolation from warehousing and logistics. The actual training is related to the specifics of warehouse management and logistics. Researchers doing work on the logistics revolution have pointed out that the logistics revolution has brought with it lower wages and poor working conditions, particularly through 'containerisation' and warehouse/distribution centres that are growing rapidly (Bonacich and Wilson 2008; Mashilo 2010). The creation of warehouse parks and automotive clusters characterises the ways in which the state seeks to attract investors by essentially lowering cost structures for those investors. These trends in structuring production, together with restructuring the labour process, have shaped the nature of skills developed in the context of increased control by logistics and engineering specialists.

TRADE UNION RESPONSES

The period from the early 1990s can be characterised as the height of trade union involvement on the discourse of skills development. In contrast, the period since the passage of the Skills Development Act of 1998 saw a decline in Numsa's intellectualisation of the skills question. This resulted in a 'lull' period till 2009 when Cosatu, realising that the skills issue had been overlooked for more than a decade, decided to convene a national conference on education and training. The multiplicity of state institutions (like Setas) had resulted in a bureaucratisation of the trade unions' approach to the skills development issue. The expansion of bureaucratic responsibilities of trade unions meant that a lot of time was allocated to the finer details of the establishment of institutions. This resulted in a declining emphasis on shop-floor issues of activism. As one former Numsa leader stated:

> Setting up the SETAs took up a lot of time, and if you have a limited amount of time should comrades be focusing on these bureaucratic structures or focus more on activism? A lot of time was spent on grant funding criteria and bureaucracy. There was also a lot of unspent funds. Then we ended up with a very complicated system. At the time this was also about the destruction of the artisan system. The argument was that to have the progression to be an artisan was important. Interesting enough, artisanship was seen to be elitist. Learnerships were more flexible; the critique of learnerships was that [they were] more beneficial to capital and would be a way of underpaying workers because artisans were expensive. If you go for learnerships, you would only pay people for the skills that they have. (Former Numsa leader 1, interview, 2014)

The artisan system is a cornerstone of the skills system. An artisan qualification is seen as the height of skill and is associated with higher remuneration. The learnerships that were introduced were not only flexible but were able to increase the number of youth accessing workplaces, albeit in a system that had less status than artisanship. The learnership system is seen as having undermined the artisanal system, and to have contributed to the weakening of artisanal training. Learnerships remain popular because the model of delivery is quicker. The programme takes only one year, provides a National Qualifications Framework level 5 certificate at completion, and attracts both employed and unemployed youth between ages 18 and 35.

Cosatu, in its self-evaluation of its role in skills development, makes a critical point:

> While many research studies have been concluded, particularly around the performance and functioning of SETAs, as Cosatu we have never concluded a proper research study on our engagement in the new skills dispensation – despite this largely being an area that we fought vigorously to influence. (Cosatu 2009, 22)

The challenge of the unions is to build adequate capacity to respond to 'production politics' in a manner that is proactive and links to the aspirations of workers on the ground. In his study of technological changes at ArcellorMittal in Vanderbijlpark, Hlatshwayo (2014, 123) found that the unions lacked capacity to engage effectively in the processes of restructuring. He maintains that the national weaknesses of the labour movement were replicated at the plant level where the union reacted to technological change, lean production and privatisation only after they had been introduced by management (Hlatshwayo 2014, 124).

There is a sign of a resurgence of focus by Cosatu on the question of skills at a systemic level, especially in relation to financing, which is a critical component of the institutional delivery mechanisms of skills development in South Africa. Nhlapho states:

> Financing is a particularly problematic aspect of the skills system. Firstly, 1 per cent[2] is inadequate to properly address the major socio-economic and inequality issues confronting South Africa. Secondly, whilst state-owned enterprises, local government and other public entities do pay levies, national and provincial government departments are not part of the levy system. This both lowers the total pot but also removes the experience in government of actual implementation reducing competence to manage the skills development system. This needs to change. We need to stand firm as labour that the skills levy needs to increase from 1 per cent to 4 per cent. (Nhlapho 2019, 32)

Numerous reports and studies have found that Cosatu and its affiliates need to build research capacity and engage with new challenges of the changing workplace environment (Webster et al. 2009; Buhlungu 2010; Hlatshwayo and Buhlungu 2016).

CONCLUSION

This chapter has traced the skills debate within the unions, signalling the extensive nature of internal contestations that shaped their ultimate position. The chapter has shown how skills discourses are deeply influenced by the global balance of forces. It has also shown that the skills issue has been strongly contested within the unions, based on ideological orientations of various strands of intellectuals within the labour movement who have over time been able to gain the support of union leaders for positions on the skills debate. The challenge for Cosatu is to revisit its vision for education and training and to look at articulating ideas that translate participation in structures like Setas – which have deep financial resources – to make meaningful changes for workers and to enhance their skills.

Labour studies can learn from this chapter how complex the question of skills is in a society like South Africa, which is characterised by the history of racialised inequalities that manifest in the labour market. Under the current policy dispensation of the democratic government, the skills question has shifted from a narrow focus on artisanal training to a wider conception and delivery through learnership programmes which cover a wider range of occupational categories. Labour studies in the future can theorise these issues further within the ongoing crises of the global capitalist economy and the nature of the state's involvement in transforming the skills development system.

NOTES

1   I borrow this definition from Webster and Von Holdt's (2005) distinction between *earning a living* and *making a living*. They argue that informal work places the emphasis on those who are making a living – the self-employed – as well as engaging in unpaid activities such as childcare and subsistence farming.

2   The Skills Development Act, No. 97 of 1998 and the Skills Development Levies Act, No. 9 of 1999 of South Africa were introduced as part of government's human resources development strategy. These pieces of legislation led to the creation of the Seta system. The current system of Setas is shaped by a levy payment by employers in the amount of 1 per cent of payroll (for companies exceeding R500 000 per annum on their payroll), and is governed through a co-determinist process involving business, labour and the state. The Setas are central to the South African model of skills development; however, in their current institutional character Setas play more of a regulatory role than an actual training role. The statutory framework together with institutional practices have resulted in a bureaucratic instrumentalism.

REFERENCES

Adler, Paul. 2004. 'Skill Trends under Capitalism and the Socialisation of Production'. In *The Skills that Matter*, edited by Chris Warhurst, Irene Grugulis and Ewart Keep, 242–260. London: Palgrave Macmillan.

Akoojee, Salim. 2012. 'Skills for Inclusive Growth in South Africa: Promising Tides amidst Perilous Waters'. *International Journal of Education Development* 32 (5): 674–685.

Barchiesi, Franco. 1998. 'Restructuring, Flexibility, and the Politics of Workplace Subjectivity: A Worker Inquiry in the South African Car Industry'. *Rethinking Marxism* 10 (5): 105–153.

Benvegnù, Carlotta, Niccolò Cuppini, Mattia Frapporti, Floriano Milesi and Maurilio Pirone. 2019. Logistical Gazes: Introduction to a Special Issue of Work Organisation, Labour and Globalisation. *Work Organisation, Labour & Globalisation* 13 (1): 9–14.

Bonacich, Edna and Jake Wilson. 2008. *Getting the Goods: Ports, Labour, and the Logistics Revolution*. Ithaca, NY: Cornell University Press.

Braverman, Harry. 1974. *Labour and Monopoly Capital: The Degradation of Work in the Twentieth Century*. New York: Monthly Review Press.

Brown, Phillip, Hugh Lauder and David Ashton. 2011. *The Global Auction: The Broken Promises of Education, Jobs, and Incomes*. Oxford: Oxford University Press.

Buhlungu, Sakhela. 2010. *A Paradox of Victory: Cosatu and the Democratic Transformation in South Africa*. Pietermaritzburg: University of KwaZulu-Natal Press.

Burawoy, Michael. 1985. *The Politics of Production*. London: Verso.

Collins, Randall. 2013. 'The End of Middle-class Work: No More Escapes'. In *Does Capitalism Have a Future?* edited by Immanuel Wallerstein, Randall Collins, Michael Mann, Georgi Derluguian and Craig Calhoun, 1–35. Oxford: Oxford University Press.

Congress of South African Trade Unions (Cosatu). 2009. 'Forward to Education and Skills Development for Working Class Power!' Paper presented at the Cosatu Education and Skills Conference, 1 July 2009, Johannesburg.

Edwards, Richard. 1979. *Contested Terrain: The Transformation of the Workplace in the Twentieth Century*. London: Heinemann.

Foley, Griff. 1999. 'Back to Basics: A Political Economy of Workplace Changes and Learning'. *Studies in the Education of Adults* 31 (2): 181–196.

Hlatshwayo, Mondli. 2013. 'A Sociological Analysis of Trade Union Responses to Technological Changes at the ArcellorMittal Vanderbijlpark Plant, 1989–2011'. PhD diss., University of Johannesburg.

Hlatshwayo, Mondli. 2014. 'Neo-liberal Restructuring and the Fate of South Africa's Labour Unions: A Case Study'. In *The New South Africa at Twenty: Critical Perspectives*, edited by Peter Vale and Estelle H. Prinsloo, 115–139. Pietermaritzburg: University of KwaZulu-Natal Press.

Hlatshwayo, Mondli and Sakhela Buhlungu. 2016. 'Work Reorganization and Technological Change: Limits of Trade Union Strategy and Action at ArcelorMittal, Vanderbijlpark'. *African Sociological Review* 20 (2): 125–152.

Kodisang, Elijah. 2018. 'The Influence of the Canadian Auto Workers Union in Debates on the South African Qualifications Framework'. Masters diss., University of the Witwatersrand.

Kraak, Andre. 2008. 'Incoherence in the South African Labour Market for Intermediary Skills'. *Journal for Education and Work* 21 (3): 197–215.

Kraak, Gerald. 1993. *Breaking the Chains: Labour in South Africa in the 1970s and 1980s*. London: Pluto Press.

Kruss, Glenda and Angelique Wildschut. 2019. 'The Need for New Kinds of Research'. In *Skills for the Future: New Research Perspectives*, edited by Glenda Kruss, Angelique Wildschut and Il-haam Petersen, 3–11. Cape Town: HSRC Press.

Kunene, Phindile and Simone Cupido. 2019. 'The "Davos Class" and the Fourth Industrial Revolution: A Technicist and Classless View of the New Capitalism'. *South African Labour Bulletin* 43 (1): 40–42.

Littler, Craig. 1982. *The Development of the Labour Process in Capitalist Societies: A Comparative Analysis of Work Organization in Britain, the USA and Japan*. London: Heinemann.

Lundall, Paul. 2017. 'Co-ordination of Enterprise Skill Formation: A Sociological and Historical Narrative of Professional, Market and State Initiatives in South Africa'. PhD diss., University of Cape Town.

Marx, Karl. [1867] 1976. *Capital: A Critique of Political Economy - Volume One*. London: Penguin Books.

Mashilo, Alex M. 2010. 'Changes in Work and Production Organization in the Automotive Industry Value Chain: An Evaluation of the Responses by Labour in South Africa'. Masters diss., University of the Witwatersrand.

Nhlapho, Bhabhali Ka Maphikela. 2019. 'Transition in Skills Development Policy in South Africa: A Worker's Perspective'. *South African Labour Bulletin* 43 (1): 30–33.

Schwab, Klaus. 2016. *The Fourth Industrial Revolution*. Geneva: World Economic Forum.

South African Automotive Masterplan (SAAM). 2018. 'Geared for Growth – South Africa's Automotive Industry Masterplan to 2035: A Report of the South African Automotive Masterplan Project'. Pretoria: Department of Trade and Industry.

Warhurst, Chris, Ian Grugulis and Ewart Keep, eds. 2004. *The Skills that Matter*. London: Palgrave Macmillan.

Webster, Edward. 1985. *Cast in a Racial Mould: Labour Process and Trade Unionism in the Foundries*. Johannesburg: Ravan Press.

Webster, Edward and Jean Leger. 1992. 'Reconceptualising Skill Formation in South Africa'. *Perspectives in Education* 13 (2): 53–68.

Webster, Edward, Alex Mashilo, Themba Masondo and Christine Bischoff. 2009. 'Changes in Production Systems and Work Methods'. In *A Report on Work Restructuring in the Auto and Components Sector: The Opportunities, Benefits, Dilemmas, and Opportunities facing Numsa*, edited by Numsa, FES, SWOP and Ditsela Research. Johannesburg: Numsa.

Webster, Edward and Karl von Holdt, eds. 2005. *Beyond the Apartheid Workplace: Studies in Transition*. Pietermaritzburg: University of KwaZulu-Natal Press.

Wildschut, Angelique and Tamlynne Meyer. 2019. 'Skills Planning for South Africa: Getting the Questions Right'. In *Skills for the Future: New Research Perspectives*. edited by Glenda Kruss, Angelique Wildschut and Il-haam Petersen, 32–47. Cape Town: HSRC Press.

INTERVIEWS

Numsa

Former Numsa leader 1. 2014. Education officer, Johannesburg, 16 July 2014. Audio 39.36.
Former Numsa leader 2. 2013. Education and training, Johannesburg, 10 May 2013. Audio 72.09.

Workers: Pretoria-based automotive assembly plant

Anonymous 1. 2013. Trainer, Pretoria, 23 May 2013. Audio 25.50.
Anonymous 2. 2013. Trainer, Pretoria, Trim & Body, 23 May 2013. Audio 28.40.
Anonymous 3. 2013. Trainer, Pretoria, 23 May 2013. Audio 27.11.
Anonymous 4. 2013. Trainer, Pretoria, 23 May 2013. Audio 18.06.

Human resources executives

Auto sector training executive. 2013. Pretoria, 21 June 2013. Audio 38.13.
Auto sector human resources executive, 2013. Johannesburg, August 2013. Audio 48.24.

6

Labour Process, Hegemony and Technology: 'Sanitised Workplace Orders' at Two South African Mines

John Mashayamombe

INTRODUCTION

The Minerals Council of South Africa (MCSA; formerly the Chamber of Mines) and its members, in what they describe as a drive to improve health and safety levels, increase productivity and remain competitive, have been advocating for the modernisation of mines (MHSC 2011; MCSA 2018a). They present a rosy picture of how the 'digitisation' and 'modernisation' of mines will lead to the 'safe', 'efficient', 'cost-effective' and 'sustainable' extraction of minerals. In their narrative, this is linked to the development of employees' skills, health and quality of life. Also, such 'smart mines' will see to the conservation of natural resources, and the preservation and restoration of the environment. They will also contribute to the development of local and labour-sending communities, recognising that metals and minerals are valuable, useful and necessary for transformation and growth as key imperatives of the mining industry and the nation (MCSA 2018a: 1). This drive, the narrative continues, is inspired by the fact that production costs have spiralled as mines get deeper, older and prone to seismic events, while unstable commodity prices and the desire for global competitiveness have contributed to the desire to prolong the life of mines (MCSA 2018a; see also Durrant-Whyte et al. 2015; Singh 2017).

Bridget Kenny and Edward Webster (2021, 13) argue that 'concerns around work reorganisation and control [in South African labour studies] have been and continue to be integrated with issues of collective identity and politics in ways that foreground an analysis of the changing dynamics of capitalist relations in space and time.' They write that there has been a return to research on the labour process in South African labour studies, and also in the context of the way in which new technologies reshape work and workplace regimes. In this chapter, I document the findings of a comparative ethnographic study of two mines as a contribution to this 'return to the labour process'. Both mines were constructed in the post-apartheid era: Zenith is an open-cast iron ore mine in the Northern Cape and Thapelo is an underground coal mine in Mpumalanga. (The names of both mines are pseudonyms.) The data was collected through participant observation, in-depth interviews, official documents and general literature between 2015 and 2018.

These new mines seem more successful at introducing new production technology than older, deep-level mines in South Africa that continue to struggle to increase mechanisation and automation for various reasons. Nevertheless, the chapter tries to navigate between the grandiose claims made by mining companies about new technology (the so-called Fourth Industrial Revolution, sometimes referred to as 4.0 or 4IR) in production and the actual way this plays out in practice. I use the concept 'sanitised workplace orders' to describe the outcome of mining companies that rely on new mining operations: these new approaches are mechanically and technologically intensive; deploy new recruitment strategies with an emphasis on education, training and diversity; utilise what mines call 'smart business operating models'; and adopt new approaches to housing, travel financing and community development (Mashayamombe 2018). These attempts at 'sanitising' mining workplaces are a response to the toxic legacy of mining during the colonial and apartheid era and its associated problems. The main focus of this chapter is on the use of technology in the workplace.

This chapter deals with two disruptions to existing workplace orders. The first relates to attempts by mining companies to move away from the way in which mines were set up under colonialism and apartheid. Second, it examines how technology is used in a very conscious way to establish new labour processes and forms of workplace surveillance. The ethnographic nature of the study allowed me to closely examine how mines implemented new technology and mechanisation in the name of 'digitisation' and 'modernisation', as well as improvements in production levels and health and safety. Of course, workers always challenge managerial attempts to control the labour process, and workplace regimes are constituted as contested terrains. Nevertheless, this resistance comes from workers directly as their trade unions are largely absent when it comes to matters of how technology affects a re-constituted post-apartheid workplace order. Individual resistance tends to be sporadic and disruptive in nature, rather than strategic and directed at long-term collective goals. As such, mining companies succeed to some extent in setting up a new hegemony, legitimated on the premise of the promise of 'smart mines', 'intelligent mines' and the benefits of the Fourth Industrial Revolution.

LABOUR PROCESS, HEGEMONY AND MINING TECHNOLOGY

Before I present the findings of this study, this section briefly discusses the theoretical framework and its historical context. Labour process theory views work organisation as a conflict-ridden terrain where workplace regimes are the outcomes of struggles between management and workers for control over production. The use of technology in the workplace has always been part of this contestation, from attempts to deskill craft work (Braverman 1974) through to the use of web-based platforms to structure service work in the gig economy (Gandini 2019). This is important given the potentially disruptive nature of new technologies and innovations and their potential impact on labour and the broader society. The labour process of technology, advocated by Richard Hall (2010), is an attempt to reinvigorate labour process theory to remain relevant and revive the fragmented social study of technology. Hall (2010) suggests that the social study of technology is fragmented, yet technology is central to the labour process, given the ways in which it is deployed by management to control production and organise work (see also Thompson and Harley 2007). Importantly, technological change has potential political impacts because it can affect material outcomes for workers in terms of their skills level, and how they experience work and the labour market, as well as various labour reactions to this (Hall 2010). In light of this, labour process of technology is central to understanding technology in the workplace because it assists in the examination of the making of characteristics of technological artefacts and investigations on the material implications of technological change in the contemporary workplace.

Struggles over technology have always been at the heart of control of mining labour processes. These struggles are circumscribed by geological factors. For over 130 years gold and other minerals have directly and indirectly shaped South Africa's economy and socio-political organisation (Singh 2017). They contributed to the institutionalisation of the oscillating migrant labour system, with its single-sex compounds and racially despotic forms of control in the workplace. Race, class, ethnic and gender identities intersected in these often violent work and residential spaces, with the conflict between mostly black workers and white supervisors being described as contending racialised masculinities (Breckenridge 1998; see also Benya's chapter in this volume). The mining operations established during the colonial and apartheid periods were labour-intensive, especially in gold, chrome and platinum group metals (Stewart 2015; MCSA 2018a). With the exception of coal mines and other mineral extractions with shallow and soft ore bodies, in which mechanisation was deployed in the early 1920s, not many significant strides have been attained at narrow-reef metalliferous underground rock faces (Stewart 2015; Singh 2017). Historical evidence shows that mechanical and technological advances on the rock face of ultra-deep, low-grade and narrow ore bodies of South African gold, and even the shallow but hard rock platinum mines, has been minimal (Stewart 2013, 119).

This is not to suggest that there have not been significant mechanical and technological innovations, such as trackless technologies, hauling, roof bolting and drilling. In fact, breakthroughs have been achieved in the few wider reefs of gold and platinum mines, but the hand-held drilling machine and blasting remain dominant (Egerton 2004; Musingwini and Minnitt 2008; Stewart 2013, 2015; Singh 2017). Furthermore, work has been reorganised away from the racial despotism characteristic of apartheid mines towards smaller teams that are increasingly motivated by production bonuses (Phakathi 2002). Intensive implementation of mechanisation and technology in gold, platinum and chrome underground mines remains an engineering and geological challenge, due to increasing depths of narrow and uneven ore reserves, uneven surfaces, high temperatures, humidity and general resistance by organised labour (Stewart 2013, 2015; Singh 2017; MCSA 2018b; Marwala 2020; see also Hlatshwayo in this volume).

The fact that deep-level mining required such large numbers of workers also had implications for the geography of mining and mining towns. As mentioned, male migrants who worked in labour-intensive mines were housed in single-sex compounds, with their families remaining in rural parts of South Africa and the rest of the sub-continent. This system came under pressure with the closure of many of these compounds in the post-apartheid era; some were converted into family units or more decent singles quarters. I mention this because, when conducting my fieldwork, I became aware of the extent to which mining companies attempt to construct a new kind of local landscape as part of an attempt to create mines that can move beyond apartheid spatial planning. So, setting up post-apartheid mines has involved the use of new technology in the workplace in order to move beyond a low-skill, labour-intensive labour market, but also setting up new communities, depending on local circumstances. It is this new workplace order, based on a combination of new technology and a different kind of internal labour market, as well as new mining communities, that add up to what I call a 'sanitised workplace order'. I limit my analysis to workplace dynamics in this chapter, but want to note this important component related to mining landscapes more broadly.

MINING, NEW TECHNOLOGY AND WORKPLACE ORDERS

South African mining companies have been more successful in mechanising mining in open-cast operations than in deep-level mining. It is interesting to note that Anglo American Platinum, historically one of South Africa's largest platinum mining companies, decided to divest from all their deep-level operations after the Marikana massacre and the strike that followed. They only maintained a presence at their Mogalakwena open-cast platinum mine near Mokopane. The company's approach suggests a preference for more capital-intensive operations. In South Africa, old and new coal mines, iron ore mines and some platinum mines have been designed with the challenges at old mines in mind. The introduction of continuous mining in underground coal mines in South Africa in the late 1950s was a game changer, as it eliminated drilling and blasting (Inch et al. 1980; Edgecombe and Guest 1986; Alexander 2001). Coal mines were the first to introduce mechanisation both on the surface and underground due to thick and shallow coal seams (Alexander 2001). The same can be said of open-cast mines extracting iron ore and platinum. New mines and old open-cast mines have been harnessing the latest mechanical and technological changes in real time to improve health and safety in the areas of ventilation, fatigue management, vehicle collision, dust control, anti-slippery mechanisms, efficient and effective production through latest trackless technologies and introduction of conveyor belts (Gumede 2018). In short, all surface mining is mechanised to semi-automated, and keeps on evolving due to new innovations.

The two mines where I did my fieldwork are both owned by a big multinational mining company and in both cases attempts had been made to construct mines that move away from the apartheid model. Zenith is an open-cast iron ore mine that was established in 2008 and started operations in 2011. It extracts ore by means of massive shovel and truck equipment with a workforce just above 1 000. The same applies to Thapelo colliery, which was established in 2008 and started operations in 2009. It had a total workforce of just under 800 at the time of fieldwork. Thapelo combines an underground and open-cast mine. However, the open-cast operations are located 20 kilometres away from the underground operations. The company refers to its operations as 'modern' and examples of what a 'future smart mine' would look like. The two mines are mechanised to a large degree, and are technology-intensive. The design, systems and processes that inform production at the two mines have been enabled by relatively shallow ore bodies; their coal seams and iron ore deposits are more accessible in comparison to gold ore reefs on the Witwatersrand basin, and platinum and chrome's Bushveld Igneous Complex that require deep shafts (Capps 2015; Stewart 2015). This does suggest that mineral extraction at these two mines is easy. However, extraction remains complex and intersects with different types of hazards. The two mines deploy the modern bulk mining approach typical of mining conglomerates to extract minerals on a massive scale, exhaust them and move to the next site as part of capital's accumulation process.

The mining method selected by mining operations plays a significant role in the optimisation of mineral reserve extraction. The Zenith iron ore mine uses the conventional open-cast mining method that involves drilling, blasting, shovel and truck loading, and hauling of waste and ore. Some machines and trucks are operated by single operators, while others have assistants. After drilling and blasting, waste is loaded by massive shovels and excavators into dump trucks and hauled to dump sites. A similar process takes place with the actual iron ore, but it is hauled to the plant where the ore undergoes primary, secondary and tertiary crushing. The crushed ore goes through scalping and screening and is then sent to a stockpile yard. The mine has a stacker-reclaiming facility where ore is processed and blended to create customer-specific grade requirements. The graded ore is loaded into goods-train wagons and freighted for export. These processes are highly automated and use intensive technology to optimise machine and labour performance to achieve high-quality production output. Given the fact that truck haulage represents the highest cost item (50–60 per cent) of surface mining operations, mining companies deploy shovel and truck operation models and optimisation approaches on allocation and dispatching of trucks to improve performance and reduce costs (Mashayamombe 2018). The company's description of its operations refers to modelling, investment in research on simulation through virtual reality and artificial intelligence, or digitisation of the specific mining operation. The company sponsored the construction of a virtual reality centre (including a dome-like theatre) at the University of Pretoria, which is used for mine design and training (Ercelebi and Bascetin 2009; Jacobs and Webber-Youngman 2017). It is in these production processes and training opportunities that various elements of digitisation are taking shape.

Thapelo colliery's underground operations deploy board and pillar mining using a Continuous Miner (CM) (Segopolo 2015). As a technology, the CM is called the 'holy grail' in the industry. It is installed with methane, water flow and water pressure sensors for safety and accuracy. These sensors are digitally synchronised and are meant to assist humans in the detection of possible fall of ground, presence of methane or water table. In a section, the CM is operated by a single operator using a remote control standing next to the CM at the coal face as it cuts coal following a set cutting sequence. The CM cuts the coal and loads it into shuttle cars, which may be four per section and operated by four operators. Shuttle cars haul the coal following set tramming routes and dump it onto a feeder breaker that crushes coal into smaller lumps; it is then hoisted to the surface through an incline conveyor belt (Mashayamombe 2018). On the surface, the belt deposits the coal into surface silos. From these silos, the coal product goes through various crushing stages and is off-loaded onto an overland conveyor belt that transports it to a coal washing plant 20 kilometres away from the colliery. At the washing plant, the coal is further processed, washed and loaded into goods train wagons and freighted to a terminal bay, from where it is shipped to various destinations (Mashayamombe 2018).

At both the mines, management uses the language of 'modernisation' and digitisation' to describe their approach. They refer to adopting business operating models that are operation-specific. There is also enthusiasm for the Fourth Industrial Revolution and the adoption of efficient operating models that are compatible with it. This, it is argued, is key to global competitiveness, improved health and safety levels, and sustainable production (Gumede 2018; Marwala 2018; Viljoen 2018). The way in which technology is used also has social implications, as argued by the labour process theory of technology. Zenith and Thapelo mines deploy operating models that integrate production systems, machines, equipment and truck optimisation, health and safety systems and labour relations. This is done in order to improve 'uptime, speed and yield'.

From a labour perspective, the mines recruit a young, educated and diverse workforce. A National Senior Certificate (Grade 12) or high school exit certificate is a minimum requirement for entry-level jobs at the two mining operations. This is a shift from the recruitment tradition at gold, platinum and iron ore mines where physical strength and home-boy networks played an important role in labour recruitment regimes. Also, the two mines deliberately hire a young and diverse workforce that represents the demographics of the country in an attempt to address historical imbalances generally visible at the old mines (Tshoaedi et al. 2017; Mashayamombe 2018). Many of these young workers buy into the idea of 'smart mines' and eagerly adopt some of the technologies. They are trained to master the business operating models, but have some leverage to negotiate the terms and conditions of work. Therefore, what has emerged is a set of contestable and collaborative workplace relations. In the language of Burawoy (1979), this younger workforce is more amenable to the company's attempts to construct management hegemony around 'smart mines' (see also Mashayamombe 2018). This can be interpreted as a positive move given the fact that South Africa's mining industry comes from a past where black African workers were excluded from decision-making processes and were believed not to be thinkers, what Burawoy (1985) refers to as 'colonial despotism' and Von Holdt (2003) as the 'apartheid workplace regime'. However, the deliberate requirement for an educated, young and diverse workforce can be seen as an attempt to control labour by bringing it closer to decision-making processes. Also, technology and automation are tools deployed by management to monitor and control labour within the labour process, although workers have historically resisted this (Webster 1985; Hlatshwayo 2013).

Attempts to automate and use technological innovation in mining are also presented as an attempt to eliminate health and safety risks to mineworkers and to 'achieve zero harm' (MacFarlane 2001; MHSC 2011; MCSA 2016). Besides the achievement of operational effectiveness and increased lifespan of mines, 'technology through innovation on health and safety systems, equipment and machinery are seen as a panacea toward achievement of Zero Harm' (Mashayamombe 2018, 219; see also MCSA 2016). Open-cast mines are generally safer spaces to work than deep-level mines. This does not suggest that there are no hazards or accidents on open-cast mines. In South Africa as a whole, mining fatalities declined from 290 in the year 2000 to 87 in 2017 (Marwala 2018). In 2019 there were 50 fatalities, but this increased again to 74 in 2021 (Stoddard 2021). The approach to health and safety training is also couched in the language of the 4IR, as well as 'smart and intelligent mines'. As mentioned, mining companies have invested in virtual reality centres where simulations of surface and underground three-dimensional models have been developed for learning and training purposes. These simulations, augmented by other cutting-edge technologies, are helping mines to predict and manage mining spaces to improve health and safety in terms of rock falls, seismicity, water flooding and dust control. In the same vein, technological innovations have been harnessed on trackless mobile machines, anti-collision devices, braking systems and early warning systems on rock falls underground and slope failures in open pits (Mashayamombe 2018).

Health and safety improvements due to technological advancement for mineworkers are generally positive. But there is also a more ominous side to this, given South Africa's high rates of unemployment. The research and development being undertaken at different institutions on artificial intelligence and the like is also directed at developing robotics that can perform tasks currently undertaken by humans. In the long run, labour could be replaced by autonomous machines and robots, with the further risk of increased unemployment and declining support for their immediate and extended families (Zuo 2016; Gumede 2018). Thus, the role and impact of the so-called Fourth Industrial Revolution on the South African mining industry must be examined carefully and systematically, as new technological innovations could potentially lead to complete automation, especially in open-cast mines. The impact on mine production of the Covid-19 pandemic and particularly of the hard lockdown of 2020 increased the case for intensified mechanisation and automation in mining operations.

With regard to health and safety monitoring, the Zenith iron ore mine introduced a fatigue management system, a comprehensive approach that monitors operators' alertness and levels of fatigue while on duty. Operator fatigue within mining's shift systems is a major contributor to mine accidents and a concern for the industry (Schutte and Maldonado 2003). Zenith mine uses the Predictive Risk Intelligent Safety Module through alertness predictive tests (Mashayamombe 2018). Most of the trucks have cameras in front of the operator's seat that monitor the operator's eye movements. Once the operator's eyes start closing frequently, the system automatically alerts a medical officer at the fatigue centre, who then informs the supervisor on duty, who will instruct the concerned operator to take a 25-minute fatigue break. In the event that an operator refuses to take a fatigue break, their truck can be remotely switched off as a safety precaution and exercise of power.

In addition, through sophisticated facial recognition technologies and data management systems, health service providers have harnessed biotechnology and generated massive amounts of data on mineworkers related to their medical reports and history. On one level, this could be seen as positive, in that the health condition of mineworkers can be monitored closely and intervention applied where necessary, and also that records are easily available to different mining operations. ('Surveillance' often takes on a positive connotation in mining health and safety language, especially when referring to diseases such as silicosis and tuberculosis.) However, fatigue monitoring and its associated surveillance technologies provide management with unprecedented control over workers in their workstations, and the disciplinary means to stretch labour to its maximum. Also, fatigue monitoring generates large amounts of data about labour, which through digitisation can be shared with different actors; workers do not have control over this process. Data privacy remains an issue on which South African trade unions still have to fully develop policies.

143

Nevertheless, as both labour process theory and labour geography argues, managerial control is usually subjected to contestation from workers. When I was conducting my ethnographic fieldwork at the mine, some medical officials complained that some operators from the mining sections abuse the fatigue management system when they do not want to work. This strategy by operators shows that labour has agency and can deploy different strategies to resist technological monitoring and control by management. Some feigned fatigue and others would declare that they were tired without the system having picked it up, thereby undermining the accuracy of camera readings. Even this is a further field of contestation, with managers discussing how to refine artificial intelligence, big data capabilities and the latest technologies using various predictive logarithms as monitoring tools under the veil of health and safety improvement.

In addition to efforts to improve health and safety, mines have employed a number of other technological solutions to production challenges. First, information and communication systems are used more readily to design operations. At Thapelo colliery the business operating model runs according to a newly introduced Operational Informative Delivery (OID) platform, which provides real-time information to personnel on the surface about Continuous Miner and conveyor belt activities underground (Mashayamombe 2018). Monitors show real-time production targets, incline conveyor belt movement in hoisting coal to surface silos, quantities of coal passing through a set point to the surface, distances in metres cut by the CM, and the general performance of machinery and equipment underground per section; these monitors are installed in the offices of shift bosses, section managers, the production manager and the general manager (Mashayamombe 2018). The availability of such information in real time enables decision-making processes on the surface, where middle managers sit, to control and monitor the labour process. These 'latest technological systems and business models' are presented as part of 'smart and intelligent mines'. Of course, the OID platform also constitutes a revitalised method of monitoring and control of labour. Surveillance is increasing in the workplace, aided by breakthroughs in artificial intelligence, and this has serious consequences for labour and the broader society (Andersen 2020). Underground to surface communication is enhanced through a combination of radio and cell phone technology. In the same space, at that time at Thapelo production, bonuses and rewards for more hours of Zero Harm[1] are used together with technology to indirectly control labour and achieve high production (Mashayamombe 2018). Labour does respond positively, as the reward system is enticing. However, when unhappy, they use the same machines to express their dissatisfaction and unhappiness (Mashayamombe 2018). They slow down production by driving slowly and carrying out mechanised tasks at their own pace, which is easily picked up on the surface's OID. This draws the attention of decision-makers and forces them to attend to the workers' issues. Furthermore, I observed similar tactics at Zenith's mining operations, where operators individually slow down the speed and pace of haulage trucks, excavators, loaders and other equipment, and slow down production as individuals or collectively, depending on conditions and agreements (Mashayamombe 2018). Upon investigation, the hierarchy then becomes aware of labour's unhappiness and attempts to address the grievances. Most of these acts of agency, that seem sporadic and sometimes uncoordinated but effective, are carried out without trade union knowledge or approval, which is a paradox.

Furthermore, there has been a push to automate production, or to create remotely controlled equipment. Again, this is done in the name of improved health and safety, but it has the added advantage (for management) of reducing labour. During the fieldwork period Zenith mine introduced automated drilling machines and drones for surveying the pits (Brown 2017; Mashayamombe 2018). Traditionally, drilling at open-cast mines has been undertaken by drilling machines operated by a single operator and an assistant to help move and position the machine. The new remote-controlled drilling machines remove the operator from the vehicle to a cabin at a command centre away from the open pit. The idea behind automated drilling is to increase efficiency, to increase operating hours and drill rates, to reduce total drills required, and to reduce exposure and possibilities of injuries and fatalities (Mashayamombe 2018). Drilling operators now work from safe spaces rather than the mining area where there are significant environmental and human-made risks of potentially fatal hazards. The same can be observed with regard to the introduction of drones to survey the mining area. Drones fitted with a Geographic Information System and other metallurgical software survey large tracts of land within a short space of time and collect data that is then used by surveyors on the computers in their offices (Mashayamombe 2018). This also reduces exposure to environmental hazards and risks they cannot control.

TRADE UNIONS AND TECHNOLOGY

In the previous section I identified sporadic and unorganised resistance to surveillance by individual workers. According to Sokutu (2018), apart from threats of shutdown and strikes, trade unions did not have a tangible plan, or the research background, to confront mining capital on matters of new technology and work. My research in the two mines confirmed this. To be sure, trade unions' responses to the threat of automation, the impact of new production technology on their members and the possibility of this leading to a declining workforce in the mining industry have been lacklustre. When interviewed, an Association of Mineworkers and Construction Union official confirmed that the union did not have a policy position in terms of how to confront and address the threats and impact of new technologies on workers and the labour process. Solidarity's general secretary Gideon Du Plessis showed an awareness of the potential dangers of automation for employment levels. He pointed out that this process was slow in South African mining and acknowledged that retrenchments were inevitable but would in all probability happen through a process of natural attrition. An official from the National Union of Mineworkers (NUM) indicated that part of the challenge at new mines (or greenfield mines) was that organised labour was not involved in the decision-making over design and mining methods. The NUM official noted that unions were only consulted when the introduction of new machines resulted in changes to production shifts, as required by section 84 of the Labour Relations Act. Furthermore, the NUM official revealed that the union had established its own internal research institute, the Sam Tambani Research Institute, to examine the role and impact of 4IR on mining in South Africa and the ability of the country to 'catch up'. Also, the Congress of South African Trade Unions has, over time, increased its internal engagements with its affiliates on 4IR; however, no clear policy position and strategy has emerged. South African trade unions' research capacity is mostly directed at matters related to immediate collective bargaining; they do not have capacity to conduct in-depth research on production-related matters. NUM acknowledged that the labour movement was reactive rather than proactive on production-related matters, with specific reference to issues related to 4IR (Hlatshwayo and Buhlungu 2017; see also Ngcwangu in this volume).

CONCLUSION

The structuring of the South African mining workplace order has been disrupted by newly designed mines and labour processes, as well as the introduction of new technology in the workplace. Drawing on the cases of Zenith and Thapelo mines, I have shown how the idea of 'smart' and 'intelligent' mines, couched in the language of the Fourth Industrial Revolution, is used to construct new forms of managerial control. These 'sanitised workplace orders' are set up as a response to the 'contaminated' legacy of deep-level mining and its migrant labour system. A younger, more diverse workforce is employed, and a combination of technologies are used to physically remove workers from the actual point of production where remotely controlled machines increasingly excavate and load ore bodies. These operators work from clean spaces – some still located on the equipment, and others in control rooms – but their movements and performance are tightly monitored in the name of 'fatigue management' and as a means to improve health and safety. Some of these young workers resist attempts to tightly control the labour process by disruptive behaviour that undermines the logic of surveillance. However, trade unions as collective forms of representation are largely absent from the wage-effort bargain and dynamics of workplace control in so far as technology is concerned.

NOTE

1   Zero Harm is a safety concept, or a safety culture movement, premised on the notion that workplaces, workers and management can create safe working spaces without harm, injuries or fatalities. In the mining sector, in South Africa and elsewhere, it is measured by hours and is linked to safety bonuses in some mining houses.

REFERENCES

Alexander, Peter. 2001. 'Oscillating Migrants, Detribalised Families and Militancy: Mozambicans on Witbank Collieries, 1918–1927. *Journal of Southern African Studies* 27 (3): 505–525.

Andersen, Ross. 2020. 'The Panopticon is Already Here'. *The Atlantic*, September 2020. https://www.theatlantic.com/magazine/archive/2020/09/china-ai-surveillance/614197.

Braverman, Harry. 1974. *Labor and Monopoly Capital*. New York: Monthly Review Press.

Breckenridge, Keith. 1998. 'The Allure of Violence: Men, Race and Masculinity on the South African Goldmines, 1900–1950'. *Journal of Southern African Studies* 24 (4): 669–693.

Brown, Justin. 2017. 'Anglo Agrees to Sell 3 Coal Mines to BEE Consortium for R2bn'. *City Press*, 9 April 2017. https://www.news24.com/citypress/Business/anglo-agrees-to-sell-3-coal-mines-to-bee-consortium-for-r2bn-20170409.

Burawoy, Michael. 1979. *Manufacturing Consent: Changes in the Labor Process under Monopoly Capitalism*. Chicago, MI: University of Chicago Press.

Burawoy, Michael. 1985. *The Politics of Production: Factory Regimes under Capitalism and Socialism*. New York: Verso.

Capps, Gavin. 2015. 'Labour in the Time of Platinum'. *Review of African Political Economy* 42 (146): 497–507.

Durrant-Whyte, Hugh, Ryan Geraghty, Feran Pujol and Richard Sellschop. 2015. *How Digital Innovation Can Improve Mining Productivity*. http://www.mckinsey.com/industries/metals-and-mining/our-insights/how-digital-innovation-can-improve-mining-productivity. Accessed 6 February 2023.

Edgecombe, Ruth and Bill Guest.1986. 'Labour Conditions on the Natal Collieries: The Case of the Dundee Coal Company, 1908–1955'. Seminar paper, African Studies Institute, University of the Witwatersrand.

Egerton, Frank. 2004. 'Presidential Address: The Mechanization of UG2 Mining in the Bushveld Complex'. *Journal of the South African Institute of Mining and Metallurgy*, 104 (8): 439–455.

Ercelebi, Selamet and Atac Bascetin. 2009. 'Optimization of Shovel-Truck System for Surface Mining'. *Journal of the Southern African Institute of Mining and Metallurgy*, 109: 433–439.

Gandini, Alessandro. 2019. 'Labour Process Theory and the Gig Economy'. *Human Relations* 72 (6): 1039–1056.

Gumede, Hlangabeza. 2018. 'The Socio-economic Effects of Mechanising and/or Modernising Hard Rock Mines in South Africa'. *South African Journal of Economic and Management Sciences* 21 (1): 1–20.

Hall, Richard. 2010. 'Renewing and Revising the Engagement between Labour Process Theory and Technology'. In *Working Life: Renewing Labour Process Analysis*, edited by Paul Thompson and Chris Smith, 159–181. Hampshire: Palgrave Macmillan.

Hlatshwayo, Mondli. 2013. 'A Sociological Analysis of Trade Union Responses to Technological Changes at the ArcelorMittal Vanderbijlpark Plant, 1989–2011'. PhD diss., University of Johannesburg.

Hlatshwayo, Mondli and Sakhela Buhlungu. 2017. 'Work Re-organisation and Technological Change: Limits of Trade Union Strategy and Action at ArcelorMittal, Vanderbijlpark'. *African Sociological Review/Revue Africaine de Sociologie* 21 (1): 126–152.

Inch, J.D., J.D. Stone, I.D. Brumby and C.J. Beukes. 1980. The Use of Continuous Miners in South African Coal Mines. *Journal of the Southern African Institute of Mining and Metallurgy* 80 (1): 5–21.

Jacobs, Jonathan and Ronnie Webber-Young. 2017. 'A Technology Map to Facilitate the Process of Mine Modernization throughout the Mining Cycle'. *The Journal of the Southern African Institute of Mining and Metallurgy* 117: 637–648.

Kenny, Bridget and Edward Webster. 2021. 'The Return of the Labour Process: Race, Skill and Technology in South African Labour Studies'. *Work in the Global Economy* 1 (1–2): 13–32.

MacFarlane, Alastair Stewart. 2001. 'The Implementation of Technology in Southern African Mines: Pain or Panacea?' *The Journal of the South African Institute of Mining and Metallurgy* 101 (3): 115–126.

Marwala, Tshilidzi. 2018. 'Mining in the Fourth Industrial Revolution'. *Independent Online*, 9 September 2018. https://www.iol.co.za/sundayindependent/dispatch/mining-in-the-fourth-industrial-revolution-16977789.

Marwala, Tshilidzi. 2020. *Closing the Gap: The Fourth Industrial Revolution*. Johannesburg: Pan Macmillan.

Mashayamombe, John. 2018. 'Sanitised Spaces: Spatial Orders of Post-apartheid Mines in South Africa'. PhD diss., University of Pretoria.

Mine Health and Safety Council (MHSC). 2011. *The Culture Transformation Framework: Changing Minds, Changing Mines*. Johannesburg: MHSC.

Minerals Council of South Africa (MCSA). 2016. *Mining in South Africa: The Challenges and Opportunities*. Johannesburg: MCSA.

Minerals Council of South Africa (MCSA). 2018a. *Mining Matters, Quarterly Update* (March 2018). Johannesburg: MCSA.

Minerals Council of South Africa (MCSA). 2018b. *Modernisation: Towards the Mine of Tomorrow*. Johannesburg: MCSA.

Musingwini, Cuthbert and Richard Minnitt. 2008. 'Ranking the Efficiency of Selected Platinum Mining Methods using the Analytic Hierarchy Process (AHP)'. In *Platinum in Transformation*, edited by the Southern African Institute of Mining and Metallurgy, 319–326. Symposium Series S52. Johannesburg: SAIMM.

Phakathi, Sizwe T. 2002. 'Self-directed Work Teams in a Post-apartheid Gold Mine: Perspectives from the Rock Face'. *Journal of Workplace Learning* 14 (7): 278–285.

Schutte, Paul and Claudio Maldonado. 2003. *Factors Affecting Driver Alertness during the Operation of Haul Trucks in the South African Mining Industry.* Pretoria: Safety in Mines Research Advisory Committee, CSIR. https://www.mhsc.org.za/sites/default/files/public/research_documents/SIM%20020502%20Factors%20affecting%20driver%20alertness%20during%20the%20operation%20of%20haul%20trucks.pdf. Accessed 6 February 2023.

Segopolo, Permla Realeboga. 2015. 'Optimization of Shuttle Car Utilization at an Underground Coal Mine'. *The Journal of Southern African Institute of Mining and Metallurgy* 115 (4): 285–296.

Singh, Navin. 2017. 'Weathering the Perfect Storm facing the Mining Sector'. *The Journal of the Southern African Institute of Mining and Metallurgy* 117 (3): 223–229.

Sokutu, Brian. 2018. 'The Planned Retrenchments could Mean up to 130 000 People Directly Affected and Probably Millions More Affected Indirectly, the Union Says'. *Citizen*, 8 August 2018. https://citizen.co.za/news/south-africa/1992946/amcu-warns-of-mass-action-over-implats-job-cuts.

Stewart, Paul. 2013. 'Kings of the Mine: Rock Drill Operators and the 2012 Strike Wave on South African Mines'. *South African Review of Sociology* 44 (3): 42–63.

Stewart, Paul. 2015. 'Accelerated Mechanisation and the Demise of a Mass-based Labour Force? Platinum Mines in South Africa'. *Review of African Political Economy* 42 (146): 633–642.

Stoddard, Ed. 2021. '72 Mine Deaths in 2021 – Industry Agrees on Urgent Measures to Safeguard Workers'. *Daily Maverick*, 13 December 2021. https://www.dailymaverick.co.za/article/2021-12-13-72-mine-deaths-in-2021-industry-agrees-on-urgent-measures-to-safeguard-workers.

Thompson, Paul and Bill Harley. 2007. 'Human Resources Management and the Worker: Labour Process Perspectives'. In *Oxford Handbook of Human Resources Management*, edited by Peter Boxall, John Purcell and Patrick Wright, 147–165. Oxford: Oxford University Press.

Tshoaedi, Malehoko, Zitha Mokomane, Christine Bischoff, Mondli Hlatshwayo, John Mashayamombe, Sandla Nomvete and Boitumelo Malope. 2017. 'Transformation in Mining: Developing Elements that will Address Racism, Sexism and All Forms of Discrimination in the Mining Sector'. Research report commissioned by the Mine Health and Safety Council. Pretoria: University of Pretoria,

Viljoen, Leon. 2018. 'What is the Fourth Industrial Revolution?' *Independent Online*, 28 March 2018. https://www.iol.co.za/business-report/opinion/what-is-the-fourth-industrial-revolution-14127465.

Von Holdt, Karl. 2003. *Transition from Below: Forging Trade Unionism and Workplace Change in South Africa.* Pietermaritzburg: University of KwaZulu-Natal Press.

Webster, Edward. 1985. *Cast in a Racial Mould: Labour Process and Trade Unionism in the Foundries.* Johannesburg: Ravan Press.

Zuo, Mandy. 2016. 'Rise of the Robots: 60 000 Workers Culled from Just One Factory as China's Struggling Electronics Hub Turns to Artificial Intelligence'. *South China Morning Post*, 26 May 2016. https://cacm.acm.org/careers/202814-rise-of-the-robots-60000-workers-culled-from-just-one-factory-as-chinas-struggling-electronics-hub-turns-to-artificial-intelligence/fulltext.

7

Trade Union Responses to Production Technologies in the Fourth Industrial Revolution

Mondli Hlatshwayo

INTRODUCTION

There has been a proliferation of discussions and debates about the future of work in the context of what is now popularly known as the Fourth Industrial Revolution (4IR) (see Mashayamombe in this volume; Schwab 2015; Balliester and Elsheikhi 2018; Lee et al. 2019; Philbeck and Davis 2019). The industrial revolutions, as described by Klaus Schwab (2017), tend to be processes in modern history triggered by technological innovations that have a direct impact on work, the economy and human lives in general. The first industrial revolution, according to Xu Min, Jeanne David and Suk Hi Kim (2018), took place between 1760 and 1840, and was driven by steam locomotive power and mechanised textile manufacturing. The second industrial revolution, beginning at the end of the 1800s and continuing into the early 1900s, involved the discovery and use of electricity in the mass production of goods (Schwab 2015). Beginning in the 1960s, the third revolution was a build-up from the second one in the sense that it concerned the use of electronics, information technology and data to improve production and its automated processes (Xu, David and Kim 2018). The Fourth Industrial Revolution, which is the current phase, takes forward the third industrial revolution. Schwab (2015, 1) explains: 'The fourth industrial revolution is fundamentally different from the previous revolutions as it is characterised by a range of new technologies that are fusing the physical, digital and biological worlds, impacting all disciplines, economies and industries.'

According to Hyeoun-Ae Park:

> Technologies such as artificial intelligence, the Internet of Things (IoT), cloud computing, social media, data science, 3D printing, connected wearable devices, quantum computing, robotics, and genetics are the driving forces of this revolution. These transformative technologies will impact all disciplines, economies, businesses, societies, and individuals. (Park 2016, 1)

However, the whole notion of a Fourth Industrial Revolution is contested; there are scholars who argue convincingly that the current phase of technological advances normally associated with the 4IR are just an expansion of the third industrial revolution (Cooper 2011; Elia, Secundo and Passiante 2017).

This chapter builds on the perspective in John Mashayamombe's chapter, and asserts that technology plays a particular role in capitalist production – an aspect that tends to be ignored by those who support the notion of a Fourth Industrial Revolution. From the beginning of the capitalist labour process until today, technology has been a tainted tool used to increase capitalists' market dominance and profits. In the struggle between workers and employers for control over the labour process, production technologies are not neutral. They are used to speed up the production process, and play a role in controlling and monitoring workers. That is why, for instance, workers have sometimes referred to robots as spies (Kunene and Cupido 2019; Ngcwangu 2019). At the same time, it has to be understood that the labour process, and the pace at which machinery and robotics are introduced into this process, is largely under the control of the employers who own the factories. Structurally, workers and their trades tend to be on the back foot – they are often only able to respond long after employers have introduced the new technologies (Hlatshwayo 2017).

Studies on the impact of 4IR technologies (such as robotics) have shown that they tend to affect workers negatively. Technology increases the pace of work, leads to the massive deskilling of the workforce and results in increased surveillance (Appolis 2018; Kunene and Cupido 2019). Contrary to arguments in support of the 4IR (Xing and Marwala 2017), technological changes and the current phase of technology make workers losers in the 'game' of the 4IR, especially in South Africa. The following section demonstrates how workers across the world – and especially in the Global South – will be negatively affected by the 4IR and its related technologies.

THE IMPACT OF TECHNOLOGICAL INNOVATION ON WORKERS: A GLOBAL OVERVIEW

In 2018, the World Economic Forum (WEF), an international organisation focusing on the global economy, published the results of a survey on technological innovation and diffusion based on the input of 313 respondents from leading global companies. The sample selected by the WEF was representative of the key sectors of the world economy, which together employed more than 15 million workers at the time. According to the WEF (2018, viii) survey, 'Nearly 50% of companies expect that automation will lead to some reduction in their full-time workforce by 2022, based on the job profiles of their employee base today'. The WEF findings seem consistent with those of the International Labour Organization (ILO 2017), which show that about 1.4 billion workers globally (accounting for 42 per cent of total employment) are in various forms of precarious employment, which includes employment that is not full-time. Technological innovation in the form of artificial intelligence, new data systems and robotics are not only going to negatively affect what is often regarded as unskilled work (ILO 2017); even employees who are considered highly skilled and highly paid are likely to have some of their functions automated, causing redundancies and job losses among this sector as well (Chui, Manyika and Miremadi 2015).

One of the WEF's (2018) key findings is that by 2022, 85 per cent of the respondents are likely to expand their use of big data analytics, which is a key component of the 4IR (see Figure 7.1). One of the possibilities here is the linking of biometrics and genetic data so that global marketing and sales decisions can be made. According to the WEF, this will increase the demand for data scientists, computer scientists, software developers and specialists in data administration and management. Figure 7.1 summarises some of the key findings from this survey.

The WEF (2018) survey concludes that 50 per cent of companies claim that technological innovation, and robotics in particular, will replace close to a billion workers worldwide by 2030. Research conducted by Citi and Oxford University suggests that 66.7 per cent of jobs could be performed by robots (*MyBroadband* 2016). While new careers and new occupations in the sphere of data, artificial intelligence,

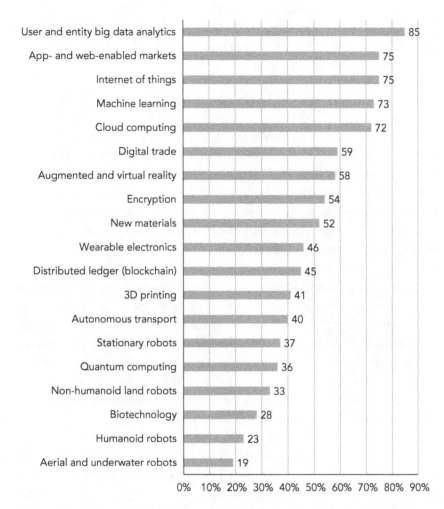

Figure 7.1: Technologies and the proportion of companies likely to adopt them by 2022 (projected) (%)

Source: WEF (2018)

robots and new technologies might be created, the disruption in occupations and job losses is more likely to affect workers negatively (Ngcwangu 2016).

Furthermore, because women are over-represented in what is often regarded as secretarial, unskilled or unpaid work, the 4IR will continue to disadvantage them. Rachel Adams asserts:

> Robots are being prepped to replace care-worker jobs. These types of professions, along with others that are particularly vulnerable to being replaced by

robotics or computers, are generally occupied by women. In South Africa, where the labour market is already more favourable to men than women, this presents a serious concern. (Adams 2019)

Another crucial question that is often ignored by 4IR promoters is the question of workers' rights in addition to human rights (Schwab 2015; Xing and Marwala 2017). The extraction of minerals used in the production of robots and other 4IR technologies is an industry riddled with extreme human rights violations, generalised violence, wars, mass rape of women and the general violation of the rights of children. For example, the extraction of coltan in the Democratic Republic of Congo, used in the manufacturing of many electronic devices, takes place in the context of armed conflict where military groups control mining in the eastern part of the country. Ann Laudati and Charlotte Mertens elaborate:

> In the last decade, the rapes [of women] in, and the metaphoric raping [of natural resources] of the Democratic Republic of Congo have received unprecedented attention from media, donors, and advocacy groups. Beginning in the early 2000s, these two narratives (the involvement of armed groups and state forces in illegal resource exploitation and the widespread prevalence of sexual violence in eastern DRC) merged to form a direct cause–consequence relationship, in which rape is framed as a tool for accessing mineral wealth. (Laudati and Mertens 2019, 1)

In addition to the adverse working conditions in the extractive industry in the Democratic Republic of Congo and the Global South more generally, workers who produce electronic gadgets also work under slave-like conditions. In China, for example, Smith (2016) describes how FoxConn, a Taiwanese multinational electronics manufacturing company with headquarters in Tucheng, New Taipei, manufactures half of the world's electronic products. In 2010, the company's complex in Shenzhen in mainland China had factories employing 430 000 workers who resided in hostels. These workers, who manufactured sophisticated and very expensive electronic equipment, were young migrant workers with no access to healthcare and education. They worked very long hours and earned low wages. Making matters worse, they were not allowed to stay with their friends and families in the city. Workers in these factories were subjected to a barbaric regime, leading to 14 workers committing suicide in 2010. In the same year, the plant managers erected nets outside workers' dormitories to prevent widespread suicide (Smith 2016; Merchant 2017).

Besides the adverse working conditions in the context of 4IR, there is also a debate about skills. This chapter asserts that skills in the 4IR context cannot be divorced from the structural economic and social divide between highly industrialised and less industrialised countries. Highly skilled workers in the Global North and in China, for example, who design robots are beneficiaries because the 4IR values their skills and work, and they earn higher wages. Their products, however, appropriate the skills of other workers. Workers who previously conducted functions such as product quality control, manual labour and other tasks in the manufacturing sector are rendered redundant. Or highly skilled, quality control scientists are replaced by computers and machines able to speedily conduct the same quality control functions. In some plants, machines now efficiently do the sorting and packaging of bolts and nuts, which was previously done manually. It can be argued that automation has led to increased efficiencies, but the biggest problem is that, in the final analysis, gains from advances in technology do not accrue to workers. Rather, it is the factory owners who benefit. In essence, the general tendency is towards a massive deskilling of workers, some of whom used to perform highly skilled work, such as quality controllers and fitters and turners, whose diagnostic functions are now being taken over by computers and machines. There is no doubt that data scientists, computer scientists, production process controllers, production managers and others involved in technical aspects of production in the Global South will benefit from the 4IR, but this is most likely to be a tiny minority of all workers and professionals. In addition, it is the big companies of the Global North, not those of the Global South, who employ these categories of skilled workers (Hlatshwayo 2017).

China and the industrialised countries of the Global North control the production of machines and other 4IR technologies, such as robots and artificial intelligence. The United States of America, one of the biggest producers of robots, has companies, such as Canvas, manufacturing sophisticated robots that use artificial intelligence and 3D technology to produce goods (Thomas 2019). The Swedish company ASEA Brown Boveri is the largest manufacturer of robots in the world, followed by the German-based Kuka, now owned by the Chinese Midea group (Shukla 2019). In the same way that these highly skilled workers in the Global North and China benefit from the 4IR because their skills are valued, so do the countries that manufacture these technologies; they reap the profits and further enhance their own technological development, making it almost impossible for countries of the Global South to catch up.

Workers who are considered to be low-skilled and who also tend to be women, especially in the Global South, do not stand to benefit from the 4IR, given that the science and technology field is dominated by men. In the Global South, women occupy precarious forms of work and this means they are even more unlikely to benefit from the 4IR. In fact, women in the Global South play a very minimal role in science and technology. Adams elaborates:

> This is a worrying oversight. The world of the fourth industrial revolution looks set to be one dominated by forms of knowledge and industries – like science and technology – that have long been dominated by men. In addition, many of the opportunities the fourth industrial revolution is thought to offer are internet based. Yet, as a recent study has shown, women tend to have less access to internet-based technologies than men do in Africa. This means that the impact on women's lives and work opportunities becomes a critical concern. (Adams 2019, 1)

TECHNOLOGY AND WORKERS IN SOUTH AFRICA

We have shown that, in the majority of cases, countries of the Global South, their workers and women in particular are not going to benefit from the 4IR. The same holds true for many workers in South Africa, a country which already faces serious problems of unemployment and poverty. When the expanded definition of unemployment is used, close to 46.6 per cent of economically active people in South Africa were unemployed in the third quarter of 2021 (Stoddard 2021). It seems as if technological innovation will most likely deepen the existing crisis. Utilising data from Statistics South Africa and an Oxford University automation index, Daniel le Roux (2018) concludes that 'occupations performed by almost 35 per cent of South African workers – roughly 4.5 million people – are potentially automatable in the near future'.

In a recent study on the impact of robots and other new technologies on South African workers and production processes, Phindile Kunene and Simone Cupido (2019) reveal that new machines have not improved the working conditions for workers in the manufacturing sector. For example, workers reported that machines increased the intensity and the pace of work, leading to workers feeling overworked because they have to keep up with the high speed of machines and robots. According to Kunene and Cupido (2019, 42), one worker stated that robots were not just taking over work previously performed by workers, they were also 'spies' that monitored the movements of workers near them. Employers then use the collected data to discipline workers.

Another complex issue when it comes to the introduction of robots, machinery and computer technologies is the crucial question of skills and occupations.

In the South African context, it has been revealed that the steel production process lags behind in so far as the introduction of robotics is concerned. On the other hand, new machinery and computer technologies have been introduced to speed up production and improve steel quality. These processes have led to massive declines in employment. For example, between 1989 and 2014, close to 50 000 jobs were lost at ArcelorMittal – previously known as the Iron and Steel Corporation, or more commonly as Iscor (Hlatshwayo 2013). A further consequence is that the deskilling of artisans and semi-skilled workers has reduced them to mere appendages in the sense that their labour processes are now dictated by machines and computers. At the same time, a tiny minority of workers who perform functions such as process controlling and production planning have become highly skilled since taking on the oversight of complex production processes. The same holds true for information technology and computer technicians, as they maintain and manage computer and data processes in firms. These observations are consistent with Mashayamombe (2020), who investigated the role of technologies in mines and concluded that new technical changes might lead to job losses in the future as jobs are taken over by machines and automation.

The question of skills, briefly mentioned earlier, has a global dimension which tends to be ignored by some scholars. Germany, the US and China, for example, produce machines, car parts and robots, giving them an advantage in terms of the 4IR. This means that skills and the value of goods tend to be largely concentrated in these countries, rather than in many countries of the Global South. In fact, production in multinational companies operating in South Africa is controlled from their headquarters, which tend to be located in the Global North (Mashilo 2010; Hlatshwayo 2013).

However, in South Africa, the car-manufacturing sector complicates the relationship between jobs, new technologies and robotics. Like other motor assembly plants, Volkswagen (VW) in Uitenhage has fundamentally revolutionised production processes in the very recent past without negatively affecting jobs. In fact, the plant has introduced 320 robots and created new jobs – something that flies in the face of the accepted wisdom that technology, and robots in particular, lead to job losses (Hlatshwayo 2017). The Automotive Production and Development Programme is responsible for job creation in the VW plant and other car manufacturing plants in South Africa. According to the state's subsidy plan, each worker is subsidised by R100 000 a year in order to sustain 28 000 jobs (Ngcwangu 2016). Despite the technological innovations which tend to decrease the number of jobs, government plans to continue with the subsidy to increase jobs to 240 000 by 2035 (Davies 2018).

TRADE UNION RESPONSES: AN INTERNATIONAL PERSPECTIVE

Table 7.1 shows a typology of trade union responses to technological innovation, which can either be proactive (by emphasising research and education in order to respond comprehensively) or reactive (by only responding after management has introduced technological changes into production). In cases where unions adopt a reactive approach, their structures tend to focus on wages at the expense of production and technology. This framework is elaborated further below through an engagement with both international and South African union experiences.

Globally, trade unions have responded in various ways to the Fourth Industrial Revolution and the introduction of new technology. In some instances, especially in Italy, unions have used strikes to defend jobs. On 14 June 2019, for example, metalworkers took to the streets of Milan, Florence and Naples in response to tech-nological change and the rise of precarious forms of work. Among other things, the strikers demanded that the state and the private sector 'use productivity gains from new technology to create new jobs, raise wages and reduce working time' (IndustriAll 2019). In addition to workplace issues, the demands also addressed the need to deal with climate change, increased job creation and the building of a socially just economy (IndustriAll 2019). While going on strike is a participatory tool used by workers to defend their jobs, strikes do tend to be a reactive, or rearguard, union response. Unions that have access to information and conduct research are more likely to devise strategies to prevent retrenchments by formulating proposals.

Table 7.1: A typology of trade union responses to technological innovation

Approach	Focus	Structures
Reactive	Based on a strategy preoccupied with increasing union members' wages.	Oriented towards wages and the politics of redistribution in the form of members' benefits.
Proactive	Wages, working conditions, technology and work reorganisation. Also general politics, aiming to forge policies that protect the interests of workers.	Able to engage with both wages and production (technology). Has a department that focuses on technological changes. Research, education and collective bargaining departments focus on technological redistribution and production issues.

Source: Hlatshwayo (2013, 78)

In these more proactive cases, strikes are used to support the concrete demands unions have formulated in advance (Hlatshwayo 2017).

It is instructive to examine how unions in Germany and the US have been grappling with technological advances in production processes. Writing about union responses to automation in the US in the 1980s, Cory Doctorow contends:

> The first wave of computerized automation caught trade unions flat-footed; already reeling from the Reagan-era attacks on labor, union leadership failed completely to come up with a coherent response to the automation of manufacturing industries (a notable exception was the Longshoreman's union, which ensured that containerization led to massive pay raises and generous retirements for the workers whose work was largely eliminated by better shipping techniques. (Doctorow 2018, 1)

This reactive approach confirms my characterisation of union responses to technological innovation (Hlatshwayo 2017). Unions are likely to be caught off guard when new technology is introduced because the production process is controlled and managed by employers whose interest it is to maximise profit in the context of market competition. In other words, in the final analysis employers do not introduce technological changes because they are concerned about the welfare of workers. The unions have the propensity to focus on wages to the exclusion of production and technologies because they tend to see technology as the preserve of managers or employers. The union response during the first wave of technological changes in the US, as elucidated by Eduardo Porter (2018), is consistent with the approach adopted by unions in India, the United Kingdom, South Africa and Nigeria (Hlatshwayo 2013).

In 2018, during the second wave of technological change in the US, trade unions representing truck drivers and service workers demanded that their members be directly involved when new technologies were introduced into their labour process. Union members wanted technology to lighten the burden of the labour process, provide more training and develop a plan to deal with the conditions of workers who might be made redundant. More importantly, the unions also demanded that workers facing retrenchment as a result of automation should be trained and relocated to other positions in their companies or be rehired by other employers. Adopting a proactive response to technological change has yielded some positive results for workers. To this end, Porter writes:

> In June [2018], the union [Unite Here] managed for the first time to include protections from technological change in its contracts

covering workers at the Las Vegas properties of MGM Resorts and Caesars Entertainment. Workers will be trained to do jobs created or modified by new technology, allowing them to share in the productivity gains. The contracts also provide for the company to try to find jobs for displaced workers. But the union's key achievement was to get 180 days' warning of technological deployments. (Porter 2018)

Unite Here – a union which represents about 300 000 workers in the hotel, food service, laundry, warehouse and casino gaming industries in the US and Canada – adopted an approach that viewed technological innovation as a crucial bargaining issue. One of the outcomes of adopting such a proactive approach was that employers agreed to give workers six months' notice before new technologies were to be introduced, allowing the unions time to formulate responses to defend jobs and advance workers' interests (Hlatshwayo 2014; Porter 2018).

Unlike the unions in the US and other countries, Industriegewerkschaft Metall (IG Metall), a German metalworkers union with two million members, has been grappling proactively with technological change since the early 1970s (Masondo 2010; Chappell 2019). From the 1960s up to the mid-1970s, IG Metall did not take issue with technological change and automation as long as these did not negatively affect employment (Masondo 2010). Social partnerships in West Germany between IG Metall, the state and employers were sustained by economic growth between the 1960s and the early 1970s, leading IG Metall to adopt a low-key approach to changes in technology in the workplace. However, the neo-liberal economic crisis of the early 1970s, which manifested in the form of work reorganisation and technological change, affected IG Metall employees negatively in the form of retrenchments and changes in occupation. In the late 1970s, IG Metal began to adopt what Themba Masondo (2010) regards as an interventionist approach towards technology and production.

The union campaigned for the expansion of co-determination (cooperation between employers and unions), which led to the amendment of the 1972 Works Constitution Act to compel employers to consult workers about plans to restructure work. Also in the 1970s, as part of developing a proactive approach towards technology in production, IG Metall initiated the Humanisation of Working Life project, whereby the union's Department of Automation, Technology and Humanisation, the Federal Ministry of Research and Technology and the Ministry of Labour developed action research. The purpose of the research was to help the union to intervene in production in a manner that would save jobs and improve workers' participation during times of technological change (Thelen 1991). Masondo succinctly sums up the aims of the 'humanisation of work' programme:

> [The aim is] to develop worker protection measures and establish minimum standards for machines, systems and plants; ... to develop humane production technologies; ... to devise and test new modes of work organisation and job structures for subsequent diffusion; and to disseminate and apply humanisation findings, and plant findings and experiences. (Masondo 2010, 68)

In explaining IG Metall's proactive approach to production technologies, I stated in earlier research:

> IG Metall initially took an apathetic attitude to technological changes in production, but the economic crisis of the 1970s compelled them to develop a proactive approach. The space to respond to technological change, as embodied in Works Councils and industry bargaining, came as a result of workers' struggles during the Second World War and tends to be regarded as part of an "historic compromise" between labour, capital and the state which provides the German unions with some breathing space. (Hlatshwayo 2014, 287)

Konrad Siegel is a former member of the Works Council (a shop-floor body of representatives elected by workers) in one of the agricultural equipment production companies in Germany; he joined the IG Metall's Automation, Technology and Humanisation Department. In the 1980s Siegel was involved with others workers and shop stewards in restructuring the plant used by the Works Council. The co-determination to realign machinery and labour process increased production by 40 per cent and saved jobs (Siegel, interview 2012).

Research conducted by Masondo (2010) shows that between 2005 and 2009 German workers in the Kassel VW plant also adopted a proactive approach to technology and were heavily involved in the restructuring of work, leading to jobs being saved and an increase in productivity. In his examination of technological changes in the Kassel plant, Masondo (2010, 89) concludes: 'All this evidence coalesces to one conclusion: workers at the VW Kassel plant are proactive and interventionist in their engagement with workplace restructuring'.

Despite the earlier successes of IG Metall's Automation, Technology and Humanisation Department, the union decided to close it down in 1997. The decision was motivated by the feeling that, because the department was able to raise a lot of money for research from the Federal Government, it had become too powerful and well-resourced. Its workplace interventions led to internal conflicts with other departments – for instance, with those dealing with collective bargaining. Subsequently, in the 2000s and in the context of increased technological changes in production in German factories, the Work and Production Innovation Department – headed by Dr Detlef Gerst, who had direct contact with the defunct Department of Automation, Technology and Humanisation – was formed to respond to technological innovation (Mashilo 2010; Masondo 2010).

It appears that the closure of the Automation, Technology and Humanisation Department in 1997 might have put IG Metall on the back foot because there was close to a ten-year period wherein IG Metall ignored technological changes; it only began to catch up in the 2000s when it re-established a department of technology. The newly found impetus to respond to technological innovation in production was prompted by the debate on the 4IR and the future of work. In 2012, IG Metall began a series of discussions on the 4IR and the impact of artificial intelligence, robotics and other production technologies on work and workers in Germany, and the world over. According to IG Metall:

> As part of the "Factory of the Future" project, key social partner IG Metall plays a vital role in helping to shape and integrate sustainable technology and workplace designs. This process involves various questions regarding employment relationships, the protection of employees, and co-determination. (IG Metall 2018, 1)

In the face of serious challenges in Germany, such as the rise of precarious work and the re-emergence of right-wing politics, IG Metall is trying to revive its proactive response to the changing nature of work and the introduction of new technologies in production. In 2017, Melissa Reuter and her colleagues (2017, 354) reported that IG Metall had approached academics and researchers in Ruhr University Bochum to develop a 'didactical approach to "Industrie 4.0" in a learning factory surrounding'. The overall aim of the project was to respond to the 4IR: 'The overarching objectives are to ensure high-level industrial value in Germany by strengthening competitiveness and innovations through secure employment and fair working conditions as well as establishing sustainable personnel development structures on a company level' (Reuter et al. 2017, 354).

One outcome of the project was the establishment of a 'learning factory' in Bochum, which develops the technological design of, for example, robots that are controlled by workers instead of robots that control workers. The learning factory is funded by the German federal government and enables workers and the union to use technologies to design work which could then be transferred to real work situations later on. However, the renewal process continues to be fragile as IG Metall faces the new challenge of precarious work, among others (Reuter et al. 2017, 354). When looking at cooperation in the context of the learning factory and borrowing from the work of David Cooper (2011), it can be argued that the collaboration between the University of Bochum, the German government and IG Metall represents a 'triple helix'. IG Metall is far ahead of other unions with its so-called 'use-inspired basic research', which is aimed at helping metalworkers respond to technological innovation and artificial intelligence in production. In other words, the union is involved in research ensuring that work in the future German context is designed so that machines and robotics are produced to improve the working conditions of human workers.

TRADE UNION RESPONSES IN THE SOUTH AFRICAN CONTEXT

Unlike IG Metall, South African unions and other unions of the Global South, especially those in the manufacturing sector, have tended to ignore production technologies as a terrain for collective bargaining, leaving management to restructure work and introduce technologies with minimum resistance. Unions in South Africa, Nigeria, India and even in the United Kingdom have tended to bargain over wages because increased wages are perceived as representing gains for their members. However, an exclusive focus on wages indirectly grants management an uncontested space in which to change production methods and technologies to the company owners' advantage (Hlatshwayo 2013). In a study on how trade unions responded to technological innovation in a steel factory near Vanderbijlpark, I argue that Solidarity, a predominantly white union, and the National Union of Metalworkers of South Africa (Numsa), a predominantly black union, were not prepared for technological changes in the production process, especially during the period of massive retrenchment between 1989 and 2001. The two unions adopted a reactive approach, which meant that they only bargained long after management had introduced the new technologies. The lack of preparedness was due to both unions seeing bargaining as limited to engaging factory owners around wages and working conditions.

Although unions in South Africa tend to adopt an extremely reactive approach to technological innovation in production, Numsa – as the leading union in the manufacturing sector and directly affected by technological change – has been developing more proactive responses in recent years. Numsa's policy now requires companies to provide six months' notice prior to the purchase of new technologies in order to allow the union some breathing space to examine the impact of automation on workers and their skills. Proposals and strategies that Numsa has adopted include calling for consultation well in advance of the introduction of new technologies in production, strengthening union research and education, and initiating international collaboration (Numsa 2012). However, research has shown that managers tend to ignore this union policy by bringing in new technologies, including robotics, without consulting the unions (Hlatshwayo 2013). For example, VW in Uitenhage brought in 320 robots in 2016 without the knowledge of the union, raising questions about the union's ability to influence production in the plant (*MyBroadband* 2016). This is the opposite of the German situation, where production issues and the introduction of new technologies are discussed in the Works Councils. IG Metall has the advantage in that German labour law calls for extensive consultation before work can be restructured and, through its own research, the union is able to formulate concrete proposals that are likely to save jobs (Mashilo 2010).

Understanding production processes and the role of technology therein is crucial to unions being able to formulate adequate responses to technological change. In other words, continuous research and knowledge of management's technological plans are factors likely to enable unions to formulate responses that can help defend workers' interests. According to Ngcwangu (2019, 45): 'Whether it is proactive work related to bargaining decisions or to general discussions over policy particularly, the union movement will require a combination of conceptual and empirical understanding of what these new technologies mean for workers'.

Research has shown that unions with the capacity to conduct their own research on technological changes in production are able to mitigate the negative effects of such change on their members (Mathews 1989; Hlatshwayo 2013). The way in which unions have responded to technological innovation in Australia and Germany demonstrates that conducting research on production as well as having a better understanding of the production process are key factors in challenging managerial control of the labour process and the distribution of labour and technology in production. A narrow focus on wages, according to John Mathews (1989) and Siphelo Ngcwangu (2019), robs trade unions of an opportunity to influence production and the deployment of technology and workers. Unions like Numsa have annual bargaining conferences on wages to inform their wage demands, showing the extent to which wages dominate South African unions' bargaining strategies. While it is understandable that wages and related monetary benefits are crucial in challenging inequality in South Africa, a unidimensional approach that emphasises wages at the expense of production, intentionally or unintentionally, grants management extreme powers to change production processes and introduce new technologies in a manner that favours and advances the interests of factory owners (Hlatshwayo 2017).

In 2013, Numsa launched its own Research and Policy Institute (NRPI), which conducts research on economic and social policy for its members (Hlatshwayo and Buhlungu 2017). However, Sakhela Buhlungu and I (2017) warn that research on automation has to be plant-specific because proposals on how to mitigate the negative effects of technologies on workers have to be clearly defined. Thus far, it does not appear as if the NRPI has conducted concrete research on how automation in specific plants affects workers.

The NRPI has, however, conducted research in the car manufacturing sector on its value chain, restructuring and technological changes, especially in the context of the 4IR. In May 2019, Numsa and IG Metall organised an educational workshop in Frankfurt, the aim of which was to share experiences on the 4IR, and the NRPI's research findings were shared in a presentation (Roy 2017). Attended by Numsa and IG Metall shop stewards and officials, the workshop shared perspectives on the 4IR and how both unions were dealing with 4IR-related challenges. As part of the workshop programme, delegates also visited IG Metall's learning factory in Buchum (Numsa and IG Metall 2019).

The Congress of South African Trade Unions (Cosatu) – the biggest trade union federation in South Africa – does not have designated worker education programmes focusing on the 4IR and technological changes in production. Unlike Numsa, which has to some extent been grappling with technological innovation and the 4IR, Cosatu lags behind in this regard. Although the union federation has shown some concerns about the impact of the 4IR on jobs and skills, its statement below seems to embrace the 4IR uncritically. In fact, the federation presents the 4IR as if it were not a tainted tool that seeks to weaken the power of labour, and workers in particular. Here is what Cosatu's president, Zingiswa Losi, states about the 4IR:

> As a federation, we're of the view that we can't avoid technology, so we must embrace it. But, as we embrace it, we should ask, what are the skills needed? What kind of workforce will we require? What are we going to do to ensure workers are skilled, reskilled and multi-skilled, to manage the changing world of work? (Losi cited in Mzekanda 2019, 1)

In the above statement, Cosatu tries to respond to concerns from workers and their affiliates about the impact of new technologies on work and jobs. However, in some instances, workers in more localised settings were beginning to respond through isolated strikes. As in Italy, employees of the Health Professionals Council of South Africa (HPCSA), a health professionals' service organisation, went on strike for almost two weeks in November 2018. Asked about the aim of the strike, Nkululeko Ntloko, a representative of the National Education, Health and Allied Workers' Union (Nehawu), responded:

> The strike action comes as a result of the arrogance and intransigence by the employer to resolve our genuine demands. The employer has unilaterally implemented the Business Process Engineering which might lead to a job bloodbath at the council. It talks to restructuring in the organisation because of automation. There are processes that were supposed to have been undertaken under a signed accord between management of HPCSA and Nehawu. (Ntloko cited in Matshili 2018)

The strike appeared to have yielded positive results when HPCSA management back-tracked. In response, the president of the HPCSA, Kgosietsile Latlape, then stated that new technology would not affect jobs. HPCSA management, however, contradicted the union's claim that they had not been consulted (Masilela 2018).

Subsequent to the massive increase in new technology usage in the banking sector and the announcement of retrenchments, the South African Society of Bank Officials (Sasbo), the biggest finance union in South Africa, announced that it would 'down tools at the end of [September] in protest over planned retrenchments in the banking sector' (*Business Tech* 2019). The union argued that it was opposed to its members being replaced by robots and other banking technologies. The union's demands included the need for consultation when new technologies are to be introduced, as well as reskilling workers and saving jobs. In a statement released by Sasbo, Cosatu (commendably) was cited as supporting its affiliate's strike. Joe Kokela (2019, 1), Sasbo's general secretary, elaborated on their demands: 'Coupled with this is our concern that the finance sector should have already taken drastic steps to upskill their workforce in preparation for the future world of work and the 4th Industrial Revolution.'

CONCLUSION

Developments of the Fourth Industrial Revolution are not, in the final analysis, concerned with resolving worldwide social, economic and ecological problems. This reality makes disruptions caused by technological change and automation susceptible to resistance and opposition from those workers most likely to be negatively affected by them. Accordingly, this chapter has demonstrated that globally, but especially in the Global South, workers are highly likely to lose jobs in the context of technological change while the companies in the Global North that manufacture robots, computers and other 4IR technologies stand to gain.

Technology has already substantially reconfigured skills and occupations. In the majority of cases, workers are deskilled when their functions and jobs are taken over by machines, automation and robots. On the other hand, a tiny minority of highly skilled workers who work as computer technologists, data scientists, designers and producers of new technologies stand to benefit from the 4IR.

Globally, IG Metall is proactively responding to automation in a manner that helps preserve jobs as a result of (1) its long history of responding to technological change; (2) Germany's particular labour dispensation, which gives unions and workers a voice in the production process; (3) the fact that Germany actually manufactures the new technologies of the 4IR; and (4) the union's capacity to conduct research. However, it has to be noted that IG Metall is also faced with the challenges associated with both the rise of precarious forms of work and the ever-changing production methods currently eroding workers' rights.

In the South African context, unions have not engaged proactively enough with the impact of new technology. Rather, their focus has been on bargaining over wages. While this focus is understandable because black workers earn low wages, ignoring technological change may lead to job losses. This situation does seem to be changing, however, since some South African unions directly affected by automation have begun to use strikes to oppose the introduction of new technology. Nevertheless, unions are limited by not adopting a more proactive approach, which would entail understanding companies' production plans and responding well in advance to new technologies being introduced.

To sum up, technology in capitalist labour processes entails profit maximisation – which serves the interests of capitalists rather than workers. On the other hand, labour, depending on the strength of its representation, can intervene and shape the use of technology in a manner that defends and advances its own interests. It is sobering to reflect that labour's intervention can only happen within the confines and constraints of capital's ultimate control. However, this chapter has demonstrated that failing to make this intervention would only be to labour's disadvantage. Therefore, the debate on technology and its role in the workplace is an issue that needs to be further interrogated by scholars and researchers, especially those focusing on labour studies and industrial sociology, as many tasks are becoming automated and digitalised. In other words, technological innovations are becoming part of the future of work, requiring specific study and grilling by trade unionists, researchers and academics. The results of such an exercise may assist South African unions in adopting a proactive approach to technological innovation, and that would be demonstrated by unions adopting technology as one of the key collective bargaining issues. Perhaps technology and labour could also be a topic that is most likely to aid and revive labour studies in South Africa.

REFERENCES

Adams, Rachel. 2019. 'Will the Fourth Industrial Revolution Leave Women Behind?' *The Conversation*, 5 August 2019. https://theconversation.com/the-fourth-industrial-revolution-risks-leaving-women-behind-121216.

Appolis, John. 2018. 'The 4.0 Industrial Revolution and Workers'. Paper presented at the Jozi Book Fair, Johannesburg, 30 August – 2 September 2018.

Balliester, Thereza and Adam Elsheikhi. 2018. *The Future of Work: A Literature Review*. Geneva: ILO.

Business Tech. 2019. 'Major Banking Strike Planned for South Africa'. 2 September 2019. https://businesstech.co.za/news/banking/338147/major-banking-strike-planned-for-south-africa.

Chappell, Carmin. 2019. 'Thousands of YouTubers want to Unionize, and They've Got the Support of Europe's Largest Trade Union'. *CNBC*, 6 August 2019. https://www.cnbc.com/2019/08/06/youtubers-want-to-unionize-and-theyve-got-the-support-of-ig-metall.html.

Chui, Michael, James Manyika and Mehdi Miremadi. 2015. 'Four Fundamentals of Workplace Automation'. https://www.mckinsey.com/business-functions/digital-mckinsey/our-insights/four-fundamentals-of-workplace-automation. Accessed 10 October 2021.

Cooper, David. 2011. *The University in Development: Case Studies Of Use-oriented Research*. Cape Town: HSRC.

Davies, Rob. 2018. 'Minister Rob Davies: South African Automotive Masterplan and Extension of Automotive Production and Development Programme'. https://www.gov.za/speeches/minister-rob-davies-media-statement-south-african-automotive-masterplan-2035-and-extension. Accessed 15 October 2021.

Doctorow, Cory. 2018. 'How Trade Unions are Addressing Automation'. *Boing Boing*, 13 October 2018. https://boingboing.net/2018/10/13/we-r-the-robots.html.

Elia, Gianluca, Giustina Secundo and Giuseppina Passiante. 2017. 'Pathways towards the Entrepreneurial University for Creating Entrepreneurial Engineers: An Italian Case'. *International Journal of Entrepreneurship and Innovation Management* 21 (1–2): 27–48.

Hlatshwayo, Mondli. 2013. 'A Sociological Analysis of Trade Union Responses to Technological Changes at the ArcelorMittal Vanderbijlpark Plant, 1989–2011'. PhD diss., University of Johannesburg.

Hlatshwayo, Mondli. 2014. 'Numsa and Solidarity's Responses to Technological Changes at the ArcelorMittal Vanderbijlpark Plant: Unions Caught on the Back Foot'. *Global Labour Journal* 5 (3): 283–305.

Hlatshwayo, Mondli. 2017. 'Technological Changes and Manufacturing Unions in South Africa: Failure to Formulate a Robust Response'. *Global Labour Journal* 8 (2): 100–119.

Hlatshwayo, Mondli and Sakhela Buhlungu. 2017. 'Work Re-organisation and Technological Change: Limits of Trade Union Strategy and Action at ArcelorMittal, Vanderbijlpark'. *African Sociological Review/Revue Africaine de Sociologie* 21 (1): 126–152.

IndustriAll. 2019. 'Solidarity with Striking Metal Workers in Italy'. *IndustriAll*, 14 June 2019. http://www.industriall-union.org/solidarity-with-striking-metal-workers-in-italy.

Industriegewerkschaft Metall (IG Metall). 2018. *Opinions on Industry 4.0 from IG Metall*. https://www.hr40.digital/en/opinions-on-industry-4-0-from-ig-metall. Accessed 13 August 2020.

International Labour Organization ILO). 2017. *The World Employment and Social Outlook 2017 – Trends 2017*. Geneva: International Labour Office. http://www.ilo.org/wcmsp5/groups/public/---dgreports/---dcomm/---publ/documents/publication/wcms_541211.pdf p2. Accessed 13 December 2021.

Kokela, Joe. 2019. 'Why the Strike?' *SASBO News* 41 (3): 1–2. https://sasbo.org.za/wp-content/uploads/2019/08/SASBO-News-v41n3-JulAug-2019-PROOF.pdf. Accessed 6 February 2023.

Kunene, Phindile and Simone Cupido. 2019. 'A Technicist and Classless View of the New Capitalism?' *South African Labour Bulletin* 43 (1): 40–42.

Laudati, Ann and Charlotte Mertens. 2019. 'Resources and Rape: Congo's (Toxic) Discursive Complex'. *African Studies Review* 62 (4): 57–82.

Lee, Keun, Chan-Yuan Wong, Patarapong Intarakumnerd and Chaiyatorn Limapornvanich. 2019. 'Is the Fourth Industrial Revolution a Window of Opportunity for Upgrading or Reinforcing the Middle-income Trap? Asian Model of Development in Southeast Asia'. *Journal of Economic Policy Reform* 23 (4): 408–425.

Le Roux, Daniel. 2018. 'Many South African Jobs could Soon be Automated, and the Country isn't Prepared'. *The Conversation*, 17 July 2018. http://theconversation.com/many-south-african-jobs-could-soon-be-automated-and-the-country-isnt-prepared-99689.

Mashayamombe, John. 2020. 'Evaluation of Labor Agency Strategy: The Case of a Strike at a South African Opencast Mine in 2012'. *Labor Studies Journal* 45 (4): 351–369.

Mashilo, Alex Mohubetswane. 2010. 'Changes in Work and Production Organisation in the Automotive Industry Value Chain: An Evaluation of the Responses by Labour in South Africa'. Masters diss., University of the Witwatersrand.

Masilela, Brenda. 2018. 'HPCSA Strike: Workers Assured Restructuring Won't Affect Their Jobs'. *IOL*, 28 November 2018. https://www.iol.co.za/news/south-africa/gauteng/hpcsa-strike-workers-assured-restructuring-wont-affect-their-jobs-18303350.

Masondo, Themba. 2010. 'Worker Participation in Workplace Restructuring in the Automotive Industry: A Comparative Study of German and South African Volkswagen Plants 1970–2009'. Masters diss., University of the Witwatersrand.

Mathews, John. 1989. *Tools of Change: New Technology and the Democratisation of Work*. Sydney: Pluto.

Matshili, Rudzani. 2018. 'Watch: Strike at HPCSA Over New Technology that could Replace Workers'. *Pretoria News*, 21 November 2018. Accessed 12 May 2023. https://www.iol.co.za/pretoria-news/news/watch-strike-at-hpcsa-over-new-technology-that-could-replace-workers-18209818.

Merchant, Brian. 2017. *The One Device: The Secret History of the iPhone*. London: Hachette Book Group.

Mzekanda, Simnikiwe. 2019. 'Technology: The Political Response'. *Brainstorm*, 3 May 2019. http://www.brainstormmag.co.za/innovation/14559-the-political-response.

MyBroadband. 2016. '67% of Jobs in South Africa can be Done by Robots'. 18 March 2016. https://mybroadband.co.za/news/business/158867-67-of-jobs-in-south-africa-can-be-done-by-robots.html.

National Union of Metalworkers of South Africa (Numsa). 2012. 'NUMSA Policy Resolutions, Edited Version'. https://www.numsa.org.za/wp-content/uploads/2013/10/Section-2-OC-CB-Edited-Version-9-consolidated-changes.pdf. Accessed 3 December 2020.

National Union of Metalworkers of South Africa (Numsa) and IG Metall. 2019. *Technology and Innovation: Workshop on Industry 4.0*. Frankfurt, Oberursel and Buchum, Germany: Numsa and IG Metall.

Ngcwangu, Siphelo. 2016. 'A Sociological Assessment of South Africa's Skills Development Regime: 1990–2008'. PhD diss., University of Johannesburg.

Ngcwangu, Siphelo. 2019. 'Responding to the Fourth Industrial Revolution'. *South African Labour Bulletin* 43 (1): 43–45.

Park, Hyeoun-Ae. 2016. 'Are We Ready for the Fourth Industrial Revolution?' *Yearbook of Medical Informatics* 25 (1): 1–3. https://www.thieme-connect.com/products/ejournals/pdf/10.15265/IY-2016-052.pdf. Accessed 4 December 2022.

Philbeck, Thomas and Nicholas Davis. 2019. 'The Fourth Industrial Revolution'. *Journal of International Affairs* 72 (1): 17–22.

Porter, Eduardo. 2018. 'Hotel Workers Fret over a New Rival: Alexa at the Front Desk'. *New York Times*, 24 September 2018. https://www.nytimes.com/2018/09/24/business/economy/hotel-workers-ai-technology-alexa.html.

Reuter, Melissa, Henning Oberc, Manfred Wannöffel, Dieter Kreimeier, Jürgen Klippert, Peter Pawlicki and Bernd Kuhlenkötter. 2017. 'Learning Factories' Trainings as an Enabler of Proactive Workers' Participation regarding Industrie 4.0'. *Procedia Manufacturing* 9: 354–360.

Roy, Melanie. 2017. '*Numsa – IG Metall Project: Building Transnational Solidarity across Global Value Chains*. Johannesburg: Numsa Research and Policy Institute. https://www.fes-southafrica.org/fileadmin/user_upload/Numsa_IG_Metall_Workshop.pdf. Accessed 12 October 2022.

Schwab, Klaus. 2015. *The Fourth Industrial Revolution: What it Means, How to Respond*. Davos: World Economic Forum. https://www.weforum.org/agenda/2016/01/the-fourth-industrial-revolution-what-it-means-and-how-to-respond. Accessed 3 October 2022.

Schwab, Klaus. 2017. *The Fourth Industrial Revolution*. New York: Crown.

Shukla, Vic. 2019. 'Top 10 Largest Industrial Robot Manufacturers in the World'. *Value Walk*, 14 June 2019. https://www.valuewalk.com/2019/06/top-10-largest-industrial-robot-manufacturers.

Smith, John. 2016. *Imperialism in the Twenty-first Century: Globalization, Super-exploitation*. New York: New York Press.

Stoddard, E. 2021. 'Economic Horror Show: South Africa's Unemployment Rate Hits New Record of 34.9%'. *Daily Maverick*, 30 November 2021. https://www.dailymaverick.co.za/article/2021-11-30-economic-horror-show-south-africas-unemployment-rate-hits-new-record-of-34-9.

Thelen, Kathleen. 1991. *Union of Parts: Labor Politics in Post-war Germany*. New York: Cornell University Press.

Thomas, Mike. 2019. '26 Robotics Companies Changing the Way We Live and Work'. *Built-in*, 13 March 2019. https://builtin.com/robotics/robotics-companies-roundup. Accessed 13 August 2020.

World Economic Forum (WEF). 2018. *The Future of Jobs Report: 2018*. Geneva: Centre for the New Economy and Society. http://www3.weforum.org/docs/WEF_Future_of_ Jobs_2018.pdf. Accessed 6 February 2023.

Xing, Bo and Tshilidzi Marwala. 2017. 'Implications of the Fourth Industrial Age for Higher Education'. https://arxiv.org/ftp/arxiv/papers/1703/1703.09643.pdf. Accessed 3 December 2021.

Xu, Min, Jeanne David and Suk Hi Kim. 2018. 'The Fourth Industrial Revolution: Opportunities and Challenges'. *International Journal of Financial Research* 9 (2): 90–95.

INTERVIEW

Mannheim, Germany

Konrad Siegel, former member of Works Council at IG Metall, 9 August 2012.

8

Emotional Labour in Government Frontline Work: The Burden of Public Call Centre Workers

Babalwa Magoqwana

INTRODUCTION

The state is South Africa's single largest employer. In his contribution to this volume, Lucien van der Walt points out that South African labour studies as a field has neglected 'the role of the long history of unions in the state, of studies of the state as workplace including via labour process theory, and of the distinctive of state activity'. He argues: 'Understanding the state on its own terms is still neglected in labour movement studies, where the state typically appears as an agent of violence, patronage, or just another employer'. In order to rectify this, he argues for 'labour process studies [that look] at the past and present of state sector work'. The aim of this chapter is to address that oversight. A secondary aim is to draw on existing labour process theories of white-collar service work, but also to disrupt this perspective by means of a case study drawn from the civil service, where the 'client' is not a consumer based in the private sector but rather the citizen of a country. Call centre work is a type of human interactive service work that requires considerable investment in emotional labour. This chapter discusses the deployment of the emotional labour in the interface between the frontline worker as both citizen and customer in the local government in South Africa. Using the concept of 'emotional labour' borrowed from Arlie Hochschild ([1983] 2003), this chapter hopes to expand the concept and application in the public sector.

Emotional labour tends to centralise the customer as the main feature of interactive work. The quality of emotional labour is measured through 'customer satisfaction'. This means that 'facial expressions, bodily postures, choice of spoken word, tone of voice and behaviour' are a central part of call centre duties for the competent performance of work (Huang and Yeoh 2007, 198). Rahmat Omar (2016, 232) tells us that 'the product of the interactive work is relationship rather than a product'. This intangible nature of the product in service work creates potential challenges in public sector call centres.

The introduction of customer cultures within the public service has transformed service work to include emotional labour, where citizens do not only demand 'care' but also emotional labour. This is based on the material conditions under which the emotional labour is deployed in the public sector, which is different from the private sector, where the 'customer is king'. I argue that the nature of emotional labour within the public sector call centre is complex, multi-layered and contested. This stems from the position of workers as customers, citizens, service providers and community members. These different and overlapping roles of the frontline worker tend to shape the interaction between the citizen/customer and the frontline worker/civil servant.

The call centre labour process is defined by the use of Automatic Caller Distribution and Interactive Voice Response software to monitor the interaction between the worker and the customer at the point of call. These technologies, which are defining features of the call centre labour process, have led to many labelling call centres as robotic, scripted and Taylorised (Poynter 2000), a digital assembly line (Taylor and Bain 1999), a panopticon with totalising control (Fernie and Metcalf 1998), electronic sweatshops (Garson 1988), gendered (Belt 2002; Patel 2014), or flat careers (Deery and Kinnie 2004). The main competencies required in the call centre job are customer interaction skills, keyboard skills, knowledge of procedures, product, services and legal regulation, and technical proficiency in programming languages and databases (Callaghan and Thompson 2002). The perceived centrality of social skills and competencies leads to management using rigorous selection and training procedures more usually associated with service jobs (Boreham et al. 2008, 74). Some of this social competency is gendered, as females are seen to possess more of the social skills required in call centres. This is one explanation for the number of women in call centre jobs. These social skills are precisely based on the management of feelings. Arlie Hochschild explains emotional management thus:

> [It is] when rules about how to feel and how to express feeling are set by management, when workers have weaker rights to courtesy than customers do, when deep and surface acting are forms of labour to be sold, and when private capacities for empathy and warmth are put to corporate uses. (Hochschild 2003, 89)

Dennis Nickson and colleagues (2001) also suggest that social skills should be extended into the service sector by including 'aesthetic labour'. This means that the 'recruitment of attitude, personality and appearance are part of the skills' (Callaghan and Thompson 2002, 234). Social skills have been critical in the recruitment, selection and training of service workers, especially on the frontline. This contributes to work production and corporate image for customer appeal. Stephen Frenkel and colleagues (1999, 19–20) emphasise the presence of the customer in the call centre labour process and how call centres are controlled by 'customer-related normative values' which supplement the 'hierarchical and bureaucratic control'. These values inform the training within call centre workplaces, as that training tends to focus on self and customer interaction rather than technical expertise and procedural knowledge (Bolton and Houlihan 2005).

EMOTIONAL LABOUR AND EMOTIONAL PROLETARIAT

Emotional labour refers to 'the management of feeling to create publicly observable facial and bodily display; emotional labour is sold for wages and therefore has an exchange value' (Hochschild 2003, 7). Emotional labour does not differentiate between types of jobs: secretaries, waiters and waitresses, salesmen, tour guides, politicians, social workers, receptionists, debt collectors and so forth all employ emotional labour to complete their tasks. Drawing on Goffman's dramaturgy, Claire Williams (2003) argues that emotional labour becomes part of organisational cultural performance. This performance includes tasks (smiling, greeting, eye contact and thanking) as well as personal rituals (negotiation), which contribute to the behaviour of the customer.

Hochschild (2003) manages to link gender and emotional labour, but speaks less about the racialised nature of emotional labour. She exposes the sexual harassment suffered mainly by female flight attendants as opposed to their male counterparts.

Emotional labour has been criticised for its racial silences and for universalising 'whiteness' within service work (Mirchandani 2004). This is taken further by Patricia Chong (2009) who asks questions about how performers of emotional labour function. Using the interlocking concepts of race, class and gender, she argues for establishing hierarchies in the performance of emotional labour. Cameron Lynne MacDonald and David Merrill (2008) use the concept of 'emotional proletariat' to refer to service jobs (waitressing, hotel desk clerk, exercise instructor, child minder and the like), which are occupied mainly by black and Latino women in the United States of America. They discovered in their research that white women employed at the bottom of the interactive service industry tend to be students, but that black women remain trapped there.

Emotional labour cannot be evaluated only along economic lines; cultural and ethnic lines also have to be taken into account (MacDonald and Merrill 2008, 122). Ultimately, gender, class, race and age affect whether and to what extent workers produce the expected emotional labour. As part of her critique of the concept of emotional labour, Chong (2009) argues that the identity of both customers and service workers influences the experience of the customer service, and thus the expression of the emotional labour. This was observed by Jeff Sallaz (2009) in his ethnographic study of the post-apartheid South African leisure resort workplace, where he noticed the racialised restrictions on the expression of emotional labour to satisfy a customer. In applying emotional labour in the public service, Mary Guy, Meredith Newman and Sharon Mastracci (2008, 7) argue that 'service exchange between worker and citizen requires the worker to sense the right tone and medium for expressing a point and/or feeling and then to determine whether, when and how to act on that analysis'.

PUBLIC CALL CENTRES AND EMOTIONAL LABOUR

Call centres in the public sector have operated in the form of small helpdesks but have increasingly embraced the concept of the sovereign customer, which seeks to produce a responsive and cost-efficient administration. Conducting research on tele-nursing, Caroline Collins-Jacque and Chris Smith (2005) caution about some instances in which call centre work might be 'inappropriate and unethical' in the public sector. Call centres form part of the 'New Public Management' influence in the public sector, where a 'discourse of efficiency' takes precedence over the collective and 'political good' of the citizens (Tsakalotos 2004). This discourse introduced private sector managerial styles of business operation into the public sector. New Public Management reforms were complemented by the electronic government notion of transparency that sought to restructure the work order in public services. Public sector call centres are generally expected to have more stable working hours and better working conditions than those in the private sector. Pia Bramming, Ole Sørenson and Peter Hasle (2009, 127) note that working conditions in the Danish government's call centres were better due to 'lack of competition in the public administration'.

In introducing the culture of the customer into local government, the post-apartheid South African government attempted to introduce reforms by putting the values of *Batho Pele* (People First) at the centre in order to change cultural conditions. As local government seeks to apply private sector principles to public service provision, they are moving from care work normally performed by public servants to the introduction of emotional labour. Call centres join this tradition within the public sector, performing emotional labour in a different socio-political context as citizens, workers and customers. In discussing the notion of emotional labour in local government call centres, one needs to look at the history of care work and those deployed to perform such work. Guy, Newman and Mastracci (2008, 3) argue that 'emotional labour is essential for job completion and is a prerequisite for quality public service'. I argue that emotional labour is a contested terrain in local government call centre workplaces as the workers in these centres occupy different yet intersecting roles. They are citizens, services providers, customers, workers and community members. Emotional labour in the public service frontline is not only about the smile and a favourable tone, but the ability to deliver the services perceived to be essential for the basic needs of the 'tax-paying' citizen. This relationship becomes qualitatively different compared to call centre work performed in the private sector.

GENDER AND EMOTIONAL LABOUR IN SERVICE WORK IN SOUTH AFRICA

Call centre work follows the tradition of absorbing black women workers as emotional labourers where performance is at the centre of the labour process. Call centres are mostly operated by young black women with matric certificates and supervised mainly by white females with post-matriculation qualifications (Benner 2006). Noticing the inclusion of the informed middle-class customer, Bridget Kenny (2005) argues that this customer has entered the production process and thereby possesses a certain measure of control in the retail sector where the mass of frontline workers are mostly black and female catering to the needs of mostly white female customers. Referring to forms of the 'apartheid workplace regime' (Von Holdt 2003) in food retail stores, she argues that 'emotional labour reinforced racial despotism as the new black interactive service workers had to cope with racist and sometimes physical abuse' at the point of production (Kenny 2004, 221). This was further observed by Edward Webster and Rahmat Omar (2003) in the post-apartheid workplace where call centre workers seemed to have a new 'boss' outside the shop floor – the customer. This tendency for the customer to express racist and abusive language towards frontline workers was labelled as part of the racial despotism defining the South African apartheid workplace. Hochschild (2003, 20) also notes that 'emotional labour affects the various social classes differently. If it is women, members of the less advantaged gender, who specialize in emotional labour, it is the middle and upper reaches of the class system that seem to call most for it'.

Webster and Omar (2003) conclude that the apartheid workplace regime existed in these (call centre) workplaces. This 'boss' mentality is also illustrated in call centres in India, where some Western customers shout insults when they hear the accent of these call centre workers, leading to Kiran Mirchandani (2004) arguing for 'locational masking' to avoid the abuse and racism of customers. The work of Miriam Tlali (1987) clearly illustrates the expression of emotional labour as a survival strategy rather than to purely satisfy the customer. In her biographical novel about the experience of Muriel, a skilled black woman clerk in a furniture shop during apartheid South Africa, Tlali (1987) details how Muriel was trained to control her emotions as she saw unequal treatment of the customers and fellow black workers. She details experiences of black customers and how they would queue after being sent threatening letters from the furniture shop to pay their debt, and how they were robbed through this racialised treatment. She mentions that many of the black workers had a language of their own to 'appear' compliant and present false acknowledgement of 'skills' in their white counterparts so they could keep their jobs. The novel details how Muriel, as the frontline worker (in the back office) had to manage her own emotions amid the racial discrimination and unfair treatment at work. She was employed to sort out the finances and record-keeping of the furniture shop, but as a skilled black woman among white women clerks who were less skilled, she was given a corner office under the stairway. It is in this novel that one begins to see the 'sovereignty' of the customer as tied to the structural conditions which necessitate the expressions of emotional labour in order to survive.

METHODOLOGY – DOING EMOTIONAL WORK ON EMOTIONAL LABOUR

I conducted a study from 2010 to 2013 as part of doctoral research on call centre work and worker experiences. The case was the City of Johannesburg Call Centre (Joburg Connect). Data was collected through semi-structured interviews, questionnaires and focus group discussions. Over 58 interviews were conducted with call centre operators, teamleaders, trade union officials, activists, researchers and municipal officials. In addition to the interviews, two focus group discussions were conducted with call centre workers who had previously completed questionnaires. The interviews were taped, transcribed and analysed using themes and coding, while the Statistical Package for the Social Sciences was used to draw comparisons from the questionnaire responses. As part of Weber's ([1964] 2008) bureaucracies that are defined by 'secrecy' and suspicion, researching local government can be described as a form of emotional work, in which the smile and friendliness of the researcher makes it easier to build trusting relations during the research process.

JOBURG CONNECT AS EMOTIONALLY CONTESTED TERRAIN

As part of their daily interaction with customers, Joburg Connect call centre operators receive calls about basic services rendered by the city – water, electricity, traffic, accounts, billing, and so on. The call centre operates 24 hours a day, 7 days a week; it was designed to centralise access for the customers of city services. Call centre operators must restrain their emotions, as customers become racist and sometimes personal in their insults. These insults and frustrations from the customer are embedded in perceived local government inefficiency. This means community members who contact the municipality are sometimes justified in being angry, which is understood by the public call centre workers. The fact that workers are not empowered with the information needed to assist customer forms a source of estrangement to the organisation itself. All the workers interviewed in this study felt that they lied when at work, because they did not have answers to the questions posed by the callers. The call centre operators argued it was disempowering not to possess the tools and information needed for effective work processes. This normally happens when the political leadership communicates with customers before the workers. This was detailed as a source of stress among public call centre workers.

Managers seemed to understand the stressful and frustrating environment in public call centres; they agreed that 'no one can work more than two years in that environment'. In training the workers to deal with angry customers, managers said:

> We simply tell them that they must treat customers like a 'madman' because you don't answer to a 'madman' ... but this is a human being. You get tired of absorbing the hurt, but I tell you after working in the call centre environment, one is able to handle any form of relations in life; working in a call centre is not easy. (Top Manager 3, interview, 2 August 2010)

In one focus group, many workers spoke of organisational inefficiency and poor communication that tended to cause frustration among the customers communicating with the city:

> We give the customers wrong numbers, and you'll find that the customer has all the numbers in your list and you pray that she does not have the next one on your list ... [One of them narrates her story:] I remember there was this guy who called in looking for some director's number. When I gave him this number he was, like, don't even try giving me that number again ... What do you do? You end up lying, giving him the Arts and Culture number ... [Group laughs]. (Focus Group Discussion 1, 3 August 2011)

These are some of the responses given by frontline workers in order to cope with poor communication and bad working conditions within the public call centre. They admit that at times they are required to 'lie' to protect the reputation of the city. This was also admitted by the manager, who claimed 'they have run out of lies' because of increased call volume during the billing crisis where customers were receiving inflated water bills due to the technological challenges in the city (*Mail & Guardian* 2011; *IOL News* 2012). One worker said:

> I used to work at WesBank in the petrol card section, and the customer will call being stuck in a garage and you will be able to say they must swipe their card and reconnect them. Here, it's different! You cannot reconnect the customer even though you feel sorry for the customer; you can try and help but it's difficult here. (Focus Group Discussion 2, 28 September 2012)

This inability to help the customer creates a sense of helplessness that sometimes translates into customer aggression towards the call centre agent. Under these conditions, call centre operators have created their own 'resistance techniques' to cope with work frustrations.

The customer has limited power to persuade the call centre operators to adhere to the 'customer is king' principle. The frontline forms of resistance place the pressure back on the managers, who have to account to politicians and media for poor service delivery. This means control is contested in the public sector call centres despite the high demands of the job. Even when the managers answered the questions on discipline, they pointed to heavy involvement of trade unions in the performance of the call centre operators:

> Labour intervention is ridiculous in the local government. It's like unions are trained to fight against management all the time, but they are supposed to be my eyes. Shop stewards are supposed to be assisting me. I personally think that unions don't understand their role. For example, when I hired temporary workers there was so much productivity in the call centre; they performed because they got paid according to their performance (Top manager 3, interview, 2 August 2010).
>
> Unions are terrible. This management is so weak, they have allowed the union to take over, they are running this place. (Top manager 2, interview, 3 July 2011)

On the other hand, managers identified political interference within local government as the source of the problems that see many calls being abandoned by the call centre operators; managers have no power to discipline the staff involved. One of the managers said she tried to discipline poorly performing call centre workers. She was then taken to the Council for Conciliation, Mediation and Arbitration by the union, and this is costly for the municipality. All the managers felt that local government's poor service delivery and customer care was partly caused by the tight controls that labour unions have on the city council:

> The difference between private and public call centres is that the latter [are] more labour-intensive, lots of consultation with the unions. You cannot move without talking to the union [here]. (Top manager 7, interview, 5 July 2011)

This was shared by workers and managers at large as they believed that the heavily politicised environment affects how work is done and managed in the public sector:

> Everything in the public sector is always problematic; even Samwu [South African Municipal Workers Union] is part of the problem. There is too much political interference. Too much focus on politics rather than communication. (Focus Group Discussion 1, 3 August 2011)

CONCLUSION

The public sector call centre labour process needs to be considered within its socio-political context rather than simply 'fitting it in' with the private sector models of call centre work. The application of the emotional labour in the public call centre is not about the 'sovereignty' of the customer; it is multi-layered and contested as the call centre workers are also paying citizens in the city. The complexity of the public call centre workplace can be considered within broader precarious working conditions in the South African labour market and crippled state services.

When applied in public sector spaces, the 'myth of the sovereign customer' creates unfairly high expectations for individual citizens and customers. This results in anger, which sometimes becomes abusive towards the frontline worker. This leads to the call centre frontline taking blame for systematic organisational failures; this produces anger and a perception of the 'uselessness' of call centre work. The operators are then accused by customers of being incompetent in conducting their tasks (Korczynski 2003).

The efficiency of running a private sector call centre might not be enough in the public sector call centres, as inefficiency can be life-threatening. A smile and polite voice does not 'fix' the basic provision of services within the household. A good deployment of emotional labour towards a customer counts for little when the customer is not quickly reconnected to basic services like water and electricity.

The limited examination of power relations between the 'dependent' customer and the call centre frontline shows that the relationship is different for private sector call centre operators who want to satisfy customers under controlling technological surveillance. In the private sector, a customer can choose an alternative service provider when unhappy about the service, which is different from public sector customers who have no alternative 'municipality' from which to source basic services.

Ian Roper (2004, 123) argues that 'the demand for public goods is inherently political'. The public call centre seeks to reduce the number of calls rather than receive more, because for the public sector call centre, 'less is good'. If the number of calls increase, it means that there is a crisis. The deployment of emotional labour in the public sector call centre is, therefore, contested as the meaning of customer takes a different meaning compared to the private call centre.

REFERENCES

Belt, Vicki. 2002. 'A Female Ghetto? Women's Careers in Call Centres'. *Human Resource Management Journal* 12 (4): 51–66.

Benner, Chris. 2006. 'South Africa On-call: Information Technology and Labour Market Restructuring in South African Call Centres'. *Regional Studies* 40 (9): 1025–1040.

Bolton, Sharon C. and Maeve Houlihan. 2005. 'The (Mis)representation of Customer Service'. *Work, Employment and Society* 19 (4): 685–703.

Boreham, Paul, Rachel Parker, Paul Thompson and Richard Hall. 2008. *New Technology @ Work*. London: Routledge.

Bramming, Pia, Ole H. Sørensen and Peter Hasle. 2009. 'In Spite of Everything: Professionalism as Mass Customised Bureaucratic Production in a Danish Government Call Centre'. *Work, Organisation, Labour and Globalisation* 3 (1): 114–129.

Callaghan, George and Paul Thompson. 2002. 'We Recruit Attitude: The Selection and Shaping of Routine Call Centre Labour'. *Journal of Management Studies* 39 (2): 233–254.

Chong, Patricia. 2009. 'Servitude with a Smile: A Re-examination of Emotional Labour'. *Just Labour: A Canadian Journal of Work and Society* 14: 177–185.

Deery, Stephen and Nicholas Kinnie, eds. 2004. *Call Centres and Human Resource Management: A Cross-National Perspective*. Basingstoke: Palgrave Macmillan.

Fernie, Sue and David Metcalf. 1998. *(Not) Hanging on the Telephone: Payment Systems in the New Sweatshops*. London: Centre for Economic Performance, London School of Economics and Political Science.

Frenkel, Stephen, Marek Korczynski, Karen A. Shire and May Tam. 1999. *On the Front Line: Organization of Work in the Information Economy*. Ithaca NY and London: ILR Press.

Garson, Barbara. 1988. *The Electronic Sweatshops: How Computers are Transforming the Office of the Future into the Factory of the Past*. New York: Simon & Schuster.

Guy, Mary E., Meredith A. Newman and Sharon H. Mastracci. 2008. *Emotional Labor: Putting the Service in Public Service*. Armonk, NY: M.E. Sharpe.

Hochschild, Arlie R. [1983] 2003. *The Managed Heart: Commercialisation of Human Feeling, with a New Afterword*. Los Angeles, CA: University of California Press.

Huang, Shirlena and Brenda S.A. Yeoh. 2007. 'Emotional Labour and Transnational Domestic Work: The Moving Geographies of "Maid Abuse" in Singapore'. *Mobilities* 2 (2): 195–217.

IOL News. 2012. 'Presidency Ask about Joburg Billing Problems'. *IOL*, 27 March 2012. http://www.iol.co.za/news/south-africa/gauteng/presidency-asks-about-joburg-billing-problems-1.1259854#.VC2bd8uKDGg.

Kenny, Bridget. 2004. 'Selling Selves: East Rand Retail Sector Workers Fragmented and Reconfigured'. *Journal of Southern African Studies* 30 (3): 477–498.

Kenny, Bridget. 2005. 'The Market Hegemonic Workplace Order in Food Retailing'. In *Beyond the Apartheid Workplace: Studies in Transition*, edited by Edward Webster and Karl von Holdt, 217–241. Pietermaritzburg: University of KwaZulu-Natal Press.

Korczynski, Marek. 2003. 'Communities of Coping: Collective Emotional Labour in Service Work'. *Organization* 10 (1): 55–79.

Macdonald, Cameron Lynne and David Merrill. 2008. 'Intersectionality in the Emotional Proletariat: A New Lens on Employment Discrimination in Service Work'. In *Service Work: Critical Perspectives*, edited by Marek Korczynski and Cameron Lynne Macdonald, 113–133. New York: Routledge.

Mail & Guardian. 2011. 'Jo'burg Billing Problems: "Please Bear with Us"'. *Mail & Guardian*, 2 February 2011. http://mg.co.za/article/2011-02-02-joburg-billing-problems-please-bear-with-us.

Mirchandani, Kiran. 2004. 'Practices of Global Capital: Gaps, Cracks and Ironies in the Translational Call Centres in India'. *Global Networks*, 57 (8): 355–373.

Nickson, Dennis, Christopher Warhurst, Anne Witz and Anne Marie Cullen. 2001. 'The Importance of Being Aesthetic: Work, Employment and Service Organization'. In *Customer Service: Empowerment and Entrapment*, edited by Andrew Sturdy, Irene Grugulis and Hugh Willmott, 170–190. Basingstoke: Palgrave Macmillan.

Omar, Rahmat. 2016. 'The New Work Order as Contested Terrain: Call Centres in South Africa'. In *The State of Labour: The Global Financial Crisis and Its Impact*, edited by Sharit Bhowmik, 228–249. New Delhi: Routledge India.

Patel, Reena. 2014, 'Today's Good Girls: The Women behind India's BPO Industry'. In *Women, Gender and Everyday Social Transformation in India*, edited by Kenneth Nielsen and Anne Waldrop, 21–32. London: Anthem Press.

Poynter, Gavin. 2000. 'Thank You for Calling: The New Ideology of Work in the Service Economy'. *Sounding Issue* 14: 151–164.

Roper, Ian. 2004. 'Managing Quality in Public Services: Some Distinct Implications for the Re-organisation of Work'. In *Contesting Public Sector Reforms: Critical Perspectives: International Debates*, edited by Pauline Dibben, Geoffrey Wood and Ian Roper, 120–136. Basingstoke: Palgrave Macmillan.

Sallaz, Jeff. 2009. *The Labour of Luck: Casino Capitalism in the United States and South Africa*. London: University of California Press.

Taylor, Phil and Peter Bain, 1999. 'An Assembly Line in the Head: Work and Employee Relations in the Call Centre', *Industrial Relations Journal*. 30 (2): 101117. DOI:10.1111/1468-2338.00113.

Tlali, Miriam. 1987. *Muriel at Metropolitan: A Novel*. Harlow, UK: Longman African Classics.

Tsakalotos, Euclid. 2004. 'Social Norms and Endogenous Preferences: The Political Economy of Market Expansion'. *The Rise of the Market: Critical Essays on the Political Economy of Neoliberalism*, edited by P. Arestis and M. Sawyer, 5–37. Northampton: Edward Elgar Publishing.

Tsakalotos, Euclid. 2004. '"Homo Economicus": Political Economy and Socialism'. *Science & Society* 68 (2), 137–160.

Von Holdt, Karl. 2003. *Transition From Below: Forging Trade Unionism and Workplace Change in South Africa*. Pietermaritzburg: University of Natal Press.

Weber, Max. [1964] 2008. *The Theory of Social and Economic Organization*. New York: Oxford University Press.

Webster, Edward and Rahmat Omar. 2003. 'Work Restructuring in Post-apartheid South Africa'. *Work and Occupations* 30 (2): 194–213.

Williams, Claire. 2003. 'Sky Service: The Demand of Emotional Labour in the Airline Industry'. *Gender, Work and Organisations* 10 (5): 514–550.

INTERVIEWS AND FOCUS GROUP DISCUSSIONS

Joburg Connect, Johannesburg

Focus Group Discussion 1, 3 August 2011.
Focus Group Discussion 2, 28 September 2012.
Top manager 2, interview, 3 July 2011.
Top manager 3, interview, 2 August 2010.
Top manager 7, interview, 6 July 2011.

PART III

NEW FORMS OF ORGANISING

9

Why Other Spaces Matter: The Case of Mamelodi Train Sector

Mpho Mmadi

INTRODUCTION

In his overview of South African labour studies in this volume, Lucien van der Walt raises the emergence of the notion of social movement unionism (SMU) as an explanatory category. He also questions the applicability of the concept in contemporary times. In this chapter, I would like to disrupt this conversation by making a geographic move. Rather than focusing on the workplace as site for union organising and the community as site for social activism, I draw on very specific worker experiences with organising in transit between home and work in order to revive and recast discussions about SMU. The Mamelodi Train Sector (MTS) was formed in 2001 in Tshwane; it organises both formal and informal as well as unionised and non-unionised workers. It is a train-based organisation focusing on commuters, and has formal links to the ruling Tripartite Alliance consisting of the African National Congress (ANC), the South African Communist Party (SACP) and the Congress of South African Trade Unions (Cosatu). The discussion is timely for three reasons. First, it takes place at time when traditional unions struggle to attract marginalised workers into their ranks. Second, there are debates around whether the SMU of the past could be revived. Third, workers' traditional forms of power are being challenged and fragmented. Drawing from MTS as a case study, this chapter attempts to demonstrate that key building blocks characteristic of the SMU of the 1980s are still prevalent within large sections of the working class in South Africa. I propose that by organising on the train, MTS has managed to keep aspects of SMU alive. Drawing on organisational repertoires characteristic of the 1980s, organisations such as MTS demonstrate that, rather than sound the alarm bells around the death of SMU, Cosatu has merely outsourced these organisational traits.

This chapter is in conversation with two recent scholarly publications interested in community–labour alliances. Marcel Paret (2015) has sought to asses prospects for union–community collaborations and, more recently, Janet Cherry (2017) explored the relationship of Cosatu members to the community and the extent to which they are two classes in South Africa. The one group is in formal employment and resides in formal townships, while many members of the community are located on the margins of the economy and are without jobs. In conclusion, Paret and Cherry raise some serious weaknesses regarding organised labour and Cosatu as a federation. Both authors, however, remain hopeful that changes of strategy or cutting ties with the ruling ANC will help facilitate a reunion between organised labour and the community (Paret 2015, 77–78; Cherry 2017, 127). I take this discussion forward by showing how community–labour ties have in fact remained a constant feature of the South African landscape, by operating in different and arguably strategic spaces such as on the trains. Drawing on the case of MTS, this chapter suggests that opportunities for revival abound. Albert Hirschman (cited in Mangcu 2017) cogently observes that energies released during the lifetime of a social movement do not disappear when that social movement becomes a spent force. They are kept in storage and become the driving force for later social movements. This process embodies what Hirschman pronounces as the principle of the conservation and mutation of social energy (Hirshman 1984 cited in Mangcu 2017, 8).

I seek to contribute to this discourse and to the 'Trade Unions and Democracy' project by showing that Cosatu's significance can be linked to the extent to which it is able to produce leaders who in their individual capacities are able to draw from Cosatu's social energy and established links with communities. Arguably, this has been a blind spot for most South African labour studies and for the 'Trade Unions and Democracy' project. Starting in 1994, this series of publications focused exclusively on Cosatu as a monolithic block comprising various unions. Using MTS as a case study, this chapter attempts to demonstrate how individual union leaders are more likely to be involved in initiating other forms of organisation outside formal workplaces and union structures. This is not surprising. Cherry (2017), for example, notes that Cosatu has maintained active links with social movements and civil society pressure groups both provincially and nationally. The union federation has engaged, and at times supported, social society movements dealing with a diverse range of issues. These include but are not limited to the Opposition to Urban Tolling Alliance (later renamed the Organisation Undoing Tax Abuse), the Anti-Privatisation Forum and the Treatment Action Campaign (Cherry 2017, 113). Despite this, Dale McKinley (2014) concludes that the momentum for labour–community alliances was buried in 2001 when Cosatu leadership failed to 'follow through' after the protest action of that year.

As a response to its contextual milieu, the South African labour movement, from the onset, has had to grapple with challenges revolving around race and class politics. For African workers, the intersection between race and class was a daily experience. The extent to which Africans, as workers, were allowed or denied industrial citizenship was influenced and shaped by their race. In this way, workplace relations were a reflection of the broader South African society in which Africans were denied basic political rights. It is in this context that the social movement unionism of the 1980s was relied upon as a power resource against both the state and capital. As such the union movement was heavily involved with community issues around transport, rent, evictions and other forms of state-led abuses against residents which led workers to package their demands as citizenship rights (Sitas 1985, 399; Seidman 1994, 3, 17). This kind of unionism was fraught with internal tensions as workers and activists debated the extent to which involvement in broader political issues was the best strategy to achieve industrial citizenship. This coalesced around what is known as the workerist vs populist[1] debate. These two currents converged in a strategic compromise in 1985 with the formation of Cosatu. It is for these reasons that the social movement aspect of Cosatu has received a great deal of academic attention.

This chapter draws on an ethnographic study conducted between October 2015 and January 2017. I employed participant observation together with one-on-one interviews as data-gathering techniques. This involved a daily commute (morning and afternoon/evening) on the Mamelodi trains, as well as attending organisation meetings one Sunday a month in a local primary school in Mamelodi township.

FORMATION OF COSATU

The 1970s presented an opportunity for black workers. Organised into various unions and having forced the state, employers and the established white labour movement into a defensive mode, black workers quickly recognised the value of power in unity. The emerging labour movement became a critical vehicle through which to channel black aspirations and anger. Following its formation in 1985, Cosatu played a critical part in the reconstruction process of South Africa. While not neglecting shop-floor mobilisation, Cosatu espoused greater affinity with the national democratic movement. Reflecting on his involvement in the labour movement as the first general secretary of Cosatu, Jay Naidoo outlines the purpose and objectives of the federation:

> Our primary focus was on the shop floor, but we also understood that our movement could not stop there, that we had to travel further, to the gates of parliament. We knew we could not deliver dignity without delivering political change first, because the country's political system was ultimately the main source of every social problem in South Africa. To end the oppression our workers lived under, we had to end apartheid first. (Naidoo 2017, 83)

According to Edward Webster (1988, 194–195), social movement unionism came about as a result of a recognition that labour is not a commodity to be bargained over but that labour is both a social and a political force. This point is further elaborated and vividly captured by Ari Sitas:

> It is wrong to suppose that trade unions equal economics whereas the community equals politics. Firstly, there is much in community mobilisation that is economics (e.g., rents, bus fares, prices, etc.) and not qualitatively different from wage struggles. Secondly, there is much that is *assumed* to be political because it confronts state institutions regulating township life (again, rents, buses, infrastructural issues, etc.). (Sitas 1985, 399)

This kind of unionism is peculiar to specific places, especially in authoritarian regimes exemplified by apartheid South Africa, Brazil and the Philippines (Lambert and Webster 1988; Webster 1988; Scipes 1992; Seidman 1994; Hirschsohn 2007). Deploying workers as foot soldiers, Cosatu was able to agitate for participatory democracy, egalitarianism, societal transformation, worker rights and dignity (Sitas 1985; Webster 1988; Seidman 1994; Hirschsohn 2007; Buhlungu 2010; Dibben, Wood, and Mellahi 2012). The aforementioned context and consequently Cosatu's achievements against state oppression require that I highlight key characteristics of SMU. This is important because by clearly delineating SMU we will simultaneously explore differences with orthodox unionism. Rob Lambert and Edward Webster (1988, 20–21) discern three types of unionism, namely orthodox, populist, and political or social movement unionism. Orthodox unionism is a form of trade unionism that focuses exclusively on workplace issues; it fails to connect production issues to wider political challenges. Members are encouraged to be politically involved without the union itself necessarily engaging in the wider political arena, believing that this is best left to other organisations more suited to the task. Lambert and Webster (1988 20–21) acknowledge that the political content of orthodox unionism differs, but that this kind of unionism pivots around institu-tionalising industrial relations conflict and reinforcing divisions between economic and political forms of struggle. Unlike orthodox unionism,

> populist unionism … is a form of trade unionism where struggles in the fac-tory are downplayed. [This type of unionism] neglects struggle over wages, supervision, managerial controls of the workplace and job evaluation. It places in its stead a political engagement that only serves to dissipate shop floor struggles. (Lambert and Webster 1988, 21)

In contrast to the two approaches discussed above, Lambert and Webster character-ise social movement unionism thus:

> It is a union strategy [that] links production to wider political issues. It is a form of union organisation that facilitates an active engagement in factory-based, production politics *and* in community and state power issues. It engages in alliances in order to establish relationships with political organ-isation on a systematic basis. (Lambert and Webster 1998, 21)

Post-apartheid South Africa has proved challenging for Cosatu in maintaining its image as an exemplar of SMU. For most observers this can be accounted for by two factors. The first factor is the federation's relationship with the ruling ANC and its failure to deal with the changing nature of work. In terms of the former, Cosatu and its affiliates have found it increasingly challenging to publicly antagonise the ruling party and have in the process failed to relate to any social formations critical of the ANC (Buhlungu 2010, 97, 176; Webster and Buhlungu 2004, 241–242; Lier and Stokke 2006, 819; Paret 2015, 55). According to McKinley:

> At the heart of the labour–community problematic were the macro-demands and impacts of Cosatu's alliance with the ANC/SACP vis-à-vis incipient struggles taking place outside of its purview. No sooner had the APF [Anti Privatisation Forum], with many more community organizations on board from 2001, begun to offer public critiques of and engage in direct action

against, the privatisation agenda of the ANC government than the various union structures pulled out. By the end of the first year of its existence, Samwu (Gauteng) [South African Municipal Workers Union], SACP Johannesburg Central Branch, the National Education, Health and Allied Workers Union (Wits Branch) and the South African Students Council (Wits Branch) had all left, charging that the APF had become too anti-ANC and anti-government. (McKinley 2014, 17)

In addition to the above, Cosatu's response to the plight of marginalised workers has been ad hoc and evidently inadequate. Those affected by the changing nature of work have found Cosatu inaccessible, a situation that Edward Webster and Sakhela Buhlungu (2004, 23) aptly refer to as a 'crisis of representation'. The rise in flexible and precarious forms of employment has deepened the economic insecurity of most workers. This is epitomised by casualisation, externalisation and informalisation (Theron 2005, 305). Employers have moved away from standard employment relationships; instead, they hire employees on a seasonal basis, they outsource non-core functions to third parties, and informal sector activities such as home-work have increased (Von Holdt and Webster 2005, 5, 7, 17–19, 22–23; 2008, 338).

Considering the above-mentioned failings, some observers have concluded that Cosatu has failed to remain a militant social movement union, noting among others, the growing distance between Cosatu and communities (Lier and Stokke 2006; Ngwane 2012; McKinley 2014; Paret 2015). However, the existence of MTS as a formally recognised structure of the alliance is a clear demonstration of how Cosatu remains an important training school for a variety of social formations in South Africa. This is because MTS is led and driven by members of Cosatu-affiliated unions and other alliance partners. This argument is not new. Buhlungu (2010) highlights how early experiences in churches, self-help societies and so on played an important formative role in the re-emergence of the unions in 1973. Cosatu's contribution to community formations should be understood in a similar vein, and not only as a formal institutional arrangement. At some level, studies carried out by Marcel Paret (2015, 65–70) and Janet Cherry (2017, 120) tentatively allude to this fact. David Lier and Kristian Stokke (2006, 821) also recognise this point and conclude that 'the historical circumstances under which the union strategy of the 1980s originated are qualitatively different from those of today'. It is for this reason that this chapter makes an argument around how Cosatu has outsourced some of its defining features of the 1980s as it moved into an alliance with the ruling elite.

MTS AND SOCIAL UNIONISM?

The history of workers organising on the trains dates back to the 1970s, at the height of the labour unrest in South Africa. Organising on the trains came about as a 'defensive unit in Pretoria as a result of what was happening on the East Rand with Inkatha' (Comrade Maphila, interview, 27 August 2016). This refers to the violence that broke out in the so-called Katorus region, an area comprising Katlehong, Thokoza and Vosloorus. (For a detailed analysis of the violence and its consequences see Segal 1991; Sitas 1996; Bonner and Ndima 1999). This defensive unit was founded with the aim of keeping workers updated with developments from various workplaces but also to provide protection. Gordon Pirie (1992, 178) finds that the train provided the legal loophole to navigate against the apartheid state's restrictions on political activities. For example, following the declaration of the State of Emergency in 1986, the train assumed a very significant role as a point of convergence (see also Shubane 1988). Because outdoor gatherings were banned, the train was utilised to subvert apartheid and its security apparatus. 'Train rallies ... [became the] new expression of the way in which public transport has long been used, both literally and figuratively, to mobilise political resistance in South Africa' (Pirie 1992, 179).

With the advent of democracy, the defensive unit was formally constituted into the Mamelodi Train Sector on 9 June 2001. It is clear that MTS took on a new role, as referred to by Comrade Maphila. It was no longer concerned with subverting the logic of the State of Emergency as observed by Khehla Shubane (1988) and Gordon Pirie (1992). Those who joined the organisation post-1994 were motivated by different reasons:

> I joined MTS in 2004, and by then, remember, the organisation was three years in existence because it was only officially launched in 2001. And I will explain some of the reasons that motivated the formation of this organisation. The organisation was formed because workers did not have a place to meet as workers only, except at the workplace. So, they started using the train as a meeting space where they can discuss workplace-related problems. Then, now it happens that because of the frustrations from work, they started to organise themselves in an organisation. That is why it was called a sector on the train. And one of the important elements of this, which I seek to bring to your attention and emphasise, is that when the organisation was formed because it was formed by members of the ANC, Communist Party and ... Cosatu; so they said ... because of the frustrations let us organise ourselves and begin to engage on issues that serve as challenges at various workplaces.

If your employer is giving you problems, you share that problem with comrades in the coach. (Comrade Segoa, interview, 14 August 2017)

I joined MTS a long time ago. It was officially launched in 2001, but I joined while still a hostel dweller located at B3. I became a hostel dweller from 1994, so I joined from 1996. So, by 1996 I was with MTS. We had an alliance with Mabopane, Ga-Rankua and Atteridgeville, and by that time they were very strong. They were having these Alliance meetings to discuss issues to do with Mabopane, Atteridgeville, Ga-Rankua and Mamelodi ... we all belonged to Tshwane Train Sector as an upper structure ... MTS is a train-based structure focused on commuters. It is not a union and it is not a political organisation ... its purpose is to mobilise workers that are inside the train and commuters. We'll touch issues that are work-related and will touch issues that are concerning us in terms of our transportation. (Comrade Mmotong, interview, 9 September 2017)

The interview extracts quoted above are an elaboration of the understanding of members of Mamelodi Train Sector and Tshwane Train Sector about the role and purpose of these sectors as advanced in the founding constitution of 2001. Clearly, the organisation can be said to be a broad church (open to all workers), with the aim of providing workers a platform from which to discuss, educate and provide guidance in relation to community and workplace challenges. However, workers' identity is presented as being inherently intertwined with that of being a commuter. Therefore, for those without workplace organisation, the contact with MTS activities was likely to influence decisions to join civic and workplace-based pressure groups. Comrade Moela had this to say of his early exposure:

Let's start by why I am a comrade. Back to my roots! See, when I was young, I grew up at a place called Mashabela near Jane Furse. When I was growing up we were not exposed to organisations such as the Congress of South African Students because we did not have them in the rural areas. But we grew up in an era in which the community of Mashabela as a whole was faced with particular kinds of social conditions. So because of those conditions we had the so-called comrades at Mashabela, some of which had been to Zambia under the military wing of the African National Congress ... After 1994 we spent a lot of time with them and they explained our past. So we adopted their mentality and grew up thinking in that mode. So I became a comrade at the age of 11 years. It was a time where I started to engage in politics. (Comrade Moela, interview, 9 August 2017)

It can be inferred that political consciousness is influenced by a number of conditions. At the very basic level, key among these is exposure. It is for this reason that Cosatu's influences is discernible in organisations like MTS.

MZABALAZO ON THE MOVE!

On 19 May 2016, in coach number 4, and as is customary, the day's proceedings were opened with the singing of the national anthem, *Inkosi sikelela' iAfrika*. During the singing of the anthem, all present rose and men took off their hats. Once completed, the chairperson opened his address by greeting fellow workers with the traditional and struggle-inspired '*Amandla!*' (Power!), followed by '*Awethu!*' (It is ours!). '*Comrades, rekgopela ditsibiso*' (comrades, can we have announcements). With no one having anything to announce, he proceeded.

> Okay, *MaCom*,[2] *nna kena le ditsibiso tše tharo* (I have three announcements to make). 1) Comrades, please be reminded the 23rd of May is the last day of voter registration and comrades must thus make an effort to register in order to be eligible to participate in the upcoming local elections. 2) The ANC will be hosting its regional manifesto launch in Atteridgeville [one of the biggest townships in Tshwane] on 29 May 2016. Comrades are encouraged to attend the event in numbers and show support for the ruling party. Sixteen buses will leave from Mamelodi on the day and details around departure points will be communicated soon. 3) On the 4th of June, ANC will be launching the provincial manifesto at the FNB stadium. Again, buses will be organised to ferry comrades to the stadium. (Observations, 19 May 2016)

Following the announcements, the chairperson appealed to his fellow commuters to bring issues forward so that they could be discussed and solutions proposed. With no one taking the stage, the chairperson proceeded to point out the problems associated with current train disruptions. Trains were always late, and the chairperson was worried that comrades would lose their jobs if the rail upgrades were not completed quickly. He shared with the coach that MTS was busy organising a community meeting to deal with this issue, and that it was important for workers to attend so that Metrorail could be made aware of problems affecting workers:

> Yesterday I knocked off work at 15:30 and only arrived home at 7 pm due to this problem with the trains. Yesterday the rand plunged yet again for

the third time this year; therefore, petrol will go up by 50c next week Wednesday. All these problems affect us as workers. Next month, Metrorail is also planning to increase train fares, yet currently the trains are disorganised. We need to organise, comrades! People always expect comrades to do something about transport problems, yet when we call out a community meeting, they don't attend. (Observations, 19 May 2016)

As can be gleaned from the 'meeting' described above, the train provides workers with an important space to discuss and strategise around workplace and community issues. Most importantly, the train is also used as a campaigning platform by the ANC and its alliance partners. This is a space for education, friendships and mobilising for community issues.

'Comrade Mama,'[3] the chairperson, called out as one lady stood up to take the floor after having put up her hand. She asked a question regarding her colleague who was given a suspension letter after a physical altercation with another colleague at work. Her grievance was that it would seem as if the employer's decision (to suspend her colleague) was biased. She emphasised the significance of her question especially because most of the workers in the coach were not unionised. She and her colleague were members of the National Education, Health and Allied Workers Union (Nehawu); her colleague had been outsourced from NetCare to Campus – but luckily, she had retained her union membership. The problem, however, was that the union was reluctant to represent her colleague at the hearing because she was outsourced, despite her being a member in good standing. This meant she was technically non-unionised. In response, the chairperson indicated that Nehawu had a duty to represent her colleague because she was still a member in good standing. 'Nehawu shop stewards must assist', the chairperson insisted.

'So, this will be tomorrow's big issue', the chairperson declared: 'When an employee is faced with a disciplinary committee hearing' – the chairperson pointed to one of the comrades, who was a shop steward, and asked him to come prepared the next day to educate fellow workers on this particular issue. The MTS chairperson cautioned against self-representation in disciplinary hearings. He pointed out the importance of being properly represented in order to avoid getting emotional and making mistakes during such proceedings. He also said, 'If you are alone in a disciplinary hearing it means you have no witnesses. Thus, in the event of a dispute, it will be your word against that of the employer, and such a scenario weakens the employee's case'. At this point the train pulled into Pienaarspoort station.

The above is a fairly typical indication of who travels on the train and to what extent trains continue to be used as spaces of social consciousness.

UNION LOCALS?

The following issues are highlighted in the literature in relation to the South African labour movement. First, there is a hierarchical class relation between union leaders and ordinary members. This hierarchy has, in fact, widened the gap between leaders and the rank and file, thus subverting democratic participation by members in decision-making. Second, the South African labour movement has been bureaucratised, with union leaders emerging as bureaucrats. A causality of the foregoing trends has been, among others, the neglect of local-level structures. This has signalled the weakening of the labour movement, as capital strengthened through the transformation of work.

The comrades' coach is a meeting place for both elected leaders and the rank-and-file membership of MTS. The participation of members is actively encouraged. For example, the weekly activities are structured in the following manner: Tuesday and Thursdays are 'complaints' days, and '*MaCom*' are encouraged to bring complaints for discussion. Wednesdays are 'big issue' days. Workers are expected to raise topical issues that speak to workplace or community concerns. The sort of interactions detailed here are reminiscent of old labour movement traditions, such as mandated report-backs. As union practices, mandated report-backs have been almost unmade by the era of bureaucratic unions (Buhlungu 2010). Once these complaints have been raised in the coach, the elected MTS leadership is expected to act upon them and to provide feedback to workers. This refers to issues of both class and politics. For example, if one had attended any political gathering of the Alliance, they would be required to brief the coach so that MTS members are up to date in respect of their Alliance partners.

ALLIANCE POLITICS

The propensity of the leadership of worker organisations to be offered political office is a well-documented practice, not only here in South Africa but throughout the entire world, and the African continent in particular. A comprehensive analysis of this trend in respect of the African continent is offered by Bjorn Beckman, Sakhela Buhlungu and Lloyd Sachikonye (2010). To be sure, MTS is expected to recruit members for the Alliance, as outlined in its constitution. This means that, by extension, members of MTS are also members of the governing party. It follows from this arrangement that those with political aspirations are afforded political office through the MTS ticket. Inevitably, the comrades' coach is a political site, and therefore provides a platform for local campaigns for political office. On 3 November 2015, the forthcoming 2016 local government elections were the subject of discussion, and comrades were reminded to go and vote for the ruling ANC the following year (Observations, November 2015). In addition, there was an appeal for comrades to stop physically attacking councillors and damaging public property:

> Comrades, let us just keep in mind that burning down schools and clinics only makes us poorer. Vandalising such infrastructures affects only us and our children. Similarly, burning down the local councillor's house is ill-advised because you put his/her children at great danger. Let's rethink our methods, comrades. (Observations, November 2015)

Clearly the message against vandalism is quite strong and a consistent position of MTS members and its leadership. On Tuesday, 24 May 2016, the chairperson, Comrade Maponya, strongly condemned events that were taking place in Vuwani, Limpopo province. He fiercely discouraged the torching of schools and other government buildings. Other leaders have made similar points:

> As MTS we do organise community protests. But we do so at the political level. At the level of the ANC. We don't organise them via train sector, even if they are led by members of the train sector, but they are organised through the ANC. As a campaigning structure, remember the protest itself is a campaign, therefore members of the train sector will fully attend such protests, as a campaign … we organise them jointly with the SACP and Sanco [South African National Civics Organisation] as well. (Comrade Segoa, interview, 14 August 2017)

Echoing the above clarion call, Comrade Segoa continued:

> We can never, as train sector, go and protest at an individual's household. Because we just don't wake up and say we're going to protest. We can never allow a situation in which a protest action is directed at an individual's home. Because we know and understand that ward councillors are employees of the municipality. Therefore, when we have issues we will take them to the municipality … our members know and are always advised to stay away from protest actions that target individual's homesteads. (Comrade Segoa, interview, 14 August 2017)

Following from the conversation above, two things are noteworthy. First, workers put local ward councillors into power. This finding is in line with the interview with Mr Maphila, who was deployed by Cosatu to stand as a ward councillor. Mr Maphila was a councillor for Ward 34 in Mamelodi West from 1994, Ward 6 in 2002 and Ward 28 in 2011 (Comrade Maphila, interview, 27 August 2016). Second, it is the same workers who demand accountability around service delivery issues. Conclusively, this makes clear the fact that the comrades' coach is not only a space for workers but also a site of community contestations. Campaigning in this space makes this point poignantly clear. The workers' active involvement in this political project can be linked to the history of Cosatu as an organisation. The general secretary of MTS addressed the coach as follows on the morning of 17 May 2016:

> Comrades, please be aware that this month of May is workers month and therefore it is incumbent upon us to do more in order to advance the interests of workers. This month is International Workers Month and we have planned to commemorate some of our former leaders who passed away. Because if we don't do this comrades, counter-revolutionary forces will up-stage us, comrades. We will wake up one day to find Inkatha Freedom Party[4] or the DA[5] busy claiming to commemorate one of our fallen leaders. (Observations, 17 May 2016)

This statement was in reference to the newly formed breakaway party, the Economic Freedom Fighters led by former ANC Youth League president, Julius Malema. The new party attempted to commemorate and honour the late ANC military wing operative, Solomon Mahlangu, who had been convicted of murder by the apartheid government and hanged in 1979. The MTS general secretary was asking MTS members to be vigilant of such attempts and telling them that they needed to reclaim the political space as workers.

In line with the general secretary's message, observations from late April into May 2016 indicate that the comrades' coach increasingly became a political platform. This finding was a distinct characteristic of the 05:45 am train number 91:16. The chairperson of the coach, Comrade Maponya, was campaigning for the position of ward councillor in Mamelodi East. Inevitably, Comrade Maponya dedicated a substantial amount of time to talking about the upcoming elections as well as to encouraging fellow comrades to register for them.

Comrade Segoa explains why MTS chose and supported Comrade Maponya to contest for a councillor position in the upcoming local elections:

> Because we are members of society, we are not only going to discuss issues affecting workers. Even social issues at home, we need to discuss those issues and political issues. One of the congress resolutions we took was that MTS shall serve as a campaigning structure of the Alliance ... As workers we can't only be active at work through unions, because at times workplace problems are linked and are as a result of political problems. People need to understand that aspect. For example, if I speak about the Labour Relations Act, that Act came about because of the political organisation currently in Cabinet [*sic*]. So, to achieve some of our objectives as workers, we needed to have influence at the political level ... So, we saw it fit, as a campaigning structure, to deepen our participation in these [political] platforms ... That is why [the] majority of MTS members are leaders elsewhere in society. We agreed that we needed to see our members in government; we are having councillors. The first thing we agreed was that let us target Ward 10. It was an informal settlement, Mandela, Lusaka[6] ... We agreed that Comrade XX,[7] who was our former president, to be a ward councillor there. He was a ward councillor [for] years and we said we could not leave that space alone. And we said Comrade [Maponya] must be a councillor because there are issues there. And we want to see Train Sector represented there because members of the Train Sector shall, from time to time represent the working class. We considered Comrade [Maponya] and we managed to be successful ... What we are doing is to encourage comrades at Ward 10 that this is a suitable candidate and we're providing them reasons for our candidate. (Comrade Segoa, interview, 14 August 2017)

For those seeking political office, the comrades' coach provides access to a captive audience with deep-rooted community ties. Generally, there exists a connection between workplace and community leadership roles. This means that an attempt to separate the world of work from the community as a place from which workers come is a naïve and futile exercise. As a space of contestation, the comrades' coach is ineluctably a site for a just social project – citizenship rights.

Because of this, the political aspect of the space is amplified and articulated through political parties such as the ANC. At an ideological level, the ANC, guided by the Freedom Charter as an economic blueprint, became an important vehicle through which full citizenship rights could be attained. This provides the motivation and premise upon which comrades seek to elect fellow workers to leadership positions. This triangular relationship between citizenship, worker and political agent is generally a key antidote against the demise of the social unionism character of the South African labour movement – Cosatu in particular.

CONCLUSION

This chapter has attempted to deepen and take further Paret's (2015) and Cherry's (2017) discussion around social movement unionism in post-apartheid South Africa. The two texts are insightful and reignite hope by demonstrating that workers still prefer to be heavily involved in community struggles. Rather than focusing on union head-office politics, the empirical contribution of this chapter is an exploration of what happens in transit between home and work. These are informal spaces, but the MTS has succeeded in establishing a measure of formal organisation that cuts across and disrupts union delimitations of industrial sector or labour market status. It is clear that Cosatu remains committed to the alliance with the ruling African National Congress and has worked hard to preserve these relations, though at times to the detriment of rank-and-file membership. On the other hand, and as the chapter has shown, it is through that very Cosatu that workers, mostly as individuals, remain highly active and involved as political agents in their respective communities. For this reason, it is too tenuous a proposition to suggest a disconnect between Cosatu, its organisational repertoires, history and community formations. Organisationally, community formations pivot around a few individuals with organisational exposure and leadership skills. In most cases, such leaders are products of Cosatu-related structures and struggles. MTS is a case in point and a valuable contribution to labour studies, which has not looked in depth at the links between community struggles and trade unions in post-apartheid South Africa.

The chapter suggests that post-apartheid South Africa requires innovative forms of engagement in order to maximise opportunities available to the working class. One such innovative form of engagement is the recognition that Cosatu has evolved and thus has had to adjust some of its strategies of engagement with the party in power, with communities and with the working class a whole.

NOTES

1   Populists argued that due to the undeniable fact that Africans were oppressed both in the workplace and in broader society, then the most plausible strategy was for trade unions to be involved in the national struggle. Populists believed that workers' struggles in factories and townships were indivisible. Fundamentally, populists were of the view that this oppression was racially motivated and thus workplace freedom without full citizenship rights was inadequate. Therefore, populists were in favour of a mobilisation strategy that went beyond the shop floor and encouraged participation in broad struggles around housing and education, as well as the struggle for national liberation. Further, alliance formations that included other groupings were viewed as important in order to achieve full emancipation of African people. The workerists, on the other hand, preferred prioritising the fight against class exploitation. The Federation of South African Trade Unions under the leadership of Joe Foster was the most vociferous protagonist from this camp. This group believed that, in order to achieve liberation, the class system had to be abolished first, thereby challenging the apartheid regime in an incremental way. For workerists, it was important for unions to focus on shop-floor bread-and-butter issues. Workerist did not eschew the nationalist goal of a non-racial South Africa, but they saw this goal as inadequate because it was not worker-led and worker-controlled.

2   'MaCom' is shorter version and a colloquial way of saying 'comrades'.

3   This refers to female comrades. Mama is a culturally respectful term meant to acknowledge women and their role as mothers or as elders.

4   The Inkatha Freedom Party (IFP), generally considered to be right-wing, is based mainly in KwaZulu-Natal, with a predominately Zulu ethnic support base.

5   The Democratic Alliance (DA) traces its roots to the apartheid years under the name United Party. In 1959, the United Party went through a split when mainly younger members broke away to form the Progressive Party, The party went through a series of mergers and further name changes and, following an alliance between the New National Party and the Federal party, the DA was born. It is currently the largest official opposition party in the South African parliament.

6   Mandela and Lusaka are some of the sections that makes up Mamelodi East. These were informal settlements before they were formalised.

7   Name concealed for ethical reasons.

REFERENCES

Beckman, Bjorn, Sakhela Buhlungu and Lloyd Sachikonye. 2010. 'Introduction: Trade Unions and Party Politics in Africa'. In *Trade Unions and Party Politics: Labour Movements in Africa*, edited by Bjorn Beckman, Sakhela Buhlungu, and Lloyd Sachikonye, 1–27. Cape Town: HSRC Press.

Bonner, Philip and Vusi Ndima. 1999. 'The Roots of Violence on the East Rand, 1980–1990'. Seminar Paper No. 450, Johannesburg: Institute for Advanced Social Research, University of the Witwatersrand. https://wiredspace.wits.ac.za/bitstream/handle/10539/8435/ISS-38.pdf. Accessed 9 November 2016.

Buhlungu, Sakhela. 2010. *A Paradox of Victory: Cosatu and the Democratic Transformation in South Africa*. Pietermaritzburg: University of KwaZulu-Natal Press.

Cherry, Janet. 2017. 'Cosatu, Service Delivery, Civil Society and the Politics of Community'. In *Labour Beyond Cosatu: Mapping the Rupture in South Africa's Labour Landscape*, edited by Andries Bezuidenhout and Malehoko Tshoaedi, 111–128. Johannesburg: Wits University Press.

Dibben, Pauline, Geoffrey Wood and Kamel Mellahi. 2012. 'Is Social Movement Unionism Still Relevant? The Case of the South African Federation Cosatu'. *Industrial Relations Journal* 43 (6): 494–510.

Hirschsohn, Philip. 2007. 'Union Democracy and Shopfloor Mobilization: Social Movement Unionism in South African Auto and Clothing Plants'. *Economic and Industrial Democracy* 28 (1): 6–48.

Lambert, Rob and Edward Webster. 1988. 'The Re-emergence of Political Unionism in Contemporary South Africa?' In *Popular Struggles in South Africa*, edited by William Cobbett and Robin Cohen, 20–41. Trenton, NJ: Review of African Political Economy/ Africa World Press.

Lier, David and Kristian Stokke. 2006. 'Maximum Working Class Unity? Challenges to Local Social Movement Unionism in Cape Town'. *Antipode*, 38 (4): 802–824.

Mangcu, Xolela. 2017. *Biko: A Biography*. Cape Town: Tafelberg.

McKinley, Dale. 2014. *'Labour and Community in Transition: Alliances for Public Services in South Africa. Municipal Services Project'*. Occasional Paper Number 24, June 2014. https://www.world-psi.org/sites/default/files/documents/research/occasionalpaper24_mckinley_labour_and_community_in_transition_alliances_for_public_services_in_south_africa_june2014.pdf. Accessed 14 May 2023.

Naidoo, Jay. 2017. *Change: Organising Tomorrow, Today*. Cape Town: Penguin Books.

Ngwane, Trevor. 2012. 'Labour Strikes and Community Protests: Is There a Basis for Unity in Post-apartheid South Africa?' In *Contesting Transformation: Popular Resistance in Twenty-first Century South Africa*, edited by Luke Sinwell and Marcel Dawson, 125–142. London: Pluto Press.

Paret, Marcel. 2015. 'Cosatu and Community Struggles: Assessing the Prospects for Solidarity'. In *Cosatu in Crisis: The Fragmentation of an African Trade Union Federation*, edited by Vishwas Satgar and Southall Roger, 54–82. Johannesburg: KMM Review.

Pirie, Gordon. 1992. 'Travelling under Apartheid'. In *The Apartheid City and Beyond: Urbanisation and Social Change in South Africa*, edited by David M. Smith, 173–182. London: Routledge.

Scipes, Kim. 1992. 'Understanding the Labor Movement in the "Third World": The Emergence of Social Movement Unionism'. *Critical Sociology* 19 (2): 81–101.

Segal, Lauren. 1991. 'The Human Face of Violence: Hostel Workers Speak'. *Journal of Southern African Studies* 18 (1): 190–231.

Seidman, Gay. 1994. *Manufacturing Militance: Workers' Movements in Brazil and South Africa, 1970–1985*. Oakland, CA: University of California Press.

Shubane, Khehla. 1988. '"Emzabalazweni!" There's Politics on the Train'. *South African Labour Bulletin* 13 (7): 43–47.

Sitas, Ari. 1985. 'Moral Formations and Struggles among Migrant Workers on the East Rand'. *Labour, Capital and Society* 18 (2): 372–401.

Sitas, Ari. 1996. 'The New Tribalism: Hostels and Violence'. *Journal of Southern African Studies* 22 (2): 235–248.

Theron, Jan. 2005. 'Employment is not What it Used to be: The Nature and Impact of Work Restructuring in South Africa'. In *Beyond the Apartheid Workplace: Studies in Transition*, edited by Edward Webster and Karl von Holdt, 293–316. Pietermaritzburg: University of KwaZulu-Natal Press.

Von Holdt, Karl and Edward Webster. 2005. 'Work Restructuring and the Crisis of Social Reproduction: A Southern Perspective'. In *Beyond the Apartheid Workplace: Studies in Transition*, edited by Edward Webster and Karl von Holdt, 3–40. Pietermaritzburg: University of KwaZulu-Natal Press.

Von Holdt, Karl and Edward Webster. 2008. 'Organizing on the Periphery: New Sources of Power in the South African Workplace'. *Employee Relations* 30 (4): 333–354.

Webster, Edward. 1988. 'The Rise of Social Movement Unionism: The Two Faces of Black Trade Unionism in South Africa'. In *State, Resistance, and Change in South Africa*, edited by Philip Frankel, Noam Pines and Swilling Mark, 33–41. London: Croom Helm.

Webster, Edward and Sakhela Buhlungu. 2004. 'Between Marginalisation and Revitalisation? The State of Trade Unionism in South Africa'. *Review of African Political Economy* 31 (100): 229–245.

INTERVIEWS

Mamelodi

Comrade Maphila, 27 August 2016.
Comrade Mmotong, 9 September 2017.
Comrade Moela, 9 August 2017.
Comrade Segoa, 14 August 2017.

10

Social Capital Unionism and Empowerment: A Case of Solidarity Union at ArcelorMittal Vanderbijlpark

Jantjie Xaba

INTRODUCTION

Mpho Mmadi's chapter in this volume makes a case for a revitalised form of social movement unionism. The aim of this chapter is to disrupt this perspective by putting on the table the idea of social capital unionism (SCU). As pointed out by Lucien van der Walt earlier in this volume, there has been very little focus in South African labour studies on trade unions beyond the tradition of the Congress of South African Trade Unions (Cosatu). This chapter focuses on the trade union Solidarity (also known by its Afrikaans name, Solidariteit) to explore an example of SCU. Since the dawn of economic liberalism in South Africa, there have been many debates about how the declining role of the 'organising model' of trade unions affects vulnerable groups of workers – the casuals, part-timers and contracted workers. Historically, trade unions were founded on the principle of worker empowerment by winning rights for members such as medical and pension benefits. However, the loss of capacity to organise members and recruit new ones reflects the breakdown of the dense networks of strong social ties on which shared interests, solidarity and collective action were traditionally based. Bruce Nissen and Paul Jarley (2005) maintain that trade unions must go beyond simple conflict escalation techniques and employ more sustainable strategies for recreating community in the workplace.

Typically for South Africa, following the 1990s market-led reforms, trade unions have embarked on wealth creation or 'labour capitalism' by establishing trade union investment as a way to generate revenue to improve the lives of members and their dependents through benefits such as bursaries, pension funds and funeral schemes (Iheduru 2001). However, this model has been marred by issues of financial mismanagement, factionalism and a lack of control by members over their own investment companies. This chapter illustrates that business unionism must be accompanied by social capital unionism that focuses on organising around people to build dense social networks among members, as well as personal relationships through frequent interactions between members both inside and outside of work.

The qualitative approach employed for this research consisted of a combination of in-depth interviews and focus groups with white workers, management, trade union officials and community representatives; archival sources, consisting of reports, newsletters, newspaper articles and speeches were also explored. Together, these sources enabled a case study of Solidarity to explain how its 'Histadrut model' served as an example of SCU that was used to benefit white workers at ArcelorMittal in Vanderbijlpark, South Africa. This contribution is important because studies on trade union revitalisation have ignored the contribution of Solidarity and simply dismissed it as a 'service union' and as a non-confrontational and politically non-aligned union (Mantashe 2008, 80). Other studies on South African trade unions have focused on the socialist and Marxist union tradition represented by Cosatu. *Labour Beyond Cosatu*, edited by Andries Bezuidenhout and Malehoko Tshoaedi (2017), never looked at Solidarity, the current incarnation of the Mineworkers Union (MWU). That will be done for the first time in this book.

RESEARCH METHODOLOGY

The material for this study is based on 74 in-depth, semi-structured interviews which were conducted between 2014 and 2018 for my doctoral study. The participants included 25 former white employees, 14 former black employees, 8 current white employees, 10 current black employees, 10 union officials and 7 community representatives. Of these, eight participants were women, while the rest were men.

In addition, two focus groups were conducted with four officials from Solidarity and six officials from the National Union of Metalworkers of South Africa (Numsa).

The officials interviewed included representatives from unions, a steel company in Vanderbijlpark and community organisations. The chairpersons of the National African Federated Chamber of Commerce, Business and Jobs Opportunity, and the Sakekamer (Chamber of Business) were interviewed to get the perspectives of the organisations working with entrepreneurs in the community. I also interviewed two professors from North-West University to get their viewpoint about the history of the town, the organisation and the community. One professor from Stellenbosch University was interviewed to understand the history and role of Solidarity in promoting social empowerment for its members. Three plant managers were interviewed; since no official from the company's Human Resources department was available, numerous company reports, minutes of meetings, newspaper articles, government reports, company presentations, journal articles and books were used as the official voice of the company.

For the white workers, men between the ages of 70 and 87 were interviewed, and three women between the ages of 70 and 75 were interviewed. Most of these individuals had worked for the Iron and Steel Industrial Corporation (Iscor, now ArcelorMittal South Africa) for more than 20 years. Some were retrenched in the early 1990s and then rehired, while others resigned. In addition, five current white employees were interviewed. The interviews were arranged with the help of two unions, as well as help from informants. White employees were represented by Solidarity. Five officials, men only, from Solidarity were interviewed. Fourteen interviews were conducted with black employees, again only men, aged between 55 and 75. In addition, interviews were conducted with five current black female employees aged between 35 and 50, who were Numsa members. Five officials from Numsa were interviewed.

In addition, nine representatives from various organisations in the Sedibeng Region were interviewed to get their experiences on how the Broad-Based Black Economic Empowerment (B-BBEE) legislation was being implemented and the challenges facing entrepreneurs as far as B-BBEE legislation was concerned. Also interviewed were two officials from the Vanderbijlpark Estate Company, a long-term subsidiary of Iscor, three officials from the National African Federated Chamber of Commerce and one from the Sakekamer. The Sakekamer was formed in 1949 by an affiliate of the Broederbond, the Federasie van Afrikaanse Kultuurvereniginge (FAK), to provide guidance and direction to Afrikaner business undertakings, and to facilitate greater contact and cooperation between local entrepreneurs and prominent business leaders nationally (O'Meara 1983, 145).

These interviews were mostly conducted in English, although some were in Afrikaans, Sesotho and isiZulu to enhance communication and gain more reliable

207

information. Questions were asked about political–legal and economic strategies and social empowerment at Iscor during the era of the National Party, as well as current political–legal, economic and social strategies in post-apartheid South Africa. Data gathered through interviews was thematically analysed.

BOURDIEU'S THEORY OF CAPITAL AND EMPOWERMENT

Scholars have debated the nature and role of social capital in promoting the long-term development of the poor. Hamidreza Babaei, Nobaya Ahmad and Sarjit Gill (2012, 119) argue that the development of social capital has contributed to economic, social and political development by enabling information-sharing, mitigating opportunistic behaviour and facilitating collective decision-making. Andy Banks and Jack Metzgar (2005, 27) maintain that trade unions could greatly increase their value and effectiveness if they paid more attention to the 'naturally occurring social networks' that tie members together in [and outside of their] workplaces. These networks are what social scientists call 'social capital'. Therefore, it is necessary to understand how institutions, networks and norms comprise social capital and how trade unions can generate and manage this capital.

According to Pierre Bourdieu (1986), there are various forms of 'capital': cultural, social and economic. Capital is accumulated labour, which can potentially produce different forms of profit (Bourdieu 1986). According to Bourdieu, all forms of capital can always be converted into economic capital, which is made possible by a conceptual break with the neo-classical economists' practice of artificially isolating the economy from cultural capital. Cultural capital has three forms of existence. It exists, first, as incorporated in the habitus – that is, a set of dispositions, reflexes and forms of behaviour that people acquire through acting in society. Second, cultural capital is objectivised in cultural articles. And finally, it is institutionalised in cultural institutions and expressed in terms of certificates, diplomas and examinations (Bourdieu 1979).

Richard Jenkins (1992, 63) defines social capital as the totality of all actual and potential resources (derived from one's belonging to a group) associated with the possession of a lasting network of more or less institutionalised relations of knowing or respecting each other. Advocates of social capital distinguish between two components: group membership and social networks. Membership in groups (such as voluntary associations, trade unions, political parties, secret societies) and involvement in the social networks developing within these and in the social relations arising from the membership can be utilised in efforts to improve the social position of the actors in a variety of different fields (Siisiäinen 2000, 12). These organisations can create a sense of solidarity among a mass of persons, give a 'name' to and institutionalise the capital that is being accumulated. Social capital is based on mutual cognition and recognition. For Bourdieu (1986), social capital can be transformed into symbolic capital – that is, capital in whatever form, when perceived by an agent endowed with categories of perception arising from the internalisation (embodiment) of the structure of its distribution. Jenkins (1992, 64) argues that the amount of social capital held by individuals depends on the extent to which they can mobilise a social network and form the capital.

Economic capital is directly convertible into money and may be manifested in family income and wealth. It is captured in part by socioeconomic status but using that as an aggregate variable is sometimes problematic as it is composed not only of a family's income, but also of the parents' education and occupational status and, therefore, it is unclear what component of socioeconomic status is responsible for a certain effect. Although Bourdieu (1986) recognises economic capital as one form of capital that is necessary to understand the social world, he did not pay specific attention to it, believing that its absence does not necessarily hinder the possession of all other forms of capital and that economic capital is insufficient in itself to understand how advantages in individuals' life opportunities are produced and reproduced (Ra 2011, 19).

The theoretical point of departure in this chapter is that the current conceptions of social capital do not pay close attention to the interconnection between economic, social, cultural and political capital. Unlike the other three forms of capital, political capital has not gained wide currency. A perspective on social capital was introduced by Robert Putnam (1993) in the final chapter of his seminal book *Making Democracy Work*, which explores the conditions for creating responsive and effective democratic institutions. Putnam (2007, 137) defines social capital as features of social organisation such as 'social networks and the associated norms of reciprocity and trust' that facilitate coordination and cooperation for mutual benefit. Putnam identifies three components of social capital: moral obligations and norms, social values (especially trust) and social networks (especially voluntary associations) as essential for improving a society's efficiency in overcoming dilemmas of collective action. The advocates of social capital argue that the institutions, social networks and norms of reciprocity comprise the sum of resources that contribute directly to empowerment at the local level, and indirectly by making institutions more responsive to the poor (Bourdieu 1986, 246; Babaei, Ahmad and Gill 2012, 119). This means that to understand empowerment it is necessary to understand whether there is a significant relationship between social capital and empowerment.

Putnam (1993) identifies three distinct types of social capital: 'bonding', 'bridging' and 'linking' social capital. Bonding social capital refers to strong, dense ties between people who know each other well, such as family members, close friends, neighbours and members of primary groups (Schuller, Baron and Field 2000; Babaei et al. 2012). Bonding capital connects individuals who are similar in terms of socio-financial position and demographic characteristics; groups defined by these relations have a high degree of homogeneity (Putnam 1993). Bridging capital refers to the building of connections between heterogeneous groups, which are likely to be more fragile, but also more likely also to foster social inclusion. Bridging social capital covers distant ties of like persons, such as colleagues and fast friends. By stressing openness towards different types of people, this form of social capital is thought to reflect generalised trust, inculcating broader identities and more generalised forms of reciprocity than occurs through bonding relations. Linking social capital pertains to connections with people in power and positions of authority or influence, whether political or financial (Jacobs 2009, 35). According to Babaei et al. (2012, 121), linking ties may include civil society organisations, government agencies, representatives of the public and the private sector. This form of social capital is vital in terms of increased access to key resources from formal institutions outside the community.

John Booth and Patricia Richard (1998) criticise Putnam for failing to specify how civil society impinges upon government, as he never elucidates how group involvement affects citizen behaviour or attitudes to influence government performance or enhance prospects for democracy. For Booth and Richard, political capital consists of four components – democratic norms, voting, campaign activism and contacting public officials – which in turn foster attitudes and behaviours that ultimately influence political regimes. Banks and Metzgar (2005, 27) add that political capital is not just about electoral or legislative politics but more about using socially developed norms of reciprocity, trust and organisational skills to achieve power and change power relations. For Bourdieu, political capital relates less to political leaders and more to the ability of citizens to translate social capital into material benefits – differences in patterns of lifestyle and consumption. Thus, understanding the three forms of capital requires a deeper understanding of the role of politics.

EMPOWERMENT

The Broad-Based Black Economic Empowerment Act 53 of 2003 established a legal framework for the promotion of empowerment, specified its purpose, policy instruments and established institutions responsible for its implementation. The Act defined empowerment as

> integrated and coherent socio-economic process that directly contributes to the economic transformation of South Africa and brings about significant increases in the numbers of black people that manage, own and control the country's economy, as well as significant decreases in income inequalities. (Department of Trade and Industry 2003: 15)

Across the world, the concept of empowerment has become an important tool for enabling marginalised people to gain access to resources and to value their own experience. However, empowerment remains an elusive and multifaceted concept. Deepa Narayan (2002, 14) defines empowerment as the expansion of assets and capabilities of poor people to participate in, negotiate with, influence, control and hold accountable institutions that affect their lives. Babaei et al. (2012, 120) describe empowerment as a social process because, in most cases, it occurs in a relationship with others. Based on their definition, empowerment is an ongoing social action process by which individuals, communities and organisations that lack an equitable share of power and valuable resources gain increased access to those resources, along with a simultaneous increase in funds of knowledge. Eventually, these gains lead to improved equity and life opportunities. Therefore, it is necessary to understand if there is significant relationship between empowerment and social capital.

In the South African context, the dominant approach to implementing empowerment is on increasing the black share of ownership in major companies. However, Stefan Ponte, Simon Roberts and Lance van Sittert (2007, 934) argue that this dominant approach is self-contradictory in that, rather than effecting structural changes in the economy, it provides 'enhanced opportunities for black elites' (who are politically connected to the ruling party) to improve their position via affirmative action. In questioning the success of empowerment, I critique the economic construction of empowerment that focuses on a system of codes, arithmetic formulas, graphs, and indices. My argument is that little or no attention is given to the social and cultural capital that enables poor people to access empowerment such as values, norms, networks, relationships and language. Importantly, the social and cultural considerations allow for a far deeper understanding of power and relations between citizens as well as how this affects their chances of empowerment.

Jo Rowland (1995) proposes a model of power that distinguishes between four types of power: 'power with', 'power within', 'power over' and 'power to'. Empowerment requires an understanding of how these forms of power are applied in society to explain how structures and relations of power affect the ability of individuals or communities to determine for themselves who they are and how they choose to relate to others – in other words, how the state and markets, including civil society organisations, operate to promote empowerment through the development of social capital. It is clear that empowerment cannot be understood and measured purely in economic terms. Cecilia Luttrell and her colleagues (2009) propose a multidimensional perspective to empowerment that shows how economic, human, social, political and cultural dimensions contribute to empowerment through mobilisation, determining hiring practices, or the development of social capital.

SOCIAL CAPITAL UNIONISM

The idea that trade unions can be used to generate social capital is not entirely unique to South Africa. Historically, trade unions functioned as 'mutual aid societies' – 'avenues' in which workers with shared interests would meet and develop strong emotional bonds infused with the reciprocity and mutuality needed for collective action (Nissen and Jarley 2005). But to change the conditions of their work and of their lives, workers had to act collectively using what Nissen and Jarley (2005) refer to as the 'organising model'. Since the dawn of economic liberalisation in the mid-1990s, many unions have lost the capacity to organise the new 'working poor'. Edward Webster and Sakhela Buhlungu (2004) maintain that casualisation and externalisation have put trade unions under enormous pressure to seek new strategies to organise part-time workers, casuals and informal sector workers.

Since the dawn of economic globalisation, there has been a wide debate about its impact on workers and trade unions. Around the world, many scholars claim that economic globalisation has reduced the power and influence of trade unions significantly, and today workers find themselves increasingly disconnected from one another. Following the decline in trade union membership, there have been widespread debates about the need for trade union modernisation, revitalisation and renewal (Webster and Buhlungu 2004; Hyman 2007). Typically for South African trade unions, especially those affiliated to Cosatu, the response came in two ways. The first response by labour is called 'strategic unionism', which means focusing on the 'human resource policies and institutions and on industrial strategy' (Misra 2008, 157), building a tripartite alliance with the African National Congress and the South African Communist Party, and shifting focus away from 'politics of resistance to politics of reconstruction' (Mantashe 2008, 5). The second response involved the realisation of the socialist vision of Cosatu to embark on wealth creation or 'labour capitalism', as Cosatu and its affiliates have established trade union investment companies. These investment vehicles are said to advance the concept of socially responsible investment and to provide independent sources of revenue for the unions and, allegedly, to promote the influence of the trade union movement in the economy. Okechukwu Iheduru (2001, 2) maintains that these strategies not only contain the impact of globalisation and neo-liberal economic reforms, but also enable the labour movement to remain relevant to the politics of transformation in the country. Unfortunately, none of these strategies considered the relationships, networks and workers' interests within and outside the workplace as a form of capital or how economic globalisation has affected worker solidarity, social networks and relationships.

Social capital unionism suggests that trade unions should strive to recreate the dense communities inside and beyond workplaces by systematically creating social networks among workers (Nissen and Jarley 2005). Nissen and Jarley (2005) maintain that the erosion of union organisation reflects the breakdown of such dense networks of strong social ties on which shared interests, solidarity and collective action were traditionally based. Accordingly, unions are compelled to go beyond simple conflict escalation techniques and employ more sustainable strategies for recreating community in the workplace – strategies that recognise the many mechanisms by which workers interact in ways that can promote generalised reciprocity norms. Unlike strategic unionism and labour capitalism, SCU favours service unions like Solidarity, which not only harness social capital to achieve concrete industrial relations outcomes (Saundry, Stuart and Antcliff 2012, 263), but also invest resources in improving service delivery and mobilising members for action. This could benefit trade unions and workers in various ways.

One such benefit is that it could allow trade unions to build capacity to 'borrow and extend the social capital of its most well-connected members' (Nissen and Jarley 2005, 12). Furthermore, social networks are not confined to purely workplace issues; they can be sustained among workers across employers, making union membership more readily 'portable across firms'. Putnam (2007) argues that individuals benefit from social capital when they participate in a variety of social networks and voluntary organisations and that a dense associational life contributes to the strength of the broader community and polity. Hyman (2007, 193–210) adds other benefits of the collective dimension of social capital, such as 'representative capacity', 'responsiveness of representatives', 'willingness to act as a social worker in dealing with issues outside of work itself' and 'the quality of the interrelationships between representatives and their constituents'.

The advocates of SCU maintain that it is necessary for the poor to form and mobilise members' connections within and between various units and outside organisations to gain access to a variety of resources (Johnson and Jarley 2005). According to Dan Cohen and Lawrence Prusak (2001), these connections are believed to be vital for the development of the shared values, trust and mutual understanding that make group cooperation and coordination possible.

The Iscor Vanderbijlpark case study was worth researching as it is remarkably unique. First, using Putnam's (2007) three types of social capital, this research found an example of social capital in Vanderbijlpark called the Iscor Club[1], which had been formed in 1944. According to Iscor (1973, 42), the club hosted facilities such as sporting codes, a clubhouse and playing fields. The Iscor Club triggered a sense of 'community' similar to what Putnam had found in the United States in the 1960s. Second, the Iscor Club served as an example of SCU by encouraging the formation of informal and formal networks of friendships, associations and relationships among white employees. With its membership open only to whites, the club contributed immensely to building and maintaining Afrikaner exclusive identity and unity among workers. Recounting the role of the Iscor Club, a former Iscor manager recalled that the club symbolised 'group identity' (Human Resources Manager [white], interview, 14 April 2015). According to the same interviewee, 'workers formed very close relations ... on Fridays workers would go out to the club and [have] a beer'.

Linking social capital involves establishing links with others outside one's immediate network who have access to power, wealth and influence. According to Babaei et al. (2012, 121), linking ties may include civil society organisations, government agencies, and representatives of both the public and private sectors. This form of social capital is vital in terms of increased access to key resources from formal institutions outside the community. One of those institutions is a trade union that acted as social capital for workers and communities in Vanderbijlpark. Using Solidarity's restructuring experience, this chapter illustrates how the union's early twentieth-century history and tradition of accumulating capital by the *Helpmekaarvereniging* and *volkskapitalisme* led to the adoption of the Histadrut model. Based on kibbutzim (communal settlements), the Histadrut was an Israeli trade union and labour federation founded by David Ben-Gurion in 1920 to solve an unemployment crisis in Palestine. Union affiliates and divisions managed hospitals, schools, banks, sporting facilities, business enterprises, assurance companies, wholesale companies, chain stores, and medical and pension schemes, and provided jobs to almost one million people (Wessel Visser, interview, 6 August, 2018).

CASE STUDY OF SOLIDARITY

Prior to 1994, different approaches were used to promote the economic empowerment of white Afrikaners, but these focused narrowly on the dominant paradigms of political–legal and economic dimensions. Instead of reducing empowerment to a mere economic construction, white Afrikaner empowerment relied on the value of people, culture and trust as resources. It also used civil society organisations to mobilise the poor, providing access to resources and the ability of communities to develop social capital. Using Solidarity as a case study, this chapter explores how the trade union generated all three forms of capital and how political, cultural and social capital were converted into economic capital to empower white Afrikaners.

Founded in 1902 as the Transvaal Miners' Association, the organisation changed its name to the Mineworkers Union in 1913. Since 1994, the MWU has undergone a major transformation. In 2001 it changed its name to MWU-Solidarity, and then to Solidarity in 2002. Solidarity is by far the oldest trade union in South Africa. The union participated in the 1922 Rand Revolt under the slogan 'Workers of the World unite and fight for a White South Africa' (Hlatshwayo 2013). In the 1930s, the leaders of the Broederbond began to impose their definition of Afrikaner nationalism on Afrikaner society by allocating jobs to members and advancing their careers by promoting or placing them in key positions and controlling all facets of Afrikaner civil society using strategically placed members.

In terms of cultural capital, the MWU benefitted immensely from the Broederbond's efforts to mobilise white Afrikaners around cultural issues. For instance, around the 1920s, the Broederbond formed the FAK to exercise control over the vast majority of Afrikaner cultural associations. One of the FAK's main tasks was to modernise Afrikaans by adapting it to an industrial society and transforming it from the 'language of the veld and farm' to the 'language of city, factory and commerce' (O'Meara 1983, 74). O'Meara (1978, 55) stresses that cultural politics provided an important ideological framework within which to forge *volkseenheid* (people's unity). During the 1930s onwards, the Broederbond raised the dangers of 'class divisions' to *volkseenheid* and the 'denationalisation' of Afrikaans-speaking workers. As a result, the Broederbond initiated two strategies: an assault on the trade unions (mobilising working-class support), and an economic movement (making explicit the economic basis and petty bourgeois character of Afrikaner nationalism). O'Meara describes the former as involvement in combatting any notion of class struggle, and replacing it with the principle of mutual cooperation and interest between workers and employers. The latter was born out of frustration that the historical trajectory of capitalist development in South Africa produced a pattern of ownership of the means of production in which white Afrikaans-speakers controlled an insignificant percentage of production in all sectors except agriculture. O'Meara (1983, 97) sums up the goal of the economic movement as 'mobilising the *volk* (the people) to conquer the capitalist system and to transform it so that is fits the [Afrikaner] ethnic nature'.

Under the United Party government (1934–1948), the Broederbond used its ideology of Christian nationalism to 'capture the control of white trade unions' or, more broadly, to 'wean the Afrikaner workers away from ideologies of class' (Lipton 1985, 270). O'Meara (1983, 86) adds that the formation of the *Blankewerkers se Beskermingsbond* (White Workers' Protection League) in 1945 was a good example of how the Broederbond sought to mobilise the whole *volk* to drive the class cancer from its national life by weaning workers from

> communist influence, to unite them with the rest of the nation and to preserve them for Christian-nationalist struggle. Many craft unions of the time, including the South African Iron and Steel Trades Associations and MWU, supported the government's policy of job reservation and monopoly of skills by whites. (Lewis 1984, 52)

Consequently, the bonds between the white Afrikaners were strengthened because the Afrikaner nationalists had the monopoly of power, and controlled and protected only a small homogeneous group.

In terms of economic capital, Solidarity benefitted from the efforts of the Broederbond to empower whites, especially Afrikaners, through the '*Reddingsdaad* (act of rescue) movement'. During the depression in the 1930s, the *Reddingsdaadbond* (Rescue Action Society) sought to help the mass of poor white Afrikaners. Its original purpose was to give Afrikaners some control over the country's business, which was previously in British hands. One of the strategies used by the *Reddingsdaadbond* was the centralisation of money-capital in financial institutions and converting it into productive capital. O'Meara (1983, 181) maintains that Afrikaners of all classes were prodded to save in various Afrikaner credit institutions. To achieve this, the Broederbond established the *Federale Volksbeleggings* (Federal People's Investments). Although it was a bank, one of its main functions was to operate as a business undertaking, geared to paying dividends to its shareholders, and to establish Afrikaner undertakings in commerce and industry through investing in shares of appropriate undertakings (O'Meara 1983, 192).

As far as political capital is concerned, the MWU benefitted immensely from the labour market policies of the Pact, United Party and National Party governments, especially in terms of job protection, skills development and support of white trade unions. Legislation such as the Apprenticeship Act (1922), the Civilised Labour Policy Act (1924), the Industrial Conciliation Act (1924) and the Mines and Works Amendment Act (1926) was enacted to ensure that 'Afrikanerdom' would remain in power for a considerable time. However, following the release of the Wiehahn Commission's report in the early 1980s, the union feared for its position. One of the recommendations of the Commission was the registration of black trade unions and the abolition of statutory job reservation. Wessel Visser (2016, 139) argues that the recommendation put the MWU into an antagonistic position with the government, and the union aligned itself with right-wing political parties and protest. The members of the MWU feared being replaced by black miners or having their wages undercut by cheap black labour, as well as job loss in relation to the South African labour force as a whole.

Visser (2016) details the history of the MWU leaders who led the union during the transition period, and outlines their different visions and strategies to develop various forms of capital for their members. One such leader was Peter Jacobus (Arrie) Paulus, Chief Secretary of the MWU in 1967. According to Visser (interview, 6 August 2018), Paulus was the first MWU chief secretary to be elected to parliament. Paulus played an important role in terms of the development of the union's political and social capital. Paulus stressed that the status quo of the Mines and Works Amendment Act (1926) with regard to job reservation should remain unchanged, as this was the only protection for the white labour minority against 'black oppression'. As 'foreigners' in white South Africa, he believed that black people could not claim trade union recognition, but should exercise their labour and political rights in the Bantustans. Paulus predicted that if blacks were appointed over MWU members in the mining industry, South Africa would know no industrial peace, and that such advancement of black labourers would lead to 'friction and labour unrest' (Visser 2006, 23).

His successor, Peet W. Ungerer (appointed in 1987), shared Paulus' vision of consolidating white union labour to protect white workers from black encroachment, but he did not believe in the alliance between trade unions and political parties. According to Visser (interview, 6 August 2018), Ungerer believed that, in the absence of effective white political power, there should be one strong labour organisation to cater for the political, economic and cultural needs of the Afrikaner working class, and to enhance bargaining power. To this end, he developed a two-pronged strategy. First, he initiated a vigorous recruitment drive to extend the union's scope to workers in the steel, chemical, distribution and other industries. Second, against the background of black trade union registration, Ungerer forced the MWU back into the fold of right-wing politics. For instance, in 1993 the MWU founded the *Afrikaner Volksfront* (Afrikaner People's Front), later renamed the Freedom Front. Nonetheless, the most prolific leader was Flip Buys who succeeded Ungerer in 1997.

Unlike the two previous leaders, Buys had the luxury of long history on his side. He observed the transition from apartheid to democracy and the impact on the white population in South Africa. He was not a miner himself, but an academically trained intellectual. His main strength was not political or social, but cultural capital. According to Visser (2016), Buys came from a new generation of white-collar trade union officials who had to function in a totally changed labour environment. As chief executive, he expanded the old Mineworkers Union into a group of organisations to build and defend Afrikaans and the interests of the Afrikaner. During his tenure, Buys grappled with the challenges of post-apartheid South African labour laws and changes in the international economy. For him, these changes meant that the MWU had to rethink its labour relations and management approach.

Buys believed that the MWU would have to establish itself as a leader on the labour front and position itself strategically at the forefront of all aspects of labour relations. A big problem was unfair racial discrimination towards whites brought by the new 'affirmative action' policy. In championing the rights of white workers, the MWU relied on the new South African constitution to counter the negative effects of affirmative action. The MWU's own constitution had to be adjusted according to the provisions of the country's constitution by scrapping the word 'white' so that membership would not be limited to a specific race (Visser 2006). This change in its constitution allowed the union to recruit blacks into its ranks. This theme featured strongly during the focus group with four Solidarity shop stewards at ArcelorMittal South Africa (AMSA) in Vanderbijlpark. One shop steward explained:

> One thing which is not understood about Solidarity is that we are a multiracial union now. Out of the 5 000 plus members here at ArcelorMittal South Africa, in Vanderbijlpark, I will easily say about 1 000 are black. So, it's not that we are racist, although in the past we were always seen as white union. (Focus Group, four Solidarity shop stewards Focus Group, 12 May 2015)

In addition, the MWU positioned itself as a free-market trade union based on the models of the *Christelijk Nationaal Vakverbond* (Christian National Trade Union) of Holland (Visser 2006, 30). This idea, however, is not new. O'Meara (1978) argues that it was used by the Broederbond in the 1930s to raise the dangers of 'class divisions' to *volkseen* (people's unity) and the 'denationalisation' of Afrikaans-speaking workers. Under the new dispensation, Solidarity continues to believe in Afrikaner Christian ideology. One shop steward explained:

> Our philosophy is that we are a Christian-driven organisation. Nothing has changed except the name of Iscor; its procedures and policies are the same. We believe in the Lord; we always open our meeting with prayers and close with prayers. We believe that what we do is the truth, is the right way; there are no hidden agendas, there is no discrimination, there is no misuse of things like this. And we feel that as long as we keep our eyes focused on the Lord, He is going to drive us where we need to be. (Focus Group, four Solidarity shop stewards, 12 May 2015)

As a free-market trade union, the MWU appointed a corps of young and energetic academically trained personnel with bachelor's degrees in industrial psychology, labour relations and communication. In terms of assisting its members to deal with the harsh economic and political realities of the post-apartheid South Africa, the MWU adopted the Histadrut model, borrowed from an Israeli trade union and labour federation.

THE HISTADRUT MODEL: AN EXAMPLE OF SOCIAL CAPITAL UNIONISM

Stressing the importance of building relationships, growing networks and developing resources to address members' interests, this study found that Solidarity played a vital role in developing social capital to empower its members, especially current and former white employees at AMSA. Since 1949, Solidarity has actively sought to address white poverty by establishing Helping Hand. According to Solidarity's website (https://solidariteit.co.za/en/who-are-we), Helping Hand is a welfare organisation that pursues the upliftment of the community based on the principles of the *Helpmekaarvereeniging* movement of 1914. Following the demise of apartheid and the rise of trade liberalisation in 1994, the trade union's influence in defending workers' rights and interests through traditional collective bargaining and political activities declined. Under the new dispensation, Solidarity resorted to the generation of social capital through the formation of dense networks and greater solidarity among members in order to survive. This included extending its traditional scope to industries beyond the mining industry, as mentioned above, and by providing legal counselling to members (Visser, interview, 6 August 2018). Based on the logic of SCU, Solidarity formed and mobilised members' connections within and between its various units and with outside organisations to gain access to a variety of resources. These connections were believed to be vital for the development of the shared values, trust and mutual understanding that made group cooperation and coordination possible.

After a visit to the Middle East in 1998, the new general secretary, Flip Buys guided Solidarity to adopt the Histadrut model (the word means 'organisation'). Visser (interview, 6 August 2018) argues that this decision was rooted in the history and ideology of Afrikaner nationalism as well as two Afrikaner traditions: first, the accumulation of capital to help people (previously started by the *Helpmekaarvereniging*), which formed the roots of *volkskapitalisme*; and second, conferences to develop a strategy for *volkskapitalisme*. Out of *Helpmekaar* came a large number of businesses that provided young Afrikaners with employment and training opportunities in business skills. This study found that Solidarity applied various strategies to empower its members.

In Palestine, the Israeli trade union and labour federation applied the Histadrut model to empower Jewish workers through a network of community organisations divided into four major areas – trade unionism; cultural and social activities (sports, newspapers, films, magazines, women's organisations); economic enterprises (agricultural enterprises and factories, credit institutions and cooperatives); and social welfare (education, unemployment relief, operation of labour exchanges). It also created Provident Funds (used as a savings method and source of credit) (Visser, interview, 6 August 2018).

In South Africa, Solidarity used the model to transform the MWU from a trade union into a labour movement and service provider based on a three-pronged approach. The first of these prongs is a vigorous national recruitment campaign to augment the union's numbers and to cater to individual members who wished to join the MWU. Second, the profit generated from *Unifonds* (a union investment vehicle, see below) were used to initiate job creation. The third prong used the organisations presence in almost 160 towns to form *WerkNet* (Work Network) – a simple, user-friendly website where job-seekers could upload their CVs and employers could advertise their jobs (see below).

Solidarity altered the definition of union activism to include acts of 'mutual aid' – similar to the 1914 *Helpmekaar* movement. These include launching *Unifonds* in 2008 to provide its members with cheaper short-term insurance, a pension and medical aid scheme, death benefits, microloans, and insurance and investment services. Further, Solidarity enhanced its instrumental and normative appeal to the membership through a conscious brokerage strategy that seeks to build bridges among workers and between workers and other organisations. This includes providing legal support to members affected by affirmative action, B-BBEE policies and other legal problems (Solidarity, https://regsdienste.solidariteit.co.za).

Building on the third prong was the union's acceptance of affirmative action in the workplace as a permanent feature of the South African labour market. Visser (2016, 16) describes the union's response as 'proactive', 'scientific' and commission-led. Rather than protest against the legislation, the union sought to prevent the creation of 'a new pool of skilled, unemployed white workers' by using the profit generated from *Unifonds* to initiate *Werknet*. *Werknet* created 100 000 jobs within the first ten years of its existence through labour placements in various companies and institutions and labour leasing of skilled unemployed persons. The union also identified a gap in the training of workers in the labour market. In 2006, Solidarity established a training institution called Sol-Tech in Pretoria. However, this private technical training institution targets only Afrikaans-speakers as it uses Afrikaans as the medium of instruction.

Under SCU, there is a realisation that the interests of members extend beyond the workplace to include community problems. The main focus of *Helpmekaar* is to solve the Afrikaner poverty crisis through a variety of projects such as: providing poverty relief through projects such as Lunchbox, Schoolbag and the #HelpHanna project for children; training children and young people to prevent them from ending up in the cycle of poverty; strengthening Afrikaans education; and job creation.

Solidarity sought to emulate the kibbutzim strategy of the Histradut model by building hospitals, schools, banks, sporting facilities, business enterprises, assurance companies, wholesale companies, chain stores, and medical and pension schemes. These are all managed by the union's affiliates and divisions, and have provided jobs for almost one million people. The findings of this study are consistent with Nissen and Jarley's (2005) observation that the revitalisation of unions includes employing more sustainable strategies for recreating community in the workplace and recognising the many mechanisms by which workers interact in ways that promote generalised reciprocity norms.

Based on the findings, this study found that Solidarity was the only white union responsible for continued contacts based on friendship, work relationships and participation in civic or leisure organisations between the current and former workers of more than 14 institutions. These include Helping Hand, AfriForum,

AfriForum Youth, FAK and Sol-Tech to name but a few used for empowering whites (see Table 10.1). One shop steward belonging to Solidarity explained:

> We no longer see our member as just an employee. We look at our member as a human being who [has] needs [some beyond the workplace], ... especially if the government and the employer don't cater to them as they did previously ... In the past, we did not have to because the state looked after and catered for our people but today that does not happen any more. We look at job creation, education, welfare, job security, fair labour practice, decent work and conditions of employment. (Focus Group, four Solidarity shop stewards, 12 May 2015)

The above excerpt illustrates the point Nissen and Jarley (2005) make about SCU, where there is a realisation that some of these interests extended beyond the workplace to include community problems.

Table 10.1: The Solidarity labour service movement

Sectors	Affiliates	Legal Services
Chemical Communication Denel, Krygkor & Aviation Electrical engineering Medical Metal and engineering Mining Professional industry	AfriForum ('civil rights' organisation) *Helpende Hand* (Helping Hand – charity organisation) Akademia and Sol-Tech (university and technical college) Solidarity Growth Fund Solidarity Investment Company Solidarity Property Company Solidarity Research Institute Virseker Trust (insurance company) Maroela Media (online newspaper) Kraal Uitgewers (publisher) Federasie van Afrikanse Kultuurverenigings (FAK) (historically an umbrella organisation for Afrikaner cultural organisations)	Solidarity labour services (140 000 members in all occupational fields, collective and professional; looks after the interests of its members and ensures the protection of their rights in the workplace) Solidarity legal services (providing legal advice on labour, civil and criminal matters)

Source: Adapted from Visser (2006) and https://solidariteit.co.za/en/who-are-we

Furthermore, the study found that current and former white employees inside AMSA and in Vanderbijlpark generally received various services from Solidarity such as study benefits, financial services, death benefits and community services.

In terms of study benefits, members can enrol at Akademia and Sol-Tech. Through these institutions, Solidarity provides financial assistance to deserving students for tertiary training; many of them are children of workers who belong to Solidarity. Akademia is a private higher education institution that offers qualifications aimed at preparing people for entry into the job market. This initiative is accredited with the Higher Education Quality Committee of the Council on Higher Education. Members of the public receive a 20 per cent discount at Akademia as well as interest-free study loans (https://solidariteit.co.za/en/study-assistance/). Through its network of institutions – such as Helping Hand, AfriForum, AfriForum Youth and FAK – Solidarity assists AMSA workers with various services such as financial assistance to deserving students for tertiary training (https://solidariteit.co.za/en/union-benefits/).

Solidarity also provides various community services to members of the public such as Support Centres for Schools, recreation and benefits related to well-being. Solidarity believes in empowering its members to be self-reliant and in mobilising its members' capital to create independent institutions through which members can realise their rights. The Support Centres for Schools entails various services such as Microsoft Office training, a Schoolbag Project which provides stationery to underprivileged Grade 1 pupils, a Lunchbox Project which feeds thousands of needy toddlers affected by poverty, mathematics courses, a reading app, as well as advice on subject choice for Grade 9 pupils (http://www.solidaritysa.co.za).

For recreation purposes, the union reports that six issues of the union's magazine, *Solidarity Magazine*, are published annually. This online magazine is available in both English and Afrikaans, and is used to communicate important labour and development issues in the labour market to its members. The benefits related to well-being include advice on medical aids, lifestyle coaching, relationships and an athletic club. Members receive discounted tariffs on consultation with a lifestyle coach and a relationship expert (http://www.solidaritysa.co.za).

During the interviews, an official from Solidarity explained that the manner in which affirmative action is currently being implemented at AMSA is causing serious discrimination:

> These laws are now being imposed and enforced by the courts on us. I have to secure our member's position within the company ... let's be honest,

if we sit back and do not fight sanctions like the B-BBEE concept and lag behind, by the time we wipe our eyes, we will have no members left of this group. That is a huge concern. (Focus Group, four Solidarity shop stewards, 12 May 2015)

During the focus group with Solidarity shop stewards, one described the work of Solidarity Helping Hand as follows:

Ja, we do have a Helping Hand. We go and dish out food to places such as Marikana. During the famous strike, we went there to dish out food every single day … we were the only union that went there. We helped everybody; it does not matter whether it's Numsa or United Association of South Africa – that's the helping hand.

Another official from Solidarity recalled:

We got 17 institutions that look at community Helping Hand, whether it is training, schooling or feeding scheme. Our mandate goes beyond feeding schemes. Every year, we give Grade 1 learners school bags; we call that "School Tassie Projek". It is for only children that do not have … Our motto is that "if you want Grade 1 to start at equal footing, you must ensure you don't have children not having basic stationery". We supplied about 3 000 bags. This year we provided bursaries, over R100 million worth of bursaries. From the poor guy to the trainee. (Focus Group, four Solidarity shop stewards, 12 May 2015)

Solidarity has succeeded in developing all three forms of capital for the upliftment of the white working class and their communities by drawing on the white Afrikaner history of accumulating capital, building social networks and ensuring greater solidarity among members. This means that the organising model of trade unions that stresses the union's ability to recruit, operate and advance the interests of their members is inadequate (Nissen and Jarley 2005). This model typically involves full-time organisers, whose task is to build confidence and strong networks and leaders within the workforce, and to involve large numbers of union members through confrontational campaigns. This study argues that Solidarity's model of SCU has worked well because of the interconnection between all forms of capital suggested by Bourdieu (1979, 1986) – namely, economic, cultural, social and political capital.

CONCLUSION

The results of this research confirm that Solidarity is a good example of a social capital union as illustrated by the unique political, economic and social services it provides to its members. As pointed out in the introduction to this chapter, social capital unionism is an area that has not received much attention in South African labour studies, a gap that this chapter has attempted to address. Historically, from 1924 until 1994, the leaders of Solidarity used politics as a form of capital – including political affiliation, institutions and legislation – to develop and accumulate benefits for its members. Trade unions such as Solidarity came from a unique tradition where white Afrikaners in the past developed institutions such as the *Helpmekaarvereniging* and the Broederbond to protect and promote the interests of the Afrikaners. Today, while other unions and their federations are losing members due to economic globalisation, and some consider union investments as an option to revitalise themselves, Solidarity is one of the few unions that has experienced growth in the number of members, due to its model of SCU. Rather than focusing on the socialist strategies and tactics used by Cosatu, Solidarity chose the Histadrut model to focus on the education, job creation and general services it provides to its members.

Indeed, white people, especially the Afrikaans-speaking population, relied on cultural organisations such as the *Helpmekaarvereniging*, the Broederbond, the FAK and trade unions like the MWU (now Solidarity) to develop cultural capital in order to protect and promote their interests. But most importantly, Solidarity succeeded in applying a form of social capital unionism because of the support from the Afrikaner nationalist ideology that saw the state passing legislation from 1948 onwards to protect and promote the interests of its supporters. After 1994, this cultural and social capital was easily converted into economic capital in terms of investment, savings and insurance as well as educational qualifications.

Solidarity's focus is not on gaining a fair share of the economy but on looking into how to build social networks that transcend employment jurisdictions, how to sustain the relationship with members, and how to 'organise' members around 'social' instead of economic issues. Today, white workers, who first joined the economy as miners, are sending their sons and daughters via social capital unionism forums such as Solidarity, not to be miners, but to gain tertiary educational qualifications to make the leap to a new social class. This is class formation in the making, which continues to rely on white privilege. This highlights a serious shortcoming in Gwede Mantashe's (2008) strategic unionism approach, as espoused by a union federation like Cosatu, which not only failed to transform the economy but also failed thousands of workers who lost their employment due to economic restructuring. In addition, strategic unionism has highlighted serious problems within unions, such as the lack of professionalism when dealing with union investment companies and corruption emanating from the alliance with the African National Congress (ANC). Solidarity, on the other hand, showed that its service model was successful because it combined the economic, social and political dimensions of SCU to build proper networks and relationships with members, to provide services and to develop better organisation and leadership capacity to survive the juggernaut of economic globalisation.

ACKNOWLEDGEMENT

While this chapter relied on the contribution of various individuals, I am particularly grateful to Professor Wessel Visser from Stellenbosch University's History Department and the shop stewards from Solidarity at ArcelorMittal South Africa, Vanderbijlpark, for their insights into the topic.

NOTE

1   The Iscor Club was similar to a country club. It was a privately owned organisation with a membership quota, and admittance was by invitation and sponsorship (by Iscor and government). The club offered a variety of recreational sports and facilities for dining and entertainment. During the restructuring of Iscor in 2005, the Iscor Club was sold to North-West University as part of the commercialisation and outsourcing of the parastatal.

REFERENCES

Babaei, Hamidreza, Nobaya Ahmad and Sarjit S. Gill. 2012. 'Bonding, Bridging and Linking Social Capital and Empowerment among Squatter Settlements in Tehran, Iran'. *World Applied Sciences Journal* 17 (1): 119–126.

Banks, Andy and Jack Metzgar. 2005. 'Response to Unions as Social Capital'. *Labour Studies Journal*, 29 (4): 27–35.

Bezuidenhout, Andries and Malehoko Tshoaedi, eds. 2017. *Labour Beyond Cosatu: Mapping the Rupture in South Africa's Labour Landscape*. Johannesburg: Wits University Press.

Booth, John A. and Patricia Bayer Richard. 1998. 'Civil Society, Political Capital, and Democratisation in Central America'. *Journal of Politics* 60 (3): 780–800.

Bourdieu, Pierre. 1979. 'Symbolic Power'. *Critique of Anthropology* 4 (13–14): 77–85.

Bourdieu, Pierre. 1986. 'The Forms of Capital'. In *Handbook of Theory and Research for the Sociology of Education*, edited by J. Richardson. Westport, CT: Greenwood.

Cohen, Dan and Lawrence Prusak. 2001. *In Good Company: How Social Capital makes Organisations Work*. Boston, MA: Harvard Business School Press.

Department of Trade and Industry, 2003. *Black Economic Empowerment Strategy*. Pretoria: DTI.

Hlatshwayo, Mondli. 2013. 'A Sociological Analysis of Trade Union Responses to Technological Changes at the ArcelorMittal Vanderbijlpark Plant, 1989–2011'. PhD diss., University of Johannesburg.

Hyman, Richard. 2007. 'How can Trade Unions Act Strategically?' *Transfer: European Review of Labour and Research* 13 (2): 193–210.

Iheduru, Okechukwu. 2001. 'Organised Labour, Globalisation and Economic Reform: Union Investment Companies in South Africa'. *Transformation* 46: 1–31.

Iron and Steel Industrial Corporation (Iscor). 1993. *Steel in South Africa, 1928–1953*. Pretoria: Iscor.

Jacobs, Cindy. 2009. 'The Role of Social Capital in the Creation of Sustainable Livelihoods: A Case Study of the Siyazama Community Allotment Gardening Association (SCAGA)'. Masters diss., Stellenbosch University.

Jenkins, Richard. 1992. *Pierre Bourdieu*. New York: Routledge.

Johnson, Nancy and Paul Jarley. 2005. 'Unions as Social Capital: The Impact of Trade Union Youth Programmes on Young Workers' Political and Community Engagement'. *Transfer* 4 (5): 605–616.

Lewis, Jon. 1984. 'Steelworkers, Craft Unions and Afrikaner Nationalism'. *South African Labour Bulletin* 8 (6): 45–58.

Lipton, Merle. 1985. *Capitalism and Apartheid: South Africa, 1910–1986*. Cape Town: David Philip.

Luttrell, Cecilia, Sitna Quiroz, Claire Scrutton and Kate Bird. 2009. *Understanding and Operationalising Empowerment*. Working Paper 308. London: Overseas Development Institute.

Mantashe, Gwede. 2008. 'The Decline of the Mining Industry and the Response of the Mining Unions'. Masters diss., University of the Witwatersrand.

Misra, Neeta. 2008. 'Strategic Unionism: The Political Role of the Congress of South African Trade Unions (COSATU) in South Africa and what it Means for Black Workers'. PhD diss, Massachusetts Institute of Technology.

Narayan, Deepa. 2002. *Empowerment and Poverty Reduction*. Washington, DC: World Bank.

Nissen, Bruce and Paul Jarley. 2005. 'Unions as Social Capital: Renewal through a Return to the Logic of Mutual Aid?' *Labour Studies Journal* 29 (4): 1–26.

O'Meara, Dan. 1978. 'Analysing Afrikaner Nationalism: The "Christian-National" Assault on White Trade Unionism in South Africa, 1934–1948'. *African Affairs* 77 (306): 45–72.

O'Meara, Dan. 1983. *Volkskapitalisme: Class, Capital and Ideology in the Development of Afrikaner Nationalism, 1934–1948*. Johannesburg: Ravan Press.

Ponte, Stefano, Simon Roberts and Lance van Sittert. 2007. 'Black Economic Empowerment, Business and the State in South Africa'. *Development of Change*, 38 (5): 933–955.

Putnam, Robert D. 1993. *Making Democracy Work: Civic Traditions in Modern Italy*. New Haven, CT: Princeton University Press.

Putnam, Robert D. 2007. 'E Pluribus Unum: Diversity and Community in the Twenty-first Century, the 2006 Johan Skytte Prize Lecture'. *Scandanavian Political Studies* 30 (2): 137–174.

Ra, Eunjong. 2011. 'Understanding the Role of Economic, Cultural and Social Capital and Habitus in Student College Choice: An Investigation of Student, Family and School Contexts'. PhD diss., University of Michigan.

Rowland, Jo. 1995. *Questioning Empowerment: Working with Women in Honduras.* Cape Town: David Philip.

Saundry, Richard, Mark Stuart and Valerie Antcliff. 2012. 'Social Capital and Union Revitalisation: A Study of Worker Networks in the UK Audio-visual Industries'. *British Journal of Industrial Relations* 50 (2): 263–286.

Schuller, Tom, Stephen Baron and John Field. 2000. 'Social Capital: A Review and Critique'. In *Social Capital: Critical Perspectives*, edited by Stephen Baron, John Field and Tom Schuller, 1–38. Oxford: Oxford University Press.

Siisiäinen, Martti. 2000. 'Two Concepts of Social Capital: Bourdieu vs. Putnam'. Paper presented at ISTR Fourth International Conference 'The Third Sector: For What and for Whom?' July 5-8, Trinity College, Dublin, Ireland.

Visser, Wessel. 2006. 'From MWU to Solidarity – A Trade Union Reinventing Itself'. *South African Journal of Labour Relations* 30 (2): 19–41.

Visser, Wessel. 2016. *A History of the South African Mineworkers' Union, 1902–2014.* New York: Edwin Mellen Press.

Webster, Edward and Sakhela Buhlungu. 2004. 'Between Marginalisation and Revitalisation? The State of Trade Unionism in South Africa'. *Review of African Political Economy* 31 (100): 229–245.

INTERVIEWS AND FOCUS GROUP DISCUSSION

Iscor Human Resources Manager, 14 April 2015.

Focus Group, four Solidarity shop stewards, ArcelorMittal, 12 May 2015 (names withheld to protect identities).

Wessel Visser, Stellenbosch University, 6 August 2018.

11

Hegemony, Counter-hegemony and the Role of Social Movements

Janet Cherry

INTRODUCTION

Growing desperation in South African society and evidence of state failure in many sectors would seem to strongly indicate the need for a counter-hegemonic project. But who will lead such a project, and what role will social movements play?[1] In May 2018, a few months before the 'Future of Labour' conference at the University of the Witwatersrand, Trevor Ngwane launched his book *Urban Revolt* at Nelson Mandela University (Ngwane, Ness and Sinwell 2017). During his presentation at the launch, Ngwane reflected on how urban social movements 'challenge the hegemony of global capital'. This provoked reflection on grassroots social movements and their relationship to the labour movement in South Africa, as well as the relationship of social and labour movements to the formal politics of representation and policy-making.

Since the conference, there have been dramatic developments that have brought inequalities and injustices in South African society (and across the globe) to the fore. Most recently the Covid-19 pandemic has resulted in new civil society coalitions that have responded to these inequalities in various ways. The climate crisis has also posed fundamental challenges to social movements in South Africa, including the labour movement. The crisis of corruption within the ruling African National Congress (ANC) has forced the labour movement to reassess its alliance with the ruling party.

The main question posed in this chapter is thus to ask whether, in the years since the 2014 trade unions and democracy survey (see Bezuidenhout and Tshoaedi 2017), a new and unified social movement led by the working class has emerged. In answering this question, new political alignments since the 'Numsa moment' are explored, including the emergence of the United Front and then the Socialist Revolutionary Workers Party (SRWP). The question is posed whether the ANC is still hegemonic and, if so, has a counter-hegemonic movement emerged? And if it has, how does the labour movement relate to this counter-hegemonic movement?

Additional questions posed are: Is there a disjuncture between the forms of organisation and mobilisation of the organised working class, employed in the formal economy (the 'labour movement') and those of the precariat (the masses of unemployed, and those in the informal economy)? Do the latter constitute a working-class movement or a social movement? Are they a movement of any kind?

The analysis below concludes that social movements in South Africa do not constitute a unified class force able to challenge the hegemony of capital; most movements are struggling for inclusion rather than for an alternative system. The space does exist, however, for the emergence of a more unified challenge to the current system, led by the working class.

The arguments below draw upon the 'trade unions and democracy' datasets since 1994 (see Ginsberg et al. 1995), in particular the responses to those questions that deal with the relationship of workers to community struggles, service delivery and the Tripartite Alliance (consisting of the ANC, the South African Communist Party [SACP] and the Congress of South African Trade Unions [Cosatu]). Research in the working-class township of Kwazakhele, including election surveys of Kwazakhele residents in each election up to and including 2019, provides corroborating empirical data. The author's involvement in, and documentation of, recent social movements in Gqeberha (Nelson Mandela Bay) provides additional anecdotal and reflective evidence.

WHAT DO THE 'TRADE UNION DEMOCRACY' SURVEYS TELL US?

The first question to be asked is, 'How has the relationship between organised labour and the broader working-class community changed over time?' The trade unions and democracy surveys since 1994 enable us to answer this question over the period of two and a half decades. It may be helpful to recapitulate briefly the findings of these surveys, the last of which was in 2014 (Bezuidenhout and Tshoaedi 2017). Reflecting on the first ten years of democracy, it was clear that 'workers do not see an "either/or" choice between electoral and extra-parliamentary strategies – they understand these strategies to be complementary' (Cherry 2006, 165). Mass action was (and still is) seen as a 'necessary form of pressure, which a vigilant civil society must bring to bear when it is failed by the government that claims to represent it' (Cherry 2006, 165). Did this change in the following decade, between 2004 and 2014?

From 2004 to 2014, the trade union democracy surveys asked workers whether they agree with this statement: 'Unions should have active links with community organisations/civil society groupings/social movements.' Over 80 per cent of workers have consistently agreed with the statement (Cherry 2017a, 113). This agreement embraces a range of forms of action, in a range of different alliances – from national leadership level partnership of (or even leadership of) campaigns for social justice, to local residents organisation campaigns for service delivery, through to the participation of individual union members in service delivery protests or in school governing bodies.

Regarding service delivery protests, probably the least organised form of working-class struggle, the 2014 survey noted that more than a quarter of the workers surveyed had participated in such protests. While lower than the 45 per cent who claimed to have participated in community protests in 2008, it remains an indication that organised workers do not understand themselves as a passive and privileged elite, but are engaged to a high degree in local struggles. This would seem to pose a counter to Mondli Hlatshwayo's argument that the unions had not only abandoned a socialist project, but had become a 'privileged elite':

> Today a wide divide seems to have emerged between unionised workers and communities. Many activists and participants in the struggles of social movements see unionised workers as a privileged elite that does not want to dirty its hands in struggles for social services. (Hlatshwayo 2005, 18)

At the same time, the surveys indicate a steady decline in support for the Tripartite Alliance. In particular, Cosatu has experienced a profound disillusionment as its faith in the Zuma-led ANC to lead a left-populist project after 2008 was steadily eroded. Since 2014, the exposure of the extent of state capture and the consequent compromise of the state's role as an instrument of redistribution has seriously challenged the relationship between Cosatu and the ANC. On the societal level, the failure of economic policies to lead to growth and redistribution has led to a widening rift between working-class and nationalist projects.

231

Ari Sitas (2017) argues that while the ANC was hegemonic until 2004, in the following decade the ANC's hegemony began to wane, and support for the Tripartite Alliance receded. He claims that 'the cement that held the ANC's hegemonic project together is crumbling as concerns organised labour' (Sitas 2017, 38).

If this is an accurate reflection of the situation in 2014, we might expect to have seen the development since then of a counter-hegemonic social movement, one in which the organised working class plays a leading role.

SOME REFLECTION ON SOCIAL MOVEMENTS SINCE 2014

The most disruptive and successful social movement from 2015 to 2017 was undoubtedly the 'Fallist' student movement. It had a dual agenda – both a reformist agenda for inclusion (into tertiary education institutions which were unaffordable to the unsubsidised lower middle class), and a radical agenda for 'decolonisation' of higher education. The movement made some significant gains with regard to the inclusion agenda (Cherry 2017b); and it can be argued even more meaningful (in material terms) gains for workers, through the successful demands for the insourcing of certain categories of labour on certain campuses. Hlatshwayo (2005) notes, 'Another indication of the retreat from socialist politics has been the labour movement's response to privatisation'. The failure of Cosatu unions to organise the cleaning staff, security guards and other vulnerable workers allowed for the alignment of students with the most marginalised casual workers, and put the unions to shame. As Savo Heleta writes:

> For years, the people who were employed to clean and take care of the campuses and ensure the safety and security of the university manage-ment, academics, staff and students have been exploited by private compa-nies selected and paid by the universities to provide these services. Hardly anyone took notice, asked about or attempted to stop this exploitation. If it wasn't for the #FeesMustFall movement, which incorporated the strug-gle of the outsourced workers into their own struggle, universities would not have done anything on their own to stop the ill treatment of the poorest of the poor. (Heleta 2016, 6)

Yet, despite revolutionary rhetoric and an agenda of radical transformation (as exemplified in Heleta's account of the #Feesmustfall movement, as cited above) and some attempts at alliance-building with civil society organisations in different cities, the movement was unable to provide leadership to a wider counter-hegemonic class project. Nancy Fraser's (2000) argument, that struggles for recognition may prove divisive and a detraction from the redistributive project, may provide some answers as to why such movements around identity (or recognition, as Fraser reframes them) are unable to create a counter-hegemonic discourse.

The other major social justice issue on the agenda since the last election was the land question, with the ANC responding to the Black First Land First movement, the pressure from various groups claiming social or demographic or geographic representivity, and the rhetoric of the Economic Freedom Fighters in parliament. This culminated in a failed attempt in December 2021 by the ANC to amend Section 25 of the Constitution to allow for expropriation of land without compensation – although it had been argued convincingly (Hall 2021) that the 1996 constitution does not prevent the state from doing so where necessary. Quite apart from the constitutional debate, land occupations (in urban and peri-urban areas in the main) have escalated, but the links to a clear movement agenda are not apparent.

Crime has led to some protests, which have tended to be polarised around racial or gender identity, an 'intersectional womin's [sic] movement against GBV [gender-based violence]' (responding to the 'Me Too' movement?) called for a 'Total Shut Down' on 1 August 2018. While it saw some effective marches, it was not really a total shutdown in the sense that production or service provision were shut down. Nor did it lead to a sustained social movement. Led in the main by middle-class black women activists, the movement was unable to mobilise women workers – or working-class communities – on any scale or in a sustained campaign. Despite the relentlessly high levels of violence against women, an effective national social movement against gender-based violence has yet to emerge.

Farm murders saw AfriForum leading a 'Black Monday' mobilisation in October 2017, which was largely supported by whites. (Interestingly, in 2017 the Philippines saw a 'black Friday' protest movement against killings of activists in the countryside; whether white farmers learned from or copied this example is not clear.) The protest saw marches and motorcades blocking roads and disrupting traffic in many towns across South Africa. Other localised campaigns against crime were organised in this period – for one example, a sustained campaign against gangster shootings in the 'Northern Areas' (a euphemism for the coloured townships of Nelson Mandela Bay). The labour movement has played little role in anti-crime campaigns, and while crime surely affects working-class communities as much, if not more, than other communities in South Africa, it does not provide the 'hinge' around which a counter-hegemonic mobilisation could easily occur.

Similarly, anti-corruption campaigns do not provide a logical focus for a working-class-led mobilisation of society. In Kwazakhele, a highly politicised working-class township in Nelson Mandela Bay, the high levels of both crime and corruption have not led to an organised challenge to ANC hegemony, as will be seen below.

In the period since 2014, there have been other significant struggles around resource access and extractive industries. Government's withdrawal of the licence to the Australian extractive giant TEM to mine the mineral sands at Xolobeni on the Wild Coast, and a victory in the High Court in November 2018 through sustained mobilisation by the Amadiba community with solidarity from broader civil society, is one such struggle. Recently, a surprisingly rapid mobilisation in opposition to Shell's seismic exploration for offshore oil and gas on the south-east coast saw an interdict granted against Shell which has, at the least, delayed the exploitation of this ocean resource. Other effective social mobilisations have been against government policies or failures. One success was that of the Opposition to Urban Tolling Alliance (OUTA), which saw, after the initial dramatic protests, a sustained form of civil disobedience as two-thirds of drivers simply refused to pay the toll fees that had been instituted on the Johannesburg–Pretoria highway.[2] Other social justice movements such as Equal Education have had some limited success in exposing government failures in providing essential infrastructure for education. The Treatment Action Campaign and the Basic Income Grant campaign (in both of which Cosatu played a leading role), and the Anti-Privatisation Forum (which saw a more militant alliance outside of the Tripartite Alliance) continued to prosecute struggles with varying degrees of success (see Pillay 2006 and Cherry 2017a for reflections on these campaigns).

Do such campaigns or issue-based movements form the basis for a counter-hegemonic project of the left? It does not seem that there is a unifying factor that can draw such campaigns together into a single movement, as was anticipated – and strategised – by the United Front. Mark Heywood, leader of both the Treatment Action Campaign and Section 27, in 2019 advanced a sharp critique of civil society and specifically of the 'left project' in South Africa, arguing that civil society has focused on political rights and neglected struggles for economic redistribution. He argued that the leaders of the left are 'incapable of a cross-class galvanising vision' (Nicolson 2019). Similarly, Fraser (2000, 108) argues that in the context of globalisation and increasing inequality, 'questions of recognition are serving less to supplement, complicate and enrich redistributive struggles than to marginalize, eclipse and displace them'.

Are Trevor Ngwane, Immanuel Ness and Luke Sinwell (2017) correct that change will come from the social movements of the precariat, what Peter Alexander (2010) terms a 'rebellion of the poor'? While it seems that service delivery protests, fragmented and spontaneous as they often are, have even less potential than the more organised social movements to be a coherent class force for change, there are other initiatives that have demonstrated potential to challenge the current hegemony. New initiatives in the organisation of precarious workers such as the Casual Workers' Advice Office (CWAO), which was formed in 2011, have had an enthusiastic response from unorganised workers.

As the CWAO claims on its website:

> The organisation was formed out of the recognition that the traditional labour movement appears incapable or unwilling to organize the new kinds of workers created by neo-liberalism. This recognition also informs the emphasis the CWAO places on precarious workers beginning to organize themselves. The old industrial model of organizing seems unsuitable for pre-carious workers. Indeed, it seems no longer suitable for traditional industrial workers themselves. The new organizational forms that will take its place will be determined by workers through struggle. (CWAO 2023)

The response to the CWAO's public information meetings, providing informa-tion about the basic rights of all workers and how workers can access these rights, has shown up organised labour for its failure in this regard. Initiatives to organise farmworkers have had some success. In the Western Cape the dramatic farmworkers' strike of 2012 led to a wage increase and the legislation of a minimum wage for farm-workers (Andrews 2013). And a strike by citrus farmworkers in the Sundays River Valley in June 2018, led by the South African National Civics Organisation, led to a R20 an hour minimum wage. These initiatives and many others such as the organ-isation of public health workers (Hlatshwayo 2018), point to the potential to bring many (hundreds of) thousands of workers into effective organisation. This can only be a positive initiative, and should not be seen as a threat to organised labour; as Lucien van der Walt (2019, 25) argues, 'Perhaps eight million workers are outside the unions. So new formations like the Simunye Workers' Forum and NGOs like CWAO can be complementary. There is enough space for a thousand initiatives'.

While the 'old' labour movement is on the defensive in the context of neo-liberal deindustrialisation, disappointingly no urban social movements have actively or effectively engaged in the politics of prefiguration, through 'seiz[ing] control or power within the commons' as Ngwane et al. (2017, 2) would demonstrate. The creation of decentralised alternatives – in the realm of the informal economy, the circular economy, the 'new economies' of decentralised production from waste, blockchain-based cooperative banking, food sovereignty and community-owned renewable energy – have been manifest only in small university-led initiatives. The existing movements have demanded inclusion into the existing system – both state and economic institutions – rather than initiating the creation of alternatives outside of the system. The labour movement, despite having significant resources at its disposal, has not managed to establish worker-owned and worker-controlled cooperatives, banks, investment companies, nor welfare measures for its members such as food distribution, health centres and medical aid societies. Instead, the highly centralised South African economy continues to concentrate capital in the hands of the elite. There is no effective cooperative movement. The South African Food Sovereignty Campaign, with its well-thought-out objectives, was not based in grassroots movements of food production and distribution until the crisis of the 2020 pandemic. The desperate situation of poor communities led to the emergence of a limited solidarity economy and a network of food production and distribution. Water and energy continue to be controlled by the state and a handful of elite private investors (in the case of Independent Power Producers).

Perhaps the most significant movement to emerge since 2014 is the climate justice movement. In South Africa this has taken the form of the Climate Justice Charter campaign, the inception of which was at the COP 17 civil society forum in Durban in December 2011. While the participation of the labour movement in what was launched as the One Million Climate Jobs campaign has been increasingly hesitant, since 2015 the campaign has gained momentum as a national alliance of grassroots organisations. As the global imperative for a 'just transition' away from fossil fuels has become apparent, the Climate Justice Charter is developing the potential to provide leadership to broader society by posing social and economic alternatives to 'carbon capitalism'. However, the absence of the voice of the main labour unions in this movement is a serious limitation.

LESSONS OF THE 2019 ELECTIONS

With organised labour being increasingly disillusioned with the Tripartite Alliance as an effective mechanism to represent labour interests in government, and millions of unemployed or casual workers not being represented by organised labour, it might have been expected that an independent labour party would emerge as a viable choice for working-class communities. It is in this context that the National Union of Metalworkers of South Africa (Numsa) formed the Socialist Revolutionary Workers Party (SRWP). Irvin Jim, Numsa's general secretary, stood as the new party's candidate in the 2019 national elections. The hope was that the union's considerable member-ship would be loyal at the ballot box, gaining the SRWP at least a voice in parliament, although this was not its primary strategy. (This hope was dashed on election day, when the party failed to gain sufficient votes for even a single seat in parliament).

Shaheen Khan of the SRWP explained the formation of the SRWP in relation to the 'Numsa moment' of 2013. 'The "NUMSA Moment" squarely raises the question of the creation of a vanguard working class party gaining a mass following in South Africa', says Khan; 'this fundamentally changes the political landscape in the coun-try' (quoted in Ismi 2019, 34).

The SRWP has an explicitly socialist agenda and intends to 'raise the con-sciousness' of the working class. Rather than pursuing votes, Khan says, the SRWP is 'focused on using every opportunity to raise the consciousness of the working class on the nature of the capitalist system and our need to organize independently outside of parliament and against it'. According to Khan, the party's aim is 'merely to secure a presence in parliament from which we can raise the working class voice and expose the capitalist nature of parliament itself' (quoted in Ismi 2019, 24).

This is in the context of the failure of both the labour movement (in the form of Cosatu) and the SACP to play this role in parliament through their alliance with the ruling ANC (Cherry, Jikeka and Malope 2017). As Ronnie Kasrils (2019) notes in his scathing post-election analysis, 'the SACP has yet again placed itself in a posi-tion of tailing behind the ANC to its detriment as would-be leader of the working class in the struggle for socialism'.

Yet, despite predictions of a significant increase in support for the Economic Freedom Fighters, given their outspoken support for land expropriation without compensation, and the considerable resources of the SRWP, neither managed to pose a significant challenge to the ANC's support from the urban working class. The SRWP's support was dismal, not even being sufficient to gain a single seat in parliament:

> It's not that it did not have funds or volunteers, courtesy of the 370,000-strong National Union of Metalworkers (Numsa). Something is indeed radically wrong since it did not benefit from that army of labour or from the endorsement of KZN's radical shack dwellers' movement Abahlali baseMjondolo. Would-be sympathisers have seen it to be sectarian and dogmatic instead of creating a broad socialist front which the country so desperately needs. (Kasrils 2019)

Irvin Jim, Numsa general secretary and SRWP leader, explained that elections, while 'not necessarily a solution', are 'a tactic that can be explored to test if we have the support of the working class' (quoted in Ismi 2019, 34). In this respect, it is clear that the SRWP failed to gain the support of the working class. Stephen Grootes (2019) identifies leadership differences, internal division and ideological rigidity as the possible reasons for the SRWP's failure to gain the support even of Numsa members in the election. However, there are other answers which are based in an understanding of the position of organised workers as members of working-class communities, situated within an understanding of the concept of hegemony.

Here, a tentative explanation is advanced by examining election results in the old industrial working-class township of Kwazakhele in Nelson Mandela Bay. Since 1994, the ANC has gained on average 85 per cent of votes from Kwazakhele residents. This electoral expression of the hegemony of the liberation movement has been consistent, despite deindustrialisation, retrenchments and unemployment levels of over 50 per cent. 'To put it bluntly: between 1994 and 2004, the ANC was hegemonic. Period', writes Sitas (2017, 38) after the 2014 trade union survey; however, he argues, by 2014 the ANC's hegemony was 'receding'.

A team from Nelson Mandela University tested this in the national elections of 2014 and 2019, and the local government elections of 2016 and 2021. Their post-election survey in Kwazakhele was corroborated against voting district results obtained from the Independent Electoral Commission (Cherry and Prevost 2017, 2020; Cherry, Brennan and Prevost 2023). The wards in Kwazakhele came up with an average 82 per cent vote for the ANC in both national elections, dropping slightly to 76 per cent in both local elections. The big change in the most recent election (2021) was the drop in the participation rate. Among those who participate in elections, it is clear that ANC hegemony is still intact. Is the left engaging in utopian thinking to imagine that a counter-hegemonic movement will come from such townships?

Do such old working-class townships have the potential to serve as centres for a new politics? The 'precariat' argument is that 'the development of a common recognition has moved the precariat closer to being a class-for-itself' and that 'the precariat could be the vanguard of a new progressive era' (Standing 2014, 12). In the South African context this would seem to indicate that it is from the 'margins of the margins' that the revolutionary mobilisation will come (Schierup 2017). This includes shack dwellers, the Abahlali baseMjondolo and other movements of the urban and rural poor, including immigrants and, critically in the context of the massive crisis of structural unemployment, the unemployed represented by movements such as the Unemployed Peoples Movement. Analyses that emphasise the divide between formal and organised labour, and between informal, casual and un-unionised labour, tend to support this argument – consistent with the old Marxist theory of a labour aristocracy which is co-opted by capital and unable to provide a revolutionary force or a vanguard leadership.

Hlatshwayo argued in 2005 that 'the lack of participation by unionised workers in struggles waged by the emerging social movements and community-based organisations' was an indicator of the co-option of the labour movement by capital: 'The drift of the trade unions, and Cosatu in particular, to the right and its acceptance of capitalism represents the end of a cycle of militant socialist struggles that began with the Durban strikes of 1973' (Hlatshwayo 2005, 18).

The implication of this 'drift to the right' is that the new social movements will have to take up the struggle where organised labour has been compromised: 'The new social movements, although still weak, represent the beginning of a new wave that is taking up struggles against globalisation and neoliberalism' (Hlatshwayo 2005, 18). This is consistent with Ngwane, Ness and Sinwell's (2017) conception of urban social movements being able to challenge capitalism.

The reality is somewhat different, however, as shown by the labour surveys over time: the complex relationship between 'labour' and 'community' is not based in geographic or income divisions. Old working-class townships where residents have property rights in the form of municipal housing – title deeds – have 50 per cent unemployed, in every household, in every ward. The 50 per cent who are employed are not only supporting those who are unemployed. They are also engaged in protests around local issues, in local policy formulation such as in Integrated Development Plans, in ward committee meetings, in school governing bodies. Informal settlement dwellers are less likely to be trade union members, to be sure.

Driving up one of the main roads through Nelson Mandela Bay's old townships, looking back towards the old power station, one is struck by the rows and rows of RDP[3] houses and old municipal houses. All these houses, old and new, are privately owned by the Kwazakhele working class. Property rights have been extended to them, along with free municipal services and child support grants. These benefits of the ANC's version of social democracy are spread across all the residents of these townships; there is no strict division between old and new residents, between proletariat and precariat. While the militant rhetoric of the Economic Freedom Fighters has attracted some of the disaffected youth, their support is not greater than 10 per cent in these townships.

Van der Walt argues that organised labour in South Africa is resilient:

> Overall, I do not find the notion that unions are in a state of collapse or demise convincing. In terms of numbers, South African unions are astonishingly stable and resilient. This is all the more remarkable given rising mass unemployment, the worst of any semi-industrial country, and a neoliberal assault from the late 1970s. (Van der Walt 2019, 25)

The idea that there is a gap between the 'old labour elite' and the 'precariat' and that the new movement will come from the latter, is disputed by Van der Walt, among others:

> Politically, the ongoing reality of three million-plus union members has to be addressed. This means, for me, an ongoing orientation towards unions, the largest formal organisations in civil society outside churches. The facts of serious corruption, the breakdown of workers' control, serious gender issues, as well as racial, ethnic and national conflicts, intolerance, gulfs between res-olutions and reality etc. are undeniable. Precarious workers may be alienated by unions, but, not surprisingly, so are a significant number of other workers, including some union members.
>
> But this does not indicate unions are hopelessly compromised or elitist. Rather, it indicates the need for a serious, nonsectarian reform project. That many unionised workers today are relatively well-paid, increasingly skilled, secure etc. is a victory, even if it should not be exaggerated. (Van der Walt 2019, 25)

A COUNTER-HEGEMONIC MOVEMENT?

Van der Walt and Ngwane, among others on the independent left, have advocated the building of a counter-hegemonic movement of the working class. Some, including communists like Ronnie Kasrils and Jeremy Cronin, agree that the SACP should lead a new and inclusive socialist movement – with or without a vanguard party. The SACP is now speaking of a 'popular left front' and the need to build unity among 'progressive forces' within and outside of the Tripartite Alliance: 'As the SACP, we will also strengthen our efforts to build a popular Left front and seek to contrib-ute towards the unity in action of the entire progressive trade union movement' (Nzimande 2021).

This raises yet more questions: What is the relationship between a movement, and gaining hegemony or building counter-hegemony? Is it necessary to have a movement in order to contest hegemony? What is a movement, after all?

Sitas (2017, 39) defines hegemony as 'the capacity of a movement to turn all possible contradictions, divisions and plausible fissures into a question of difference and through that establish an emotive and cognitive sway over and a unity between people'.

Among academics, there is a clear understanding of the difference between national liberation movements, labour movements and social movements (Prevost 2006).

While some political activists, including many within the ANC itself, argue that the ANC maintains the character of a revolutionary and/or a liberation movement, and as such should provide the leadership of an inclusive national project (ANC 2001; Gaba 2011), it is hard for many working-class people, whether in organised labour or in the precariat, to accept that the ANC is a movement of any kind (see Lehulere 2005 for a left-labour critique). It is now a political party, and operates according to the dictates and conventions of liberal democracy. Raymond Suttner (2016, 2022), Ronnie Kasrils and others on the left have argued convincingly for the defence of this democracy, whatever its weaknesses.

Suttner (2022) argues that 'the failure of the ANC to meet the aspirations of the majority has been accompanied by lack of confidence displayed in the electoral alternatives'. While defending the democratic gains of 1994, Suttner makes the important point that 'power can be manifested outside of electoral democracy, and it need not be a negation of the power of the vote, that was an important historical gain in South Africa'. He thus writes of the need to look at 'what organisational forms can be developed to augment electoral politics' and refers to a 'new alignment of forces' that is 'dedicated to revitalising democratic life and defending the Constitution'. Suttner (2022) argues that the labour movement, even in its weakened and compromised state, 'needs to be an important part of such forces'.

A movement can be defined as a sustained mobilisation around a strategy to achieve an objective. Not only is it unnecessary to have a political party represent the working class; perhaps it is not necessary to have a unified working-class movement at all in order to effectively contest hegemony. The labour movement (which is itself not unified), an ecofeminist movement organising women in mining-affected communities, a food sovereignty movement (which is struggling to gain traction), a cooperative movement (which has not taken off), a climate justice movement (which has a global agenda as well as many local campaigns around different issues), a movement demanding or occupying land, a peasant movement – one cannot assume that they can unite and become an inclusive movement under the leadership of the working class. This does not, however, mean that they cannot contest the hegemony of the ruling class.

Furthermore, the strategy of occupying centres of power, favoured by communists, is not necessarily the most effective way of contesting hegemony. It is possible that decentralised contestation of power through taking control of resources at local level – including land, water, energy production, food production and distribution – could change the balance of class forces, redress inequality and transform the economy. This refers not only to 'the commons' but also to productive forces, technology which is seen as a threat to the working class but has the potential to transform labour and relations of production. The easily-spoken phrase 'radical economic transformation' is potentially given substance through such processes – what Gillian Hart (2013, 192) is perhaps referring to when she avers that Gramsci did not use the term 'counter hegemony' but rather envisaged an 'alternative proletarian hegemony grounded in the philosophy of praxis'.

INCLUSION OR TRANSFORMATION?

Social movements, though, have not focused on such transformation, but rather on inclusion into the existing hegemonic system. One needs only to review debates around land, housing policy and property rights in South Africa to understand this crucial point (see Schneider 2004 on the Grootboom case). The protests and demands of Abahlali baseMjondolo and the precariat, the marginalised, the unemployed and the homeless are, almost universally, for inclusion. This inclusion takes many forms: demands for an elusive title deed to a house, however tiny, and thereby to Hernando de Soto's (2006) precious legal ownership as means of class mobility; demands for electricity provision (not only via pre-paid metres but also to middle-class access to an electricity account which is paid monthly); for a salary rather than a wage, and thereby to a credit card, a housing bond, credit for a vehicle purchase, a private school and a private medical aid. The structure of these institutions makes this a rational course of action.

Social justice movements have also, by and large, focused on extension of rights or holding the state to account in realising existing rights; the Treatment Action Campaign and Equal Education are examples of this. Similarly, the established labour movement is defensive in the context of global contraction and job losses, and attempts to organise precarious workers focus on including such workers into the protection of existing labour legislation. While such organisation and mobilisation to demand inclusion, extension of rights and state accountability are all meaningful and empowering for those who benefit, they do not in themselves constitute a counter-hegemonic project. Similarly, struggles around recognition usually pose their demands in terms of inclusion rather than posing a radical re-ordering of the economic system; in this respect they cannot be considered counter-hegemonic, even though their struggles may be just. As Fraser argues (2000, 120), we should not 'reject the politics of recognition *tout court*. That would be to condemn millions of people to suffer grave injustices that can only be redressed through recognition of some kind'. However, this does not mean that all such struggles, even if just, can combine to constitute a counter-hegemonic project. Can the 'hard' struggles of the precariat, the shack dwellers and the unemployed constitute such a counter-hegemonic project?

Gillian Hart (2013) and others see local government and service delivery as the 'key site of contradictions' where hegemony is contested. How is hegemony understood? My reading of the Gramscian notion of hegemony understands a contestation for class leadership of the society (that is, capitalist society), that either the bourgeoisie or the working class is hegemonic in the sense that other strata and sectors of society are mobilised around the 'class project' of the dominant class. The defensive struggles of shack dwellers or the unemployed for inclusion cannot, in this sense, be understood as a counter-hegemonic project; they are neither unified nor consciously providing leadership to civil society as a whole. To take the argument further, a counter-hegemonic mobilisation would pose an alternative which is convincing to the majority, and convincing not only at the level of ideas but because it provides a demonstrably viable alternative to capitalism. As Van der Walt (2019, 24) states, 'I argue against reliance upon the state, and for re-building unions – and other workers' movements – to maximise direct action, autonomy, and education, so laying the basis for direct workers' control over production and the economy, rather than nationalisation'.

The Rojava eco-socialist movement in the autonomous region of north-eastern Syria may be understood as such a counter-hegemonic movement, although complicated by its nationalist separatist framework. While it is important to engage with such 'current debates, like disconnecting from the state as raised by, for example, Occupy and the Rojava Revolution' (Van der Walt 2019, 25), in South Africa we are not looking at any territorially separate experiment with alternatives, but instead a demonstration of the viability of such alternatives within the civil society space provided by the liberal democracy that exists. Given the evidence of working-class support for the ANC as documented above, it seems necessary to listen to SACP stalwart Jeremy Cronin (2019) who, in his recent debate with Ronnie Kasrils, argues that 'in the South African context the struggle from within the ANC and ANC-led state and the struggle from without are both essential. We need to find better ways of making them complementary'. I would argue that the seizure of state power through electoral or other means should not be the focus of theoretical debate on the left. Instead, 'The challenge for the left is to create a broad-based, united, people-centred, grassroots movement under working-class leadership for democratic socialism – political, social, cultural, gender, youth and environmental renewal – and an alternative economy' (Kasrils 2019).

There seems to be an emerging consensus among left and labour activists both within and outside the Alliance on the need for such a new formation, although the precise form it would take has not been agreed. Some are arguing for an independent socialist or eco-socialist party (Satgar 2021). The SACP, as argued by Cronin, must lead 'a new front for socialism; a Left front, a unity of Left and all progressive formations' (quoted in ANA 2017). Cronin articulates this in terms of building working-class hegemony both in the state and in 'all sites of power': 'Our strategic objective in regard to state power is to secure, not party political, but working class hegemony over the state, as part of our wider medium-term vision to build working class hegemony in all sites of power' (quoted in ANA 2017).

Others from the anarchist left argue that:

> What is needed is a serious, organised, non-sectarian project of democratic reform and political discussion that spans the unions. This would include a rank-and-file movement and would allow multiple views and foster critical thought. It means replacing reliance on the state and parties with struggle, and destructive inter-union rivalry with a serious project of working-class counter-power. (Van der Walt 2019, 25)

However, both the ANC and Cosatu still speak the language of 'social compact', and emphasise the urgent need for a social compact to respond to the current crisis of unemployment in the wake of the Covid-19 pandemic. In the ANC's statement of 8 January 2022, President Ramaphosa identified the social compact as the number one priority of the ANC, and noted the urgency of the following tasks:

> 3.2 Mobilise social partners to urgently finalise a social compact to reduce unemployment, poverty and inequality.
> The NEC and all other structures of the organisation must ensure that all social partners, including business, labour and civil society forge a compact to deal decisively with economic exclusion, poverty, unemployment and inequality.

This is supported by Cosatu's Zingiswa Lozi who, while harshly critical of the ANC, agreed that 'we need a social compact with government and business where they commit to halting retrenchments and creating jobs' (quoted in Mkentane 2022).

Yet, while Cosatu wants every sphere of government and state-owned enterprise to have 'job creation and economic growth at the heart of their work' and argues that 'both the public and private sectors need to accelerate the implementation of the economic reconstruction and recovery plan and ramp up local procurement' (quoted in Mkentane 2022), it should be noted that certain public sector unions have been implicated in the state capture of the previous ANC administration under President Zuma. As former Numsa leader Dinga Sikwebu (2022) argues, 'there is denialism and ambivalence about state capture within the labour movement'. In a scathing critique of public sector unions – arguably Cosatu's strongest constituency – he writes:

> In a country with a strong union presence in state-owned enterprises (SOEs), how did all this happen without unions sounding the alarm bells? Active unionists sit on boards and other policy forums of SOEs. Unlike in the private sector, where unionisation rates hover at about 20%, union representation in the public service stands at about 70%. With its state-centred perspective of development and a history of casting its eyes beyond the workplace, the expectation was that the labour movement would pay attention to changes at the state level and jealously guard the SOEs on behalf of society. (Sikwebu 2022)

Cosatu and the SACP, as members of the Tripartite Alliance, are thus still trapped in an old conundrum: as civil society they are part of anti-corruption alliances, but at the same time they are bound to the ruling party in myriad ways. It is hard to see how a unified labour movement will be possible in this context. It is also hard to see how Cosatu would be able to provide leadership to a new alignment of left forces, as the late Oupa Lehulere warned back in 2005. Similarly it is hard to see how a social compact between labour, business and government will be realisable.

CONCLUSION

In summary, the dominant position of the ANC and Cosatu – representing government and labour, respectively – is in favour of a social compact. Whatever its weaknesses, this is the hegemonic position. The positions on the left of the Alliance and labour – including elements of the SACP and the South African Federation of Trade Unions – are in favour of a 'left popular front' (the SACP position) or a 'new alignment of left popular forces' outside of political parties. Others on the left argue for a new 'labour/left' party to contest elections. None of these as yet constitute a counter-hegemony to the social compact of the Alliance.

However, the outlook for social movements is positive. The evidence above suggests that there is indeed space within a consolidated liberal democratic system such as South Africa for movements for social and climate justice. This suggests a strategy of working within the constraints of parliamentary democracy, flawed as it is, and using the space it allows the working class (both employed and unemployed) to engage in strategic building of counter-hegemony through socialist experiments 'on the ground'. This does not mean that a single popular movement is necessary or desirable; there may be a multiplicity of social movements contesting power in different spaces and around different issues. This does not mean electoral politics, nor taking 'centres of power' in government or even in local government, but rather building independent worker-controlled institutions that are not in direct conflict with existing laws and policies. Using available land, resources and infrastructure – the abandoned schools, the dumpsites, the hundreds of thousands of municipal houses that are now owned by the working class, the water and electricity infrastructure which is accessed to advantage by the middle class – it may be possible for the working class to take some decentralised control over aspects of the economy.

Through such movements, the hegemony of the ruling class is not directly challenged, as Ngwane suggested in 2018, but rather indirectly challenged – a subtler and less obviously revolutionary process of building the institutions of a different society and a different economy, more appropriate for the future. The real challenge is not to build a working-class political party, but rather to mobilise the working class around the material issues of the day.

NOTES

1   This chapter is based in the first instance on some thoughts contributed to a panel on 'Issues of social justice and social movement unionism' at the conference *The Future of Labour*, held at the University of the Witwatersrand, 6–7 September 2018. My brief was to 'reflect on the past and future of labour's links to communities and issues of social justice'.

2   The campaign was later expanded, and OUTA changed its name to Organisation Undoing Tax Abuse.

3   In common parlance, RDP refers to a government-subsidised low-income housing programme that formed part of the first ANC government's Reconstruction and Development Programme from 1994.

REFERENCES

African National Congress (ANC). 2001. *Through the Eye of a Needle? Choosing the Best Cadres to Lead Transformation*. September 2001. Johannesburg: ANC. https://www.ancpl. org.za/wp-content/uploads/2019/09/Eye-of-the-needle.pdf. Accessed 7 February 2023.

African National Congress (ANC). 2022. 'January 8 Statement'. https://www.anc1912.org.za/ statement-of-the-national-executive-committee-on-the-occasion-of-the-110th-anniversary-of-the-anc-2022. Accessed 7 February 2023.

African News Agency (ANA). 2017. 'SACP Unlikely to Contest State Power for Now'. *Polity*, 13 July 2017. https://www.polity.org.za/article/sacp-unlikely-to-contest-state-power-for-now-2017-07-13. Accessed 7 February 2023.

Alexander, Peter. 2010. 'Rebellion of the Poor: South Africa's Service Delivery Protests – A Preliminary Analysis'. *Review of African Political Economy*, 37 (123): 25–40.

Andrews, Mercia. 2013. *Sleeping Giant is Stirring: Farmworkers in South Africa*. https://viacamp-esina.org/en/wp-content/uploads/sites/2/2013/05/EN-09.pdf. Accessed 7 February 2023.

Bezuidenhout, Andries and Malehoko Tshoaedi, eds. 2017. *Labour Beyond Cosatu: Mapping the Rupture in South Africa's Labour Landscape*. Johannesburg: Wits University Press.

Casual Workers' Advice Office (CWAO). 2023. 'About the Casual Workers Advice Office'. http://www.cwao.org.za/about.asp. Accessed 7 February 2023.

Cherry, Janet. 2006. 'Workers and Policy-making'. In *Trade Unions and Democracy: Cosatu Workers' Political Attitudes in South Africa*, edited by Sakhela Buhlungu, 143–166. Cape Town: HSRC Press.

Cherry, Janet. 2017a. 'Cosatu, Service Delivery and the Politics of Community'. In *Labour Beyond Cosatu: Mapping the Rupture in South Africa's Labour Landscape*, edited by Andries Bezuidenhout and Malehoko Tshoaedi, 111–128. Johannesburg: Wits University Press.

Cherry, Janet. 2017b. 'The Successes and Failures of South Africa's Student Movement'. *Waging Nonviolence*, 29 June 2017. https://wagingnonviolence.org/2017/06/south-africa-fees-must-fall. Accessed 7 February 2023.

Cherry, Janet, Patrick Brennan and Gary Prevost. 2023 (forthcoming). 'Battle for the Bay Revisited: The 2021 South African Local Elections in the Nelson Mandela Bay Municipality'.

Cherry, Janet, Nkosinathi Jikeka and Tumi Malope. 2017. 'The Politics of Alliance and the 2014 Elections', In *Labour Beyond Cosatu: Mapping the Rupture in South Africa's Labour Landscape*, edited by Andries Bezuidenhout and Malehoko Tshoaedi, 85–110. Johannesburg: Wits University Press.

Cherry, Janet and Gary Prevost. 2017. 'Kwazakhele after Twenty Years of Democracy: The Contradictory Development of Political Pluralism and Political Alienation'. *Transformation* 94 (1): 1–27.

Cronin, Jeremy. 2019. 'A Response to Ronnie Kasrils' Response to Me'. *Daily Maverick*, 24 May 2019. https://www.dailymaverick.co.za/article/2019-05-24-a-response-to-ronnie-kasrils-response-to-me. Accessed 7 February 2023.

De Soto, Hernando. 2006. *Realising Property Rights*. Peru: ILD.

Fraser, Nancy. 2000. 'Rethinking Recognition'. *New Left Review* 3 (May/June): 107–120.

Gaba, Mzukisi. 2011. 'Revolutionary Discipline: Perspectives of the ANC'. *Polity*, 31 October 2011. https://www.polity.org.za/article/revolutionary-discipline-perspectives-of-the-anc-october-2011-2011-10-31. Accessed 7 February 2023.

Ginsberg, David, Edward Webster, Roger Southall, Geoff Wood, Sakhela Buhlungu, Johann Maree, Janet Cherry, Richard Holmes and Gilton Klerck. 1995. *Taking Democracy Seriously: Worker Expectations and Parliamentary Democracy in South Africa*. Durban: Indicator Press.

Grootes, Stephen. 2019. 'End of the Road for the Socialist Revolutionary Workers Party? And What Future for NUMSA?' *Daily Maverick*, 20 May 2019. https://www.dailymaverick. co.za/article/2019-05-20-end-of-the-road-for-the-socialist-revolutionary-workers-party-and-what-future-for-numsa. Accessed 7 February 2023.

Hall, Ruth. 2021. 'Why the Expropriation Bill is Needed – And Why it is Not Enough'. *Business Day*, 11 February 2021. https://www.businesslive.co.za/bd/opinion/2021-02-11-why-the-expropriation-bill-is-needed-and-why-it-is-not-enough. Accessed 7 February 2023.

Hart, Gillian. 2013. *Rethinking the South African Crisis: Nationalism, Populism, Hegemony*. Durban: University of KwaZulu–Natal Press.

Heleta, Savo. 2016. 'Decolonisation of Higher Education: Dismantling Epistemic Violence and Eurocentrism in South Africa'. *Transformation in Higher Education*, 1 (1): 1–8.

Hlatshwayo, Mondli. 2005. 'From Socialist Politics to Business Unionism'. *Khanya Journal* 8 (May): 16–18. http://khanyajournal.org.za/from-socialist-politics-to-business-unionism. Accessed 7 February 2021.

Hlatshwayo, Mondli. 2018. 'The New Struggles of Precarious Workers in South Africa: Nascent Organisational Responses of Community Health Workers'. *Review of African Political Economy* 45 (157): 378–392.

Ismi, Asad. 2019. 'South Africa's New Revolutionary Party takes on a Corrupt System'. *Monitor* 25 (6): 34–35. https://www.policyalternatives.ca/sites/default/files/uploads/ publications/National%20Office/2019/03/CCPA%20Monitor%20Mar%20Apr%20 2019%20WEB%5B1%5D.pdf. Accessed 7 February 2023.

Kasrils, Ronnie. 2019. 'A Curate's Egg of an Election'. *Daily Maverick*, 14 May 2019. https:// www.dailymaverick.co.za/opinionista/2019-05-14-a-curates-egg-of-an-election. Accessed 7 February 2023.

Lehulere, Oupa. 2005. 'Social Movements, Cosatu and the "New UDF"'. *Khanya Journal* 11 (December). https://khanyajournal.org.za/the-new-social-movements-cosatu-and-the-new-udf-2. Accessed 7 February 2023.

Mkentane, Luyolo. 2022. 'The ANC is Dying, Says Cosatu'. *Business Live*, 23 January 2022. https://www.businesslive.co.za/bd/politics/2022-01-23-the-anc-is-dying-says-cosatu.

Ngwane, Trevor, Immanuel Ness and Luke Sinwell. 2017. *Urban Revolt: State Power and the Rise of Peoples Movements in the Global South*. Johannesburg: Wits University Press.

Nicolson, Greg. 2019. 'Civil Society must Face its Failures – Mark Heywood'. *Daily Maverick*, 17 May 2019. https://www.dailymaverick.co.za/article/2019-05-17-civil-society-must-face-its-failures-mark-heywood.

Nzimande, Blade. 2021. 'SACP Statement on the 28th Annual Chris Hani Commemoration'. *South African Communist Party*, 10 April 2021. https://www.facebook.com/permalink. php?story_fbid=3172830049486852&id=609064382530111. Accessed 5 March 2023.

Pillay, Devan. 2006. 'Cosatu, Alliances and Working Class Politics'. In *Trade Unions and Democracy: Cosatu Workers' Political Attitudes in South Africa*, edited by Sakhela Buhlungu, 167–198. Cape Town: HSRC Press.

Prevost, Gary. 2006. 'The Evolution of the African National Congress in Power: From Revolutionaries to Social Democrats?' *Politikon*, 33 (2): 163–181.

Satgar, Vishwas. 2021. 'Without a Serious Challenge from the Left, the Political Field in South Africa Could See the Emergence of A Neoliberal Right'. *Daily Maverick*, 18 November 2021. https://www.dailymaverick.co.za/article/2021-11-18-without-a-serious-challenge-from-the-left-the-political-field-in-south-africa-could-see-the-emergence-of-a-neoliberal-right.

Schierup, Carl-Ulrik. 2017. 'Under the Rainbow. Migration, Precarity and People Power in Post-apartheid South Africa'. In *Politics of Precarity: Migrant Conditions, Struggles and Experiences*, edited by Martin Bak Jorgenson and Carl-Ulrik Schierup, 276–315. Amsterdam: Brill.

Schneider, Daniel. 2004. 'The Constitutional Right to Housing in South Africa: The Government of the Republic of South Africa v. Irene Grootboom'. *International Journal of Civil Society Law* 2 (2004): 45–62.

Sikwebu, Dinga. 2022. 'Were Unions Complicit in the State Capture Project?', *City Press*, 30 January 2022. https://www.news24.com/citypress/voices/dinga-sikwebu-were-unions-complicit-in-the-state-capture-project-20220130.

Sitas, Ari. 2017. 'The Social Character of Labour Politics'. In *Labour Beyond Cosatu: Mapping the Rupture in South Africa's Labour Landscape*, edited by Andries Bezuidenhout and Malehoko Tshoaedi, 37–47. Johannesburg: Wits University Press.

Standing, Guy. 2014. 'The Precariat'. *Contexts* 13 (4): 10–12. https://journals.sagepub.com/doi/full/10.1177/1536504214558209. Accessed 7 February 2023.

Suttner, Raymond. 2016. *Recovering Democracy*. Johannesburg: Jacana Media.

Suttner, Raymond. 2022. 'The Crisis of Our Times Cannot be Resolved Simply by Electing New ANC Leaders – We Need a New Alignment of Forces'. *Daily Maverick*, 17 January 2022. https://www.dailymaverick.co.za/article/2022-01-17-the-crisis-of-our-times-cannot-be-resolved-simply-by-electing-new-anc-leaders-we-need-a-new-alignment-of-forces.

Van der Walt, Lucien. 2019. 'Rebuilding the Workers' Movement for Counter-power, Justice and Self-Management: A Contribution to the Debate'. *Amandla*, 63: 24–25.

12

Competing Interests: Investment Companies and the Future of Labour

Sandla Nomvete

INTRODUCTION

The Covid-19 lockdown and subsequent economic disruptions caused by rising energy prices following the war between Russia and the Ukraine did not only affect the economy and the workplace, but also trade unions themselves. Trade unions are complex formal organisations that are funded from various sources. At the heart of unions' finances is the idea that members should pay dues and that the payment of membership fees (or withholding of fees, by resigning from the union) is a form of control that members have over their representative organisations. This principle was so important at the time of the formation of the Congress of South African Trade Unions (Cosatu) in 1985 that the federation made 'paid-up membership' one of its core principles. One of the reasons for this is the need for unions to be independent and free from outside interference. The rise of union investment companies in the post-apartheid era was seen as a way for the labour movement to take advantage of Black Economic Empowerment initiatives in the economy; this introduced a new dynamic to this equation. This chapter considers the role that union investment companies play in the internal dynamics of trade unions, with a particular focus on union finances.

Proponents of union investment companies argue that they allow for an opportunity to grow the economy's 'social sector', as well as an opportunity to use profits to benefit union members and their dependents (Cosatu 1997, Chapter 2; Golding 1997; Copelyn 1997). The scholarship programmes of both the Southern African Clothing and Textile Workers' Union and the National Union of Mineworkers (NUM) are often mentioned as successful examples (Copelyn 2016). On the other hand, opponents of union investment companies point to the dilution of unions' mandate to represent the working class, and raise the potentially corrupting influences of unions getting too close to capital and thereby becoming employers of other workers themselves. This, it is argued, constitutes a fundamental conflict of interest (McKinley 1999; Nattrass and Seekings 2016).

The aim of this chapter is to situate the emergence of union investment companies within a historical focus of shifts in trade union finances more broadly, and to draw on a number of interviews with trade union officials and office-bearers to reflect on how trade unions themselves understand and explain the impact of trade union investment companies on the nature of trade unionism. Interviews were conducted with officials and office-bearers from unions affiliated to Cosatu, the South African Federation of Trade Unions (Saftu) and the National Council of Trade Unions (Nactu). In addition to this, media reports are used to describe a number of high-profile cases where trade union investment companies became so controversial that internal contestations within trade unions themselves over the corrupting influence of their investment companies spilled over into the public domain.

The trade union movement in South Africa has historically been viewed as the vanguard of the working class. However, post-apartheid developments that saw the diversification of the unions' profile as more than just worker and political organisations, but also as entities with businesses interests of their own, however, present a new challenge to the ability of unions to maintain a moral voice. Leaders are often tainted by public allegations and internal battles around benefits derived from close links to decision-makers in their unions' business dealings. This situation runs the risk that unions may be viewed by some as spaces of business, and unionists are seen as business opportunists 'covered in worker blankets'. As is the case in political parties and government, high-profile union leadership battles often settle scores by means of selectively exposing alleged corruption. The interests of union leaders are then seen to be driven by personal business and political aspirations, thereby contradicting workers' interests (Inhedru 2001; Buhlungu 2010).

This chapter commences with a summary of key historical labour activities which offer a context to union operations and how that evolved over time. The subsequent section discusses how union finances were used in the past and how they are used in the present in running and sustaining union operations. Subsequently, the chapter discusses union investment companies which have become 'central to union finance viability and operations' today (Nomvete 2018; Iheduru 2001). The section offers insights into how union investment companies came into existence in South Africa with the aim of illuminating successes and challenges tied to their prevalence. The final part of the chapter presents solutions to mitigating complexities presented by the evolved nature of union finance.

UNIONS FINANCES UNDER APARTHEID

The labour movement in South Africa has a well-documented and dynamic history (see Lucien van der Walt's chapter in this volume). An important theme in this history is the rise and decline of trade unions, with moments of social movement unionism followed by decline, often due to union leaders losing touch with their membership base and the decline of formal organisational capacity due to maladministration and corruption. At other times, union organisation has been disrupted by state repression, primarily though the imprisonment of union activists, the assassination of activists, or the departure into exile of union activists in order to escape state repression (Buhlungu 2010).

Trade unions that mobilised against colonialism and apartheid, and that primarily focused on organising the black working class, date back to the formation of the Industrial Workers of the World (South Africa) in 1910, the Industrial and Commercial Workers' Union (ICU) in 1919, the Federation of Non-European Trade Unions in 1928, the Council of Non-European Trade Unions in 1941, and the South African Congress of Trade Unions (Sactu) in 1955 (Friedman 1987; Baskin 1991; Van der Walt 2007). Following the 1973 Durban strikes and the organisation of workers into a new set of independent trade unions, union activists looked back at this history of movements on the rise, followed by decline, and attempted to strategise accordingly. These lessons related to the need for union democracy and worker control over the activities of full-time union officials, as well as careful considerations around the relationships (or alliances) between unions and political organisations (Buhlungu 2010).

From the early days, unions such as the ICU had to adapt to the ever-changing face of work and society. While their existence sought to deal primarily with shop-floor issues, those could not be divorced from societal issues. Sakhela Buhlungu (2010, 58) argues that 'this was to be expected given that black workers were denied both industrial and political citizenship'. Owing to the political atmosphere at the time, unions had to reimagine themselves as both worker and societal organisations. In facing severe forms of racial oppression, the ICU initially took on the form of social movement unionism, implying that trade unionism was not only about representing workers at their place of work, but also had to address the need to challenge the system as a whole. Like other South African labour movements, the ICU was most successful when it was able to balance workplace and political campaigns. However, it was a general union, organising in all industries, which limited its ability to provide the kind of industry-specific workplace representation that workers often require. To be sure, Sakhela Buhlungu (2010) and Steven Friedman (1987) both argue that the ICU, at crucial times, focused on political battles at the expense of struggles at the workplace. Also, at the time, unions were dependent on membership dues that were collected at the level of union branches. As such, members had a form of control over their organisations. The ICU eventually collapsed when the leadership became detached from the base and engaged in corrupt practices involving union finances (Bonner 1978; Bradford 1987).

In the period between the collapse of the ICU and the introduction of formal apartheid from 1948 onwards, it became increasingly difficult for trade unions to organise black members. Following labour legislation that outlawed trade unions organising across colour lines, the Trade Union Council of South Africa followed a policy of parallel unions, while its opponent, Sactu, focused on organising black workers as part of a commitment to national liberation. The Trade Union Council eventually became top-heavy and bureaucratic, and the federation's detachment from its membership meant that it was unable to withstand the dynamism of a new wave of militant trade unionism that emerged in the 1970s. Sactu, on the other hand, was forced to go underground and eventually had to operate from exile, with little real formal structure in the country itself (Friedman 1987; Baskin 1991).

During the periods subsequent to the formation of the first black unions, unionism endured for 50 years, but the repressive apartheid regime led to a significant decline in union activism during the 1960s and the early 1970s. As mentioned, Sactu as a labour federation essentially operated from exile or through underground structures. Following the 1973 Durban strikes, however, things started to change. The recognition of black trade unions after the Wiehahn Commission in the late 1970s opened up new space for formal union organisation. Drawing on earlier lessons, union activists followed a number of strategies to build organisation from the ground up. In response to the ICU's rapid growth as a general union and the lack of direct links with their members as a result of being overstretched, the majority of post-1973 unions set up industrial unions. Also, in response to what had happened to Sactu and in anticipation of state persecution of union leaders, the new unions emphasised building strong and durable shop-floor organisation through intensive workers' education programmes, and inculcating the idea of workers' control over elected officials. Shop stewards could be recalled if they acted outside of mandates given by members. Then there is the matter of union involvement in the liberation movement. In the 1970s and early 1980s, a number of union officials strategically did not reveal their associations with the liberation movement in order to maintain unions as legal structures, whereas others (called 'workerists', as opposed to 'populists') argued for a socialist path independent from the liberation movement and what was seen as its middle-class and nationalist origins. These new militant unions were therefore characterised by a flat structure, limited bureaucracy, accessible leadership and power that rested with the workers (Webster 1988; Von Holdt 2002; Buhlungu 2010; Pillay 2012).

How was the trade union movement able to survive and see to its day-to-day operations during the apartheid era? Given that the colonial and apartheid regimes refused to grant political citizenship to black workers and to blacks in general, it was impossible that black unions would benefit from government funding or any form or subsidy within South Africa at the time. Nevertheless, unionism led by black and white South Africans on the left continued. It is common knowledge that unions operated primarily on subscription fees from their members. These subscriptions fees in the early unions were collected by hand by shop stewards, and then handed over to the union's treasurer general by local organisers. This was due to the absence of stop-order facilities at the time. This method of collection was a time-consuming exercise that opened the union to possibilities of corruption, maladministration and lack of accountability, as those in charge could choose what was recorded on the books (Molete and Hurt 1997). On the other hand, because union officials had to physically collect union dues from branches, the practice maintained continued personal contact between union officials and members. This meant that branches had some control over the activities of head-office officials (Theron 2017). Nevertheless, reflecting much later on its two years of existence, a report by the National Education, Health and Allied Workers' Union (Nehawu), captured in a book by Martha Molete and Karen Hurt, read:

> Our union is still very poor ... Out of 18 000 members, only 1 500 are paying subs to the union ... Our office does not have equipment, our organisers do not reach certain areas on time because of lack of own transport, workers are not well-serviced in general terms ... Whilst our staff are busy negotiating wages for workers, organisers earn as little as R450 per month. They sometimes run for three months without even getting that money.

We then experience a dropping down of morale and eventually people will leave our union with skills that they have gained through Nehawu and go and use them somewhere else with unions who can offer more for their skills. In fact, the situation is so critical that most of our accounts, like stationery, have not been paid. The union can be taken to court at any moment from now; we cannot keep the photocopier running and do union work. (quoted in Molete and Hurt 1997)

Even though Nehawu was formed in 1987, at a time when, it could be argued, unions had gained momentum, the above quote gives an indication of what the situation was like at the embryonic stages of the union movement. The issue of union subscription fees was but a microcosm of a deeper issue of bad administration (see Molete and Hurt 1997 and Friedman 1987 on early union administrative matters). To further illustrate the dilemmas associated with union finances, the following extract is from an interview conducted more recently with a senior Cosatu official. When asked how unions maintained self-sufficiency, particularly with regard to finance, this official replied as follows:

Those unions in the past were thriving more on donor funding but after 1994 the avenues of donor funding went dry because the donors were now funding more the democratic government … Why the NGOs [non-governmental organisations] had more funding was because the donors were not recognising the state then. So, they opted for the NGOs; they were building them up to challenge the state then. So what the donors are saying now is that we will fund the state and you will get your monies from the state … So, trade unions of the 70s, 60s and 80s were thriving on donor funding; if you go back to their finances you will realise that they were thriving on donor funding, they were not self-sufficient, and they were not thriving on subscription fees. It was difficult under the apartheid government to even get subs on a regular basis from those companies, so it is not true that those unions were surviving only on subscription. Their main revenue stream was donor funding. (Cosatu official, interview, 16 October 2019)

The point about donor funding in the apartheid period is an important one, since receiving funding from external sources introduced additional political dynamics, also due to the Cold War between the West and the Soviet bloc. Okechukwu Iheduru (2001) writes that most unions in South Africa under apartheid survived from funding that came from communist parties around the world, as well as funding from Scandinavian countries. In addition, the emerging independent unions received significant support from unions in the West, due to the fact that those unions, unlike those in the Communist world, organised in multinational corporations that had investments in South Africa. The first recognition agreement between a trade union in South Africa and a textiles company (at Smith and Nephew, in 1973) was concluded after considerable pressure on the company from workers in the United Kingdom to recognise their South African counterparts as negotiating partners (Byrne and Ulrich 2016). This pioneered numerous other such recognition agreements, that also allowed unions to use office space and resources from companies where they organised members.

Equally significant, and as mentioned in the interview quoted above, the emerging unions received funding from international donors. These included funds from the American Federation of Labor and the Congress of Industrial Organizations (AFL-CIO), the main trade union federation in the United States. This was a controversial funding source, since it was criticised by the Soviet bloc and independent left groupings as being a covert source of funds from US imperialism. (The US federation was sometimes mockingly referred to as the AFL-CIA, referring to its assumed covert relationship with the Central Intelligence Agency). Nevertheless, in an analysis of this period, Southall (1995) argues that Cosatu and its predecessors were able to avoid trade union imperialism and could draw on this funding without being influenced politically. They also had a diverse range of funders from numerous other countries and trade unions as part of a global anti-apartheid movement, and significant global support for the role of trade unions in resisting apartheid. Their mandate was clear; it entailed the struggle for workplace democracy and political freedom, and as unions grew in strength and commanded more resources, they were able to turn solid organising at workplaces into powerful industrial unions that operated at the national level. From a position of strength, Cosatu adopted the Freedom Charter at its congress in 1987, thereby openly aligning itself with the African National Congress (ANC) and the South African Communist Party in exile.

A point has to be made about the cost of union bureaucracies in the apartheid era. Full-time union officials were paid relatively low salaries, at times pegged to a maximum of the highest paid workers in the union's bargaining unit. Union officials did not have medical aid or provident funds and there were no internal grading systems with wage differentials or notches linked to performance. Union offices were in areas where the rent was cheap, close to the workplaces organised by unions. They rarely owned these buildings. Put differently, there was little social distance between union organisers and members, apart from the social cleavages between white union officials and black members (Buhlungu 2006, 2009).

To summarise, the independent unions that emerged after the 1973 strikes were able to rely on a combination of funds derived from membership dues (collected in person), considerable donor funding (global solidarity directed against apartheid) and limited use of company resources (resulting from recognition agreements between unions and companies). Because dues had to be collected from the branches, this required routine contact between branches and the union's full-time bureaucracy, which provided branches with a certain degree of leverage over full-time officials and national office-bearers. An important qualifier has to be made here. Mainstream unions – that is, white unions – had additional sources of funding, including significant investments in property. These unions owned assets that put them in a strong position to reinvent themselves in the post-apartheid era (Visser 2006, as well as Jantjie Xaba's chapter in this volume).

UNION FINANCES AFTER APARTHEID

With the transition from apartheid to a democratic order, it became clear that the day-to-day operations of the union movement were about to change (Baskin 1991; Buhlungu 2010). The trade union movement became bigger, more complex, and therefore needed to be better organised. In the same vein, it had to shape itself for South Africa's imminent reintegration into the mainstream global economy. Following the formal end of the apartheid regime in 1994, critical questions had to be asked in the labour movement:

> How do we reposition ourselves for relevance in a country that allows trade unions to organise freely? How do we deal with the swelling numbers within unions? How do we organise ourselves better as organisations and, importantly, how do we sustain ourselves financially? (Cosatu 1997)

Handling growing numbers of union members was addressed through the educational empowerment of union officials, improved organising and the much-debated bureaucratisation of the trade union (Buhlungu 2010). Whereas unions had relied primarily on membership dues and donor funding during the apartheid era, the transition to democracy presented new challenges, but also provided new funding opportunities.

First, where union dues were once physically collected at the branch level, by the time of the transition from apartheid the banking system had changed in such a way that dues could be collected via stop orders or debit orders. PK (a pseudonym), a former NUM Regional Treasurer, Deputy Chairperson and Chairperson at the time of his retirement in 2015, stated during an interview that union finances were centralised at the head office. Unlike the case of Nehawu in the late 1980s, he states that when he worked as Regional Treasurer in the early 1990s, collection of subscription fees happened via debit orders. The job of Regional Treasurers, then and now, is to audit debit-order sheets and make sure that companies have collected subs from all members. They also double-check if the finances have been forwarded to the union's head office. Consistent with the quote from Nehawu, Jan Theron (2017) states that in the past union monies collected by hand rested with the branches. Thus, the branches had autonomy on how the money would be used. Theron further argues that the introduction of stop-order facilities contributed to giving head offices power, ultimately contributing to centralisation. Asked about how they received money in regions and what it was used for, PK reaffirmed the point of centralisation. He stated that it was the head office of the union that allocated budgets to regional offices. He said that allocations were based on the size and needs of each branch, and that allocation was not based on a blanket approach. When probed further on what union monies were used for, he identified important administrative components central to union work. PK stated that monies allocated to the regions paid rent, telephone bills, travelling for cases, stationery, petrol and union staff. He further clarified that those at the union branches were paid by the companies and that administrative costs of the union office were also handled by the company as per clauses in the recognition agreements. Other union expenses such as hiring venues for conferences, union regalia, food and the like were all funded by companies.

Second, whereas the apartheid state had been hostile to the labour movement, the state now supported selected union activities. One example would be Ditsela, which became an important institutional base for worker education. Another would be research funding from government departments such as the Department of Trade and Industry, which allowed unions to prepare for policy engagements with employers and the state in tripartite and multipartite forums such as the National Economic Development and Labour Council. This also meant that union head offices had more power to allocate these resources and training opportunities.

Third, a clause in the Labour Relations Act (1995) allowed for unions with majority representation in certain industries and workplaces to collect union dues from non-members (agency shop agreements). In some cases these amounted to considerable resources, and the agency shop funds were paid into trusts, which unions could access for organising and education. These agency shop trusts became controversial, since there were tussles between union branches and head offices over control of the funds.

But in addition to these new sources of funding, Cosatu and its affiliates thought about the question of union financial surpluses, with NUM raising this towards the end of the 1980s and debating in the 1990s whether to set up a trade union investment company (Botiveau 2017). Cosatu-linked union investment companies were envisaged as vehicles that would empower labour to transform the economy, to expedite skills transfer to those in need, to support regional economic integration and to generate jobs. Importantly they would enable the transmission of the means of production to workers and thus assist in socialising the economy (Cosatu 1997; Golding 1997). It was clear in this vision, however, that union investment companies were not to become capitalist in the process of democratising the economy (Dexter 1999). The reality turned out to be more complicated.

Discussions about setting up union investment companies took place within the context of growing unions and a shift in power from branches to head offices. Iheduru (2001) notes that union investment companies have always existed in countries such as Spain, the United States, Israel, Canada, Australia, Scandinavia, Portugal, and China (see also Ellerman 1990; Quarter 1995; Howard 2000). He also states that globalisation and global economic reforms expedited their formation. They were formed, he states, for purely profit-making reasons, to supplement wages of worker-owners. Moreover, there was hope and interest in creative collective ownership. What then about South Africa?

South African organised labour, although maintaining its stance on socialism, also decided to follow the path of 'wealth creation for workers' – something that came to be known as labour capitalism (Inhedru 2001). These investment companies and other businesses were formed with the understanding that they would go on to become sources of revenue for the union and subsequently benefit the previously disadvantaged workers (Iheduru 2001). But have South African trade unions achieved these desired outcomes?

Melikaya Rubushe (2009) and Sakhela Buhlungu (2010) characterise the issue of investment companies and union business wings as having become a thorny one that has placed officials and unions under scrutiny over the years. This has been the result of misappropriation of union funds and loss of sight of the core union business by some union officials. Rubushe (2009) identifies what he views as contradictory to union ethos, given that unions tend to invest monies in businesses that go against their very foundations. One of the fundamentals identified by Rubushe (2009) is worker control, a phenomenon that does not seem to have a role in the decisions relating to union business and investment companies. Extending from this, while speaking to Rubushe, Dinga Sikwebu, a trade union stalwart, lamented that union businesses sought profits and did nothing towards furthering a socialist agenda, which is what trade unionism was founded on. This is even though subscription fees from union members alone have been identified as inadequate in running the modern day-to-day business of the union. To solicit fresh responses from senior leaders of labour federations, questions were asked about why South African unions needed to do business.

Among other things, it emerged in the responses that the recognition of unions in the late 1970s and the formation of labour federations such as Cosatu, Nactu and the Federation of Unions of South Africa (Fedusa) in the mid-1980s was met with great enthusiasm. This was seen as a plus by the large membership in the face of a union movement that was still struggling administratively and financially. Many unions at this point still did not have adequate resources such as office space, stationery, vehicles and other necessities for running what was going to be a bigger union movement across the country. For those unions that enjoyed donor funding and financial support from international socialist organisations, such as those in the Scandinavian countries and the East, the financial sympathy that came because of political repression would soon wane with the dawn of democracy. Unions, therefore, had to plot their transition towards self-sufficiency. Doing business through investment companies would be the ultimate vehicle towards self-sufficiency (Inhedru 2001). A senior Saftu official, who at the time of this transition was a member of the National Union of Metalworkers of South Africa (Numsa), unpacks how and why this became necessary.

> In 1993 Numsa held a historic congress and began to grapple with the post-colonial and post-apartheid South Africa – how do we reposition ourselves as the trade union movement? We were also considering that trade unions were funded by the Scandinavian countries, similar to the ANC as an anti-apartheid movement. So, there was a strong feeling that after the attainment of democracy unions must be on their own, financially and otherwise. So, we envisaged a new South Africa and were under no illusion that the ANC government would do everything … So, the union began to grapple with the fact it would require more resources with the new dispensation, such as capacity to do research. Here we were talking about a country that would be reintegrated into the global economy and so you were going to need research capacity, you are going to need competent staff. Moreover, there was also a sense that the union was going to lose a lot of people to government or the private sector; some people call it the 'brain drain'. It became a massive exodus. We lost a lot of people; among others were the likes of [Enoch] Godongwana, and this crippled the union movement

because you have these people where you invested not only technically but ideologically … and these are the people who understood the national discourse. So, then there was a big discussion on how we get organisations to survive and sustain themselves because we would be competing with government and the private sector … So that was the basis! It became clear that we cannot over-rely on subscriptions because they were beginning to dwindle because of globalisation that came with automation and flexible work. (Saftu official, interview, 18 October 2019)

This quote raises important justifications of why unions had to go into business, and mirrors the assertions of Iheduru (2001, 2) where he states, 'these businesses were established to provide independent sources of revenue for the unions and, allegedly, to enable workers to share in the economic opportunities that have opened up for previously disadvantaged individuals in the country'. The following expands from this and deals more with the technical necessities.

I will speak for Cosatu largely, and briefly for unions in general. Unions generally have a problem of financial survival. The reason for union investment companies is to ensure that revenue streams come into the union, but those revenue streams do so much more than simple union work of running the office, servicing members and other administrative work. They also look at other sister unions, in European countries for example, and think they must have schemes to protect those that have retired, they must have strike funds so that when there is a strike workers can go home knowing they can at least get things like food parcels during strikes because they know that those are the things that demotivate workers during a strike programme. Unions must have buildings and they must have assets. That is why unions started investment companies in the main. As unions they were aware that they had been left out of the mainstream economy and that is the basic reason in my understanding. (Cosatu official, interview, 16 October 2019)

Given this context, unions needed to reconsider how they would maintain financial survival given the turn of events that we could argue threatened their very existence and relevance in a democratic state. The transition into a democratic regime meant diversification in terms of union operations. The introduction of the Labour Relations Act in 1995 meant unions could represent workers at different levels of work, something that would need officials to be trained, including in specialised skills in litigation. Moreover, the emulation of unions elsewhere in the world in terms of providing back-up and support for its workers during strike season, as quoted above, meant that unions had to look beyond union subs. Given this position of the union, union leaders were therefore asked what the unions had managed to achieve since union investment companies and other business wings took off. The question of desired outcomes solicited mixed replies from the different officials:

> I do not think the trade union movement achieved what it set out to achieve with the union investment companies. In fact, I think these investment companies constitute a major contradiction of what the trade union movement stands for. In a sense that the leadership of the union is elected either after three or four years, and each leader when they come in, they have a completely different vision. When they are coming they do so because their thinking is that there is money there ... This has completely demotivated and defocused the trade union in general, and members as well. For instance, in the case of Nactu the investment of money was doing general union work, paying staff, paying this and that. At a critical point, when we were supposed to reap off on the investment, the money was now stuck in the hands of white corporates because we were selling shares to stay afloat and doing damage control. Workers got nothing! This is a typical example. (Nactu official, interview, 21 August 2019)

The Nactu situation represents one of the worst-case scenarios. The official further elaborated that the federation had underdeveloped leadership to oversee its investments, and hence every challenge within the union that required funds was dealt with by selling shares, which ultimately saw them lose absolute control of their investment wing. To the same question a Saftu official replied:

> The question of the desired outcomes will depend on union to union. Some unions got a lot of money, your NUM and the likes, but that is because they invested in leadership on guys such as Gwede Mantashe and going through university. Some unions invested in property, such as the Numsa property after we realised that the rental was becoming too expensive. So, when you invest in own property you cut out the middleman. But when it comes to dividends, you will not find anything ... For workers directly you will find benefits such as the Mbuyiselo Ngwende bursary scheme, Doves Funeral Services [a company in which Numsa investment company has shares]

as well as the Medical Aid scheme courtesy of the financial services wing …
but I don't want to delve into that controversy. (Saftu official, interview,
18 October 2019)

The above reflects some of the best practices on the side of the union investing in
property and thus avoiding unnecessary expenditure for the union in the future.
Sharing similar sentiments on the fruits of these companies, the Cosatu official
stated:

> Well, to an extent there are benefits for workers in these investment
> companies and I am not even going to lie about it. I mean many unions –
> Sactwu, NUM, Numsa and many other unions – run bursary schemes.
> The NUM one is the most spoken of; they have the JB Marks and the Elijah
> Barayi bursary schemes, they have resource centres … Workers here benefit
> directly because they can study for free with the support of these invest-
> ment companies, but that is not enough!! (Cosatu official, interview, 16
> October 2019)

As one of the unionists above has mentioned, there have been varying outcomes
when unions do business. Some have taken this business model and attempted to
get the best outcomes from it, whereas for others there have been failures owing
to lack of training of company administrators. In the interviews with union officials it also emerged that the existence of these investment companies had fractured
union leadership. As pointed out above, for some in the trade unions the investment
companies have become the priority while worker interests are secondary. That is,
the interest of some who get into the union movement lie in being parachuted to
directorship of those companies and thus improved proximity to finances rather
than worker interest.

One of the most striking revelations in the conversation with these officials was
how the chief executive officers of the investment companies influence democratic
processes of the unions. It emerged that, among other things, some executives
attempted to sustain their positions by influencing congress through funding
certain individuals for certain positions. This is even though union companies
in general are said to be independent from the union. Scholars have attempted
to conceptualise the nature of this type of unionist and unionism that is defined
by business and the self-interest of union leaders. Buhlungu (2010, 126) defines
this type of unionist as an Entrepreneur Unionist, and among the characteristics is
'individualistic and manipulative empire builders that use unions as steppingstones

in upward social mobility. They are opportunistic, driven by personal interest and see the union as a business organisation'. Bezuidenhout has similarly defined this type of unionism as Entrepreneurial Unionism. He argues:

> It moves the focus from members to the interests of the official. At times the union may look like a social movement union and may be characterised by leaders who make appeals to notions of social justice or even socialism, but the internal practices of the unions do not conform to basic standards of democratic representation and their finances are not open to outside scrutiny or review by members. (Bezuidenhout 2017, 221)

A Cosatu union official corroborates Bezuidenhout's assertion around lack of basic democratic practices and financial transparency which governed the traditional union. He asserted:

> Many workers are not even aware of these union investment companies because it's an issue of accountability; no one wants to account. I mean, many of them [workers] don't even read or get their financial statements … Okay, let us go back. Many of the shop stewards by virtue of their positions must hold regular workplace-based meetings; they don't! And because of that, much of the information rests with the executives at the branch, regional and national level. It is never cascaded down to workplaces. Go to any union, go to any militant union and workplace, and ask workers when was the last time they got a congress report from a person they had delegated to a congress – simple things! A congress report is the most topical because it does two things; it writes up policy and elects new leadership. Now think about finances and think about the degree of feedback from executive structures … There is no accountability to workers whatsoever. (Cosatu official, interview, 16 October 2019)

This response came after a question was posed as to whether union members were aware of the union investment companies, and whether they knew where their subscription fees were going. One may perhaps view the line of questioning as impractical, particularly because unions and their companies are 'separate entities'. Be that as it may, unions are well-represented on the boards of their investment companies and therefore it can be argued that those representatives who sit as union national office bearers have the responsibility of at least filtering the necessary information down so that workers are in the know about their monies and therefore people can account. Lack of transparency on these monies has therefore opened up a can of worms for the union. To demonstrate some of the issues that have followed unions in doing business, the chapter refers to some cases reported on by the media over the years.

CASE STUDIES OF UNION INVESTMENT COMPANIES AND COMPETING INTERESTS

In the past, the South African Transport and Allied Workers' Union (Satawu) has been battling in the courts over alleged missing monies that amounted to millions of rands. In February 2013, Satawu national office bearers appeared in court for allegations of fraud that saw R8 million missing from the union's account when they were office bearers (Maphumulo 2013). A sister trade union, the South African Municipal Workers Union (Samwu), was also hit by a scandal where an estimated R140 million was unaccounted for. The union president at the time of the allegations, in 2014, suggested that they were 'baseless and unfounded'. In an attempt to find facts about the alleged missing monies, the provincial leadership of Samwu suggested that the national leadership conduct an independent forensic audit. The national leadership refused to do so. Those that challenged the union leadership on the matter were suspended and later expelled from the organisation. Nevertheless, the requested audit was eventually conducted, although it was an internal audit which found no evidence of missing money (Marrian 2015).

Around the same period, the Chemical, Energy, Paper, Printing, Wood and Allied Workers' Union leadership was at loggerheads with the union's lawyers over the control of its investment arm worth over R1 billon, according to Solly Maphumulo (2013). This squabble for control escalated to the courts, with the union's deputy general secretary filing a court application that the union get independent trustees to control the investments (Maphumulo 2013). While they were battling for investment control in the courts, the Department of Labour was threatening to deregister the union following its failure to submit an audited financial statement. In the country's second largest federation. Fedusa, a senior official was suspended and subsequently expelled from his position as general secretary of the union following alleged misconduct. He was alleged to have pushed Fedusa to do business with a company that had ties with his own personal business (Smit 2019).

From the above cases, it is clear that the trade union movement is confronted with something of a dilemma regarding its business wings. Union officials were asked, therefore, how this situation could be mitigated in order to ensure that it does not continue to erode trade union credibility. There were contrasting points of view, as is evident in the quotes below. We hear first from the Cosatu official:

> First you need to make sure that investment companies are operating on the strict mandate of the unions. It is not a standalone business that should be a free-for-all just because it operates in the market. It operates in the markets so that it manipulates the market so that it brings back money to the union, so each and every high structure must always discuss the investment company – where does it invest, what are the returns there and what is the direction of the company? So, every time the company must come here and account, it must be discussed, and a mandate must be given. The second thing is that the people you send to those companies must be given the technical capacity, the human capital. They must not go there and be swallowed by smart thinking, but also the ones that stay behind must not fail to manage those that have been sent to the companies. And maybe just thirdly, we must make sure that the revenues that [are] made by those companies are regularly sent in the direction of the union, because one of the biggest problems currently with the union investment companies is that the leaders are the ones that benefit from them and not the regular members, and that is why recent fights in the unions have been about investment companies more than anything else. (Cosatu official, interview, 16 October 2019)

The views in the latter part of the above quote were also expressed by a Satawu official in 2013, when interviewed for the 'Taking Democracy Seriously' study. He stated:

> Unionists in investment companies want to maximise kickbacks for them to benefit. They use the banner of the union to build more networks for them and not the organisation. The focus is no longer what they were mandated to do, but the focus now is on what they want to achieve using the banner and platform of the trade union. (Satawu official, interview, 3 February 2013)

The Saftu official shared his own position on how the issue with the investment companies and the controversies around them could be dealt with. He said:

> The birth of Saftu, also in the context of asking ourselves what can we shape, all these problems in the union, are a microcosm of what is happening in the country. What happens in the ANC, what happens in state institutions is exactly

what is happening in unions. We have leaders who are corrupt, leaders who are substandard, who want resources, who want opulence and to control shop stewards in different industries for their interest. So, it is quite tricky; it will require a particular call of a type of comrade that will take risks. But if you are found you must know that it is easy to draft a charge sheet that says you have done the so-called gross insubordination. (Saftu official, interview, 18 October 2019)

The quotes above acknowledge that unions are indeed in trouble where investment companies are concerned. They postulate some of the possible solutions, but also warn that people who challenge the status quo may be victimised by those nursing their self-interest. In the main, these assertions suggest the existence a new type of unionist and unionis.

CONCLUSION

The current nature of the trade union movement in business leaves us with more questions than answers. There is a general sense and agreement coming out of this chapter that trade union business wings have brought forth a multitude of problems that require thorough organisational introspection. The shift in the ideological character of these trade unions has not been given sufficient scholarly attention. It seems, as suggested by Buhlungu (2010) and others, that trade unionism over the years has travelled through different layers of ideologies, from social movement and political unionism through to entrepreneurial unionism. It seems to me, therefore, that with the change in ideological lenses, trade unions may have entangled themselves in a situation that they might not fully understand and, more significantly, one of which they are not sure how to rid themselves. This is because there was no conscious effort to shift the type of unionism from the outset; they occurred rather due to chance and to the political atmosphere of the time. Unions only reacted to political shifts that needed them to do business. Although there were discussions leading them to this conclusion, it does not seem that the unions envisaged the challenges that would arise at both operational and ideological levels. As it stands, it is clear that there are competing interests among unionists and other trustees on matters relating to investment companies. Personal interests have overshadowed the interests of workers and led to the harm eloquently described by union officials in this chapter. It seems that many unionists directly involved in the running of these organisation have succumbed to ideological poverty and have completely lost the union ethos that was founded on a workerist and socialist agenda. What therefore for the future of unionism? The current crop of workers is becoming increasingly literate and arguably have improved their understanding of administration, finance and the general functioning of the union. If this trajectory persists, unions risk losing more workers to private litigators such as Clientele and LegalWise, among others. Trust in the trade union movement may very well thin out, which might then lose overall credibility.

REFERENCES

Baskin, Jeremy. 1991. *Striking Back. A History of Cosatu*. Johannesburg: Ravan Press.
Bezuidenhout, Andries. 2017. 'Labour Beyond Cosatu, other Federations and Independent Unions'. In *Labour Beyond Cosatu: Mapping the Rupture in South Africa's Labour Landscape*, edited by Andries Bezuidenhout and Malehoko Tshoaedi, 217–234. Johannesburg: Wits University Press.
Bonner, Phil. 1978. 'The Decline and Fall of the ICU – A Case of Self-destruction?' In *Essays in Southern African Labour History*, edited by Edward Webster, 114–120. Johannesburg: Raven Press.
Botiveau, Raphaël. 2017. *Organise or Die? Democracy and Leadership in South Africa's National Union of Mineworkers*. Johannesburg: Wits University Press.
Bradford, Helen. 1987. *A Taste of Freedom. The ICU in Rural South Africa, 1924–1930*. New Haven and London: Yale University Press.
Buhlungu, Sakhela. 2006. 'Rebels without a Cause of their Own? The Contradictory Location of White Officials in Black Unions in South Africa, 1973–1994'. *Current Sociology* 54 (3): 427–451.
Buhlungu, Sakhela. 2009. The Rise and Decline of the Democratic Organizational Culture in the South African Labor Movement, 1973 to 2000'. *Labor Studies Journal* 34 (1): 91–111.
Buhlungu, Sakhela. 2010. *A Paradox of Victory: Cosatu and the Democratic Transformation in South Africa*. Pietermaritzburg: University of KwaZulu-Natal Press.
Byrne, Sian and Nicole Ulrich. 2016. 'Prefiguring Democratic Revolution? "Workers' Control" and "Workerist" Traditions of Radical South African Labour, 1970–1985'. *Journal of Contemporary African Studies* 34 (3): 368–387.
Congress of South African Trade Unions (Cosatu). 1997. 'The Report of the September Commission on the Future of the Unions to the Congress of South African Trade Unions'. Johannesburg: Cosatu.
Copelyn, Johnny. 1997. 'Seizing the Moment: Union Investment Companies'. *South African Labour Bulletin* 21 (2): 74–78.
Copelyn, Johnny. 2016. *Maverick Insider: A Struggle for Union Independence in a Time of National Liberation*. Johannesburg: Picador Africa.
Dexter, Phillip. 1999. 'Union Investment Companies: Business Unionism or Union Business?' *South African Labour Bulletin* 23 (6): 82–84.
Ellerman, David. 1990. *The Democratic Worker-owned Firm: A New Model for East and West*. Boston: Unwin Hyman.
Friedman, Steven. 1987. *Building Tomorrow Today: African Workers in Trade Unions 1970–1984*. Johannesburg: Raven Press.
Golding, Marcel. 1997. 'Pioneers or Sellouts? Exploring New Lands'. *South African Labour Bulletin* 21 (3): 85–90.

Howard, Michael. 2000. *Self-management and the Crisis of Socialism: The Rose in the Fist of the Present*. New York: Rowman and Littlefield.

Iheduru, Okechukwu. 2001. 'Organised Labour, Globalisation and Economic Reform: Union Investment Companies in South Africa'. *Transformation* 46: 1–31.

Maphumulo, Solly. 2013. 'More Millions Missing in Satawu Fraud Case'. *Business Day Live*, 28 February 2013. https://www.iol.co.za/business-report/economy/more-millions-missing-in-satawu-fraud-case-1478609.

Marrian, Natasha. 2015. 'Fighting for Control'. *Business Day*, 22 July 2015.

McKinley, Dale. 1999. 'Union Investment Companies: Business Unionism or "Social Capitalism"?' *South African Labour Bulletin* 23 (6): 85–90.

Molete, Martha and Karen Hurt. 1997. *Nehawu History, the Unfinished Story: The History of the National Education, Health and Allied Workers' Union*. Johannesburg: Nehawu.

Nattrass, Niccoli and Jeremy Seekings. 2016. 'Trade Unions, the State and "Casino Capitalism" in South Africa's Clothing Industry'. *Review of African Political Economy* 43 (147): 89–106.

Nomvete, Sandla. 2018. 'Where is Trade Unionism Going? A Brief Analysis'. *South African Labour Bulletin* 42 (1): 10–13.

Quarter, Jack. 1995. *Crossing the Line: Unionized Employee Ownership and Investment Funds*. Toronto: James Lorimer.

Pillay, Devan 2012. 'Between Social Movement and Political Unionism: Cosatu and Democratic Politics in South Africa'. *Rethinking Development and Inequality* 2: 10–27.

Rubushe, Melikhaya. 2009. 'Trade Union Investment Schemes: A Blemish on the Social Movement Unionism Outlook of South African Unions?' Masters diss., Rhodes University.

Smit, Sarah. 2019. 'Dennis George "Shocked" in the Wake of Fedusa Sacking'. *Mail & Guardian*, 20 May 2019. https://mg.co.za/article/2019-05-20-dennis-george-shocked-in-the-wake-of-fedusa-sacking.

Southall, Roger. 1995. *Imperialism or Solidarity? International Labour and South African Trade Unions*. Cape Town: University of Cape Town Press.

Theron, Jan. 2017. *Solidarity Road: The Story of a Trade Union in the Ending of Apartheid*. Johannesburg: Jacana Media.

Van der Walt, Lucien. 2007. 'Anarchism and Syndicalism in South Africa, 1904–1921: Rethinking the History of Labour and the Left'. PhD diss., University of the Witwatersrand.

Visser, Wessel. 2006. 'From MWU to Solidarity: A Trade Union Reinventing Itself'. *South African Journal of Labour Relations* 30 (2): 19–41.

Von Holdt, Karl. 2002. 'Social Movement Unionism: The Case of South Africa'. *Work, Employment and Society* 16 (2): 19–41.

Webster, Edward. 1988. 'The Rise of Social Movement Unionism: The Two Faces of the Black Trade Union Movement in South Africa'. In *State, Resistance and Change in South Africa*, edited by Philip Frankel, Noam Pines and Mark Swilling, 174–196. London: Croom Helm.

INTERVIEWS

Cosatu House, Saftu head office, Nactu head office, Satawu head office, Johannesburg

Cosatu official, 16 October 2019.
Nactu official, 21 August 2019.
Saftu official, 18 October 2019.
Satawu official, 3 February 2013.

Going Global, Building Local: A Southern Perspective on the Future of Labour Internationalism

Edward Webster

INTRODUCTION

The distruption to global supply chains caused by lockdowns in response to the Covid-19 pandemic has created new challenges for trade unions' involvement in transnational organising. But new ways of communicating in response to lockdowns have also opened up new opportunities for labour internationalism. This context provides new impetus for labour studies to train a new generation of trade union activists, as well as to develop a clear research agenda. Nevertheless, the idea of worker solidarity, the idea that the strong should help the weak to realise their collective power, continues to inspire trade unionists across the globe. Indeed, the idea goes back to the beginnings of industrial capitalism. It is best captured in Karl Marx's well-known slogan, workers of the world unite! In South Africa this call for worker unity took a peculiar form when, in the general strike of 1922, white workers mobilised around the slogan 'workers of the world unite for a white South Africa'. Those early revolutionary socialists who brought the idea of labour internationalism from Europe to Southern Africa failed to persuade their fellow white workers – the colonisers – that their destiny lay with black workers – the colonised. The white workers defended their position on the grounds that they were being undercut by cheaper black labour (Webster 1978, 14–16).

This segmentation of the working class – by race, gender, language, skill and, above all, between the Global North and the Global South – remains the central challenge in building international worker solidarity. There is no homogeneous working-class condition, here or anywhere else in the world; just as in the late nineteenth century, in many parts of the world today for many working people a bad job is better than no job. Indeed, in the age of neo-liberal globalisation the movement of jobs from developed countries to developing countries has put workers in direct competition with each other. In such circumstances workers in one country begin to see workers in other countries as the enemy, rather than uniting to challenge capital. The result is a 'race to the bottom' where, Jan Breman and Marcel van der Linden (2014, 928) suggest, the 'main burden falls on the lowest and the poorest masses in the globalised workforce'. 'It doesn't seem to be far fetched to argue', they continue, 'that labourers in the West contribute to the exploitation of their work mates in South Asia … The regime of informality has hit the West with full force and is making serious inroads into all sectors of employment' (Breman and Van der Linden 2014, 928).

In response to this growing insecurity worldwide, we have seen the emergence of a kind of populism fuelled by nationalist entrepreneurs favouring isolationism and xenophobia. It was expressed most dramatically in Donald Trump's America but it is present in India, in South Africa, the United Kingdom and in Europe:

> In Europe "Blut und Boden" (blood and soil) jargon has indeed a stark fascist slant; it feeds on sentiments which resist integration in a united Europe and reject forces of globalisation even more strongly in an ideology that brazenly postulates fundamental inequality between creeds and races. (Breman and Van der Linden 2014, 936)

They conclude that 'there seems to be a close relationship between the unfettered free market mechanism and religious or ethnic fundamentalism' (Breman and Van der Linden 2014, 936).

In this chapter I reflect on the changing nature of the global economy and how a more labour-friendly world order could be created. The chapter fills a gap in the 'Taking Democracy Seriously' study by addressing the international dimension of labour politics and how the Covid-19 pandemic has presented new challenges, but also opportunities for labour.

I begin in Part One by exploring the contradictory processes within the global economy, those forces pulling workers together, what could be called convergence, and those forces keeping workers apart, or what could be called divergence. In Part Two I distinguish between three different types of international solidarity, focusing on what I call the regulatory approach and the possibility of a strategy aimed at the formalisation of labour rights at the global level. This, it is argued, could be done through the construction of a global social floor driven by a 'drastically reformed and reorganised international trade union movement' in coalition with popular movements (Breman and Van der Linden 2014, 937). In Part Three, I identify examples of transnational worker solidarity through new sources of power as well as an attempt by the Global Labour University (GLU) to develop union organisers able to 'go global' while being embedded in local workplaces and communities. I conclude by arguing that this will require overcoming the biggest obstacle to a truly global labour internationalism, the on-going North–South divide.

PART ONE: CONVERGENCE AND DIVERGENCE

Globalisation has drawn large parts of the globe that were previously insulated from global capitalism, such as Central Europe and the former Soviet Union, India and China, into possible sites for penetration by global corporations and hence the global labour market. As Thomas Friedman observes:

> In 1985 "the global economic world" comprised North America, Western Europe, Japan, as well as chunks of Latin America, Africa and the countries of east Asia. The total population of this global economic world, taking part in international trade and commerce ... was about 2.5 billion people. By 2000, as a result of the collapse of communism in the Soviet empire, India's turn from autarky, China's shift to market capitalism, and the population growth all over, the global economic world expanded to encompass 6 billion people. This meant that another roughly 1.5 billion new workers entered the global economic labour force. (Friedman 2005, 182)

The crucial point is that these 'new' workers, in a global population in 2023 of 8 billion, came into the labour market 'unprotected', without the rights and protections that workers had won in North America and Western Europe. As a result they are often seen as a threat to organised labour in the Global North. In his account of the way in which globalisation is 'flattening the world', Friedman introduces, halfway through his book, a note of caution to his over-optimistic celebration of globalisation. He mentions a conversation with his two daughters in which he bluntly advises them, 'Girls, when I was growing up, my parents used to say to me "Tom, finish your dinner – people in India and China are starving". My advice to you is, Girls, finish your homework – people in China and India are starving for your jobs' (Friedman 2005, 237).

But of course the world, or more specifically the global economy, is not flat; it is highly uneven and the impact of globalisation has different implications for workers. As Ben Scully argues:

> As precarity has come to be analysed as a global phenomenon, there has been a tendency to employ a somewhat simplistic assumption of global convergence. While precarious work has been on the rise throughout the world, fundamental differences in the histories of work, and of workers, in the Global North and South should caution against viewing precarity as a universal phenomenon whose meanings and implications are cognate for workers everywhere. (Scully 2016, 161)

To illustrate this difference in the impact of informalisation of the economy on workers, my colleagues and I studied the production of white goods – namely fridges, washing machines and microwave ovens – in three countries as a lens to show how the responses of workers diverged (Webster, Lambert and Bezuidenhout 2008). In Electrolux Australia we found resignation in the face of the relocation of the plant to China. Most workers interviewed felt fatalistic about the future of the plant and intended to fall back on the modest social protection provided by the Australian welfare system (Webster et al. 2008, 141–146). In South Korea workers responded to intensified international competition by working harder. Overtime increased and workers responded to the threat of downsizing by investing in individual insurance and pension schemes (Webster et al. 2008, 127–140). In South Africa, on the other hand, workers retreated into the household in order to engage in various survivalist–type strategies in the informal economy (Webster et al. 2008, 108–126).

We framed the study in terms of Karl Polanyi's notion of a 'double movement' whereby ever wider extensions of free market principles generated countermovements to protect society, suggesting that this period of neo-liberal globalisation could best be described as the Second Great Transformation (Webster et al. 2008, 4–5). We did find modest experiments and initiatives to protect society against the unregulated market, but in general workers' responses to global restructuring were localised. The only attempt to challenge global restructuring was an initiative at Electrolux in Orange, Australia, to globalise their struggle. Through the Internet they were able to establish contact with workers in Electrolux Greenville, a small town in Michigan, United States, and workers at the home of Electrolux in Sweden. But this attempt at building worker-to-worker solidarity in production failed. The leadership of the Swedish union was too close to management not to see the advantages to the company of relocating to China.

But 'successful failures' can provide the basis for the next step in a struggle. We remember the Montgomery bus boycott in the civil rights campaign in the southern United States, but Aldon Morris has shown that it was preceded by several other 'unsuccessful' and little-remembered bus boycotts (Morris 1984, cited in Clawson 2010). What can we learn about international worker solidarity from our study of labours' divergent responses to globalisation in the white goods industry?

The expansion of the global labour market has presented the international labour movement with a paradox. On the one hand, it has deepened the exploitation of labour on a global scale, while ironically, on the other hand, it has led to opportunities to transcend past constraints through the emergence of new sources of power and forms of organisation. Here are three examples of new opportunities for transnational solidarity:

- The technological revolution brought about by globalisation can be used to the advantage of workers – email, WhatsApp, Zoom and satellite television provide opportunities for global networks and campaigns (Webster et al. 2008, 186–211).
- Global supply chains create new vulnerabilities for capital. By linking production globally through global value chains, companies have become vulnerable to new sources of power. A delay in the delivery of an engine part from South Korea to an assembly line in Australia can force employers in both Australia and South Korea to the bargaining table. New sources of power have emerged in the age of globalisation.
- New global workplace norms worldwide – such as international labour standards, codes of conduct and international framework agreements – provide a new benchmark for labour. There is a new logic at work in the global economy, a logic that argues that international labour standards must be introduced to prevent a race to the bottom.

What are the implications of these new opportunities for transnational solidarity?

PART TWO: TYPES OF TRANSNATIONAL SOLIDARITY

It is useful, in thinking about transnational solidarity, to distinguish between three different types. The first type I will call the humanitarian type. These are acts of solidarity in defence of victims of human rights abuses, such as victims of racism or child labour or struggles for union recognition by a group of workers. The crucial characteristic of this type of solidarity is that it is driven by moral claims. It can be very powerful, as the successful anti-apartheid movement has shown. This solidarity can take the form of a consumer boycott or campaigns, such as the campaign against the global mining corporation Rio Tinto over basic worker rights (Webster et al. 2008, 197–201). These campaigns are relatively easy and inexpensive to organise in the age of the Internet. The Rio Global Union Network was coordinated in cyberspace by a graduate student in California, and the Network demanded a commitment by the corporation to core labour conventions as outlined by the International Labour Organization (ILO) (Webster et al. 2008, 197).

An important factor in the victory of the anti-apartheid movement was international solidarity. The campaign to boycott South Africa and impose financial sanctions was crucial in persuading the apartheid government to negotiate with the African National Congress under the leadership of Nelson Mandela. The solidarity shown, for example, by dock workers in San Francisco when they refused to unload South African goods is one among many examples of international solidarity (Cole 2013). More recently we have seen successful boycott campaigns, including the Burma Campaign, the campaign against the fur trade and the Body Shop campaign.[1] Boycotts have a long and important history of contributing to international solidarity, as well as succeeding in their more immediate goals.

The victory of the African National Congress in 1994 was a precarious victory, as it was won in a world where power had shifted decisively to capital. South Africa was experiencing a double transition (Webster and Adler 1999). On the one hand, it was a transition to democracy where a militant labour movement had won significant rights. On the other hand, it had entered the global economy where international competition was forcing employers to cut costs through bypassing the newly won labour rights so that they could produce at the 'China price'.[2]

The second type of transnational solidarity I will call the production approach. Here acts of solidarity are between workers on a factory-to-factory basis. These acts of solidarity are the most difficult to organise, as the example of the failed attempt by Electrolux Australia workers to globalise the struggle illustrates. The internationalisation of production has created a competitive logic between countries. If General Motors goes on strike, for example, other motor car producers will sell more vehicles.

But in spite of these obstacles, there is a growing coordination of transnational solidarity in production. Volkswagen workers from Germany, Brazil, India and South Africa gather worldwide every year to coordinate their demands across Volkswagen factories. Seafarers were the first sector to engage in global collective bargaining. Inspectors from the International Transport Workers Federation carry out inspections on vessels when they dock in port. In this way they are able, for the first time in history, to agree on a minimum global wage in a sector and enforce it among seafarers across the globe (Croucher and Cotton 2009).

These new forms of transnational organisation challenge the conventional national-based forms of organisation that prevailed in the twentieth century. According to an older model of international solidarity, such links tended to be channelled through specialised international departments and were more likely to be between the leaders of trade union federations. Instant communication through email, WhatsApp smart phones and Zoom has changed all this. These new forms of transnational action are decentralised and are as likely to be bottom-up as top-down.

The third type of solidarity I will call the regulatory approach. This approach is not an attempt to bring workers together in production but rather tries to build a common body of soft law such as global rights and labour standards or new rules of governance through International Framework Agreements. The GLU's launch in June 2015 of its online course for trade unionists, which focuses on workers' rights in the global economy, is an example of the regulatory approach.[3] The fundamental principles of international labour standards, ILO Convention 87 (freedom of association; workers' rights to join organisations of their own choosing), ILO Convention 98 (collective bargaining rights to ensure that unions are not dominated by employers), and ILO Convention 151 (the rights of public sector workers), provide the foundations for this approach.

The ILO Commission on the Future of Work built its proposals around the idea of a Universal Labour Guarantee. In terms of this proposal 'all workers, regardless of their contractual arrangement or employment status, should enjoy fundamental workers' rights, an "adequate living wage", maximum limits on working hours and protection of safety and health at work' (ILO 2019, 4).[4]

An innovative example of the regulatory approach is the implementation in the Global South of the idea of a global social floor. The International Labour Conference in June 2012 adopted Recommendation 202 on National Floors of Social Protection (ILO 2012) that aims to provide coverage of people at all stages of the life cycle – a child grant, a right to a pension, access to healthcare, and a basic minimum of income whether through a job guarantee or a direct cash grant. Barrientos and Hulme (2009, 5) suggest that a 'quiet revolution' is taking place in social policy in the South. The Bolsa Familia programme in Brazil is thought to be the highest social transfer scheme in the world and presently covers some 46 million people. The Mahatma Gandhi National Rural Employment Guarantee Scheme in India entitles every rural household to a hundred days of work per year. The Community Work Programme in South Africa provides two days a week of public employment, in a scheme similar to that of the rural guarantee scheme in India (Webster and Bhowmik 2014, 14).

Veteran scholars of the labouring poor in the developing world, Jan Breman and Marcel van der Linden (2014, 935–940), argue something similar to the regulatory approach when they suggest the need to 'return to the social question at a global level'. In addition to a universal right to social security, they suggest a global strategy aimed at 'the formalisation of labour rights' through 'a minimum labour price indexed to the variable cost of living, employment which is not flexible but regular, dependent … proper jobs rather than endless drifting around short term worksites…' (Breman and Van der Linden 2014, 935).

These attempts at establishing a global social floor are examples of the embryo of an alternative approach to the global economy, in Polanyi's terms a countermovement, a response aimed at protecting society against the unregulated market (Harriss 2010). However, as Kaustav Bannerjee points out, rights from above remain merely words on paper, 'until assertions of these rights by people from below establishes them in practice'; he describes this as a 'double movement from below' (Bannerjee cited in Webster and Bhowmik 2014, 15). Breman and Van der Linden (2014, 937) make a similar point when they argue that 'pressure from below … will be of the utmost importance in … a drastically reformed and reorganised international trade union movement'.

But none of the above authors provide us with any ideas of what a feasible movement from below would look like. Indeed, Breman and Van der Linden (2014, 937) argue that with 'the rapid spread of informality from the global South to the Atlantic basin … the West is more likely to follow the Rest … than the other way round'. They then identify 'several critical differences between the current global economy and the nineteenth and early twentieth century', concluding on a deeply pessimistic note that the 'the working classes are trapped in a trajectory of exploitation and forced together into a race to the bottom' (Breman and Van der Linden 2014, 938). At the centre of their pessimism on the possibilities of formalising labour rights globally is that 'at the globalized heights there is no public governance to rein in the freebooting operations of capital' (Breman and Van der Linden 2014, 938).

I turn now to how a new labour internationalism is being constructed through the implementation of the regulatory approach in the Global South.

PART THREE: CONSTRUCTING A SOUTHERN LABOUR INTERNATIONALISM

Jamie McCallum (2013), in an in-depth study of Group 4 Securicor, demonstrates how labour can become an agent of global governance through implementing the regulatory approach. Workers, McCallum suggests, are not simply victims of the global juggernaut; they can change the rules of global engagement.[5] Global framework agreements, he suggests, are part of this strategy to expand the bargaining power of national unions over entire industries by forcing major companies to play by union rules. McCallum illustrates this theoretical argument through an analysis of a global campaign led by a global union, Union Network International, against the multinational Group 4 Securicor, the largest employer in Africa and, surprisingly, also listed as the largest employer on the London Stock Exchange.

The centre of McCallum's argument is that the campaign did not win new rights, but instead used global power to make new rules of engagement for local unions. He calls this new approach 'governance struggles'. Governance struggles refer, he says, 'broadly to the exercise of power in the absence of an overarching political authority, usually by a constellation of institutions that make decisions and enforce compliance with norms and rules at the supranational level' (McCallum 2013, 12). This allows him to theorise global unions themselves as potential agents of governance. McCallum has identified a new source of power: global associational power. This is an important insight, as it allows us to go beyond the widespread view that globalisation disables labour – the left pessimism of, among many others, Breman and Van der Linden – and to begin to explore the new sources of vulnerability and the strategic possibilities that globalisation has created for labour.

The point is that globalisation is not only a constraint; it also opens up new sources of power.[6] For example, workers in the large grape farms in north-eastern Brazil have been able to maintain high wages and permanent employment by taking advantage of the pressures on suppliers to deliver high-quality grapes on time for the European market (Selwyn 2012). The large-scale commercial farmers, who export this produce, are subject to quality pressures from retailers in Europe and need a permanent workforce that is trained and possesses the required skills. This has given the workers structural power – that is, workplace bargaining power at the heart of the production process, not unlike the pressures that workers could bring to bear on Fordist production – as well as marketplace bargaining power (through employers' need of their skills). These previously low-paid farm workers can disrupt or thwart production if they are not satisfied with their working conditions, and employers cannot afford to allow this to happen given the strict delivery requirements of the retailers.

Another example is that of informal workers in India. Rina Agarwala (2013) challenges the conventional view that informalisation is the 'final nail in the labour movement's coffin'. Informal workers, she demonstrates, are creating new institutions and forging a new social contract between the state and labour. She shows that informal worker movements are most successful when operating within electoral contexts where political parties must compete for mass votes from the poor. Agarwala calls this 'competitive populism'. These informal worker organisations are not attached to a particular political party, nor do they espouse a specific political or economic ideology. In this way, they have successfully organised informal workers.

But the most fundamental challenge to a new labour internationalism remains that of bridging the North–South divide. As Harvey (2002) shows, global corporations are effectively exploiting 'the geography of difference', low-waged zones of the globe, in ways that undermine core labour standards. Giovanni Arrighi and Beverly Silver (2001, 530) argue that a North–South divide continues to be the main obstacle 'to the formation of a homogenous world-proletarian condition' and are sceptical of a new labour internationalism based on a Red/Green alliance between Northern and Southern workers. Indeed, Silver (2003, 13) raises the question of 'whether struggles by Northern workers aimed at reforming supranational institutions are more likely to be steps towards the formation of a global working class "for itself", or signs of an emergent, new form of national protectionism'. Gay Seidman (2004) expresses a similar scepticism, highlighting the potential tensions between a language of universal rights and citizenship claims within the nation state. She articulates the distrust that many developing countries hold of US campaigns for human rights in the Global South, in particular whether transnational monitoring campaigns empower global managers and consumers in advanced industrial societies, rather than workers in the factories and unions in the South.

The challenge of empowering labour in the age of globalisation was taken up by the ILO in 2004 when it launched, under the directorship of Frank Hoffer and Christoph Scherrer, the Global Labour University (Webster 2008). Its central aim has been to build capacity among trade unionists to develop policy expertise through a Master's programme on labour policy and globalisation. The rationale for a partnership with universities is that new knowledge needs to be acquired and new strategies developed for labour to engage effectively with neo-liberal globalisation. This new knowledge, it is believed, cannot be adequately achieved by traditional union education programmes. But, and this became a central challenge for GLU, this knowledge is either rapidly disappearing from universities or still needs to be created; the older generation of labour academics have reached retirement age and a new generation needs to be created. So, in addition to teaching, a crucial part of GLU involves joint research, faculty and student exchange, and the organisation of conferences for GLU alumni on global labour.

GLU soon expanded beyond Germany to include the Global South – first South Africa in 2007, and then India, Brazil and the United States – as it realised the need to develop partnerships with labour scholars and their institutions in the Global South. An early challenge that GLU faced was that many unionists in the South did not have the necessary formal academic qualifications to meet the requirements for entry into a university Master's programme, yet they were the key target for any programme to transform the labour movement. As a response to this challenge, in 2010 GLU introduced the ENGAGE programme, an Empowerment and Capacity Building Network for Global Trade Unionists and Labour Activists. In 2013 ENGAGE was relocated to the University of the Witwatersrand in Johannesburg.

ENGAGE South Africa has been designed to provide experienced trade unionists from around the world (and in particular from Africa) access to high-level academic, theoretical and research training. The programme is aimed at providing participants with opportunities to tackle the impact of neo-liberal globalisation on work. The first module of the course is on Global Governance and focuses, inter alia, on the growing informalisation of work and the need to 'close the representation gap' (Webster and Bischoff 2011). A crucial part of ENGAGE is to ensure the transfer of the skills developed by the participants to their unions in their country of origin. The skill introduced to 'close the representation gap' is that of mapping, both vertical and horizontal. Mapping is used as a tool to facilitate the organisation of vulnerable workers.[7]

Drawing on trade unionists in sub-Saharan Africa and elsewhere, ENGAGE has been able to develop the skills for a new type of union organiser, one who understands the global context but who is rooted in the local community. There are five ways in which this is being achieved. First, the participants are able to identify, through horizontal mapping, new constituencies of precarious workers, such as truck drivers in Malawi, domestic workers in Lesotho, private security guards in Swaziland, cleaners in Zambia and hospitality, retail and street vendors in South Africa (ENGAGE Transfer Project, Joint seminars, 25–26 November, 2014 and 16–25 November 2015, Johannesburg).[8] Importantly, the participants are identifying what Jennifer Chun (2012, 40) calls the 'new political subjects of labour … women, immigrants, people of colour, low paid service workers, precarious workers … groups that have been historically excluded from the moral and material boundaries of union membership'. Second, it forced the union organisers to interact with vulnerable workers face-to-face and to become aware directly of their work and living conditions. Third, vertical mapping is especially useful in plotting supply chains and discovering the way globalisation functions in the southern African region. Fourth, through responding to the questionnaire, those interviewed have begun to develop an identity as workers. Fifth, the process has helped workers to frame their grievances and sense of injustice in ways that enabled them to organise collectively.

This experiment in building a new labour internationalism is a modest first step. The long-term aim of the course is to develop a cohort of trade union organisers who could run a regional campaign to organise vulnerable workers (McGregor and Webster 2021). As the organisers of the global research network, Women in Informal Employment: Globalizing and Organizing (Wiego), frame the challenge:

> There is no single easy, one-step way to formalise informal employment. Rather, it should be understood as a gradual, on-going process of incrementally incorporating informal workers and economic units into the formal economy through strengthening them and extending their rights, protection and benefits. (Wiego 2014, 1)

CONCLUSION

I have identified three different types of labour internationalism – humanitarian, production and regulatory. These different types are not necessarilty mutually exclusive. For example, in the struggle against apartheid, humanitarian support was given to the anti-apartheid movement through consumer boycotts. There were also factory-to-factory links to strengthen shop-floor struggles of black workers in multinational companies such as Volkswagen, what I call the production approach. Third, the emerging black unions drew on the ILO's international labour standards as a way of legitimating their demands, what we call the regulatory approach (Southall 1995; Webster and Forrest 2020).

I have focused in this chapter on the regulatory approach with its emphasis on building a new global system of labour standards and a labour-friendly system of global governance. However, unless this attempt at going global is accompanied by strong organisation at the local level, it will not reverse the 'race to the bottom'. The All-China Federation of Trade Unions is a case in point. In spite of the fact that China is in breach of international labour standards as it lacks an independent trade union movement, the international trade union movement, with the exception of the International Union of Food Workers, have 'normalised' relations with the Chinese federation (Lambert and Webster 2018).

Constructing a new labour internationalism does not involve a choice between going global or remaining local; it requires that unions navigate between the local and the global. This combination of the local and the global has led to the emergence of what Sydney Tarrow (2005, 42) calls 'rooted cosmopolitans'. Rooted cosmopolitans, Tarrow says, are activists who think globally, but are linked to very real places. In his words, 'they move physically and cognitively outside their origins, but they continue to be linked to place, to the social networks that inhabit that space, and to the resources, experiences, and opportunities that place provides them with (Tarrow 2005, 42).

The most difficult question raised by this chapter is how to build international worker solidarity across the North–South divide. There are two different interpretations of worker solidarity that emerge from the analysis. The first is value-based, where solidarity implies that you place yourself in the other person's position, realising that you are both human beings, having equal value. This was described earlier as the humanitarian approach to labour internationalism. This approach defines solidarity as a 'moral imperative that is a fundamental value in all the major religions of the world; do unto the other what you would like her to do to you; love your neighbour as yourself' (Lindberg 2014, 136).

The interpretation of worker solidarity that emerges from this analysis is different from the humanitarian approach as it rests on mutual self-interest. Lindberg writes:

> Solidarity in a union context means moving from an individual self-interest, or the self-interest of a smaller group, to a broader self-interest, perhaps of all metalworkers in Sweden or all dockworkers in Europe. Perhaps to the mutual self-interest of a global working class? But even so, union solidarity will always have an element of shared self-interest. Unions are interest-based organisations. (Lindberg 2014, 136)

I have shown how a global regime of informality now defines work and labour worldwide through a thoroughly flexible labour market. But I have also demonstrated the ways in which new forms of transnational solidarity are emerging, which recognise that the interests of workers can best be defended by going global. These forms of action take as their point of departure the assumption that the labour movement was built around its capacity to disrupt the economy (its structural power within the economy). While structural power has been weakened by neoliberal globalisation, and associational power (the ability to organise collectively into trade unions and political parties) is under attack by the ideologues of the 'free market', new strategies, organisations, institutions and sources of power can be identified that are rebuilding labour (see Ronaldo Munck 2018 for a similar argument).

The situation worsened with the arrival of Covid-19 at the end of 2019. Clearly the impact of the pandemic has been devastating for the lives and livelihoods of working people. The high proportion of informal workers in sub-Saharan Africa, estimated at 80 per cent, has made the impact of Covid-19 especially harsh.[9] If you are, for example, a street trader and you can no longer earn an income on the street, you face hunger and deepening poverty. Covid-19 has revealed the weakness, or non-existence, of an adequate social protection system in Africa.

A key question is whether the pandemic and its associated responses offer the opportunity for a revitalisation of labour in Africa, or a further weakening.

Covid-19 has brought to the fore opportunities to revitalise worker organising. I identify four.

First, new technology opens up the opportunity for digital organising; this is not a substitute for face-to-face to organising but online organising can reach a much larger number of people at dramatically reduced cost. However, it is important to recognise that Internet penetration is very uneven in Africa. Disparities are even larger when one looks at Internet usage. In South Africa, for example, it is estimated that 56 per cent of the population has access to the Internet. However, if one looks at coverage at the household level, only 11 per cent of households have access. Although South Africa has higher levels of Internet coverage than most countries on the continent (Castel-Branco, Mapukata and Webster 2020), access is concentrated in a minority of households.

Second, the experience of Covid-19 has broadened the demands emerging from workers. In particular, it has highlighted the global nature of the challenges workers face and the need for them to deepen international connections.

Third, Covid-19 has widened the constituencies of labour. There has been a major shift in the recognition of the informal economy, particularly in areas such as food production and distribution. These 'essential workers' are often in sectors dominated by women workers, such as retail, hospitality and varieties of paid and unpaid care work.

Fourth, the growth of working from home during Covid-19 opens up an opportunity for worker organising. Home-workers are workers, and should be recognised as such. This has been recognised by the ILO as long ago as 1996 in the Home-Work Convention (No.177). Trade unions need to recruit home-workers as members, and employers need to recognise the existence of home-based workers in their value chains and ensure they get a fair income. National governments should include home-based workers in their national statistics on the labour force and give them a voice in decision-making (Delhi Declaration of Home-Based Workers, New Delhi, 9 February 2015).

The argument raised in this chapter suggests that the divisions between the North and the South are too great to be explained by institutional differences. The history and legacy of colonialism as well as the policies of liberalisation have affected the Global South in ways that are different from the North. It is not only that there has never been a 'golden age' of decent work in the colonial workplace (Scully 2016). When you go beyond the workplace into the hidden abode of reproduction, the household and the community, these differences become clear (Lee and Kofman 2012, 393). In the Global South the crisis is not simply over jobs; it is a crisis over the very reproduction of society itself (Webster and Von Holdt 2005). The result is that the politics of labour, and the possibilities of an agreement around the formalisation of labour rights at the global level, will have to go beyond a compromise between organised labour and organised capital. In the Global South a compromise will have to be struck 'between the state, urban classes, and class fractions (including workers, the informal economy, the unemployed) and domestic and international capital' (Webster and Adler 1999, 353–354). Whether this 'return to the social question at a global level' can win the battle against those working people in the North and in the South who are turning inwards and xenophobic, is the central question facing the advocates of a new labour internationalism.

ACKNOWLEDGEMENT

I dedicate this chapter to my late colleague, comrade and friend Rob Lambert who was, until his retirement in 2018, the Winthrop Professor of Employment Relations at the University of Western Australia's Business School. Rob did more than anyone else I know to develop a Southern approach to labour internationalism. He conceived and developed a little-known but imaginative attempt to bring together over a 30-year period a network of democratic trade unions in the Global South – the Southern Initiative on Globalisation and Trade Union Rights (SIGTUR). This inspiring story of women and men who continue to believe in the common fate of humanity and the obligation of the strong to support the weak is captured in Robert O'Brien's recently published book, *Labour Internationalism in the Global South: The SIGTUR Initiative*, Cambridge University Press, 2018.

NOTES

1   Animal welfare activists called for a boycott of the Body Shop after its founder
     Anita Roddick and fellow shareholders sold out to French cosmetics giant L'Oreal.
     The animal welfare groups oppose L'Oreal's policy on the testing of cosmetic ingredients
     on animals.

2   The current marketised employment relations in China is the cornerstone of the neo-
     liberal restructuring of the global economy, and this has implications for the price of
     labour everywhere. The Chinese system is a cornerstone because the political com-
     mitments to neo-liberalism across the globe (the removal of all protections in trade,
     investment and finance) have created perfect conditions for global corporations to
     exploit the uneven geography of labour (Harvey 2002, 31).

3   This certified course consists of six modules. It is designed to help unionists understand
     global workers' rights and the institutional structure of the ILO as the key player in set-
     ting international labour standards. It is aimed at deepening unionists' understanding
     of the concepts behind the fundamental rights of freedom of association and collective
     bargaining.

4   The ILO's focus on working hours is pertinent. In the findings of research projects
     on workers in Johannesburg, as part of GLU's ENGAGE programme at the University
     of the Witwtarersrand, the researchers found that taxi drivers were working as much
     as 17 hours a day, market vendors from 12 to 14 hours a day and car guards 10.5 hours
     a day (Global Labour University, University of Witwatersrand, Research Presentations,
     26 April 2019).

5   The following two paragraphs are taken from my chapter in Bieler, Erne, Golden, Helle,
     Kjeldstadli, Matos and Stan, 2014 (Webster 2014).

6   I have drawn the following two examples from my article (Webster 2015, 33).

7   There are two ways of conducting mapping – horizontal and vertical. Horizontal map-
     ping refers to the method used to document and identify the characteristics of the work-
     ers, their location and industry sector, by contacting individuals in their homes or
     communities. This type of mapping focuses on gathering data on demographic char-
     acteristics of workers, their home situation, their work processes, their employment
     relationships, payment amounts and processes, and the problems and issues that they
     face. In contrast, vertical mapping refers to a process that identifies the chain of produc-
     tion linking home-workers, subcontractors, intermediaries, buyers and brand owners
     (Burchielli, Buttigieg and Delaney 2008, 169).

8   The organisation of the ENGAGE transfer project was undertaken by Warren
     McGregor, the GLU coordinator. I would like to thank him for the crucial role
     he played in running workshops in the nine countries and then ensuring that the 40
     participants reported on their successful transfer of mapping as an organising tool
     in their home countries.

9   The ILO (2019) estimates that 89.2 per cent of employment in sub-Saharan Africa is infor-
     mal. It should be noted that informalisation is uneven across Africa; highest in Western
     Africa (92.4 per cent) and lowest in Southern Africa (40.2 per cent).

REFERENCES

Agarwala, Rina. 2013. *Informal Labour, Formal Politics, and Dignified Discontent in India.* New York: Cambridge University Press.

Arrighi, Giovanni and Beverly Silver. 2001. 'Capitalism and World (Dis)order'. *Review of International Studies* 27: 257–279.

Barrientos, Armondo and David Hulme. 2009. *Social Protection for the Poor and the Poorest in Developing Countries: Reflections on a Quiet Revolution.* Oxford Development Studies Occasional Paper. Oxford: Oxford University Press.

Breman, Jan and Marcel van der Linden. 2014. 'Informalizing the Economy: The Return of the Social Question at a Global Level'. *Development and Change* 45 (5): 920–940.

Burchielli, Rosaria, Donna Buttigieg and Annie Delaney. 2008. 'Organizing Home-workers: The Use of Mapping as an Organising Tool'. *Work, Employment and Society* 22 (1): 167–180.

Castel-Branco, Ruth, Sandiswa Mapukata and Edward Webster. 2020. 'Work from Home Reserved for the Privileged Few in South Africa'. *Business Day*, 17 September 2020. https://www.businesslive.co.za/bd/opinion/2020-09-17-work-from-home-reserved-for-the-privileged-few-in-sa.

Chun, Jennifer. 2012. 'The Power of the Powerless: New Schemes and Resources for Organising Workers in Neoliberal Times'. *In Cross-national Comparisons of Social Movement Unionism; Diversities of Labour Movement Revitalisation in Japan, Korea and the United States,* edited by Akira Suzuki, 37–60. Oxford: Peter Lang.

Clawson, Dan. 2010. 'False Optimism: The Key to Historic Breakthroughs? A Response to Michael Burawoy's From Polanyi to Pollyanna: The False Optimism of Global Labour Studies'. *Global Labour Journal* 1 (3): 398–400.

Cole, Peter. 2013. 'No Justice, No Ships Get Loaded: Political Boycotts on the San Francisco Bay and Durban Waterfronts'. *International Review of Social History* 58 (2): 1–33.

Croucher, Richard and Elizabeth Cotton. 2009. *Global Unions, Global Business: Global Union Federations and International Business.* London: Middlesex University Press.

Friedman, Thomas. 2005. *The World is Flat: A Brief History of the Globalised World in the 21st Century.* London: Allen Lane.

Harriss, John. 2010. 'Globalization(s) and Labour in China and India: Introductory Reflections'. *Global Labour Journal* 1 (1): 3–11.

Harvey, David. 2002. *Spaces of Hope.* Edinburgh: Edinburgh University Press.

International Labour Organisation (ILO). 2012. *Work for a Brighter Future: Global Commission on the Future of Work.* Geneva: ILO.

International Labour Organisation (ILO). 2019. *ILO Centenary Declaration for the Future of Work: A Roadmap for a Human-centred Future.* Geneva: ILO.

Lambert, Robert and Edward Webster. 2018. 'The China Price: The All-China Federation of Trade Unions and the Repressed Question of International Labour Standards'. *Globalizations* 14 (2): 313–326.

Lee, Ching Kwan and Yelizavetta Kofman. 2012. 'The Politics of Precarity: Views Beyond the United States'. *Work and Occupations* 39 (4): 388–408.

Lindberg, Ingemar. 2014. 'Unions and Trade: What Kind of Solidarity?' *Globalizations* 11 (1): 131–142.

McCallum, Jamie. 2013. *Global Unions, Local Power: The New Spirit of Transnational Labor Organising.* Ithaca, NY: ILR Press.

McGregor, Warren and Edward Webster. 2021. 'Building a Regional Solidarity Network of Transnational Activists: An African Case Study'. *Tempo Social, Revista de Sociologia da USP* 33 (2): 15–36.

Munck, Ronaldo. 2018. *Rethinking Global Labour: After Neoliberalism*. Newcastle upon Tyne: Agenda Publishing.

Scully, Ben. 2016. 'Precarity North and South: A Southern Critique of Guy Standing'. *Global Labour Journal* 7 (2): 160–173.

Seidman, Gay. 2004. 'Deflated Citizenship: Labour Rights in a Global Order'. In *People out of Place: Globalization, Human Rights and the Citizenship Gap,* edited by Alison Brysk and Geshon Shafir, 109–129. London and New York: Routledge.

Selwyn, Ben. 2012. *Workers, State and Development in Brazil: Powers of Labour, Chains of Value*. Manchester: Manchester University Press.

Silver, Beverley. 2003. *Forces of Labor: Workers' Movements and Globalisation since 1870*. Cambridge: Cambridge University Press.

Southall, Roger. 1995. *Imperialism or Solidarity? International Labour and South African Trade Unions*. Cape Town: UCT Press.

Tarrow, Sidney. 2005. *The New Transnational Activism*. Cambridge: Cambridge University Press.

Webster, Edward. 1978. 'Background to the Supply and Control of Labour in the Gold Mines'. In *Essays in Southern African Labour History* edited by Edward Webster, 9–19. Johannesburg: Ravan Press.

Webster, Edward. 2008. 'Shop Floor and Chalk-face: A New Partnership'. *South African Labour Bulletin* 32 (3): 45–48.

Webster, Edward. 2014. 'Labour after Globalisation: Old and New Sources of Power'. In *Labour and Transnational Action in Times of Crisis,* edited by Andreas Bieler, Roland Erne, Darragh Golden, Idar Helle, Knut Kjeldstadli, Tiago Matos and Sabina Stan, 109–122. London: Rowman & Littlefield.

Webster, Edward. 2015. 'The Shifting Boundaries of Industrial Relations: Insights from South Africa'. *International Labour Review* 154 (1): 26–36.

Webster, Edward and Glenn Adler 1999. 'Towards a Class Compromise in South Africa's "Double Transition": Bargained Liberalisation and the Consolidation of Democracy'. *Politics and Society* 27 (3): 347–385.

Webster, Edward and Sharit Bhowmik. 2014. Work, Livelihoods and Insecurity in the South: A Conceptual Introduction. In *Socio-economic Insecurity in Emerging Economies: Building New Spaces,* edited by Khayaat Fakier and Ellen Ehmke, 1–18. London: Routledge.

Webster, Edward and Christine Bischoff. 2011. 'New Actors in Employment Relations in the Periphery: Closing the Representation Gap amongst Micro and Small Enterprises'. *Relations Industrielles/Industrial Relations* 66 (1): 11–33.

Webster, Edward and Kally Forrest. 2020. 'The Role of the ILO during and after Apartheid'. *Labour Studies Journal* 46 (4): 325–344.

Webster, Edward, Robert Lambert and Andries Bezuidenhout. 2008. *Grounding Globalisation: Labour in the Age of Insecurity*. Oxford: Blackwell Publishers.

Webster, Edward and Karl von Holdt. 2005. *Beyond the Apartheid Workplace: Studies in Transition*. Pietermaritzburg: University of KwaZulu-Natal Press.

Women in Informal Employment: Globalizing and Organizing (Wiego) Network Platform, 2014. 'Transitioning From the Informal to the Formal Economy in the Interests of Workers in the Informal Economy'. Document distributed at the Vulnerable Workers Task Team workshop, Cosatu, Johannesburg, June 2014.

PART IV

LABOUR AND LOCKDOWN

14

The Labour Movement's Response to the Covid-19 Pandemic

Christine Bischoff

INTRODUCTION

The severe restrictions placed on all but essential types of economic activity during South Africa's first lockdown during the Covid-19 pandemic in 2020 exposed not only the frail forms of livelihood tactics adopted by so many South Africans, but also revealed many issues that South African trade unions had not faced up to previously. Those who work in retail, as well as teachers, nurses and doctors faced the crisis head-on, delivering essential services during the Covid-19 crisis. Workers in jobs that permitted them to work from home, such as professionals and managers, were more fortunate than others during the lockdowns. However, workers in elementary occupations and plant and machine operations, as well as those in occupations such as community, social and personal services, mineworkers, private households and manufacturing could not work remotely (Benhura and Magejo 2021). Trade union members and their trade unions faced many challenges during the Covid-19 crisis, but even those on opposing sides of the ideological spectrum have taken the opportunity to forge working-class unity as they have found common ground to respond collectively, which is what this chapter focuses on.

THE IMPACT OF THE NATIONAL LOCKDOWN IN SOUTH AFRICA

The President of South Africa, Cyril Ramaphosa, declared a State of Disaster on 15 March 2020, and the country went into lockdown at midnight on 26 March 2020. The initial lockdown lasted 35 days at alert level five, which was the most restrictive phase. The national lockdown affected economic activity, and some people were threatened with retrenchment or lost their jobs and their income. The result was that they, together with their households, went without food. These were workers who were vulnerable to job loss as they could not work from their homes or they were in low-skill occupations, representing roughly 10.5 million workers or 63 per cent of the workforce. Workers in low-wage sectors such as hospitality and entertainment, catering, construction, the informal economy and domestic work were particularly affected by the lockdown. They had no option but to stay at home. Many did not get paid during the lockdown, or their salaries were cut.

Utilising data from the Quarterly Labour Force Surveys, it is estimated that in 2020, 26.7 per cent or 4.5 million workers in employment prior to the lockdown were employed in essential industries or occupations (Kerr and Thornton 2020). It is these workers, considered as performing essential services or producing essential goods, who carried on working during the lockdown. It is estimated that about two million South Africans, or 13.8 per cent of workers, could work from home; their incomes were not adversely influenced by the lockdown. This was particularly the case for the professionals and those with high-level skills.

Not all essential industries ran at full capacity under the lockdown. To be precise, essential workers comprised approximately 750 000 agricultural workers, 650 000 health workers and 600 000 security guards. In addition to this, there were 400 000 essential workers in food and beverage manufacturing, 300 000 in food retail and petrol stations, 250 000 mineworkers, 200 000 minibus taxi drivers and 100 000 spaza shop owners. Police officers, members of the South African National Defence Force, correctional services workers, and workers in banking and insurance make up other substantial groups, with another 500 000 in various smaller industries (Kerr and Thornton 2020). While private schoolteachers could initially work from home and conduct online learning, most primary and secondary teachers in the public sector could not do the same, due to a lack of access to Internet which was true for their learners, too.

A ban was also placed on the sale and distribution of alcohol from the end of March 2020 until the beginning of June 2020, as it was feared that alcohol-connected trauma cases would place an immense burden on health services during the increase in Covid-19 infections. The ban was lifted for about a month before it was put in place again in July 2020, as the number of infections had increased at this time.

After the first three weeks of the lockdown there was pervasive food insecurity among a substantial portion of the population, which incited anger and protests (Bhorat 2020). Wages were cut and some employers reneged on negotiated increases via collective agreements. The cost of the average household food basket increased from R3 856.34 in October 2020 to R4 018.22 in November 2020 (Pietermaritzburg Economic Justice and Dignity Group 2020). Forecasts predicted that economic growth would decline by 7 per cent and that economic contraction in the South African economy would be similar to that in 1960 (Bhorat 2020). The state responded to the magnitude of the socioeconomic destruction by revealing a massive stimulus package of approximately R328 billion. This package comprised a substantial increase in social assistance and a national wage subsidy programme, making South Africa's relative spending on Covid-19 the highest when compared to the other emerging markets in the world (Bhorat 2020). The independently administered Solidarity Fund, Unemployment Insurance Fund (UIF), Temporary Employer/Employee Relief Scheme (TERS), tax relief and a loan guarantee scheme, in partnership with big banks, were put into place. (TERS was a stipend intended to assist employees who could not be paid by their employers when operations shut down during the lockdown. The scheme was financed from the UIF, which had amassed a considerable amount over the years.) In addition to this, the National Empowerment Fund provided loans to black-owned businesses to manufacture and provide a variety of medical products to support the essential healthcare sector.

Under Covid-19, 'business as usual for trade unions went out of the window in 2020' (Mthethwa 2020). Trade unions had to urgently re-assess how they were going to continue delivering value to their members and recruit new members under pandemic conditions. Union officials, many of them working remotely, had to deal with a plethora of issues such as the non-payment of UIF-TERS, retrenchments and non-compliance with Covid-19 occupational safety and health guidelines in workplaces.

Methodologically, the material for this chapter was drawn from responses by various labour federations and their affiliates to the severe restrictions put into place in the various phases of the Covid-19 lockdown during 2020. This material was gathered through monitoring newspaper media reports as well as the official Facebook pages of the labour federations.[1]

LABOUR FEDERATIONS AND THEIR AFFILIATES: RESPONSE TO THE COVID-19 PANDEMIC

The monitoring of the responses of labour federations and their affiliates focused predominantly on those of their members who were designated as essential service workers during the Covid-19 crisis. These included employees in the public sector, as well as private sector employees in fields where there were large workforces, such as in mining, and employees who worked for state-owned enterprises.

Congress of South African Trade Unions

A key affiliate of the Congress of South African Trade Unions (Cosatu), the South African Commercial, Catering and Allied Workers Union (Saccawu), organises workers in the retail sector, Saccawu was alarmed about the lack of personal protective equipment (PPE) for retail workers, essential workers at various retail outlets such as Spar, Makro, Dischem, Pick n Pay and Shoprite. The union also noted that the retail sector was short of preventative measures and plans for Covid-19 for the workforce. Some Saccawu members stated that if they wanted to visit health facilities, employers were using the principle of no-work-no-pay, even if the workers tested positive for Covid-19. Furthermore, they had no guaranteed income if they were quarantined or hospitalised. Saccawu committed to seeking legal counsel on these matters and stated it would contact the offices of the Presidency and the Ministries of Employment and Labour as well as that of Trade and Industry to bring their attention to the challenges that the union's members faced.

In the mining sector, the National Union of Mineworkers (NUM) and Harmony Gold reached an agreement that all workers in all Harmony Gold operations in South Africa would return to work early in May 2020. Harmony Gold had paid mineworkers their salaries during the lockdown period. Both NUM and the company had agreed that rigorous screening had to be carried out to test the workforce for Covid-19 as soon as they reported for work. Those who tested positive would be quarantined immediately and those who were ill would be hospitalised. The company agreed to implement stringent measures in all its operations to guarantee the health and safety of workers. The union's Health and Safety structures and the management at Harmony Gold operations set up task teams to gauge and observe that the company followed the Health and Safety standards for all workers who had returned to work. The company also launched an education programme about the virus for returning workers. Health workers were trained and prepared to manage the virus, and they were constantly tested for the virus. Sanitisers and masks would be made available to all employees, social distancing would be meticulously followed in the workplace and body scanners would be set up at the company's big mines.

In Cosatu, public sector trade unions now have the largest membership and wield considerable power and influence within the labour federation, launching major strikes (Bischoff and Maree 2017). As will be shown below, Cosatu was in the lead in responding to the Covid-19 pandemic in the educational and healthcare sectors in the course of 2020.

When President Ramaphosa announced financial relief packages for workers, the Democratic Nursing Organisation of South Africa (Denosa) pointed out that nurses, their members, had been excluded from this. There were numerous reasons for this but, in short, nurses' salaries were not adjusted according to the deadline in the collective bargaining agreement reached in the public sector a few years earlier. Because of the lockdown's restrictions, including a curfew, on public transport, which many Denosa members used, their transport expenditure had increased as the trips took longer to reach their places of work, for which they were not compensated. As their salaries had not been adjusted, nurses were not given tax breaks. More worryingly, many nurses worked without PPE, which further exposed them to the risk of being infected. Denosa had called for the payment of a Risk Allowance for these essential workers but this was not addressed. In facilities that were short-staffed and were admitting Covid-19 patients, no additional staff had been employed, although funds had been set aside for this. Denosa called on all its members not to treat any Covid-19 patients if they were not given PPE. Nurses at an Eastern Cape hospital, where there had been a spike in Covid-19 infections, duly refused to treat Covid-19 patients. Some healthcare facilities had been declared ready to handle the virus, but when the Minister of Health visited one of the hospitals in the Eastern Cape in April 2020, he was shocked to discover that the hospital was not prepared despite the provincial health department declaring that it was.

Denosa and other unions decided to declare a dispute at the Public Service Co-ordinating Bargaining Council (PSCBC) against the government as the government had not honoured its side of the agreement for salary increases. The Denosa Student Movement expressed concern at the decision to reopen higher learning institutions for the coordinated return of final-year Clinical Training (medical) students to help with the health management campaign of the Department of Health. Although the medical students formed part of the frontline and thus were at risk of being infected, they were not insured for this. Furthermore, the nursing colleges did not have the necessary infrastructure to adapt to online learning, as other higher education institutions had done during the lockdown period. Because student nurses had to undertake clinical duties for experiential learning as part of their training, they were carrying out essential work but only received a bursary payment for this, despite being exposed to the dangers.

In April 2020, 200 Cuban medical doctors arrived in South Africa to assist with the treatment of Covid-19. This was despite the fact that there were many vacancies for health workers. Denosa was aware that about 100 000 applications had been made by South African doctors and health professionals, including nurses, in response to these vacancies. Simultaneously, many healthcare workers were leaving South Africa for overseas jobs. The South African government had a staff retention strategy especially for nurses, but this had not been renewed since its expiry in 2012. The World Health Organization released a report in April 2020 on the World State of Nursing, and it disclosed that there was a shortage globally of 5.9 million nurses, of which 5.3 million were in poorer countries.

The South African Emergency Personnel's Union called on its members to be cautious when they responded to calls during this lockdown period, as some had been hijacked and robbed in the ambulances when attending to emergencies.

The National Education, Health and Allied Workers' Union (Nehawu) were displeased at the non-implementation of salary increases for public servants that were due at the beginning of April 2020, even though a binding collective agreement had been signed by all parties in 2018. Nehawu members were also frontline workers against Covid-19. The union planned to take the then Minister of Health, Dr Zweli Mkhize, and his department to court to force them to comply with the Occupational Health and Safety Act (No. 85 of 1993) during the Covid-19 crisis, and this was supported by Cosatu.

The South African Local Government Bargaining Council urged the country's 257 municipalities to hold talks with two recognised trade unions in the sector – the South African Municipal Workers Union and the Independent Municipal and Allied Trade Union (which is an independent trade union, established in 1996). The intention was to discuss the possibility of danger allowances for municipal employees who were defined as essential service workers.

All schools closed on 18 March 2020. The rapid closure of schools saw some move learning online or carry out distance learning. This occurred in both private and public sector basic educational institutions, most notably in the quintile five schools that are located in wealthier areas. This revealed the vast inequalities in the educational sector, among the private and public schools, and even within the public schools themselves. The South African Democratic Teachers Union (Sadtu) posted the Department of Education's daily television and radio lessons on their social media accounts, and Sadtu members communicated with their students through a variety of messaging platforms such as WhatsApp, the D6 School Communicator, Google Classroom and Microsoft Teams. This required that both teachers and learners have adequate data and devices and at least a cell phone. Sadtu noted that it was a struggle to make contact with learners living in rural areas and in informal settlements as there was poor infrastructure, such as electrification, in those places.

The Minister of Basic Education announced early in May 2020 that schools would reopen in June, with a phased in return to school for learners. To prepare for schools to reopen, the school management team (SMT) (which is responsible for planning the timetables and receiving the teachers and support staff), the teachers and administrative staff would return in the middle of May. However, Sadtu pointed out that the law stipulated that the employer – that is, the state – was responsible for ensuring that the workplace for employees was safe, and it instructed its members that they should not return to schools until these non-negotiables were successfully fulfilled. Some schools also needed their infrastructure fixed (such as installing of proper toilet and ablution facilities), as well as the installation of sanitisers and the deep cleansing (fumigation, disinfection) of the schools. This was eventually carried out by the Department of Public Works and the infrastructure unit of the Department of Basic Education. The role of the SMT would be to ensure that all the essentials were comprehensively delivered. Added to this, the Department of Basic Education still had to clarify the plans for adherence to social distancing inside classrooms and on playgrounds, the cut-back in class sizes, provision of soap and sanitisers, availability of masks, and the screening of learners, teachers and support personnel. Some schools were asked to get parents involved in the cleaning of schools or to use the budget set aside for other purposes (such as printing) to hire cleaning staff. It was also expected that schools in areas with a high infection rate, which was mostly the metro areas, would not reopen while schools in other areas with low infection rates could. Sadtu was worried that the provincial departments were ill-prepared with regard to the provision of health and safety essentials, which had to be in place in the learning institutions at least two weeks before any activity could commence. Until these concerns were met, Sadtu proposed that no school should reopen.

Sadtu emphasised that 14 minimum conditions had to be met before schools could reopen. On 19 May 2020, the Minister for Basic Education confirmed that schools would reopen on 1 June 2020 and that Grades 7 and 12 would return first, with plans for the phasing in of other grades and special needs schools to be published later on in the month. The minister also clarified that the essential items needed for the reopening of schools would be sent using a just-in-time process as many schools had been vandalised over the school closure period. Compounding this was the fact that many schools did not have adequate storage facilities.

In response to this, Sadtu reported that it had received reports of school readiness from the provinces and was concerned about the variation in the state of preparedness among the schools. Union leaders feared that this would have a further impact on the pre-Covid-19 inequalities in the education sector. Furthermore, Sadtu was of the opinion that consultation by the minister with the teacher trade unions had not been collaborative, and this view was shared by all the other educational trade unions. To be clear, the reopening plans were announced at the national level – for example, that the SMTs would return on 11 May 2020 – but at the provincial level some of the essentials to secure the return of SMTs were not in place. Within provinces, there were contradictory circulars on the state of preparedness. The general secretary of Sadtu reported that some principals, afraid of the consequences of not complying, had embellished their state-of-preparedness reports, and teachers had returned before the school had received PPE, sanitisers and thermometers. This meant that, even before they opened, some schools were not complying with the department's health and safety legislation nor with the Covid-19 national regulations.

Sadtu stated on 18 May 2020 that it was not prepared to comply with the proposed reopening of schools. Instead, the union committed to continue gathering data from their members. Sadtu stated that its local structures would assist the department to monitor and evaluate, but they made it clear that the health and safety of learners and educators would take priority over completing the 2020 academic year. The Gauteng Department of Education issued an invitation to unemployed youth in the province, between the ages of 18 and 35, to apply to become part of the Covid-19 Brigades Programme. They would receive a stipend for their services. As there was an existing shortage of support staff at schools, and as community transmission was still high, they would be recruited to assist in screening staff and learners, monitoring data, and ensuring compliance to social distancing and sanitising once learners returned to school in June 2020.

South African Federation of Trade Unions

At the end of April 2020, the South African Federation of Trade Unions (Saftu) launched a campaign on PPE, which it considered a fundamental right for the safety of all health and care workers and for the safety of the communities they served.

The Democratic Municipal and Allied Workers Union of South Africa reported that its members – frontline workers such as those who worked in the safety and security departments – were working in unsafe conditions; about 24 employees had already contracted the virus. The union pointed out that the City of Cape Town had overlooked health and safety regulations in relation to the Covid-19 pandemic. It called on the Department of Labour to shut Metro Police stations until a risk assessment could be carried out, and this was supported by Saftu.

The National Union of Public Service and Allied Workers (Nupsaw) criticised the reopening of schools, nurseries and day-care centres by the Department of Basic Education. Nupsaw felt it was too early as the pandemic was still far from over. The union believed that the department was only concerned with saving the 2020 academic year, but was unable to reopen the schools safely. Like their Cosatu counterparts, Nupsaw advised that schools only reopen when the authorities could issue a guarantee that they were absolutely safe. Nupsaw felt that the government had not paid attention to the health, well-being and emotional resilience of the learners, staff and parents, who were afraid to send their children back even if a phased reopening took place. This was because certain issues like revision of school schedules, methods to curb infection – including increased spacing between desks, pupils attending schools on different days or times of the day, and how to structure playground time – had not been provided by the educational authorities.

Approximately 600 workers and members of the Food and Allied Workers Union working for South African Breweries faced retrenchments at the beginning of May 2020 due to the ban that had been placed on alcohol sales and distribution. The union also demanded that workers who came to work and risked contracting the virus because they had to work with others in factories or deal with customers in retail stores also be paid a danger allowance and receive an income tax break.

Saftu rejected the South African Airways (SAA) business rescue practitioner's recommendations that approximately 10 000 workers accept retrenchment packages during the lockdown period or the airline would be liquidated. SAA was connected to over 34 000 jobs along the value chain, as its subsidiaries (SAA Technical, Air Chefs and Mango) were also affected by its closure. Saftu regarded this as an attempt to privatise SAA, a state-owned enterprise which Saftu regarded as a very important national asset. Even though there was concern about how the ANC government had eroded state-owned enterprises through corruption, Saftu ideologically opposed privatisation as it felt that such enterprises played a vital role in developing the economy and that they would be strategic in the drive to re-industrialise in the post-coronavirus phase.

The National Union of Metalworkers of South Africa (Numsa) reported that during the lockdown period, Village Main Reef Tau Lekoa mining company (in Sedibeng region) did not pay their employees and served workers with a section 189 notice (warning them of possible retrenchment). Numsa's members at the Target branch of the mine, situated in the Free State, had been informed that they must prepare to return to work but that the company had not applied the essential safety steps to guarantee that the workplace was safe. Numsa unsuccessfully attempted to open a case against the company, alleging the company's contravention of the Disaster Management Act (No. 57 of 2002). Numsa urged its members not to return to work. It also insisted that the company pay employees their full salary for the duration of the lockdown, and then claim back the funds form the Department of Labour through the TERS relief scheme. Numsa condemned the company's attempts to coerce those who were not working to apply for leave for the period of the lockdown.

The Young Nurses Indaba Trade Union demanded improved protection for all frontline workers – nurses, doctors and other healthcare workers. Apart from receiving inadequate PPE and that vulnerable medical staff were not supported mentally during a very stressful time, the union called for a danger allowance and asked that adequate transport arrangements be made for nurses, especially at night after their shifts. It called on President Ramaphosa to give frontline staff an income tax break of six months. The motivation for this demand was that nurses were poorly paid when compared to other healthcare professionals; they came from poor backgrounds, had many dependents and were not receiving a salary increase for the 2020/2021 financial year.

Federation of Unions of South Africa

The Federation of Unions of South Africa (Fedusa) called on the South African Nursing Council to increase demands for the Department of Health to provide PPE to nurses and other healthcare workers on the frontline at each health institution in the country – this as the world marked International Nurses Day on 12 May 2020, amid the Covid-19 crisis. On 1 May, Fedusa had launched a R100 000 Isibonelelo Fund to support its members who were on the Covid-19 frontline. This fund could be used to procure vital PPE as the economy re-opened under Level 4 of the lockdown, which saw a further 1.5 million workers return to work without the necessary support in place. Fedusa televised video clips throughout the month of May to inform members and their communities about hygiene methods and other safety precautions to keep themselves safe from infection. Fedusa also acknowledged that many women and children were subjected to abuse during the lockdown restrictions, and urged them to take a stand against gender-based violence.

The South African Typographical Union demanded that the board of Media24 give the union and its members clarity on the rationale to give notice of Section 45(5) of the Companies Act (No. 71 of 2008), as the Covid-19 pandemic had seen a global decline in advertising spending. This section of the act enables the provision of financial assistance to directors or officers of the company, or to related companies. The union urged that as Media24 workers were at the forefront as essential service workers in the media industry, they be assisted financially before the executives and shareholders were assisted

The National Tertiary Education Union, which organises academic and general staff workers in universities and other institutions in the tertiary sector, approved of the Minister of Higher Education's emphasis on safety first. The union anticipated that the higher education institutions would observe the necessary safety measures, which involved the thorough sanitisation of campuses and suitable supply of PPE to all staff. However, union leaders were aware of the immense inequalities within higher education, as 14 universities had not been able to conduct online teaching. The union pledged to provide its support to the ministerial task teams and the department to address the imbalance and not lose the 2020 academic year.

The South African Teachers' Union (SAOU) insisted that the safety and health of education staff and learners had to be the main priority for when schools reopened at the end of level five lockdown. Many schooldays had been lost but SAOU felt that the prevention of infections was the most complex issue and had to be adequately dealt with. SAOU's 21 890 members had participated in an electronic poll and agreed that no school could re-open until:

- the pre-sanitisation of schools had taken place,
- the supply of adequate sanitation packages and equipment for the daily sanitisation of schools had been delivered,
- the provision of cloth masks and hand sanitisers to staff and learners had occurred,
- thermal scanners had been delivered to schools,
- the provision of instructions for compliance with social distancing on and off the school premises had been made,
- isolation areas for persons who were identified as infected at the school were allocated, and
- acceptable safety protocols and appropriate communication to staff, parents and learners were issued.

SAOU pledged to request that the courts release an appropriate instruction that assured compliance with these requirements.

TRADE UNIONS: COVID-19, SOURCES OF POWER AND WORKING-CLASS UNITY

Cosatu public sector trade unions have drawn on their numerical strength to successfully negotiate higher salaries for their members. Due to the transformation of labour relations in the public service, the Labour Relations Act (No. 66 of 1995) granted the same labour relations and collective bargaining rights to all employees in the public service. Once collective bargaining took off in the public sector, multi-year wage agreements were reached for public sector employees such as teachers and nurses. The result was that the bulk of state expenditure on basic education was dedicated to salaries; this has negatively affected the provision of essential services to public schools. The strength of these essential public service workers is unlike that of other service workers who, Chun (2009) argues, are marginalised. Indeed, organised public sector workers in South Africa have structural power, as conceptualised by Silver (2016). Added to this, the teacher trade unions in South Africa do not compete for members as they come from different political traditions that have persisted into the democratic era.

The public sector is a significant employer in the South African economy; the proportion of employment in the public sector grew by four per centage points, from 16 per cent to 20 per cent, between 2009 and 2015 (Kerr and Wittenberg 2017). Thus the marketplace bargaining power of public sector employees is high. There have been a number of protracted strikes in the public sector in the post-apartheid era, most notably by the teachers and nurses in 2007 and in 2010. In 2007, 700 000 public sector employees went on strike for 28 days and it is estimated that 8.1 million working days were lost. At the heart of the strike was a dispute over wage increases (Maree 2017). Organised public sector employees have workplace structural power. Taken together these are two important bases for public sector employees' power.

The education trade unions took a united position, and agreed not to adhere to the instruction given by the Minister of Basic Education to prepare for the reopening of schools until certain conditions were met. A joint statement was issued by the National Professional Teachers Organisation of South Africa, Sadtu, SAOU, the National Teachers Union, and the Professional Educators Union; these are unions from across the ideological spectrum and from different labour federations. Their statement read as follows:

> As the Covid-19 pandemic wreaks havoc around the world, we are experiencing the greatest display of solidarity in human history. This is the solidarity we expect in our education institutions and we, as education trade unions, felt that we should jointly respond to the ministers' plans. (Africa News Agency Reporter 2020)

This illustrates that not all workers are in competition with each other globally – for example, those in service work and place-based jobs, as Evans (2014) points out.

The Covid-19 pandemic also exposed that the public sector trade unions across the federations have what Silver (2016) calls ambiguous structural power. These unions are powerful and have been successful in delivering salary increases to their membership through the collective bargaining apparatus. Yet the state has often been a hostile partner in these negotiations in not conceding to the demands made by the trade unions and offering much lower increases (Maree 2017). At the start of the South African level five lockdown, it was clear at the PSCBC held on 17 March 2020 that the state would be reneging on the final year of the 2018 agreement by not paying public servants a wage increase in 2020/2021 (Nicolson 2020). The agreement stipulated that the government give an increase for the years 2018/2019, 2019/2020 and 2020/2021. This affected approximately 400 000 teachers as well as nurses and the police, all essential service workers in the struggle against Covid-19 (Mahlaka 2021). Even though an econometric analysis conducted in 2015 by the Public Service Commission and the Financial and Fiscal Commission had established that the current high expenditure on employee salaries had no statistically significant effect on economic growth, the report recommended that a shift in expenditure take place to improve the productivity of health and education. This meant dedicating more of the budget to non-wage components such as health technologies and technologies for e-education, which were both sorely lacking, as exposed by the Covid-19 pandemic.

National Treasury declared that no additional funding would be made available to directly fund costs associated with implementing the last leg of PSCBC Resolution 1 of 2018. Subsequently, negotiations reached a deadlock at the PSCBC over the government's refusal to abide by the wage agreement it had signed in 2018. The finance minister indicated that he also intended to reduce the public sector wage bill by R160 billion over the following three years as it was the biggest part of government expenditure, at R639 billion for the 2020/2021 financial year (Mathe 2020).

The government approached the Labour Court to seek an order to declare the wage agreement null and void. Because public sector employees did not receive salary increases as promised by the state, the united position taken by all the teacher unions was to consider the possibility of declaring a dispute.

The Auditor General released the report of an investigation into the use of R500 billion, which was a Covid-19 fiscal package. The report found many cases of the overpricing of products, such as in the procurement of PPE in the education sector. Many beneficiaries of this government tender also had familial connections to ruling politicians, which enraged Cosatu. As many senior politicians and businesspeople were implicated in the alleged corruption, Cosatu insisted that President Ramaphosa mobilise the Special Investigative Unit to look into claims, including allegations that some employers had misappropriated funds from TERS.

Finally, in October 2020, a strike was called by Cosatu, Saftu and Fedusa in protest against the 'rampant corruption and looting of COVID-19 funds, and the government's failure to honour a 2018 wage agreement in the public sector' (Kulkarni 2020). The General Industries Workers' Union of South Africa (Giwusa) was the first Saftu affiliate to announce its full support of Cosatu's call. Giwusa stated that it was encouraged that Cosatu was

> … becoming conscious of the class character of the ANC government and will not defer to it the historic demands of the working class. Giwusa hopes that this decisive action shall spark the beginning of a sustained collaboration between the two biggest federations in the country. History is calling us to act decisively and we dare not fail. (Giwusa quoted in Kulkarni 2020)

Saftu and Fedusa undertook to hold demonstrations and pickets on 7 October 2020.

When South Africa reached level one of the lockdown later in 2020, President Ramaphosa pronounced that the UIF Covid-19 TERS payments would be cancelled. Both trade unions and businesses were alarmed that such a decision had been taken without discussing this with the social partners, as it had been understood that President Ramaphosa intended that TERS continue along with the extension of the State of Disaster. TERS has prevented many employees, some of them trade union members, from being retrenched, but so many more would face retrenchment if it was rescinded. However, it emerged that during the lockdown period the government had wanted to cut funding in June 2020. All the labour federations and organised business at the National Economic Development and Labour Council urged the government to extend its relief for workers in distress, as jobs were being lost and the country was traversing an economic crisis.

Saftu and Cosatu also took a united stand to defend the Commission for Conciliation, Mediation and Arbitration (CCMA).[2] Part of the austerity measures implemented by the government had severely impacted key labour institutions such as the CCMA. The CCMA's budget of R1 billion was reduced by R99 million and more cuts of R170 million and R231 million were planned to take place over the following two years. The CCMA was under immense pressure as it strained to deliver on its authorised mandate, as more and more workers were being retrenched.[3] Analysing wage agreements reached in 2020, the Labour Research Services confirmed that the largest percentage increase in wages was 8 per cent and the lowest 3.8 per cent.[4] Some bargaining councils and companies postponed salary or wage increases due to financial distress and the Covid-19 pandemic (Mthethwa 2020). Many companies have cited financial restraints and the need for retrenchments or restructuring because of the Covid-19 pandemic.

The rate of unemployment in South Africa during the Covid-19 crisis worsened quarter by quarter, as reported by Statistics South Africa in its 2020 Fourth Quarterly Report. Indeed, unemployment was at 32.5 per cent, and as high as 42.5 per cent if the expanded unemployment rate (which includes discouraged job seekers) was taken into consideration (Stats SA 2021). The garment manufacturing industry took immense strain under the Covid-19 lockdown. The Southern African Clothing and Textile Workers Union (Sactwu) was relieved when the decision to offer duty-free imports on woven fabrics was taken by the government on 5 February 2021, and called this a 'breakthrough that will save garment and textile jobs' (IndustriALL 2021). According to Sactwu, this policy move will foster growth in the textile and garment manufacturing sectors, and it encourages local procurement. This was the result of four months of negotiations with social dialogue partners that comprised retailers, garment manufacturers and textile mills, facilitated by the Retail, Clothing, Textile, Footwear and Leather (R-CTFL) Masterplan.[5]

Andre Kriel, Sactwu general secretary, reported:

> The consensus reached in this industrial development agreement is unprecedented. Together, these employers and labour organizations constitute the most representative industry voice on this rebate matter. Importantly, the imported fabric can only be used by companies that are signatories to the R-CTFL Masterplan and are compliant with it. (Kriel quoted in IndustriALL 2021)

In the case of clothing and textiles manufacturing, Covid-19 had disrupted imports and this prompted the industry to reconsider its options. Yet what this also reveals is that collective bargaining needs robust trade unions. Indeed, to be more effective stakeholders in responding proactively to Covid-19, trade unions needed to be more informed than ever before. They should request company information in the case of proposed retrenchments so that they are aware of the 'bargaining benchmarks' that would help them to respond constructively. The Covid-19 crisis showed that trade unions should revisit their existing collective agreements in order to build in a disaster management clause if there is not one in place (Mthethwa 2020).

CONCLUSION

The Covid-19 pandemic and the crisis that swiftly unfolded in South Africa changed the tide for all the trade unions. The crisis has aided the labour movement to unite in its response to the state and to employers. The trade unions in the education sector were united about the proposed return to school. In the health sector, the unity among the various trade unions stemmed from demands that health workers be sufficiently protected in the fight against Covid-19. The health workers were the recipients of the first batch of vaccines. Trade unions recognised how the onus of the Covid-19 crisis had been placed on the shoulders of the working class. Cosatu has openly stated that the African National Congress has 'betrayed the country's working class' (Kulkarni 2020). On the one hand, this might raise questions about the stability of the alliance between the African National Congress, the South African Communist Party and Cosatu. On the other hand, it has opened up the space for greater unity in the trade union movement, which faced divisions over the issue of continued support for the ruling party. Post the pandemic, trade unions are now faced with both shielding their members from retrenchments and dealing with employers who are only proposing marginal percentage increases equivalent to or less than the rate of inflation during wage negotiations.

The Covid-19 pandemic has also shown how the collective agreement continues to be a strategic tool for trade unions to contest threats to workers' rights and compel employers to respond. The labour movement in South Africa has used the crisis to concentrate on rebuilding a working-class solidarity that seems to be transcending their ideological differences. Worker solidarity can be further advanced by centring working-class interests; in the absence of wage increases, the unions could make non-wage demands such as the provision of quality PPE, subsidised transportation and a food allowance to assist workers disadvantaged by the crisis (Mthethwa 2020). Trade unions need to sustain their responses to the Covid-19 crisis as tensions in the workplace continue to mount around wage reductions and as more retrenchments loom.

NOTES

1 The responses of trade unions and labour federations to the Covid-19 pandemic, the lockdowns and the restrictions was gathered from their Facebook accounts, as the unions used these to disseminate information and keep their members updated on important developments that affected them and their work.
2 The CCMA administers over 200 000 cases annually including unfair dismissals, wage disputes and retrenchments.
3 Mthethwa (2020) reports that from 1 April to 31 May 2020, the CCMA received over 23 500 referrals for retrenchments and unfair dismissals.
4 Even the Labour Research Service has noted that more unions are approaching them for advice on how to manage retrenchments.
5 The Masterplan was initiated by the Department of Trade, Industry and Competition with the objective of cultivating the textile and garment value chain. The value chain incorporates spinning, weaving, dyeing, knitting and finishing of natural and synthetic fibre inputs and leather tanning. Cut-make-trim operators, design houses, garment and household textile manufacturers, and leather and shoe manufacturers are included in the value chain. Locally sourced and imported products are part of the value chain as well.

REFERENCES

Africa News Agency Reporter. 2020. 'Education Unions Demand Clarity and More Discussions on Reopening of Schools'. *IOL News*, 2 May 2020. https://www.iol.co.za/news/politics/education-unions-demand-clarity-and-more-discussions-on-reopening-of-schools-47467830.

Benhura, Miracle and Prudence Magejo. 2021. 'Who Cannot Work from Home in South Africa? Evidence from Wave 4 of NIDS-CRAM'. National Income Dynamics Study (NIDS) – Coronavirus Rapid Mobile Survey (CRAM) Wave 4, 29 January 2022. https://cramsurvey.org/wp-content/uploads/2021/05/2.-Benhura-M.-_-Magejo-P.-2021-Who-cannot-work-from-home-in-South-Africa_-Evidence-from-wave-4-of-NIDSCRAM..pdf. Accessed 7 February 2023.

Bhorat, Haroon. 2020. 'Economic Fallout is Ferocious, but Health Crisis must be Focus'. *News24*, 10 May 2020. https://www.news24.com/news24/Analysis/haroon-bhorat-economic-fallout-is-ferocious-but-health-crisis-must-be-focus-20200507.

Bischoff, Christine and Johann Maree. 2017. 'Public Sector Unions in Cosatu'. In *Labour Beyond Cosatu: Mapping the Rupture in South Africa's Labour Landscape*, edited by Andries Bezuidenhout and Malehoko Tshoaedi, 170–190. Johannesburg: Wits University Press.

Chun, Jennifer Jihye. 2009. 'Legal Liminality: The Gender and Labour Politics of Organising South Korea's Irregular Workforce'. *Third World Quarterly* 30 (3): 535–550.

Evans, Peter. 2014. 'National Labour Movements and Transnational Connections'. *Global Labour Journal* 5 (3): 258–282.

IndustriALL. 2021. 'Agreement on Duty Free Woven Fabrics is a Breakthrough in Saving South African Jobs'. 24 February 2021. http://www.industriall-union.org/agreement-on-duty-free-woven-fabrics-is-a-breakthrough-in-saving-south-african-jobs. Accessed 24 February 2021.

Kerr, Andrew and Amy Thornton. 2020. 'This is Who is Most at Risk of Losing a Job due to Covid-19 Lockdown'. *Business Day*, 22 April 2020. https://www.businesslive.co.za/bd/opinion/2020-04-22-this-is-who-is-most-at-risk-of-losing-a-job-due-to-covid-19-lockdown.

Kerr, Andrew and Martin Wittenberg. 2017. *Public Sector Wages and Employment in South Africa*. SALDRU Working Paper 214. Cape Town: Southern Africa Labour and Development Research Unit, University of Cape Town.

Kulkarni, Pavan. 2020. 'South African Unions Prepare for Historic Strike on October 7'. *Peoples Dispatch*, 4 October 2020. https://peoplesdispatch.org/2020/10/04/south-african-unions-prepare-for-historic-strike-on-october-7/. Accessed 16 May 2020.

Mahlaka, Ray. 2021. 'More Damage to South Africa's Labour Market as Unemployment Hits New High'. *Business Maverick*, 23 February 2021. https://www.dailymaverick.co.za/article/2021-02-23-more-damage-to-south-africas-labour-market-as-unemployment-hits-new-high/.

Maree, Johann. 2017. 'Internal Democracy in Cosatu: Achievements and Challenges'. In *Labour Beyond Cosatu: Mapping the Rupture in South Africa's Labour Landscape*, edited by Andries Bezuidenhout and Malehoko Tshoaedi, 146–169. Johannesburg: Wits University Press.

Mathe, Tshegofatso. 2020. 'Mboweni Plans to Freeze Public Sector Wage Increases for the Next Three Years'. *Mail & Guardian*, 28 October 2020. https://mg.co.za/business/2020-10-28-mboweni-plans-to-freeze-public-sector-wage-increases-for-the-next-three-years.

Mthethwa, George. 2020. 'Covid-19 Support Measures for Workers in South Africa'. *Labour Research Service*, 30 November 2020. https://www.lrs.org.za/2020/11/30/covid-19-support-measures-for-workers-in-south-africa.

Nicolson, Greg. 2020. 'South Africa: "We are Dying"' – Nehawu Gears to Strike as Frontline Workers Battle Covid-19'. *Daily Maverick*, 21 August 2020. https://allafrica.com/stories/202008210049.html.

Pietermaritzburg Economic Justice and Dignity Group. 2020. 'Pietermaritzburg Household Affordability Index, November 2020'. https://pmbejd.org.za/wp-content/uploads/2020/09/PMB-September-2020-Household-Affordability-Index_30092020.pdf. Accessed 7 February 2023.

Silver, Beverly. 2016. 'The Remaking of the Global Working Class'. *Roar: The Future of Work*, Issue 2. 19 August 2021. https://roarmag.org/magazine/the-remaking-of-the-global-working-class. Accessed 7 February 2023.

Statistics South Africa (Stats SA). 2021. 'Quarterly Labour Force Survey Quarter 4: 2020'. 23 February 2021. Stats SA. Statistical Release P0211.

Questions, Answers and New Directions

**Andries Bezuidenhout, Christine Bischoff
and Malehoko Tshoaedi**

INTRODUCTION

The chapters collected in this volume raise new topics for South African labour studies, but they also point to the need to return to past debates. In this concluding chapter, we provide an overview and highlight some of these new foci and how they relate to more established (and at times forgotten) debates. We are interested in challenges posed by this to both the labour movement and to South African labour studies more generally. We introduced the volume with an appreciation of the challenge posed to South African workers and the labour movement by the Covid-19 pandemic. All of this happened in the context of a fragmented labour movement, described by labour scholars and in the popular media as being weak and lacking direction. Not surprisingly, both the virus and the lockdown that was intended to slow its spread had major negative impacts. Like the rest of the world, we have experienced the shock of family, friends and colleagues dying because of the pandemic, of fellow workers losing their jobs and livelihoods, as well as the tragic death of a number of prominent union leaders, including the general secretary of the National Union of Mineworkers. But we also argued that the pandemic, probably ironically so, posed challenges to the labour movement that focused the minds of members and leaders alike, and led to the emergence of renewed interest in working-class unity. Old and new enemies jointly participated in some of the campaigns that challenged government's response to the pandemic. All of this happened while South Africans, in lockdown mode, were following the drama on television and other media platforms around state capture in the form of the Zondo Commission of Enquiry.

Much of the research for the chapters in this volume started before the Covid-19 pandemic, and not all the chapters deal directly with this topic and its fallout. Nevertheless, they all highlight in some way that a major international health crisis, which also precipitated an economic crisis, tended to be felt along the contours of existing fault lines. A crisis tends to focus our attention on questions that have lurked in the background. So we start our discussion here with the chapter preceding this one, where Christine Bischoff clearly illustrates this point about fault lines. As could be expected, vulnerable workers in vulnerable sectors were affected more severely than others. She researched and wrote this chapter during the course of the pandemic and the national state of lockdown, keeping track in real time of events as they unfolded. She offers that the severe restrictions placed on all but essential types of economic activity during South Africa's lockdown due to the Covid-19 pandemic in 2020 exposed the frail forms of livelihood tactics adopted by so many South Africans, but it also revealed many issues that South African trade unions had not faced up to.

The main burden of the Covid-19 crisis has been placed on the shoulders of the working class, especially those more vulnerable because of precarious contracts in precarious sectors, and this has changed the tide for all trade unions. The labour movement has united to respond to the state and to employers on many issues, such as the return to work, the adequate protection of the workforce and the non-payment of wage increases. However, in 2022, as the lockdown ended, trade unions were still faced with shielding their members from retrenchments and dealing with employers who only proposed marginal percentage wage increases. Nevertheless, as pointed out in the introduction to this volume, after the lockdown period there were a number of joint campaigns between competing unions (such as the National Union of Mineworkers and the Association of Mineworkers and Construction Union) and rival federations (such as the Congress of South African Trade Unions [Cosatu], the South African Federation of Trade Unions [Saftu] and the Federation of Unions of South Africa [Fedusa]). One could argue that the labour movement in South Africa has used the crisis to begin a process of rebuilding working-class solidarity despite ideological differences.

Is this reading overly optimistic? Maybe so. So let us, for a moment, delve into those differences that prevent working-class solidarity. We reflect here on three areas of division that have been explored in labour studies more generally. We first explore how unions have traditionally related to strategies of organising economic sectors. We then turn to how unions approach political involvement and political parties. Finally, we look at unions and ideological differences. All these factors have contributed to working-class fragmentation and a lack of unity, but falling back on older ideas of working-class unity will again fail to deliver a stronger labour movement. Society, the economy and how we approach politics have all changed rapidly, and fixating nostalgically on old ways of doing things will deliver just that – old ways of doing things. We argue here that the chapters collected in this volume present a number of critical questions that could assist in developing a revitalised approach both to organising workers and to understanding attempts at organising better. We also use this scoping exercise as an opportunity to highlight silences and areas of interest that should be on the agenda of a revitalised labour studies agenda. (For background on South African labour studies, see Lucien van der Walt's chapter in this volume, as well as Webster 1991, 1999, 2018; Buhlungu 2009; Freund 2013).

TRADE UNIONS, ORGANISING AND ECONOMIC SECTORS

The history of trade unionism can be traced back to how unions responded to the reorganisation of work under capitalism. Here we draw a distinction between craft unions, industrial unions, general unions and advice bureaus. Of course, all these categories are ideal types, as Max Weber would refer to such categorisations (Stewart 2018). The earliest unions in countries that industrialised first emerged out of guilds, and were called craft unions. They controlled access to their ranks through their role as masters of apprentices; in order to maintain their power in the workplace, they limited the number of apprentices they were willing to train. This gave them immense marketplace bargaining power, since they generally possessed scarce skills. We refer here to carpenters, millwrights and the like. Of course, their power was a major irritation to industrialists, and the emergence of scientific management – the breaking down of the production process into measurable tasks – successfully broke the power of many of these craft unions. Henry Ford added the moving assembly line – or machine-paced production – in order to further tighten control over the labour process in production. Harry Braverman (1974) famously referred to this combination of Taylorism and Fordism as a process of deskilling – over time the working class would lose their skill, as they became merely appendages to production machinery (see also Webster 1985).

At the time, many predicted the end of trade unionism, because trade unions were seen as craft unions by definition – they were *trades* unions after all. But craft unions did not die out entirely. In the professions – nurses, doctors, engineers, teachers and the like – many employees are still represented by professional associations that operate like craft unions. They set certain occupational standards and restrict access to their professions through the registration of members with professional associations as a way to guarantee professional and ethical and standards and as a way to bargain for decent remuneration and working conditions. The privatisation and commodification of healthcare in many parts of the world have put doctors and nurses in opposition to their governments, with such professionals going on strike in order to protect their professions.

Three of the chapters in our volume, discussed below, raise these issues, but in a new context. These chapters point to the need for a more comprehensive and critical understanding of how work in the civil service is changing. Here we refer to new technologies such as the rise of e-government and the use of algorithms in administrative and surveillance systems, as well as the challenge that welfare systems that include an element of state employment pose to the labour movement and labour market regulation more generally.

Babalwa Magoqwana considers the links between emotional labour and gender relations in precarious service work jobs. She argues that the performance of service work is carried out for reasons of survival rather than pleasing the customer. Focusing on local government call centres in post-apartheid state workplaces, Magoqwana argues that the introduction of a customer culture within the public service has changed care work into emotional labour, as citizens/customers demand both care and emotional labour from the call centre agents. Her research opens up an interesting new avenue to explore the impact of new technology on work, including in the context of the civil service.

This brings us to Nomkhosi Xulu-Gama and Aisha Lorgat's chapter, which explores the challenging contradictions posed by government welfare programmes that operate on the 'right to work' principle – which characterises the state as an employer of last resort in cases where citizens are not able to secure jobs in the private sector. In South Africa this takes on the form of Community Works Programmes. It raises a conundrum. Are people employed through these programmes welfare recipients, or are they workers that should therefore be represented by unions? Xulu-Gama and Lorgat explore the question of what happens when there are no jobs in communities, which results in survival strategies, such as 'volunteerism' and solidaristic practices, being deployed. They focus on the experiences of community health workers, mostly comprised of unemployed black youth, mostly women, who become 'employed' under the auspices of the Department of Health in Gauteng province. These individuals have struggled to improve their working conditions. Xulu-Gama and Lorgat assert that the volunteerism undertaken by the healthcare workers has taken the pressure off the government to assign resources to sufficiently train and compensate professional health workers. The authors point out that these are survival strategies in the context of little or no work and where the responsibility of care has been put onto community and household members.

Siphelo Ngcwangu revives an interest in issues of skill and deskilling with his contribution. He contends that there has been a noticeable decrease in activities that engage with the question of skill within the trade union movement, which has opened up space for a far more technical orientation on the issue. Ngcwangu examines the technological changes that are taking place in the automotive assembly sector, how workers are grappling with these changes and how these changes are shaping the organisation of trade union responses. He concludes that the challenge for the unions is to build adequate capacity to respond pre-emptively to 'production politics' and to connect to the objectives of workers on the ground.

These chapters introduce new empirical realities, but they also reintroduce to our research agenda questions around skill and deskilling. In addition, they point to the continued relevance of trade unions raising issues of civil service professionalism and the importance of craft unionism in the contemporary era.

Nevertheless, despite craft unionism's relevance in professional sectors, in much of the manufacturing sector a new kind of unionism has emerged as a response to the rise of mass production. So, with the demise of craft unionism under the rise of mass production, there were two responses from trade unions, with two traditions emerging – at times competing for dominance.

First, a number of socialist labour activists felt strongly that workers should not be divided by craft or industrial affiliation, so they formed general unions. Such unions were often based on the emerging nation states, but internationalist in orientation. Others formed local unions based on towns, cities or districts. The idea was to be close to members, and workers' power would reside in their ability to organise across the economy and enable general strikes – or associational power. A good example of a general union in South Africa is the Industrial and Commercial Workers' Union. It collapsed when it grew too large and became unaccountable to its members. Later on, from the 1970s onwards, the General and Allied Workers' Union followed a similar strategy, but was overshadowed by its industrial union rivals.

Second, for industrial unions, the position workers occupied in the production process was used as a source of power – workplace bargaining power. In this case, workers' strength resided in how well entire industries were organised. In the 1970s and 1980s industrial unions became the heartland of union organising. The Metal and Allied Workers' Union (which later became the National Union of Metalworkers of South

Africa [Numsa]) and the Chemical Workers Industrial Union – which later merged with the Paper, Printing, Wood and Allied Workers' Union to become the Chemical, Energy, Paper, Printing, Wood and Allied Workers' Union – are important examples. These industrial unions had a strong focus on the workplace, and built up their strength as national unions by building density workplace by workplace, and then taking on entire industries through the old Industrial Councils (later reconstituted as Bargaining Councils). This was during a time when production processes were based on integrated factories in nation states. South Africa's economy was also isolated through sanctions against apartheid. So, if workers in an auto assembly plant's paint shop went out on strike, the entire plant came to a standstill. This is an example of structural power residing in the workplace. In South Africa, and much of the world, industrial unions became the dominant form of trade unionism and to some extent still are, even though many of these unions are currently in crisis due to automation and the globalisation of production systems. Cosatu took industrial unionism so far as to make it one of their core principles – one industry, one union. Numsa's movement away from this – to organise along value chains, rather than industrial demarcation – is one of the reasons given for it being expelled from Cosatu. Of course, this is only part of the story. It is well known that the South African Clothing and Textile Workers' Union, still affiliated to Cosatu, also organised along value chains and has signed up members in the agriculture and retail sectors that are linked with textile and garment production.

But there is a danger that if trade unions leave the focus that industrial unions had on the workplace behind, it might be to the detriment of their members. We have already mentioned Siphelo Ngcwangu's chapter on skills and technology in the workplace, and we draw attention to it again here. Two additional chapters in this volume highlight this point, as well as the need to return to some of the debates of the past related to workplace restructuring, but perhaps also in new ways. Both these chapters raise the issue of what has become known, controversially so, as the Fourth Industrial Revolution.

Mondli Hlatshwayo asserts that, in the struggle between workers and employers for control over the labour process, production technologies are not neutral. These technologies are utilised to speed up the production process and to increase control over workers. The pace at which machinery and robotics are introduced into the labour process is controlled by the employers. Furthermore, workers and their trade unions are only able to respond long after employers have initiated the new technologies. Thus Hlatshwayo concludes that technological changes and the current phase of technology make workers losers in the 'game' of the Fourth Industrial Revolution in South Africa.

John Mashayamombe examines what he terms the two-faced nature of the Fourth Industrial Revolution through mechanisation, automation and increased use of various technologies at two new mining companies in the coal and iron ore commodities industry. Mashayamombe argues that this has had many advantages, in that it has led to improved health and safety levels, higher remuneration, efficient and quality production, the upskilling of labour, and even the enhancement of workplace relations. However, it also means that new employees are not being hired, that the workforce is shrinking, that there is increased monitoring and control of employees beyond the workplace through sophisticated technologies, and that work has become depersonalised. These swift changes are also occurring in a context where the education, training and regulatory authorities as well as the trade unions are only managing these changes through reactive approaches as they have not developed concrete solutions. Covid-19 presents additional challenges to the struggling mining industry as production and supply chain were disrupted by lockdowns. In addition to this, infections and, in some cases, deaths, and regulations associated with physical distancing have affected the labour process.

We end this section on trade unions and how organising relates to economic sectors with a brief examination of the relevance of advice bureaus. To be sure, it might be somewhat controversial to include advice bureaus as a kind of trade unionism. These forms of labour movement activism emerge during times when trade unions are weak, or are not addressing the concerns of certain segments of the labour market. At times, they also function as a non-membership-based form of representation, when being a union member may lead to persecution. This persecution may be due to either authoritarian regimes that target union members, or labour brokers that flout the letter and spirit of labour laws in order to provide their clients with a non-unionised workforce. The most prominent such bureau in the South African context is most probably the Casual Workers' Advice Office in Johannesburg, whose offices were burned down during the lockdown. They have won a number of battles against the abuse of labour broking and are a vociferous critic of existing unions. More research has to be done on these new forms of organising (in fact, a revival of an older mode of organising). Edward Webster's chapter looks at combining new forms of knowledge production with labour organising.

Lucien van der Walt's chapter highlights the silences in labour studies of the past and in the present, and we address this here by way of a mapping exercise. In Tables C1, C2 and C3, we summarise the main points, but the discussion leaves us with the question as to whether we should perhaps start exploring value chain trade unionism as a category wedged between industrial unionism and general unionism.

Table C1: Trade unions and industrial modes of organising

Craft Unionism	Industrial Unionism	General Unionism	Advice Bureaus
Doctors' and nurses' associations	Most South African unions belonging to Cosatu, Saftu, Fedusa and Nactu	Numsa still rooted in industrial unionism, but moving in this direction Sactwu organising along value chains	Casual Workers' Advice Office

TRADE UNIONS, POLITICAL PARTIES AND MOVEMENT POLITICS

In post-independence Africa, immense pressure was applied to African unions to connect with the objectives of national development, as outlined by the new political elite. In some African countries, workers' well-being would be guaranteed by some sort of affiliation of their union to the ruling political party, and ministerial posts were given to trade unionists in exchange for pledging industrial peace. Nevertheless, trade unions and wage workers were central to the project of development after independence. Many trade unions in post-independence Africa relied on their alliances with ruling parties to affect public policy. However, where the elites needed to assert political control to advance nation-building, they subordinated trade unions to the national development project. The outcome of this effort was varied but many trade unions in Africa remain linked to nationalist political parties, and it was nationalism that was the political form of the working-class struggle for democracy across the African continent. Trade unions then had to grapple with the decline of the interventionist state, the introduction of structural adjustment policies, political authoritarianism and the intensification of neo-liberal policies. In so far as trade unions, political parties and movement politics are concerned, we drew a distinction in our previous volume – *Labour Beyond Cosatu*, edited by Andries Bezuidenhout and Malehoko Tshoaedi (2017) – between:

1. social movement unionism (unions as part of a broader coalition directed at social transformation);
2. political unionism (unions associated with or affiliated to political parties);
3. economic unionism (unions narrowly focused on the workplace and workplace representation); and
4. entrepreneurial unionism (trade unions where the officials and office-bearers use union resources for their own benefit).

We would like to rename this last category 'parasitic unionism', since it is a more accurate description of this kind of unionism, where corruption is integrated into the mode of operation.

During the anti-apartheid struggle, South African trade unions took on a social movement character, and the waning of this tradition has been described and analysed in detail. Two of the contributions to this book put new evidence and analysis on the table. First, Janet Cherry looks at how, after Numsa's expulsion from Cosatu, a new political alignment took place with the emergence of the United Front and the Socialist Revolutionary Workers Party. Cherry's analysis of these new formations reveals that the new social movements in South Africa do not represent a unified class force able to contest the hegemony of capital nor that of the hegemony of the African National Congress (ANC). Cherry concludes that most movements are struggling for inclusion rather than for an alternative system, but that the space does exist for the emergence of a more unified and working-class-led opposition to the current system. Furthermore, some dramatic developments have brought inequalities and injustices in South African society (and across the globe) to the fore. Most recently the Covid-19 pandemic has resulted in new civil society coalitions that have responded to these inequalities in many ways.

Then, in a fresh new empirical and analytical contribution, Mpho Mmadi analyses the emergence of Mamelodi Train Sector, which was formed in 2001. It is a train-based organisation that focuses on commuters, and has formal links to the ruling Tripartite Alliance. It emerged at a time when traditional unions struggled to attract marginalised workers, such as informal sector workers, into their ranks. This was also a time when debates were taking place around whether the social movement unionism of the 1980s could be revived, as workers' traditional forms of power had been challenged and fragmented. Mmadi uses the case study to demonstrate that the key building blocks characteristic of social movement unionism are still prevalent within large sections of the working class in South Africa. He also shows how community–labour ties are a persistent feature of the South African landscape, but that they now operate in different and more strategic spaces such as the train.

Another contribution sheds light on the darker side of trade unionism – what we called entrepreneurial trade unionism in the previous volume, but that should perhaps be called parasitic trade unionism. Sandla Nomvete looks at union investment companies and union business wings that have emerged in the post-apartheid South African labour movement. Nomvete argues that some trade unionists are more interested in the union investment companies and that this has overshadowed workers' interests. This is especially the case where unions had a workerist and

Table C2: Trade unions, movements and politics

Social Movement Unionism	Political Unionism	Economic Unionism	Parasitic Unionism
Little evidence of this, although there is some form of social movement character in the ethnic mobilisation of Solidarity	Cosatu

Saftu

Nactu | Fedusa

Consawu (including Solidarity) | Some elements of this in most unions |

socialist agenda. Overall, although trade union business wings are a formidable source of income for trade unions, the mismanagement of the finances by union officials is deeply problematic and has undermined the labour movement. Nomvete's contribution highlights the need for a much more systematic research focus on union finances and how this relates to union organising and models of trade unionism. In researching this chapter, Sandla and we as editors were struck by the lack of hard empirical data on this topic.

Finally, in an original contribution, Jantjie Xaba reflects on the model of business unionism and presents a case study of Solidarity Union and its 'Histadrut model'. This serves as an example of social capital unionism, which has benefitted white workers at ArcelorMittal in Vanderbijlpark. Xaba's study shows how building up finance capital by trade unions does not translate into the broad-based empowerment of workers. Rather, it is the investment in social networks, relationships, trust and mutual obligation that leads to the direct empowerment of workers and their communities, as the Histadrut model clearly demonstrates. South African labour studies has neglected unions beyond the Cosatu tradition, and this study is a welcome correction. Xaba's chapter also raises the question about a potential new category, which we have termed economic unionism (see Table C2).

TRADE UNIONS AND IDEOLOGICAL TRADITIONS

In South Africa, historically, trade unions were split along national and racial lines. Among white workers, British chauvinism and the ideology of Afrikaner nationalism played a more significant role in the struggle against racial solidarity than did the ideology of socialism. Afrikaner nationalists battled to draw unionised white Afrikaans-speaking South Africans into an ordered nationalist movement. White workers viewed African workers as their adversaries as they were perceived to be the allies or tools of capitalism that were used against white workers.

Within both the South African Communist Party and the black trade union movement, African trade unions were deeply moulded by the politics of national liberation, although non-racialism was central to unionisation. Nationalist strands formed the background against which union mobilisation was conducted.

In terms of political thinking within the trade unions concerning the relationship between unions and the national liberation movement, there were two broad groupings. One grouping adopted Marxist politics; it was termed the 'workerist' tendency, and rejected the national democratic struggle (as embodied by the ANC) in favour of a democratic socialist revolution. The other grouping, the 'populists', opted for links with the national liberation movement whose key objective was to tear down the apartheid state (Forrest 2005).

Founded in 1985, Cosatu adopted the ANC's Freedom Charter, which was seen as a 'stepping stone to socialism' (Pillay 2011). This represented both the entrenchment of a 'strategic compromise' for Cosatu as it acknowledged the popular alliance between the ANC and the South African Communist Party, but with the firm idea that an independent labour movement was very important. While the bulk of Cosatu trade unionists viewed themselves as radical socialists with worker-centred policies, many affiliates adhered to the national democratic political narrative, and so it has become a significant political tradition within the South African labour movement. At Cosatu's 13th national congress in 2018, reported membership figures for the federation were above 1.7 million across 21 affiliates (Cosatu 2018).

Many and competing types of African nationalism developed, such as those between the ANC and the Pan Africanist Congress, but there were other forms of black nationalism, such as Black Consciousness which also challenged national oppression. The United Workers' Union of South Africa was formed in 1986 for Zulu workers as an independent trade union backed by the Inkatha Freedom Party and its political ambitions. The union was set up in opposition to Cosatu but it never constituted an actual threat to Cosatu unions in the factories (Forrest 2005). During the same time, the National Council of Trade Unions (Nactu) was formed out of a merger between the Council of Unions of South Africa and the Azanian Confederation of Trade Unions, both with mainly black members. These federations were guided by Africanism and the Black Consciousness Movement, and while they support non-racialism, they enforced black leadership of the federation. Nactu is independent, but some affiliates have politically associated themselves with the Pan Africanist Congress, which has been a source of conflict internally among its leadership; others within the federation have endorsed Black Consciousness organisations such as the Azanian People's Organisation. However, the Black Consciousness group in Nactu linked up with the workerists in Cosatu. Nactu has 22 affiliates and has a membership of 400 000 (Nactu 2018).

The Federation of Unions of South Africa (Fedusa) emerged in post-apartheid South Africa, but was external to the Tripartite Alliance and was multi-racial in its composition. Being non-aligned and independent, it adheres to a more liberal ideology such as a belief in the free market. Fedusa resulted from a merger between the Federation of South African Trade Unions and the Federation of Organisations Representing Civil Employees (Fedusa 2021). Significantly, Fedusa trade unions favour a conservative approach to wage demands and so tend to negotiate rather than embark on strikes. Fedusa has 19 affiliates and 700 000 members (South African History Online 2017).

In 2006, Fedusa merged with Nactu and the Confederation of South African Workers Union (Consawu) to establish a larger umbrella federation, namely the South African Confederation of Trade Unions. However, the federations did not reach an agreement about the details of the merger, and so all the federations continue to function as distinct entities (South African History Online 2017). Formed in 2003 as an independent and non-aligned trade union, Consawu has 27 affiliates and claims 300 000 members; it has no website (Mail & Guardian 2006).

Solidarity considers itself as an ethnically based Christian trade union and is one of the oldest independent trade unions, emerging from the racially exclusive Mineworkers Union that was formed in 1902. It supports minority rights and the Afrikaans language, and so is an example of a trade union that ideologically promotes ethnic nationalism. Solidarity focuses on workers' rights, but its broader focus involves defending its members' civil rights (there are approximately 34 staff members in its legal division). Solidarity affiliated to Consawu in 2006. It has 200 000 members (Solidarity 2022).

After Cosatu expelled one of its largest affiliates, Numsa, in 2013, Saftu was established in 2017. Saftu is independent but is political, with a socialist orientation that believes trade unions should be worker-controlled. It adheres to the principles of non-racialism and non-sexism. It has 21 affiliated trade unions and a membership of 800 000 workers (Saftu 2022).

Table C3 provides a summary of the ideological affiliations of the main South African trade union groupings.

Table C3: Trade unions and their ideological orientations

	Collectivist ideology			Individualistic ideology
		Nationalism		
Socialism	Pan-Africanism	Black Consciousness	Ethnic nationalism	Liberalism
Cosatu, Saftu	Nactu		Solidarity	Fedusa

What is clear from this discussion is that trade unions have structured their ideological affiliations along the lines of race and class – in South African language, and taking a cue from Lenin, what is known as the 'national question'. However, what we have been consistently highlighting in our research series is the importance of an intersectional analysis of the labour movement and workers' experiences in the workplace (Buhlungu and Tshoaedi 2012; Bezuidenhout and Tshoaedi 2017). An intersectional approach to labour studies has allowed us to look at the voices and experiences of different workers within the unions and the workplace (Tshoaedi 2012, 2017; Benya 2013, 2015; Kenny 2016). In addition to race and class, capitalist exploitation is intersected by workers' various identities – generation and gender, or being a queer, a migrant worker or a disabled worker. Capitalist power relations of domination and exclusion of the marginalised groups in society is the biggest problem for the labour movement of the twenty-first century. With a history of colonial and apartheid domination, the African labour movement has a responsibility to engage in meaningful struggles that seek to end the continued dehumanisation of marginalised groups in society. Trade union renewal must be founded on building new solidarities, where difference is recognised as strength for building powerful working-class movements of the twenty-first century. Such solidarities have the potential to be powerful and strategic in broadening workers' issues as well as broadening alliances outside the workplace and across borders.

The focus on gender in the labour movement has revealed the continued limitations within the labour movement in terms of prioritising the representation of women workers. Asanda-Jonas Benya raises the matter of the intersections between race, class and gender. She examines women mineworkers' experiences of their work underground and their responses to the mining unions. Drawing from research conducted in platinum mines in South Africa between 2008 and 2019, Benya asserts that unions, as boy's clubs, promote both the production of unequal power relations at work and gender inequity, and they maintain gender inequity by fostering hetero-patriarchal norms. Furthermore, the shop-floor class tradition that trade unions have relied on does not serve the interests of their women members. Both employers and mining unions reproduce a culture that disempowers and neglects women mineworkers. Benya concludes that to effectively serve their women members, unions have to address the connections between class and gender oppressions.

In addition to gender, insufficient attention has been paid to generational differences, specifically when it comes to organising younger workers as the future of trade unionism. In one of her chapters, Christine Bischoff asserts that even though the Employment Tax Incentive was introduced in 2014 to persuade employers to hire young and less experienced work-seekers, the South African government is struggling to put unemployed youth into jobs. The youth are extremely unlikely to find employment, and they faced the greatest risk of losing employment during the Covid-19 pandemic. The youth lack the necessary skills and experience, are more vulnerable to unemployment, and tend to be employed in low-skilled and semi-skilled jobs. Many young people remain discouraged with the labour market, and are not developing their skills base via education and training. Bischoff finds that there are low union density rates among the employed youth, and the labour movement is failing to close the representational gap, leaving employers to determine conditions of employment and wages for employed youth.

Globalisation and capitalist expansion presents trade unions with peculiar challenges, especially for workers and the labour movement in developing nations. While the impact of globalisation and the changing nature of work has produced instability for all workers across the globe, there are variations in how workers in developing nations are affected. The changes in the nature of work require a different kind of worker, one who is highly educated and armed with technical skills; this has been a major challenge for African workers. It has pushed many of them into the informal sector, which is highly unpredictable in terms of working conditions and income. Unions in the African context are organising under extremely difficult challenges when compared to their counterparts in developed nations. And this needs to be taken into account in terms of the type of trade unionism that is required for an African context. For instance, our surveys have shown that most workers' wages support more than one household (Buhlungu and Tshoaedi 2012; Bezuidenhout and Tshoaedi 2017). Research continues to show that unemployment in the African context is often subsidised by workers who are already earning low wages (Bezuidenhout and Fakier 2006; Mosoetsa 2011; Kenny 2020). The issue of social security and welfare in the African context is relevant to trade unions in Africa, and this was even more pronounced during the Covid-19 economic shutdown. The experience with the Covid-19 pandemic and the compulsory lockdowns resulted in many workers being out of jobs and without income for extended periods. It is estimated that between 2.2 to 2.8 million adults in the country lost their jobs from February to April 2020 as a result of the lockdown (Posel, Oyenubi and Kollamparambil 2021). Through pressure from civil society and the labour movement, some economic relief arrangements were organised for workers and businesses. However, this experience was significant in terms of the need for trade unions to redefine their mobilisation strategy outside of the workplace. The traditional forms of mobilisation, which focus on the workplace, are being challenged by the new complexities we face in our society.

Finally, there is the matter of trade unions organising beyond the borders of their own countries. In the era of Brexit and new economic nationalism – including working-class nationalism – this issue has become more important than ever. With increasing migration within the continent and across the globe, the meaningful involvement of migrant workers in the labour movement could potentially strengthen unions on transnational collaborations on specific campaigns. With deepening globalisation and inequalities, migration across the globe presents opportunities for the labour movements to expand membership through the inclusion of migrant workers and activism on issues that go beyond national borders. In his chapter, Edward Webster focuses on the international dimension of labour politics and the implications of new opportunities for transnational solidarity. He maintains that the most fundamental challenge to building a new labour internationalism remains that of the North–South divide. To bridge this, Webster recommends the regulatory approach, with its emphasis on building a new global system of labour standards and a labour-friendly system of global governance. He identifies how the Covid-19 pandemic and its responses presents an opportunity for the revitalisation of labour in Africa and how home-workers, informal sector workers performing essential work in the retail and hospitality sectors, or those who undertake paid and unpaid care work, can be organised by trade unions. Webster identifies how the Covid-19 pandemic provides an opportunity for trade unions to increase worker participation, and examines the counter strategy to retrenchments of one of South Africa's largest union's in this regard.

Our aim with this volume was to bring together a range of chapters that reflect new directions in South African labour scholarship, but that are rooted in past debates and concerns. We note that our intervention here represents but part of the field. We would like to mention two examples. First, our focus on women has to be supplemented by a broader focus on gender and sexualities in working-class politics. Second, we also have to take seriously the interface between labour movement politics and the environmental movement (see Cock 2022). Nevertheless, our survey of the lay of the land has identified a number of disruptions in the order of things, and how these disruptions point to new directions for both the labour movement and labour scholarship. The Covid-19 pandemic and the lockdown that was intended to contain its spread exacerbated the existing economic and social crises of poverty, unemployment and the unequal distribution of resources. This was followed by large-scale social unrest, as well as environmental catastrophe in the form of floods. In all of this, the state struggled to respond, in part due to the fact that its capacity was hollowed out by rent-seeking and corruption. In this context, a united and mobilised labour movement that forms part of a broader civil society coalition would be an asset. Unfortunately, the labour movement has lost much of its former dynamism. In spite of this, as we hope we have shown, there are signs of revitalisation. But a precondition for these signs of revitalisation to flourish into movement dynamism is a realisation among trade unions, and us as labour scholars, that the world has changed and that old ways of doing things are no longer sufficient.

REFERENCES

Benya, Asanda. 2013. 'Gendered Labour: A Challenge to Labour as a Democratising Force'. *Rethinking Development and Inequality* 2: 47–62.

Benya, Asanda 2015. 'The Invisible Hands: Women in Marikana'. *Review of African Political Economy* 42 (146): 545–560.

Bezuidenhout, Andries and Khayaat Fakier. 2006. 'Maria's Burden: Contract Cleaning and the Crisis of Social Reproduction in Post-apartheid South Africa'. *Antipode* 38 (3): 462–485.

Bezuidenhout, Andries and Malehoko Tshoaedi, eds. 2017. *Labour Beyond Cosatu: Mapping the Rupture in South Africa's Labour Landscape*. Johannesburg: Wits University Press.

Braverman, Harry. 1974. *Labor and Monopoly Capital: The Degradation of Work in the Twentieth Century*. New York: Monthly Review Press.

Buhlungu, Sakhela. 2009. 'South Africa: The Decline of Labor Studies and the Democratic Transition'. *Work and Occupations* 36 (2): 145–161.

Buhlungu, Sakhela and Malehoko Tshoaedi. 2012. *Cosatu's Contested Legacy: South African Trade Unions in the Second Decade of Democracy*. Cape Town: HSRC Press.

Cock, Jacklyn. 2022. 'Sociological Engagement with the Struggle for a Just Transition in South Africa'. In *Critical Engagement with Public Sociology*, edited by Andries Bezuidenhout, Sonwabile Mnwana and Karl von Holdt, 123–143. Bristol: Bristol University Press.

Congress of South African Trade Unions (Cosatu). 2018. 'Organisational Report on the Federation's Activities: Consolidated Departmental and Provincial Reports towards the COSATU 13th National Congress. Book 3'. *Report*. http://mediadon.co.za/13th-national-congress. Accessed 20 August 2020.

Federation of Unions of South Africa (Fedusa). 2021. *About Fedusa*. http://www.fedusa.org.za. Accessed 20 August 2020.

Forrest, Kally. 2005. 'Power, Independence and Worker Democracy in the Development of the National Union of Metalworkers of South Africa (NUMSA) and its Predecessors: 1980–1995'. PhD diss., University of the Witwatersrand

Freund, Bill. 2013. 'Labour Studies and Labour History in South Africa: Perspectives from the Apartheid Era and After'. *International Review of Social History* 58 (3): 493–519.

Kenny, Bridget. 2016. 'The Regime of Contract in South African Retailing: A History of Race, Gender, and Skill in Precarious Labor'. *International Labor and Working-class History* 89: 20–39.

Kenny, Bridget. 2020. 'The South African Labour Movement: A Fragmented and Shifting Terrain'. *Tempo Social, Revista de Sociologia da USP*, 32 (1): 119–136.

Mail & Guardian. 2006. 'Solidarity joins Consawu'. *Mail & Guardian*, 25 July 2006. https://mg.co.za/article/2006-07-25-solidarity-joins-consawu/

Mosoetsa, Sarah. 2011. *Eating from One Pot: The Dynamics of Survival in Poor South African Households*. Johannesburg: Wits University Press.

National Council of Trade Unions (Nactu). 2018. *Our Affiliates.* https://nactu.org.za/affiliates. Accessed 20 August 2020.

Pillay, Devan. 2011. 'The Enduring Embrace: COSATU and the Tripartite Alliance during the Zuma Era'. *Labour, Capital and Society.* 44 (2): 57–79.

Posel, Dorit, Adeola Oyenubi and Umakrishnan Kollamparambil. 2021. 'Job Loss and Mental Health during the COVID-19 Lockdown: Evidence from South Africa'. *PLoS ONE* 16 (3): e0249352. https://doi.org/10.1371/journal.pone.0249352.

Solidarity. 2022. *Who is Solidarity?* https://solidariteit.co.za/en/?gclid=Cj0KCQiA_8OPBh-DtARIsAKQu0gZMDF0x3J3t5jnx4yY7gjEPXxJckqMQM9FElrLWH-I6Z3M78-v3yh-gaAmDEEALw_wcB. Accessed 20 August 2020.

South African Federation of Trade Unions (Saftu). 2022. *Saftu Affiliates.* https://saftu.org.za/affiliates. Accessed 20 August 2020.

South African History Online. 2017. *Federation of Unions of South Africa (FEDUSA).* https://www.sahistory.org.za/article/federation-unions-south-africa-fedusa. Accessed 20 August 2020.

Stewart, Paul. 2018. 'Sociological Theory'. In *Sociology: A Concise South African Introduction,* edited by Paul Stewart and Johan Zaaiman, 1–44. Cape Town: Juta.

Tshoaedi, Malehoko. 2012. 'Making Sense of Unionised Workers' Political Attitudes: The (Un)Representation of Women's Voices in Cosatu'. In *Cosatu's Contested Legacy: South African Trade Unions in the Second Decade of Democracy,* edited by Sakhela Buhlungu and Malehoko Tshoaedi, 90–109. Cape Town: HSRC Press.

Tshoaedi, Malehoko. 2017. 'The Politics of Male Power and Privilege in Trade Unions: Understanding Sexual Harassment in Cosatu'. In *Labour Beyond Cosatu: Mapping the Rupture in South Africa's Labour Landscape,* edited by Andries Bezuidenhout and Malehoko Tshoaedi, 129–134. Johannesburg: Wits University Press.

Webster, Edward. 1985. *Cast in a Racial Mould: Labour Process and Trade Unionism in the Foundries.* Johannesburg: Ravan Press.

Webster, Edward. 1991. 'Taking Labour Seriously: Sociology and Labour in South Africa'. *South African Sociological Review* 4 (1): 50–72.

Webster, Edward. 1999. 'Race, Labour Process and Transition: The Sociology of Work in South Africa'. *Society in Transition* 30 (1): 28–42.

Webster, Edward. 2018. 'Culture and Working Life: Ari Sitas and the Transformation of Labour Studies in South Africa'. *Journal of Contemporary African Studies* 36 (2): 163–174.

CONTRIBUTORS

Asanda-Jonas Benya is a senior lecturer in the Department of Sociology at the University of Cape Town. Her work focuses on the intersection of gender, class and race. She has published in labour and feminist journals in areas of women in mining, gender and the extractive industries, labour and social movements, social and economic justice. She is currently working on a book project based on her ethnographic study on women underground miners.

Andries Bezuidenhout is Professor of Development Studies at the University of Fort Hare. He holds a PhD from the University of the Witwatersrand, Johannesburg. Previously he worked at the University of Pretoria and as a researcher at the Society, Work and Development Institute at the University of the Witwatersrand, to which he is still attached as an associate.

Christine Bischoff is a sociologist at the University of the Witwatersrand, Johannesburg. She holds a PhD in Sociology from the University of Pretoria. She has published on labour in journals such as the *International Labour Review* and *Work and Occupations*. Her main areas of research are trade unions and employment relations.

Janet Cherry is a South African socialist activist and academic. She is currently Professor of Development Studies at the Nelson Mandela University in Gqeberha. She has a PhD in political sociology from Rhodes University, Grahamstown. Her main areas of research are sustainable development, political economy of development, democratic participation and social and political history. She has published two books as well as a number of articles and chapters in books on South African history, labour, women's and social movements, transitional justice and sustainable development.

Mondli Hlatshwayo is a senior researcher in the Centre for Education Rights and Transformation at the University of Johannesburg. Previously he worked for Khanya College, a Johannesburg-based NGO, as an educator and researcher. His areas of research include precarious work, migrant workers, world cup and stadia, unions and technological changes, workers' education, trade unions and social movements. Hlatshwayo's doctoral thesis, which he completed in 2012, was on trade union responses to technological changes. He has published peer-reviewed journal articles and book chapters, and is co-editor (with Aziz Choudry) of *Just Work? Migrant Workers' Struggle Today* (Pluto Press, 2015). In 2019 the *Review of African Political Economy'* awarded him the Ruth First prize for his article 'The New Struggles of Precarious Workers in South Africa: Nascent Organisational Responses of Community Health Workers.' It was published in *ROAPE* 45(157) in Autumn 2018.

Aisha Lorgat is a researcher at Chris Hani Institute, Johannesburg. She is in the process of completing her PhD with the University of Cape Town. Her research focus is the socioeconomic rights of migrant workers, with a particular focus on the right to work and rights in the workplace. She is an executive member of the South African Sociological Association Council. Her research interests include migration, precarious workers and socioeconomic justice.

Babalwa Magoqwana is the interim director of the Centre for Women and Gender Studies at Nelson Mandela University in Gqeberha. She is a fellow of the African Humanities Programme and a research associate of the South African Research Chairs Initiative Chair in Social Policy at the University of South Africa. Magoqwana is the principal investigator of the Catalytic Project on Maternal Legacies of Knowledge in the Eastern Cape, supported by the National Institute for the Humanities and Social Sciences. She was also a recipient of the National Research Foundation/First Rand Foundation Sabbatical Grant for her project on 'Women-centred Vernacular Sociology of the Eastern Cape'.

John Mashayamombe is a sociologist by training. He completed his undergraduate degree at the University of Zimbabwe and postgraduate degrees at the University of Pretoria. His research and writing interests are around worker and workplace issues, technology and machines, health and safety, housing, and the environment within the mining sector. He also focuses on student movements and student accommodation.

Mpho Mmadi is a senior student adviser in the Faculty of Natural and Agricultural Sciences, University of Pretoria. He holds a DPhil from the University of Pretoria. His research interests focus on working-class struggles, unions and other forms of worker organisation. He has a keen interest in student support and development.

Siphelo Ngcwangu is currently a senior lecturer in the Department of Sociology at the University of Johannesburg. He teaches sociology at the undergraduate level and supervises at postgraduate level. His research focuses on skills development, education and the economy, youth unemployment, racial inequality and the restructuring of work. He has published a range of journal articles, book chapters and monographs in his areas of research.

Sandla Nomvete is an Institutional Researcher in the Office for Institutional Strategy at Nelson Mandela University, Gqeberha. He is currently completing his doctoral studies in sociology at the University of Pretoria and has recently published on the 2015 #FeesMustFall movement in South Africa. In addition to student and social movements, his research interests lie in the areas of work and mining migrant labour post-apartheid.

Malehoko Tshoaedi is an associate professor in the Department of Sociology at the University of Johannesburg. She holds a PhD in Political Science and Gender studies from the University of Leiden, the Netherlands. She is a member of the Ministerial Task Team on Gender-based Violence and Harassment in Higher Education. She is the former vice-president of the South African Sociological Association. She is co-editor with Trevor Ngwane of *The Fourth Industrial Revolution: A Sociological Critique* (Jacana, 2021); with Andries Bezuidenhout of *Labour Beyond Cosatu: Mapping the Rupture in South Africa's Labour Landscape* (Wits University Press, 2017); and with Sakhela Buhlungu of *COSATU's Contested Legacy: South African Trade Unions in the Second Decade of Democracy* (HSRC Press, 2012).

Lucien van der Walt is Professor of Economic and Industrial Sociology, and director of the Neil Aggett Labour Studies Unit at Rhodes University, Grahamstown. He has published widely on labour, the left and political economy, and is involved in worker and union education. His books include *Anarchism and Syndicalism in the Colonial and Postcolonial World, 1870–1940: The Praxis of National Liberation, Internationalism, and Social Revolution* (Brill, 2010) with Steve Hirsch, *Negro e Vermelho: Anarquismo, Sindicalismo Revolucionário e Pessoas de Cor na África Meridional nas Décadas de 1880 a 1920* (UFSC, 2014) and *Politics at a Distance from the State: Radical and African Perspectives* (Routledge, 2018) with Kirk Helliker.

Edward Webster is Distinguished Research Professor in the Southern Centre for Inequality Studies and founder of the Society, Work and Development Institute at the University of the Witwatersrand. He was a Senior Fulbright Scholar at the University of Wisconsin (Madison) in 1995–1996. Webster was the first Ela Bhatt Professor at the International Centre for Development and Decent Work at Kassel University, Germany, in 2009–2010. His research interests lie in the world of work, labour movements and social inequality. In 2009 his co-authored book, *Grounding Globalisation: Labour in the Age of Insecurity* (Wiley, 2008) was awarded the prestigious American Sociological Association award for the best scholarly monograph published on labour. In 2017 he co-edited two volumes, *The Unresolved National Question: Left Thought under Apartheid* (Wits University Press) and *Crossing the Divide: Precarious Work and the Future of Labour* (University of KwaZulu-Natal Press).

Jantjie Xaba is a lecturer in the Department of Sociology and Social Anthropology at Stellenbosch University. He lectures at undergraduate level on Crime and Deviance, Poverty and Inequality, and Industrial Sociology. His involvement at the postgraduate level includes offering an elective course for honours and masters students, as well as supervision and examination. He is also a specialist in the sociology of work in South Africa. His previous research was on worker restructuring in the metal industry, and his PhD research broadened and deepened this through a comparative study between Afrikaner Economic Empowerment and Black Economic Empowerment. He has also published on the informal economy for the ILO, restructuring of work, the impact of retrenchments on miners, employee assistance programmes and globalisation, and has been part of an international research project on global cities.

Nomkhosi Xulu-Gama is a senior lecturer at the University of Cape Town. She is also a research associate at the Durban University of Technology. Her book, *Hostels in South Africa: Spaces of Perplexity* (University of KwaZulu-Natal Press, 2018) has redefined scholarship in the field. Her research interests are related to issues of migration, housing, rural–urban connections, gender, household relations and everyday lived experiences.

INDEX

Printed in the USA
CPSIA information can be obtained
at www.ICGtesting.com
JSHW021954231023
50693JS00002B/6